THE

Kidnapping OF *Edgardo* *Mortara*

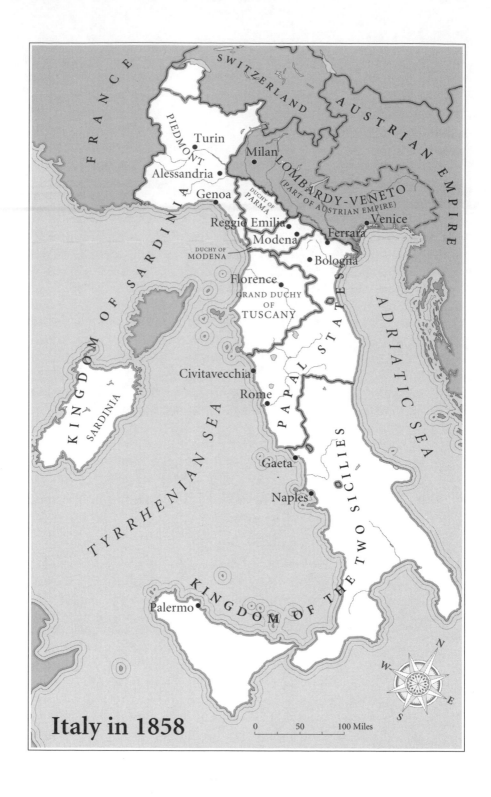

Italy in 1858

THE
Kidnapping
OF *Edgardo*
Mortara

DAVID I. KERTZER

Alfred A. Knopf   NEW YORK   1997

THIS IS A BORZOI BOOK
PUBLISHED BY ALFRED A. KNOPF, INC.

Copyright © 1997 by David I. Kertzer
Maps copyright © 1997 by David Lindroth, Inc.

All rights reserved under International and Pan-American Copyright
Conventions. Published in the United States by Alfred A. Knopf, Inc.,
New York, and simultaneously in Canada by Random House of Canada
Limited, Toronto. Distributed by Random House, Inc., New York.

http://www.randomhouse.com/

Library of Congress Cataloging-in-Publication Data

Kertzer, David I.
The kidnapping of Edgardo Mortara / by David I. Kertzer.—1st ed.
p.   cm.
Includes bibliographical references and index.
ISBN 0-679-45031-9.—ISBN 0-679-76817-3 (pbk.)
1. Mortara, Pio, d. 1940. 2. Jews—Italy—Bologna—Conversion to
Christianity—History—19th century. 3. Converts from Judaism—
Italy—Bologna—Biography.
I. Title.
DS135.I9M595   1997
945'.004924—dc21   96-39159
                                                                CIP

Manufactured in the United States of America
First Edition

To my father, Morris Norman Kertzer,
and to my daughter, Molly Emilia Kertzer,
with love and appreciation

CONTENTS

*Maps will be found opposite the title page
and on pages 249 and 269*

PROLOGUE

*I*T WAS the end of an era. Regimes that had lasted for centuries were about to be swept away. On the Italian peninsula, the old world of papal power and traditional authority uneasily faced the disparate progeny of the Enlightenment, the French Revolution, and the champions of modern industry, science, and commerce. The proud warriors of the old and the new viewed each other warily, in mutual incomprehension. Each side waved its own flags, intoned its own verities, worshipped its own icons, sang praises to its heroes, and heaped scorn on its enemies. Revolutionaries dreamed of utopic futures, far different from the oppressive present; liberals envisioned a new political order, based on constitutional rule; and even conservatives began to wonder whether the old order could stand much longer. New gods were being born, new objects of adulation. In Italy, out of the patchwork of duchies, grand duchy, Bourbon and Savoyard kingdoms, Austrian outposts, and the pontifical state itself, a new nation-state was soon to take shape whose boundaries were as yet unknown and whose nature was as yet unimagined. Subjects would soon become citizens. Yet for the mass of illiterate peasants, nothing much would seem to change.

Nowhere in the West was the chasm between the old world and the new so wide as in the lands of the pope-king. Where else, indeed, could rule by divine right be so well entrenched, so well justified ideologically, so spectacularly elaborated ritually? The Pope had been a worldly prince, a ruler of his subjects, for many centuries, and the contours of his domain in 1858—stretching from Rome in a crescent sweeping northeastward around the Grand Duchy of Tuscany and up to the second city of the Papal States, Bologna, in the north—were much the same as they had been three and a half centuries before. The Pope ruled his state because that was what God willed. The revolutionary notions that people should choose their own rulers, that they should be free to think what it pleased them to think, believe what they chose to believe—these were not simply wrongheaded but heretical, the devil's work, the excrescences of Freemasons and other enemies of God and religion. The world was as God had ordained it. Progress was heresy.

But while the pontifical state still stood in 1858, it had not survived the previous seven decades unbattered. When French soldiers streamed down the Italian peninsula in 1796–97, the Papal States were gobbled up; in the years that followed, two popes were driven from Rome into humiliating exile, and Church property was auctioned off to the highest bidder, swelling Napoleon's coffers. Although with Napoleon's collapse Pope Pius VII returned to the Holy City in 1814 and the Papal States were restored, what had once appeared so solid—a product of the divine order of things—now seemed terribly fragile. Conspiracies against the Pope's worldly rule sprouted; revolts broke out. At midcentury another pope was forced to flee Rome, this time fearful of murderous mobs, and had to rely on foreign armies to restore his rule and then protect him from his own mutinous subjects.

Among those subjects—though, for the most part, far from mutinous—were the Jews, "the Pope's Jews." Having lived in Italy since before there were any Christians, they nonetheless could not shake off their status as outsiders, petitioners for the privilege of being allowed to remain where they were. Few in number—fewer than fifteen thousand in all the Papal States[1]—they were high in the clergy's consciousness, occupying a central, if unenviable, position in Catholic theology: they were the killers of Christ, whose continued wretched existence served as a valuable reminder to the faithful, but who would one day see the light and become part of the true religion, helping to hasten the Redeemer's return. Since the sixteenth century, the popes had confined them to ghettoes to limit the contagion. No Christian was allowed in their homes; theirs was a society apart. Still, life in the ghetto had its joys and consolations. There the Jews had a rich communal life, their own institutions, their own synagogues, rabbis, and leaders, their own quarrels and triumphs, their own divinely ordained rites that structured each day of their lives and each season of the year.

But the Jews, too, saw a new world come into view as French troops, spreading the secular trinity of *liberté, égalité, fraternité*, swept through the continent, hauled down the ghetto gates, and burned them in a purificatory blaze for popular edification. In the soldiers' wake, sometimes with Christian neighbors looking ominously on, the Jews—some exhilarated, others terrified—began to take their first halting steps out of a world that was the only one they and their ancestors had ever known.

The events chronicled here, which together form a strangely forgotten chapter in the battle that spelled the end of the old regime, began in the porticoed city of Bologna, indeed in the very heart of its medieval center of cobbled streets and piazzas, in 1858. In Rome, Pope Pius IX sat on St. Peter's throne as French troops patrolled the Eternal City. Two of the three most powerful men in Bologna were cardinals: the Archbishop, the city's spiritual leader, and the Cardinal Legate, representing the papal government, the civil ruler. The third was a military man, an Austrian general, whose troops (along with the French forces in Rome) ensured that the tottering papal government did not fall.

Directly across the street from the general's headquarters stood Bologna's justly famous Dominican church, San Domenico, where Saint Dominic himself died and where his bones are to this day reverently encased. There lived the Inquisitor, charged by the Congregation of the Holy Office in Rome with combating heresy and defending the faith. Among his tasks was ensuring that the restrictions imposed on the Jews were obeyed.

For two centuries, Bologna's inquisitors had had little reason to worry about the Jews, for in 1593 the Pope had expelled all nine hundred of them from the city and its surrounding territories. In the wake of the French occupation of the 1790s, a few adventurous Jews made their way back, but once the Papal States were restored, their status again became tenuous, their right to live in the city less than clear. Yet, by 1858 close to two hundred of them lived in Bologna, merchants for the most part, carving out a comfortable niche for their families. Given Church authorities' mixed feelings about their presence in the formerly forbidden city, the Jews had no desire to call attention to themselves, and so had neither synagogue nor rabbi.

Like many of these Jews, immigrants from the ghettoes of other cities, Momolo Mortara and Marianna Padovani Mortara had moved to Bologna from the nearby duchy of Modena. They lived with their children and their Catholic servant in a building in the center of the city. Their obscurity was about to come to a painful end.

THE
Kidnapping
OF *Edgardo*
Mortara

CHAPTER 1

The Knock at the Door

THE KNOCK CAME at nightfall. It was Wednesday, June 23, 1858. Anna Facchini, a 23-year-old servant, descended a flight of stairs from the Mortara apartment to open the building's outer door. Before her stood a uniformed police officer and a second, middle-aged man of martial bearing.[1]

"Is this the home of Signor Momolo Mortara?" asked Marshal Lucidi.

Yes, Anna responded, but Signor Mortara was not there. He had gone out with his oldest son.

As the men turned away, she closed the door and returned to the apartment to report the unsettling encounter to her employer, Marianna Mortara. Marianna sat at the living room table, busily stitching, along with her twin 11-year-old daughters, Ernesta and Erminia. Her five younger children, Augusto, aged 10, Arnoldo, 9, Edgardo, 6, Ercole, 4, and Imelda, born just six months before, were already asleep. Marianna, a nervous sort anyway, wished that her husband were home.

A few minutes later, she heard sounds of feet climbing the back stairs, which could be reached through her neighbor's apartment. Marianna stopped her stitching and listened carefully. The knocking on the door confirmed her fears. She approached the door and, without touching it, asked who was there.

"It's the police," a voice said. "Let us in."

Marianna, hoping though not really believing that the policemen had simply made a mistake, told them what she prayed they did not know: they were at the back door of the same apartment they had visited just a few minutes before.

"It doesn't matter, Signora. We are police and we want to come in. Don't worry; we wish you no harm."

3

Marianna opened the door and let the two men in. She did not notice the rest of the papal police detail, some of whom remained on the nearby stairs while others lingered on the street below.

Pietro Lucidi, marshal in the papal carabinieri and head of the police detail, entered, with Brigadier Giuseppe Agostini, in civilian clothes, following him in. The sight of the military police of the Papal States coming inexplicably in the night filled Marianna with dread.

The Marshal, not at all happy about the mission before him, and seeing that the woman was already distraught, tried to calm her. Pulling a small sheet of paper from his jacket, he told her he needed to get certain clarifications about her family and asked her to list the names of everyone in the household, beginning with her husband and herself, and proceeding through all her children, from oldest to youngest. Marianna began to shake.

Walking home beneath Bologna's famous porticoes with Riccardo, his 13-year-old son, that pleasant June evening, Momolo was surprised to find police milling around his outside door. He hurried up to his apartment and discovered the police officer and the other strange man talking to his frightened wife.

As Momolo entered the apartment, Marianna exclaimed, "Just listen to what these men want with our family!"

Marshal Lucidi now saw that his worst fears about his mission would be realized, but felt even so a certain relief at now being able to deal with Momolo, who was, after all, a man. Again he stated that he had been given the task of determining just who was in the Mortara household. Momolo, unable to get any explanation for this ominous inquiry, proceeded to name himself, his wife, and each of his eight children.

The Marshal checked all these names on his little list. Having noted all ten members of the family, he announced that he would now like to see each of the children. His request turned Marianna's fright to terror.

Momolo pointed out Riccardo, Ernesta, and Erminia, who had gathered round their parents, but pleaded that his other children were asleep and should be left alone.

Moved, perhaps, but undeterred, the Marshal remained firm. Eventually the Mortaras led the two policemen through the door into their own bedroom, with the three oldest children and the servant trailing them in. There, on a sofa-bed, slept 6-year-old Edgardo. His parents did not yet know that on the list the Marshal had brought with him, Edgardo's name was underlined.

Lucidi told Anna to take the rest of the children out of the room. Once they had left, he turned back to Momolo and said, "Signor Mortara, I am sorry to inform you that you are the victim of betrayal."

"What betrayal?" asked Marianna.

"Your son Edgardo has been baptized," Lucidi responded, "and I have been ordered to take him with me."

Marianna's shrieks echoed through the building, prompting the policemen stationed outside to scurry into the bedroom. The older Mortara children, terrified, sneaked back in as well. Weeping hysterically, Marianna threw herself into Edgardo's bed and clutched the somnolent boy to her.

"If you want my son, you'll have to kill me first!"

"There must be some mistake," Momolo said. "My son was never baptized. . . . Who says Edgardo was baptized? Who says he has to be taken?"

"I am only acting according to orders," pleaded the Marshal. "I'm just following the Inquisitor's orders."

Lucidi despaired as the situation seemed to be slipping out of control. In his own report, he later wrote: "I hardly know how to describe the effect of that fatal announcement. I can assure you that I would have a thousand times preferred to be exposed to much more serious dangers in performing my duties than to have to witness such a painful scene."

With Marianna wailing from Edgardo's bed, Momolo insisting that it was all a horrible mistake, and the children crying, Lucidi scarcely knew what to do. Both parents got down on their knees before the discomfited Marshal, begging him in the name of humanity not to take their child from them. Bending a bit (and no doubt thinking this was all the Inquisitor's fault anyway), Lucidi offered to let Momolo accompany his son to see the Inquisitor at the nearby Convent of San Domenico.

Momolo refused, afraid to let Edgardo into the Inquisitor's hands.

Lucidi recalled: "While I waited for the desperate mother and father, overcome by a terrible agony, to return to reason so that the matter could be brought to its inevitable conclusion, various people began to arrive, either on their own or because they had been called there."

In fact, with Lucidi's permission, Momolo had sent Riccardo to alert Marianna's brother and uncle, and to fetch their elderly Jewish neighbor Bonajuto Sanguinetti, whose wealth and community position, Momolo hoped, might ward off the impending disaster.

Hurrying back to the cafe where, less than an hour before, he and his father had left them, Riccardo came upon his two uncles, Angelo Padovani, his mother's brother, and Angelo Moscato, husband of his mother's sister. Moscato later described the encounter:

"As I sat with my brother-in-law at the Caffè del Genio on via Vetturini, my nephew Riccardo Mortara came running up, in tears and disconsolate, telling me that the carabinieri were in his house, and that they wanted to kidnap his brother Edgardo."

The two men rushed to the Mortaras' apartment: "We saw the mother, devastated, and in such a sorry state that it's impossible to describe. I asked the marshal of the gendarmes to explain what was going on, and he responded that he had an order—though he never showed it to me—from the Inquisitor, Father Pier Gaetano Feletti, to take Edgardo because he had been baptized."

Marianna was "desperate, beside herself," as her brother, Angelo Padovani, recalled. "She lay stretched out on a sofa which they also used as a bed, the sofa on which Edgardo slept, holding him tightly to her chest so that no one could take him."

Trying to find some way to stop the police from making off with Edgardo, Padovani and his brother-in-law persuaded the Marshal not to remove the child before they could consult with their uncle, who lived nearby. The uncle, Marianna's father's brother, whose name was also Angelo Padovani, was still at work in the small bank he ran in the same building in which he lived.

After his nephews filled him in on the dramatic events at the Mortara home, Signor Padovani decided that their only hope was to see the Inquisitor. While the younger Padovani rushed back to inform the Marshal of the need for further delay, the other two men made their way to the convent.

At 11 p.m., they presented themselves at the forbidding gate of San Domenico and asked to be taken to the Inquisitor. Despite the hour, they were rushed up to the Inquisitor's room. They implored Father Feletti to tell them why he had ordered the police to take Edgardo. Responding in measured tones, and hoping to calm them, the Inquisitor explained that Edgardo had been secretly baptized, although by whom, or how he came to know of it, he would not say. Once word of the baptism had reached the proper authorities, they had given him the instructions that he was now carrying out: the boy was a Catholic and could not be raised in a Jewish household.

Padovani protested bitterly. It was an act of great cruelty, he said, to order a child taken from his parents without ever giving them a chance to defend themselves. Father Feletti simply responded that it was not in his power to deviate from the orders he had received. The men begged him to reveal his grounds for thinking that the child had been baptized, for no one in the family knew anything about it. The Inquisitor replied that he could give no such explanation, the matter being confidential, but that they should rest assured that everything had been done properly. It would be best for all concerned, he added, if the members of the family would simply resign themselves to what was to come. "Far from acting lightly in this matter," he told them, "I have acted in good conscience, for everything has been done punctiliously according to the sacred Canons."

Seeing that it was impossible to get Father Feletti to reconsider his order, the men pleaded with him to give the family more time before taking the boy. They asked that he suspend any action for at least a day.

"At first," Moscato later recounted, "that man of stone refused, and we had to paint a picture for him of the sad state of a mother who had another child she was nursing, of a father who was being driven almost out of his mind, and of eight [sic] children clutching at their parents' and the policemen's knees, begging them not to take their brother away from them."

Eventually, the Inquisitor did change his mind and allowed them a twenty-four-hour stay, hoping that in the meantime the distraught mother could be made to leave the apartment, thereby heading off what threatened to become an unfortunate public disturbance. He asked Moscato and Padovani to promise that no attempt would be made to help the boy escape, an assurance they gave only reluctantly.

Father Feletti later recounted what went through his mind as he weighed the risks of permitting the delay. He knew full well, he said, of the "superstitions in which the Jews are steeped," and so he feared not only that "the child might be stolen away," but indeed that he might perhaps even be "sacrificed." His was a belief shared widely in Italy at that time, for it was thought that Jews would rather murder their own children than see them grow up to be Catholic. He would take no chances. In the note he prepared for Padovani to give to Lucidi, he ordered the Marshal to keep Edgardo under constant surveillance.

Meanwhile, the vigil at the Mortara apartment continued as other friends and neighbors converged on the home. Among these was the Mortaras' 71-year-old next-door neighbor, Bonajuto Sanguinetti, like Momolo a transplant from the Jewish community of nearby Reggio Emilia, in the duchy of Modena. Sanguinetti had already gone to bed when Riccardo, after fetching his two uncles at the cafe, came to his home and told the servant what was happening.

Sanguinetti described his first reactions when his servant woke him up: "I went to the window and saw five or six carabinieri walking about under the portico, and at first I was a little confused, thinking that they had come to take one of my own grandchildren."

He rushed to the Mortaras' home: "I saw a distraught mother, bathed in tears, and a father who was tearing out his hair, while the children were down on their knees begging the policemen for mercy. It was a scene so moving I can't begin to describe it. Indeed, I even heard the police marshal, by the name of Lucidi, say that he would have rather been ordered to arrest a hundred criminals than to take that boy away."

At half past midnight, the eerie vigil at the Mortara home was interrupted by the arrival of Moscato and Padovani, brandishing the piece of paper that they had extracted from Father Feletti. Marshal Lucidi was astonished that the Jews had had any success with the Inquisitor. He had assumed that he would not be leaving the apartment that night without the boy.

"I could see," the Marshal later recalled,

that Signor Padovani was an erudite person, of dignified demeanor, a man who was looked up to and respected by his coreligionists, and they counted heavily on him. Indeed, they had good reason to do so, for it must have taken someone of great influence to obtain a stay in the decree, and in my opinion others would not have succeeded in getting one, all the more so when I learned that the order came from the highest level, and that the Father Inquisitor himself was not in a position to change it.

When the Marshal departed, he left a scene that he described as a *teatro di pianto e di afflizione*, a "theater of tears and affliction." Aside from the ten members of the Mortara family and the two policemen guarding Edgardo, he left behind Marianna's brother, her brother-in-law, her uncle, and two family friends.

Momolo reacted to the news of the stay with relief, saying later it gave them "a ray of hope." He was less happy, though, to discover that in putting into effect the Inquisitor's admonitions to guard Edgardo closely, the Marshal had ordered two of the policemen to remain with the child in the Mortaras' bedroom.

It was a terrible night for Momolo and Marianna: "Both of the policemen stayed in our bedroom, with the guard changing from time to time with others replacing them. You can imagine how we passed that night. Our little son, though he didn't understand what was happening, slept fitfully, shaking with sobs every now and then, with the soldiers at his side."

The only hope left to the family was finding someone in a position to overrule the Inquisitor and vacate his order. There were only two men in Bologna who, in the view of the men of the Mortara and Padovani families, might have such power: the Cardinal Legate, Giuseppe Milesi, and the city's famous but controversial archbishop, Michele Cardinal Viale-Prelà. Encouraged by the diplomatic success enjoyed by Marianna's brother-in-law and uncle the night before at San Domenico, Momolo and Marianna asked them to undertake this new mission. In midmorning, on June 24, they set out.

They did not have far to go. Indeed, Angelo Moscato had been sitting practically in the shadow of the imposing building in which the Cardinal Legate worked when, the previous evening, the breathless Riccardo had brought the news about Edgardo.

The hulking government palace, the old Palazzo Comunale, loomed over the city's central square, the Piazza Maggiore. Opened as the center of government in 1336 and built up further over the next two hundred years, it was as much a fortress as an administrative center. Its opening had coincided with the completion of the vast, imposing wall that surrounded the city, a wall nine meters in height that made a lopsided circle seventy-six hundred meters around the old city. Each night the great gates closed their portals to protect the city's inhabitants (and rulers) from their enemies. When the palace and the outer wall were built, Bologna was an autonomous city-state, battling, among others, papal forces that sought to subdue it. It was a struggle that the city ultimately lost, and with the triumphal entry of Pope Julius II into Bologna in 1506, the city and its territories were annexed to the Pontifical State.

Giuseppe Milesi Pironi Ferretti had come to Bologna just two months earlier, having at age 41 been simultaneously named a cardinal and appointed legate to the province of Bologna. Arriving to take up his new duties in Bologna on the evening of April 30, 1858, he was met with due ceremony as he made his way to his offices and apartment in the government building. The resident Austrian troops sounded an artillery salute.

Not everyone in Bologna, however, was pleased about the Cardinal Legate's arrival, for hostility against papal rule, and against the Austrian troops who for years had enforced it, pervaded the city. Enrico Bottrigari, one of those Bolognesi influenced by the ideas of the Risorgimento, the national unification movement that one day in the not very distant future would help drive Milesi out of the city, described the Cardinal Legate's arrival:

"Hardly had he arrived in his quarters when the senior senator of Bologna came to pay his respects in diplomatic style, followed by many noble personages and citizens, the usual ones who bow before power! Those who have seen him say that the new legate, at first sight anyway, has the appearance of a man cold as ice, a person graced with little intelligence."[2]

The Inquisitor had given both Cardinal Milesi and the Archbishop advance notice of the planned seizure of the Jewish child. When Angelo Padovani and Angelo Moscato reached the gate of the Cardinal Legate's head-quarters, they were told that His Eminence was not in Bologna. There was little they could do but try to find the one other person they believed could help them: Bologna's archbishop, the redoubtable Michele Viale-Prelà.

Once again, they did not have far to go, for the archdiocesan head-quarters, connected to the cathedral of San Pietro, was no more than a stone's throw from the government palace. The two Jews were not optimistic, for in the brief time that the famous cardinal had been in Bologna, he had developed a reputation as the leader of the Church movement against liberalism, a crusader for religious purification and morality, a friend of the Inquisition, and a steadfast warrior in the battle to protect the Pope's position as a temporal ruler.

The previous night, when the Mortara family and their friends in Bologna's tiny Jewish community had gathered at their home, desperately casting about for a way to prevent the police from taking Edgardo, Sanguinetti had suggested that they try to bribe someone in the Church hierarchy. The idea was not shocking to them, for it was an approach that Italian Jews over the past centuries had occasionally used with success, even with popes. However, no one thought Viale-Prelà was the sort to be bought off.

As it happened, Padovani and Moscato would not even have the chance to try, for they received the same reception at the Archbishop's as they had at the Cardinal Legate's: they were told that the Archbishop was on a trip outside Bologna and would not be available that day.[3] The priest with whom they spoke, upon hearing what lay behind their pressing request to see the Archbishop, threw up his hands and told them he had no idea what they could do.

It was noon by now and time was running out. Angelo Moscato gave up: "Seeing that all hope was lost, we decided to let things take their unhappy course. I decided not to return to the Mortara home, for it would have only made me more bitter."

At the Mortara apartment, the tension was unbearable. Marianna's sister, Rosina, arrived in midmorning and found Marianna still clutching Edgardo, sobbing. As Rosina moved to comfort Edgardo, he gave his aunt a kiss and, gesturing toward the policemen who remained ever at his side, told her simply, "They want to take me away."

Rosina did the only thing she could think of to help. She took her other nieces and nephews back to her home to join her own six children. "I didn't want them to see their mother in such a state any longer," she said.

While Rosina took the children away, the men gathered in the apartment decided that something had to be done about Marianna herself. She had spent all night in Edgardo's sofa-bed with him in her arms and still would not let go of him. They feared what would happen if she were home when the carabinieri came that night to tear her son from her grip. And they were worried, too, about little Imelda, whose hungry cries were being ignored by her preoccupied mother.

Momolo explained: "As the day passed, amidst anxiety and fear, seeing my wife in a deplorable state, indeed driven almost insane, I decided it was best if she were taken from the house so that she wouldn't be made to see the separation, for the sight would have killed her." The Mortaras' 52-year-old friend Giuseppe Vitta, a fellow Jew from Reggio who lived near the Mortaras in Bologna, offered to take Marianna to his own apartment, where his wife was waiting. Vitta, along with Momolo and Marianna's brother, spent two hours trying to convince her that it would be best if she left: there was nothing she could do there, and Imelda's health depended on her getting away.

Finally, Marianna relented, but as Vitta waited for her she found it hard to stop kissing Edgardo. The men had to carry her out of the building and into the closed carriage, for her strength had left her. As they took her out, she cried so pitiably, said the family's servant, that it broke the hearts of all who heard her. Indeed, during the short trip to the Vitta home, Marianna's wails were so piercing that, although the carriage was covered, the unsettling noise brought people throughout the neighborhood hurrying to their windows.

Momolo had one last hope: the Inquisitor. Only he could call a halt to the looming disaster. Accompanied by Marianna's brother Angelo, Mortara set out for San Domenico.

At five o'clock, the two men arrived at the convent and were ushered into the Inquisitor's rooms. Momolo, in a loud but unsteady voice, declared that there had surely been some mistake about the supposed baptism of his son, and asked Father Feletti to tell him what grounds he had for thinking that the child had been baptized. The Inquisitor would not respond directly. The rules of the Holy Tribunal had been scrupulously followed, he said, and there was no point in asking for any further explanation. When Momolo begged for another delay, Father Feletti told him it would serve no purpose.

Momolo should not worry, the Inquisitor said, for his son would be treated well; indeed, little Edgardo would be under the protection of the Pope himself. He suggested that Momolo prepare some clothes for the boy; he would send someone to pick them up. Having a nasty scene when the police took Edgardo away, the Inquisitor warned, would benefit no one.

When Momolo returned home, he realized that time had run out on him. The house had emptied. Marianna and baby Imelda had been taken to the Vitta home; the rest of the children were with their aunt. Other relatives and friends had found the Mortara home too painful to endure and so remained at home, awaiting word of what was to come. Aside from the two policemen, who would not even allow Edgardo to go to the lavatory by himself, there remained only Momolo, his brother-in-law Angelo, and Giuseppe Vitta, back after having delivered Marianna to his wife's care.

Marshal Lucidi had meanwhile prepared carefully for the child's departure. Brigadier Agostini, Lucidi's silent companion of the night before, was assigned the task of driving Edgardo away, and for this had been given the best coach the Bologna police possessed. Lucidi came in a separate carriage, with a supporting police contingent. He arrived at the apartment at about eight o'clock. Accompanied by a number of his men, he climbed the stairs. In the apartment, Momolo held Edgardo in his arms; the boy remained calm, perhaps not comprehending what was about to happen. When Lucidi took Edgardo from his father's trembling arms, tears flowed from the eyes of the two policemen who had been guarding the boy.

Vitta ran desperately down the stairs first, followed by the policemen, and then a stricken Momolo. The sight of his son being carried off, draped from the policeman's shoulders, drained Momolo of his little remaining strength, and as he followed Edgardo he fell in a dead faint. As the boy was passed to Brigadier Agostini in the carriage, Vitta tried to calm him. "Don't worry," he said, "your father and I will follow you in another carriage." Vitta assumed, as did the rest of the Mortara family, that Edgardo's ride would be a short one, that his destination lay within the city walls. In this they were mistaken.

On the sidewalk, the frantic Vitta spied a Catholic neighbor, Antonio Facchini, a 31-year-old merchant, who happened to be passing by. Facchini tells of the startling encounter:

> As I was walking down via Lame, I found a carriage standing in front of the house that the Mortaras were then living in, and I saw a policeman stationed at the door. I was stupefied by this, all the more so when I heard shouts coming from the stairs from someone, and then I saw another person rushing out of the door calling to me, "Come! Come see, Facchini! what a pathetic picture!" It was the Jew Vitta, a friend of mine. When I asked him what was going on, he told me to come in. I went into the building with him, and saw at midstairs a policeman who was coming down with a boy in his arms, and just behind him, out cold and lying across the stairs, the Jew Mortara. . . . We rushed to help him, and carried him into his home, where we put him down on a sofa.

When Vitta explained what had happened, Facchini became enraged, and rushed to spread the word at the nearby Caffè del Commercio. There, he said later, "if I'd only found a couple of dozen of my friends, I would've tried to follow the carriage, stop it, and take the boy so that he could be given back to his poor parents." Whether this was simply braggadocio on Facchini's part, we do not know.

CHAPTER 2

Jews in the Land
of the Popes

*B*ologna la grassa, Bologna la dotta—Bologna the fat, Bologna the learned. Second only to Rome itself in population and social, political, and economic importance, Bologna had never been fully digested by the Papal States. The site of booming international commerce even before it was enveloped by the papal forces in the early sixteenth century, and home of Europe's oldest university—whose thousands of students from throughout the continent were hiring their own professors and running the school until the clerics took charge—Bologna, and not Rome, was the site Charles V chose for his consecration as emperor of the Holy Roman Empire in 1530.

At the time Charles received Pope Clement VII's blessing in the massive San Petronio basilica on the Piazza Maggiore, Bologna had a bustling Jewish community, immersed in the city's famed trade and commerce. Eleven synagogues dotted the central quarter, where most of the city's eight hundred Jews lived. Hebrew book printers and famed Jewish scholars complemented Bologna's reputation as a center of learning.

The sixteenth century, however, was not kind to Italy's Jews. The Roman Church, besieged farther north in Europe by Lutherans, Calvinists, and other heretical reformers, counterattacked. The campaign to enforce orthodoxy had as one of its victims the Jews, long an anomaly in Christian Europe.

For Bologna's Jews, the result was catastrophic. In 1553, their Hebrew books, including hundreds of copies of the sacred Talmud, were publicly burned by orders of the Pope and the Holy Office of the Inquisition. Three years later, the Jews were told to move to a single, walled-in zone, in the shadow of Bologna's famed two towers. The 1555 papal decree calling for the confinement of the Jews, *Cum nimis absurdum*, grew out of basic Church theology: "It is absurd and utterly unacceptable that the Jews, who due to their own guilt were condemned by God to eternal slavery, can, with the excuse of being protected by Christian love and thus tolerated living in our midst, show such ingratitude toward the Christians." No more would the Jews be allowed to mingle with the Christians; they were to be shut up into ghettoes.[1]

Scarcely had they begun to adjust to this life of confinement when, in 1569, came the first papal order for their expulsion from Bologna. A thousand Jews, their worldly possessions strapped to their backs or swaying atop wooden carts, left the city behind them. Amidst the packs of their clothes, books, and kitchen utensils were nestled the bones of their ancestors. Pope Pius V offered the Jewish Cemetery of Bologna as a gift to the nuns of the convent of Saint Peter the Martyr, telling them "to destroy all graves . . . of the Jews . . . and to take the inscriptions, the memorials, the marble gravestones, destroying them completely, demolishing them . . . and to exhume the cadavers, the bones and the fragments of the dead and to move them wherever they please."[2] After seventeen years in exile, the city's Jews were permitted to return in 1586, but in 1593 Pope Clement VIII ordered them out of Bologna again and indeed expelled them from the pontifical state, excepting only the capital of Rome and the Adriatic city of Ancona, where ghettoes would be allowed to remain. The Spanish Bourbon rulers of the Italian south, inspired by Spain's example, had earlier in the century expelled Jews from their entire territory, from Naples to Palermo. The south, which up through the eleventh century had been the home of Italy's most thriving Jewish communities, now had no Jews at all.

Fortunately for Bologna's dispossessed Jews, just to the northeast and northwest of Bologna lay Ferrara and Modena respectively, lands still under the control of the Estensi dukes. When forced for the second time to leave Bologna, most of the displaced Jews headed not to Rome or Ancona but out of the Papal States altogether, seeking refuge in the Estensi lands. Although Ferrara was itself soon swallowed up by the Papal States, the popes left that city's Jews where they were, and Ferrara's Jewish communities—swollen by the immigrants from Bologna and other lands where Jews had been expelled—lived on.

When the Estensi lost control of Ferrara in 1598, the ducal family moved its home to Modena. The duchy of Modena encompassed not only the city of that name, thirty-nine kilometers from Bologna, but the city of Reggio Emilia, twenty-four kilometers farther northwest in the Po Valley. In the centuries when Jews were barred from living in Bologna, both Modena and Reggio had flourishing Jewish communities, and it was from these that Edgardo Mortara's family came. In 1858, Bologna, unofficial capital of the pontifical state's northern territories, known as the Legations, was ruled by Pope Pius IX. Modena and Reggio lay in the domain of Duke Francesco V.[3]

Momolo Mortara was born in Reggio just two years after the Estensi duke had been restored to power in Modena following Napoleon's fall and the withdrawal of French troops from the duchy. Momolo's father, Simon, born in 1797, had had little experience with the legal restrictions of ghetto life, for his birth had coincided with the arrival of French troops, the burning of the ghetto's gates, and the abolition of all restrictions on the Jews.[4] Like many of Reggio's 750 Jews, Simon owned a small shop, where he was assisted by his wife and four children. His family had lived in Reggio for well over a century, but they felt part of a much wider Jewish community. Along with the other Jews of the peninsula, they shared the burden of the laws aimed against them and the sense of living as not entirely welcome guests in a land belonging to others. They were united, too, by the manifold ritual prescriptions they followed, the teachings of their holy texts.

When, in 1814, the Duke of Modena returned to power, he put most of the old discriminatory regulations back into effect. Under these laws, Jews could not spend the night outside the ghetto or own stores outside its walls. Christians were forbidden to venture into the ghetto after dark, nor could they work as servants for Jewish families. On the other hand, Christians were warned not to harass the Jews or make fun of them. This was especially a problem in the duchy, as throughout Italy, during Carnival and Lent, times when it was a valued part of popular tradition to taunt Jews. To avoid provoking the Christians, the law forbade Jews to leave the ghetto for the duration of Holy Week.

The ducal decree of 1814, after condemning the Jews' collaboration with the French-installed regime, reinstated the old code but abrogated some of its most irksome features, including the obligation to close the gates of the ghetto at sundown and to return to the ghetto before nightfall. Also abolished was the centuries-old requirement that Jews wear a distinctive emblem on their clothes so that all would know that they were Jews. In Modena, this emblem had consisted of a red ribbon, which Jews wore prominently atop their hats. Although the prohibition on Jewish residence and ownership of stores outside the ghetto remained technically on the books, it was suspended in exchange for a hefty annual payment from the Jews to the Duke. And so, after the fall of the French, the Mortaras were among the Reggio Jewish families who continued to live and keep their store outside the ghetto walls.[5] All in all, the duchy's Jews could have been worse off. In Rome, restoration of papal power in 1814 not only led to reghettoization, but the city's rabbis were once again required to make their humiliating appearance at Carnival. Forced to dress in grotesque black outfits, with short pants and a little cloak, they were made to march through the streets as part of popular festivities, their loose neckties serving as a target for rotten food and other missiles hurled by the jeering throngs.[6]

When it was time to find a husband or a wife, a Reggio Jew could draw on a dense kin network that extended indifferently across political borders. It went without saying that the spouse should be Jewish, not only because this was required by Jewish law but because marriage of a Jew to a Christian was forbidden by the state as well.

A woman moved to her husband's home upon marriage. Momolo's grandfather married a woman from Mantua, who moved to Reggio in 1789; his father married a woman from Verona in 1815, and she likewise moved. When it was time for Momolo to marry, in 1843, his bride, Marianna Padovani, from a family of successful merchants herself, moved from Modena to join him.

It was common for Jews in Modena and Reggio to live in large, extended families. Momolo followed this tradition, bringing his new bride into his parents' home. Their marriage was blessed with many children. By the time their fourth child, Augusto, was born, in 1848, the house was getting crowded. In addition to Momolo, Marianna, and their children, it included Momolo's father and mother, his 26-year-old bachelor brother, Abram, and another brother, Moses Aaron, with his new bride, Ricca Bolaffi. When, just a month after Augusto's birth, Moses and Ricca had their first child, Momolo and Marianna must have felt not only that their living quarters were tight, but that the store which provided all of them with their living could no longer do so. It was time to move.

Generations of marriages linking men and women from different ghettoes produced far-flung networks, stretching from Rome and Ancona through Livorno and Florence to Ferrara, Turin, and Venice. In deciding where to move, Momolo and Marianna acted no differently than their fellow Jews, no differently than their ancestors had: they turned to these networks. In discussions with kin and friends, the attractions of Bologna became clear.

The young couple knew a number of Jewish families, including Marianna's wealthy Modena neighbors the Sanguinettis, who had recently moved to Bologna. Much larger than either Reggio or Modena, and a much more important center of commerce, Bologna offered broader scope for an enterprising young man like Momolo. The very fact that there were hardly any Jews in the city—a result of two centuries of banishment following 1593 and the renewed government restrictions on Jews in the Restoration years—meant that the economic niche occupied by Italy's Jews in local commerce was largely open. Of course, this also meant that the thick web of Jewish social, economic, and religious institutions familiar to Momolo and Marianna in Reggio and Modena would not be found in Bologna. But the Mortara family would not be alone in their new home. It was a family decision. Around the same time that Momolo and Marianna arrived with their children, Marianna's parents, her uncle, and her married brother and sister also moved there.

As they were debating the move, dramatic events unfolding in the larger world could not be ignored. The year 1848 was one of upheaval and revolt throughout Europe, when rulers were chased from their palaces. In Modena and Bologna people rebelled, and armed revolt blended with general chaos. The very month that the Mortaras' son Augusto was born, the Duke of Modena, Francesco V, fled his capital, alarmed by reports that insurrectionary forces from throughout his dukedom were marching on Modena, together with hundreds of armed rebels on the move from Bologna. In both Modena and Reggio, civil militias filled the vacuum, installing a provisional government committed to constitutional law and individual rights.

The center of the uprising was the city of Bologna itself. Although part of a different state, it exercised considerable influence over Modena. Little more than three decades earlier, during the years of French rule, the two areas had been joined together in a single government.[7] When papal rule was restored in 1814 at the end of the Napoleonic wars, the Church had tried to impose tighter control over the rebellious northern Legations. These efforts were met with resistance by the Bolognesi: the years of French occupation had left a legacy of liberal ideas among the upper classes, and a growing cadre among the educated in this university city regarded papal temporal rule as an insufferable anachronism.

Publicly organized resistance was, of course, viewed by the authorities as treason, so the political opposition formed secret societies, including the famed Carbonari. Revolts against the old order in Naples and Turin in 1820–21 prompted Pope Pius VII to excommunicate members of the Carbonari. In the ensuing police inquiries into the secret society, one of those whose names came up most often in Modena was a member of the Sanguinetti banking family.[8]

Leo XII, elected pope in 1823, decided that extraordinary measures were required. In his five-year reign he canceled the modest reforms that had been enacted by his immediate predecessors, and imposed heavy-handed police surveillance. He demanded that the old measures against the Jews be enforced, and that the rest of the population be watched carefully to ensure that Church precepts with regard to fasting and religious observance were followed. Practices identified with modernity—and so deemed at odds with divinely ordained ways—were attacked. Even smallpox vaccinations were halted.⁹

To deal with the unrest in the Romagna area—the portion of the Legations that stretched from Bologna across to Ravenna and Ferrara—the Pope appointed Agostino Cardinal Rivarola as his *legato straordinario*. The Cardinal was to have unlimited powers, and he quickly acquired a reputation for brutality and repression. In 1825, after summary trials, he oversaw the sentencing of five hundred men from Romagnola for participation in *carbonarismo* and conspiracy. A year later, in return for his efforts, the Cardinal Legate was the target of an assassination attempt in Ravenna; after a narrow escape, he fled the Legations, but his replacement continued his iron-fisted policies, executing four of the men judged guilty for the attempt on the Cardinal's life.

Despite the campaign to stamp out political opposition, the next decade began with a new wave of unrest in the Legations. In early 1831, local elites led an uprising aimed at winning greater liberty and constitutional rule. In February, a nervous Cardinal Legate abandoned Bologna, and people rushed into Piazza Maggiore to celebrate the end of papal rule. They ripped the papal insignia from atop the door of the government palace and hoisted in its place an Italian national tricolor. Amidst the revolutionary fervor, papal troops fled the city, and a provisional government was formed, headed by the prominent local jurist Giovanni Vicini. When Duke Francesco IV of Modena heard about the successful revolt in Bologna, he hurriedly departed his capital. In Reggio the tricolor replaced the Duke's flag, and while his officers joined him in flight, the bulk of the troops joined the rebels.

On February 6, 1831, the very day that cardinals gathered in Rome to install Gregory XVI, the new pope received the news of the revolt in Bologna. Two days later, Vicini's provisional government declared an end to papal rule over Bologna. On February 19, seeing the Legations slipping away from him, Gregory urged Austria to send its troops to crush the rebellion. Two weeks later, thousands of Austrian soldiers poured into the duchy of Modena to retake it for the Duke, who had ties of blood to the Habsburg throne. On March 24, Austrian troops entered Bologna, and Vicini and his colleagues fled.¹⁰

This was not the first time that Vicini had provoked the wrath of papal authorities. Just five years before the 1831 revolt, he had been punished for his notorious public defense of Jewish rights in the Papal States. His action was prompted by a sermon given during Lent in 1826 by Ferdinando Jabolot, a monk known for his oratorical zeal, in Bologna's San Petronio Church. To make the sermon's message available to a wider audience of the faithful, the monk had it published. His topic was the Jews, who were, he pronounced, the plague of humanity, a bunch of filthy usurers and lawless ruffians, richly deserving of the divine punishment that had been meted out to them.

The roots of Jabolot's diatribe lay in centuries of Church dogma concerning the Jews. In Catholic theology, embodied in papal declarations of various kinds over the centuries, Jews were a people to be tolerated, but only within strict limits. As the people from which Jesus sprang, and a people whose Bible formed one of the Church's holy books, they enjoyed a special place that other non-Christian peoples did not. Yet they also bore a special guilt, for they were responsible for the crucifixion of Jesus. While the Jews were once God's favored people on earth, they had become God's enemies. Their temples in Palestine had been destroyed as divine punishment, and they were consigned by God to be perpetual wanderers, leading a wretched life.

Until the mid-sixteenth century, Church policy toward the Jews showed a certain restraint. They were allowed to practice their rituals, to have their synagogues, for they were a people who had played a special role in God's work on earth, and their continued existence bore testimony to that historic role. Yet the day would ultimately come when the Jewish people would see the true way, embrace God's Church, and in this way help to usher in the Second Coming. This attitude, however, changed dramatically with Pope Paul IV's declaration in 1555 consigning the Jews to ghettoes. Their conversion was no longer something to await passively; it was to be pursued vigorously.[11]

Vicini, reacting to the anti-Semitic campaign in Bologna and to the discriminatory laws directed against the Jews in the Papal States, published his own views in 1827, in the form of a brief on a thorny legal question that had recently come up. Giuseppe Levi, a converted Jew, had died without a will. He left behind three brothers; one of these had also converted, but the other two remained Jews. The prevailing juridical view in the Papal States was that only the brother who had converted should inherit, because, according to canon law, in the act of being baptized converts severed ties with their Jewish kin. As Vicini put it in his 154-page analysis of the case, the central issue was "whether the baptism of a member of a Jewish family dissolves the ties of kin and of blood that he has with the members of his family who remain Jews." Vicini's opinion was that they did not, and that consequently the Jewish brothers should be allowed to inherit.[12]

Bologna's legal profession, or at least that part of it identified with the government, was scandalized by Vicini's claims. The city's most distinguished expert in civil law, Vincenzo Berni degli Antonj, a professor at the University of Bologna, prepared a denunciatory reply, published that same year. Following the time-honored Church credo on the Jews, he denied, first of all, that Jews had any rights of citizenship. He dismissed Judaism as a vicious religion, and Jews as a people condemned by God to wander homeless across the land, an object of scorn among God-fearing peoples.

The professor went on to enunciate the following basic legal principles:

1. That Jews in the Papal States are simply slaves to be tolerated.
2. That they have no right to share along with Christians in the intestate inheritance of a Christian relative.
3. That the Jews themselves, in order to fulfill the nefarious requirements set down by a religion marked by an implacable hatred of Christians, are called upon to treat them with all manner of trickery, of treachery, and of torture, and to work tirelessly to reduce Christians to perpetual slavery.
4. That the restrictions under which Christians permit Jews residence are entirely necessary in order to avoid the deadly effects of their religion.[13]

The Inquisition in Bologna, only recently back in business at the Dominican monastery after being abolished during the period of French occupation, took a dim view of Vicini's heresy. Both he and the printer who published his defense of the Jews were found guilty and condemned to spend eight days confined in a convent to reflect on their sin.[14] Three years after this sentence, Vicini had the satisfaction—albeit short-lived—of pronouncing the end of papal rule in Bologna.

The Austrian soldiers who retook Bologna remained in the city for another half-dozen years to ensure that there would be no further challenge to the rule of the Cardinal Legate. But barely a decade after their departure, Bologna once again rose in revolt, this time along with much of the rest of the peninsula.

The Italian revolts of 1848–49 followed insurrections elsewhere in Europe in that fateful year. In February, an uprising in Paris spawned a new Republic; the next month a revolution in Berlin led to the granting of a constitution and the installation of a liberal government in Prussia. Most important of all for Italy—most of which came under Austrian influence in one way or another—a revolt in Vienna in March brought about the fall of the redoubtable Prince Metternich and the formation of a liberal government there as well.

In Italy itself, the Sicilians were in revolt for their freedom from the inept Bourbon rulers of the Kingdom of the Two Sicilies. When the revolt spread to the capital, Naples, King Ferdinando II was forced to grant a constitution, and his example was followed by the other rulers on the peninsula, unnerved by the prospect of popular revolt: Carl Albert, King of Sardinia, with his capital in Turin; Leopold II of Tuscany; and the Pope himself, Pius IX, who had ascended St. Peter's throne just two years before.

The Viennese uprising in March prompted a revolt against Austrian rule in Milan, center of the Austrian territory of Lombardy-Veneto, which stretched across the northeast of what would become the new Italian state. Those who dreamed of a unified Italy, free of foreign tyrants, called on the Savoyard king of Sardinia to help them throw out the Austrians and their lackeys. The creation of an Italian nation ruled only by Italians seemed to be within reach. In Milan, people threw up barricades and began to fight the Austrian troops. Fourteen days after Augusto Mortara's birth, Duke Francesco V of Modena fled his duchy. By the end of March, the Austrian troops had been driven from both Milan and Venice, and provisional governments were formed to replace the old regimes. King Carl Albert decided to send his soldiers to Lombardy, hoping to rout the Austrians and expand his kingdom. Newly installed governments from Modena to Venice deliberated the annexation of their lands to the Sardinian kingdom, to make Carl Albert the king of all Italy. By the beginning of April, volunteers from Modena and Bologna were heading north to join the war against the Austrians.

The war for national unification, the end of foreign rule, and the achievement of a state based on constitutional principles guaranteeing basic rights to its citizenry were initially viewed by most partisans of Italian unification as having the Pope's blessing. When he had assumed the papacy two years earlier, Pius IX had been widely regarded as a champion of reform and modernity. Some, indeed, had imagined that he would serve as honorary head of a confederation of constitutional states that would together make up the Italian nation. These hopes were dashed for good, however, when, at the end of April 1848, Pius IX announced his opposition to involvement of the Papal States in the war against the Austrians. In Rome and throughout the Papal States, the rebels found that they had a new target: the pope-king himself.

In Bologna, enthusiasm for the war against Austria ran high, while the Pope's announcement of late April undermined the moderates, who had been preaching the compatibility of a united Italy with continued papal rule. When, later in the spring, Austrian troops began to take the offensive and news of the first reverses of the Piedmontese forces began to come in, Bologna was in turmoil. Increasing numbers of defeated soldiers flooded into the city, and reports that Austrian troops were heading for Modena and Romagna left the population nervous and afraid.

In early August, the Austrians marched into Modena and reinstated the duke. They then moved on to Bologna, where, after a fierce battle against a rapidly mustered, largely civilian force, they were repulsed from the city. Tales of the Austrians' cruelty as they retreated—sacking houses and killing people on the way—fueled popular hatred.

Rome's increasingly tenuous hold on Bologna gave way in the fall when, following the assassination of his prime minister and facing the threat of a popular uprising, Pope Pius IX fled Rome and the Papal States altogether, seeking refuge in Gaeta, a fortified coastal town north of Naples. Demonstrations in Bologna forced the conservative city council to resign. In February 1849, following Giuseppe Garibaldi's arrival in Rome, the victorious rebels announced the birth of a new Roman Republic, while in Bologna there appeared the first decree of the Roman Constitutional Assembly:

> Article I. The papacy's rule and temporal power over the Roman
>   State is declared over.
> Article II. The Roman Pontiff will have all the guarantees necessary
>   for his exercise of spiritual authority.
> Article III. The form of the government of the Roman State will be
>   pure democracy, and will take the glorious name of the Roman
>   Republic.

In Bologna—although conservatives warned of impending anarchy—demonstrators rushed to the city's public buildings, removed the papal insignias from their portals, piled them up in the middle of Piazza Maggiore, and lit a great fire.[15]

Three days later, Bologna's newly elected council proclaimed the city's proud adherence to the Roman Republic. But however joyous the night of celebration that followed, it could not hide the widespread conviction that, in the face of opposition from the Austrians as well as the French, the new government would not last long.

Indeed, Bologna had little defense, other than its wall, against the Austrian troops who, in the name of the Pope, soon marched on the city. After an eight-day siege in mid-May 1849, the Austrians entered Bologna, restored the papal insignias, prohibited all public gatherings, required all residents to be off the streets by midnight, reinstated censorship of the press, and banned all displays of the national tricolor. Bologna was once again part of the Papal States. Two weeks later, Francesco V reentered Modena to take back his duchy. A month after that, French troops marched into Rome, destroying the last remnants of the republic and sending Giuseppe Garibaldi and Giuseppe Mazzini into exile.[16]

Too weak to stand on its own, papal rule in Bologna would now be ensured by the presence of a large, permanent force of Austrian troops and a reign of repression. In 1850, with order returning, the Mortaras made their move from Reggio to a home in the center of Bologna. Although they followed political developments with interest, they were preoccupied with the tasks of caring for their five small children and getting a new business started. They avoided the attention of the Austrian troops and the papal police as much as they could.

CHAPTER 3

Defending the Faith

WHILE AUSTRIAN TROOPS maintained their vigil in Bologna, Marianna Mortara went on busily bearing more children. Having given birth to Arnoldo shortly before moving to Bologna, Marianna bore her first child in Bologna, Edgardo, in 1851. Just a few months after Edgardo's birth the family acquired a new servant, Anna Morisi, a girl from the nearby rural town of San Giovanni in Persiceto. Anna, who, like all her kin and friends, was illiterate, was 18 years old, although she herself had only a hazy idea of her age.

No self-respecting family of merchants, of however modest means, would do without a domestic servant in Bologna. It was the servant's task to keep the house clean, do the laundry and much of the daily shopping, run errands, and help take care of the children. While the wealthy and the aristocrats had both male and female servants, the middle class had only women, most often unmarried and young. Anna was a typical case. Her parents, by sending Anna and her three sisters to the city to work as servants, saved the cost of feeding them while allowing the girls to save, from their modest pay, for their trousseaux and dowries so that one day they could marry. All the Morisi sisters followed this path, three of them returning to San Giovanni to marry. Only unlucky Maddalena never made it back: she died from the bite of a rabid dog.

Following Edgardo's birth, on August 27, 1851, Marianna again found herself pregnant, giving birth to Ercole late in 1852, and then, in 1856, after a four-year hiatus, to the ill-fated Aristide, who would die a year later. The household had grown large, with six boys along with their twin sisters. Riccardo, eldest of the eight, was only 12 years old.

Stability had meanwhile returned to Bologna, although hatred of the occupying Austrian forces remained strong. In 1855, Carlo Cardinal Oppiz-zoni, who had served as Archbishop of Bologna for an incredible fifty-two years, died two days short of his eighty-sixth birthday. Having survived the depredations of the city's churches at the hands of Napoleonic troops—who turned some of them into stalls for their horses—early in the century, having endured the revolts that flared up over the ensuing decades, and having weathered opposition from the more intransigent members of the Church hierarchy for his live-and-let-live attitude, Oppizzoni represented, for the people of Bologna, the benign side of Church authority, a Church that was an inextricable part of their lives.

His successor was a man of a very different stamp. At the time when he was named archbishop of Bologna, Michele Viale-Prelà was one of the conti-nent's best-known cardinals. As papal nuncio to Vienna—the Pope's ambas-sador to the Austrian Empire—he had just concluded a concordat between Austria and the Vatican that was hailed as a great triumph for the Church. It was an achievement that crowned a brilliant career as a papal diplomat.

On the first of November, All Saints' Day, 1856, the new archbishop made his triumphal entrance into Bologna, capped by his solemn entry into the cathedral. The following morning all the church bells of the city rang, joined by the sounds of Austrian artillery blasts, as a long procession of priests, monks, and local dignitaries, together with the entire university faculty, clad in their academic gowns, marched to San Petronio, in the Piazza Maggiore, to meet the new archbishop and escort him back to the nearby cathedral.

Viale-Prelà cut an imposing figure in his purple robes. A tall, slender man whose eyes radiated intelligence, he gave the impression of always being in control of himself, always acting with self-conscious dignity. His forehead was large, his face thin. He dressed with exquisite care. Although he smiled benev-olently when the occasion called for it, those who knew him could not re-member ever seeing him laugh. Having spent years in the highest diplomatic circles, Viale-Prelà was known for his erudition, his familiarity with history, art, and literature. He was a serious man; indeed, many thought he was too serious, a man unbending in his commitment to the Church.[1]

The new archbishop's entrance into the cathedral was witnessed by Enrico Bottrigari, an acute, if less than sympathetic, observer: "A solemn mass was celebrated, with grand music. In the middle of the mass His Eminence read a long sermon, full of repetitions, and boring not only in its content, but also because of the orator's monotonous voice. At the end, he gave the papal blessing to the numerous people in attendance." The Archbishop then retired to his official residence while a choir gathered outside to sing a song in his honor. That night his palace was ablaze, illuminated by gaslights.

Bottrigari concluded: "The reputation that our new pastor brings with him is not particularly flattering. They say he is too fond of the Jesuits, and an overly zealous priest. The work he did in Austria, with the all-too-famous Concordat, tells us what we need to know about him!" In a city that had suffered seven years of occupation by Austrian troops, the Archbishop's famed friendship with Prince Metternich and the rulers of the Austrian Empire did little to endear him to his new flock.[2]

Michele Viale-Prelà was the second of four sons of a wealthy Corsican family of Genoese origin. Born in Bastia, Corsica, in 1798, he was virtually pre-destined for high clerical office. His maternal uncle, Tomaso Cardinal Prelà, was physician to two popes, Pius VI and Pius VII. In deference to his uncle's role in his upbringing, Michele added his mother's maiden name to that of his father, Paolo Viale. Once ordained, in 1823, Michele entered the fast track of the papal diplomatic corps, serving from 1828 to 1836 as assistant to the papal nuncio to the Swiss Confederation. After two years back in Rome working with the papal Secretary of State, Viale-Prelà was sent to Munich, where he became nuncio himself and was named a bishop. Finally, in 1845, he moved to Vienna to become nuncio to the Imperial Court of Austria. While there, in 1853, he learned he had become a cardinal.[3]

Word of his appointment as Archbishop of Bologna reached Viale-Prelà in Vienna as bishops were gathering from throughout central Europe for the signing of the concordat he had negotiated. Accompanied by a personal note from Pope Pius IX, the news was an unwelcome surprise. The Cardinal had thought that, after all his years of service abroad, it was time for him to return to Rome. He had looked forward to this prospect not only for professional reasons but for personal ones as well. He had lived for much of his youth in Rome and would have enjoyed spending the rest of his years in the Eternal City. There was also the attraction of being close to his brother, Benedetto, who was a professor of medicine at the University of Rome and, continuing the family tradition, physician to Pius IX.

Viale-Prelà's appointment as spiritual leader of the contentious Bologna diocese was surprising for another reason, for in his brilliant career the Corsican priest had never had a pastoral role. He was a man clearly suited for the highest positions of Vatican governmental service; indeed, he was rumored to be the leading candidate to replace the widely reviled but powerful Secretary of State, Giacomo Antonelli. Those who favored such a move suspected that behind the unexpected assignment of Viale-Prelà to Bologna was none other than the crafty Secretary of State himself. They were sure that Antonelli had used his much-lamented influence with the politically naïve pope to keep his Corsican competitor far from his fellow cardinals, foiling their efforts to plot against him.

Although the new archbishop of Bologna was no more enthusiastic about his arrival in the towered city than were many in his new flock, he nonetheless threw himself into the task. As he saw it, his predecessor, well-meaning but overly indulgent and in failing health in recent years, had left him with a population that had slid perilously away from proper religious observance.[4]

The result, according to some Bolognesi, not averse to hyperbole, was a drive reminiscent of the worst days of the Inquisition. Indeed, in a typical account, Cardinal Viale-Prelà was charged with working closely with the Dominican inquisitor, Father Pier Gaetano Feletti, to introduce more effective surveillance of the population. The Cardinal issued large manifestos, which were attached to the doors of all diocesan churches, sternly reminding his flock of the requirements of the Friday fast. He was said to send olfactory spies around the diocese on Fridays, sniffing out those boiling pots from which wafted the odor of forbidden meats. Viale-Prelà's authoritarian reputation was not helped by reports that one day shortly after his arrival, spotting a man who failed to doff his hat as he passed by, the Cardinal had stopped his entourage and ordered the man to uncover his head.[5]

Viale-Prelà also became known for his displeasure with the proliferation of popular theater in Bologna. He could not have been pleased to learn that, at the time of his arrival to take the helm of his archdiocese, the talk of the town was the sensational American Miss Ella, performing at the dazzling Teatro del Corso. The Bolognesi were smitten by the amazing acrobatic feats she performed—with a ballerina's grace—while riding on the back of a horse.[6]

A glimpse of the austere orthodoxy promulgated by the Archbishop can be gleaned from his annual pastoral letters. In the letter he sent to all the diocesan clergy to be read to the faithful on Christmas 1858, he explained his view of Church teachings. "No," Viale-Prelà exhorted his flock, "this life has not been given to us so that we can use it to enjoy the pleasures of this world, pleasures that alienate us from God, that pervert the heart, that cloud our judgment, that overwhelm our will, pleasures that unfortunately simply pro- duce agitation, rancor, competition, jealousy, affliction, and unhappiness."

In that same end-of-year message, the Archbishop stressed that there was no higher or more noble human activity than the winning of the souls of unbelievers to the mercy of Jesus Christ through baptism. He made no men- tion of the case near to home, although by the time this letter appeared, the controversy over Edgardo Mortara's baptism and kidnapping was creating a great uproar.

The baptismal program outlined by the Archbishop was not aimed at Bologna's few Jews, but it was based on the same theology that lay behind the boy's abduction. Since his arrival in the city, Viale-Prelà had sought a way to involve the children of his diocese in his missionizing efforts, for he was troubled by the sad moral state of the youth. Clearly they were in dire need of religious education. He had begun the initiative shortly after arriving, and in a letter he sent to all parish priests in the diocese in September 1858, three months after Edgardo was taken, Viale-Prelà instructed all parishes to participate.

The letter alerted his flock to the barbarous custom in China of abandoning babies, a practice found all too frequently among the world's non-Christians. "This execrable custom is so widespread among those teeming hordes," he wrote, "that we see hundreds of thousands of these poor little creatures, shortly after birth, being drowned in the sea, or in the rivers, or eaten by animals, or trampled by carriages or by horses." He called on every child in the diocese to make a small weekly contribution to the Church's effort to save these unwanted children. Not only would their lives be spared if the Church could find them in time, but "in addition, they can be regenerated through the waters of Holy Baptism, so that if they die at an early age, they become little angels who fly up to heaven, and should they survive, they will be educated in the true faith, destined to spread Christianity in those lands in which today reigns an idolatry both sacrilegious and stupid. . . . Oh, what a blessing God will bestow on our families whose contributions will have sent Angels to Heaven!"[7]

The Archbishop made his own modest, if unusual, contribution to the winning of heathen souls in the year of Edgardo's abduction, a victory that gave him particular satisfaction because it came at the expense of just the kind of public indecency he was committed to curbing. One of the many circuses that traveled town to town in Italy had set up its show of wild animals and wonders in Bologna. Among its biggest attractions was a black youth touted as a real live cannibal. Indeed, he looked fierce, dressed in an animal-pelt outfit reeking of savagery. Word of the display reached the Archbishop, who had the matter looked into. The "cannibal," it turned out, was an illiterate boy of sixteen. Investigation revealed that he had indeed come from Africa and was not baptized. In order to get the boy away from his French keepers—for it was a French circus troupe—the Archbishop had to buy him, at considerable cost.

Thus procured, the boy was sent to a local Church institute where he was instructed in the catechism and the principles of the Catholic religion and then baptized. The following summer, in 1859, the circus manager paid an unexpected visit to the Archbishop. It seems the circus was suffering as a result of the loss of its most exotic attraction, but his pleas that the "cannibal" be returned were refused. The young convert, described by the priest in charge of his education as blessed with a gentle and loyal disposition, became a servant for one of Bologna's most illustrious families.[8]

Viale-Prelà's arrival was a boon to the demoralized corps of conservative Catholics in Bologna. Among his most ambitious efforts was the founding of a newspaper, *L'osservatore bolognese,* designed to combat the liberal ideas that had gained so much currency. The first issue of the weekly appeared on April 9, 1858, two and a half months before Marshal Lucidi appeared at the Mortara home. Its first article on the Mortara case did not appear until early October, when the paper expressed its shock over the massive scale of the protests against the Mortara abduction, which had spread throughout Europe and beyond. Titled "The Jew of Bologna," the article dismissed the hundreds of critical stories devoted to the case as a jumble of "fantasy, tall tales, insolence, blasphemies," and branded the papers that published them as "irreligious, heretical, Judaic."9

To nourish a renewed religious commitment, the Archbishop also organized a campaign of missions to the parishes of his diocese. In this, he joined a larger movement that was sweeping Catholic Europe. Skilled Church orators—typically Jesuits—traveled from parish to parish organizing brief periods of intense preaching and prayer. Cardinal Viale-Prelà's reputation among his critics for excessive attachment to the Jesuits was reinforced by his heavy reliance on the order for this campaign, inaugurated in April 1857. The Jesuits began their work of proselytizing and spiritual renewal by visiting each of the city's parish churches in turn. Bologna liberals' views of the campaign are pithily reflected in Bottrigari's diary: the Jesuits, he wrote, were spreading "ideas that were not only retrograde but entirely opposed to people's civil and moral progress."10

The Archbishop's spiritual-regeneration campaign had scarcely begun when exhilarating news arrived: the Pope had decided to make a journey to the Legations, and would be spending a full two months in Bologna, aimed at showing the world how fond his subjects were of him and how committed they were to continued pontifical rule.

It was the papal Secretary of State's idea that a grand tour of this kind be made. Not only did Cardinal Antonelli hope to shore up internal support for papal rule in the Legations, he was also worried about the Holy See's precarious diplomatic position. The previous year, 1856, Europe's major powers had gathered at the Congress of Paris, where they heard formal protests on behalf of the people of Bologna and the rest of the Legations. The petitioners accused the papal regime of administrative ineptitude, financial mismanagement, and an inability to curb rampant lawlessness. Only the presence of Austrian troops, the petitioners argued, prevented the Pope's disgruntled subjects from rising in revolt. The prelates were no longer capable of governing; the territories should be freed from papal rule. At the same conference, Count Camillo di Cavour, representing the kingdom of Sardinia, had pressed for the annexation of the duchies of Modena and Parma to the Piedmontese state, and the withdrawal of Austrian forces from the peninsula.

The Pope was stung by these attacks and by the reproaches voiced by the English and French delegates to the conference, who blamed the Vatican's governmental incompetence for provoking the prolonged Austrian occupation of the Legations. Pius IX was also worried about the movement for national unification, which was showing signs of new vigor in the peninsula. It was, in fact, in 1857 that the National Society was formed, based in Turin and dedicated to the unification of the Italian nation under the crown of Victor Emmanuel II, king of Sardinia.[11]

Of course, the idea of a caravan carrying a divinely ordained ruler to bless his far-flung subjects is an ancient one, the royal progress long a favored means of "demonstrating sovereignty to skeptics," in Clifford Geertz's felicitous phrase.[12] The Pope had a recent example before him, for earlier in 1857, the Austrian emperor, Franz Joseph, had visited his own restless subjects in Lombardy and Venice. The idea, in short, was to stimulate popular enthusiasm throughout the Pope's realm and convince England, France, and Piedmont of the solidity of his rule.

Bologna was to be the principal destination of Pius IX's voyage, and the Archbishop, the Cardinal Legate, and the local Austrian military command worked hard to make the occasion sufficiently magnificent. The Austrian general wanted to deploy heavy artillery in the middle of Piazza Maggiore to discourage would-be protesters during the Pope's visit, but Church officials, sensitive to the unfortunate impression this might create, prevailed on him to find a less visible site for his cannons.

Pius IX's procession into Bologna the evening of June 9 was suitably grand. Striding in front of the beautiful horse-drawn coach bearing the Pope down the old Roman road, Strada Maggiore, military trumpeters announced the Pontiff's impending arrival. His coach was surrounded by a guard of nobles, with a high official of the pontifical militia riding alongside one door and an Austrian official aside the other. Behind the coach rode an impressive assortment of full-dress generals, followed by coaches bearing members of the noble papal court, and then, stretching far down the road, a line of carriages carrying the local nobles who had come to greet the Pope.

As the lurching procession neared the city, it came to a triumphal arch, constructed just for this occasion, covered with buntings on which the colors of Bologna and the papacy were superimposed. There the carriages stopped, and the Pope was welcomed by a delegation of the city's nobility, who presented him the key to the city, nestled atop a plush cushion. Pius IX ascended a luxurious throne by the side of the arch and proceeded to give his blessing to the assembled dignitaries. He then returned to his carriage, in which the archbishops of Ferrara and Pisa awaited him. The papal procession got moving again, making its way through the great Porta Maggiore and into the city, passing through streets festooned with brightly colored banners and buntings. The papal carriage finally stopped at Bologna's cathedral, where Cardinal Viale-Prelà extended his arm to help the Pontiff out. Together they entered the church, where fourteen bishops greeted them.

Just what impression the Pope's arrival made on the people of Bologna is difficult to say. The many hagiographic accounts of the triumphal entry published by the Church in the wake of the visit paint a moving picture of adulation and devotion. In a typical example of this genre, the streets were described as lined with a multitude of people, "full of life, energized, happy, prostrating themselves as the papal carriage passed in a sign of religious reverence." The author recounts that the people appeared as "children happily pressing up to their father, and in every possible way showing their joy." The presence of "a few angry souls who tried to somehow disturb that joy" was unhappily noted, and likened to the lamentable presence, in even the best of families, of the occasional undisciplined child.[13]

Enrico Bottrigari, who also witnessed the evening's events, paints a different portrait. "In the soul of the crowd," he observed, "one saw the stimulus of curiosity rather than devotion, much less enthusiasm."[14]

The evening proceeded in eye-popping, ear-splitting style. After saying mass in the cathedral, the assembled clerics made their way to the nearby Piazza Maggiore, where a multitude of military and civilian bands played. The festivities stopped long enough to allow the Pope, from a balcony above the central piazza, to bless his subjects. The displays that followed were indeed impressive, with the Austrian troops marching through the square on horses decked with colored lanterns and torches. The spectacle pleased the Pope, who smiled his delight from the window, his hand held up in benediction.

Although government authorities from Rome had prohibited any signs of protest in the towns that lay along the Pope's route, a petition of grievances had been drawn up in Bologna, signed by a hundred of the city's elite. The petitioners' plan to present it to the pontiff during his visit, however, came to naught.[15]

The Pope did meet some prominent critics while he was in Bologna, men who begged him to reform the Papal States before it was too late. Among these was Count Giuseppe Pasolini, who a few years later would join the cabinet of the new Italian government. At the time, though, the Pope considered him a loyal friend. Indeed, the Count had briefly served as his minister of commerce in 1848. The meeting was an emotional one, two luminaries of an older world uncertainly confronting the new.

Pius IX was pained to hear Pasolini's view that the Pontiff was set on a disastrous course of intransigence, and that he was unwittingly playing into the hands of revolutionaries bent on destroying the old order. At the end of the unhappy encounter, the embattled and emotional Pope, in tears, asked, "So you too, my dear Count, are leaving me?" "No, Your Holiness," Pasolini replied, "it is not we who are leaving you, but you who are abandoning us."[16]

While the Pope was in Bologna, the monks of San Domenico invited him to join them in celebrating Saint Dominic's day, on August 8. Along with his Dominican brothers, Father Feletti—until recently prior of the convent as well as its longtime inquisitor—was thrilled to hear that the Pope would indeed be coming.

The Dominicans were doubly pleased about the Pope's visit, because they hoped to enlist his aid. Since the Napoleonic army had evicted them from their church and convent at the end of the previous century, they had succeeded in regaining only a part of their former vast complex. Unfortunately for them, the Austrians' military headquarters for Bologna was across the street, and a substantial portion of the Dominicans' buildings had been converted to barracks for the troops.

Following the celebration of a mass honoring their founder, the Dominicans took the Pope on a tour of their library. Once one of Italy's foremost book collections, it had been sadly reduced as a result of the Napoleonic depredations. Not only had large portions of it been carried off by the French, but a good deal of the rest had been seized to stock the city's municipal library. After the tour, the monks took their guest to a reception in his honor. There they asked him to order the removal of the Austrian troops from their convent.

To show their appreciation, Father Feletti and the other convent leaders presented the Pontiff with a beautiful reliquary in which they had placed a fragment of Saint Dominic's bones. There was no greater gift they could offer. Although San Domenico boasted many treasures, none was more precious to the monks than the holy remains of their founder.[17]

Pius IX accepted the reliquary with gratitude, for he was a man with a deep appreciation of the holy and a firm belief in the powers of the spiritual realm. Two years later, the Dominicans' wish would be fulfilled, and the entire Austrian military force in their complex hustled out, though hardly in the way they anticipated on that glorious August morning.

A week later, Pius IX left Bologna. His old friend Count Pasolini sadly described the scene: "A touching and lonely departure. You could see Pius IX's hand reach out from the door of the papal carriage, blessing the German troops who, silent, standing at attention, in single file, presented their arms. Nobody else was on the roads."[18]

CHAPTER 4

Days of Desperation

FRIDAY, June 25, 1858, the day after 6-year-old Edgardo rode down Bologna's cobblestone streets in the arms of the police, Momolo was still bewildered. He did not know who was supposed to have baptized his son, when they had done it, or how the Inquisitor had come to hear of it. The one thing he did know—he thought—was that his son was still somewhere in the city, most likely in the convent of San Domenico itself. Just before Marshal Lucidi took Edgardo away, Momolo's friend Vitta demanded a receipt for the boy. The note Lucidi scrawled read: "I have received and been consigned by Sig. Momolo Mortara his son Edgardo, aged 7 [sic], who by order of the Holy Father Inquisitor General is to be deposited in that Convent."[1]

At the moment, Momolo's only hope of contacting his son was through Father Feletti. Momolo recalled the Father's suggestion that he prepare some clothes for the boy, and although the Inquisitor had said that he would send someone to pick up the package, Momolo decided to take it to the convent himself to see if he could learn where his son was.

After lunch, he prepared a little bundle—the boy had left with only what he was wearing—and asked his brother-in-law, Angelo Moscato, to return with him to San Domenico. When they arrived at the splendid church courtyard, a lay Dominican brother informed them that Father Feletti was away and suggested they come back the next day. On their return the next morning, Edgardo's clothes again in hand, they were ushered into the In-quisitor's quarters.

Father Feletti received them graciously, but told Momolo that his son would have no need of the clothes after all. Edgardo was doing just fine, although just where the boy was, the Inquisitor would not say. I have entrusted your son, he reassured Momolo, to someone who is a good family man himself, a man who can be counted on to treat Edgardo with a father's care. What Momolo was not told was that the family man in question was a person he had recently met—Brigadier Agostini.

Momolo and his brother-in-law could get nothing more from the Inquisitor and returned dejectedly home, where friends and neighbors soon brought the news that the carriage that had made off with Edgardo had been spotted as it sped out of the city. It had not gone to San Domenico at all.

Momolo was in shock. His wife, Marianna, was, according to some reports, going out of her mind. They knew only too well the fate that had befallen them, for it was one that they, their relatives, and their Jewish friends had feared all their lives.

Once a Jewish child had been baptized, the child was in the eyes of the Church no longer a Jew and could not remain with his or her parents. In Catholic theology, baptism is viewed as a practice instituted by Jesus himself; its effects are instantaneous and irreversible. Through baptism, the individual becomes part of the mystical body of Jesus Christ and thereby a member of the true Church. Baptism releases the recipient from original sin and all other sins committed up to that time, and allows the beneficiary to enjoy eternal life. The practical requirements of the ceremony are modest. Water must be sprinkled on the person's head while the words "I baptize you in the name of the Father, the Son, and the Holy Ghost" are said. Although sanctified water is preferred, the baptism is valid regardless of the kind of water used. Under normal circumstances a priest should officiate, but anyone can carry out the rite as long as the baptizer has the proper intention. Indeed, not only can baptism be performed by someone who is not a priest; it can be performed by someone who is not even a Christian.[2]

Reggio and Modena, where Momolo and Marianna had grown up, were no strangers to such cases of police appearing in the night and demanding that a baptized Jewish child be turned over to them. They could scarcely have forgotten what had happened in Reggio less than a month before their first child was born there.

It was the evening of July 12, 1844. Police appeared at the home of Abram Maroni and his wife, Venturina, and informed them that their 19-month-old daughter, Pamela, had been secretly baptized. They wrested the child from her parents' arms and left. Abram learned that the alleged baptism had been administered by a young Catholic woman who had worked in their home for a few days. The family's protests—to the Archbishop, the Duke of Modena, and even the Holy Office of the Inquisition in Rome—were to no avail. Pamela was taken to the local Casa dei Catecumeni—House of the Catechumens, the Church institution founded in the sixteenth century for the conversion of Jews and other infidels—and her parents were forbidden to see her until she became an adult.[3]

Another Reggio case was no doubt known to Momolo, although he was not yet aware of its uncanny similarities to his own predicament. One day in November 1814, the Governor of Reggio ordered that a 7-year-old child, Saporina De'Angeli, be removed from her Jewish parents. A few days after police took her, the Reggio Jewish community helped the distraught father send a plea to the Governor of the province. It began: "A poor but honest man, intensely observant of the Law of Moses, yet having full respect for those principles that are professed by Christianity, Abram has been blessed by Providence with seven children, the oldest of whom has barely reached his tenth birthday. But in the midst of this, a great calumny was silently being plotted, which would reduce him to desolation and tears."

The villain in this piece, as in the taking of Pamela Maroni in the same city three decades later, was an illiterate young Catholic woman: "It is said that a woman of the lowest classes, of whose name and morals the unfortunate man remains ignorant, claims that, on some occasion vaguely recollected in the past, she secretly baptized his daughter named Saporina. And this was enough for the police to be sent to tear the daughter from the arms of the weeping mother, and take her to the Casa dei Catecumeni."

The woman in question was a former family servant. She claimed to have baptized Saporina years before, when she was a baby. She performed the rite, she said, because the child was ill, and she feared the consequences if the little girl died unbaptized. The protests of Saporina's parents were in vain, and, indeed, the deputies of the Jewish community who helped them were sharply rebuked by the secretary of the Duke of Modena's cabinet for interfering in the matter.[4]

Rather than a flickering vestige of the dark days of the Counter-Reformation, the taking of Jewish children was a common occurrence in nineteenth-century Italy. So frequent had such cases become that in October 1851, a few weeks after Edgardo's birth, the leaders of the Jewish communities of Reggio and Modena drew up a joint petition, which they presented to Francesco V, duke of Modena. Their supplication began with the usual profession of loyalty and appreciation but then called on the Duke to do something about "an extremely grave evil that in the recent past has afflicted us many times." They went on: "We speak of the horrible danger that we face even today of, from one moment to the next, finding ourselves bereft of our offspring due to clandestine baptism. Experience teaches us that it is in the power of even the most abject and infamous person to reduce, in but a moment, a family to desperation, a whole Nation to mourning and fear."[5]

The appearance of the police that June night on the Mortaras' doorstep, and the Marshal's request to see their children, were, far from being baffling, all too readily decipherable by Marianna and Momolo. Indeed, the carabinieri's knock on their door came in the wake of yet another case that had struck close to home, a case that was unusual only in being publicly discussed at the highest levels of government.

On June 9, 1858, barely two weeks earlier, a member of the Piedmontese parliament, that is, the parliament presided over by Cavour and reporting to King Victor Emmanuel II, rose to speak. "In Modena," he told his fellow deputies, "many cases have occurred of Jewish children being baptized because of a vendetta, or from stupidity, or due to the fanaticism of some servant. If this extralegal action had no outcome other than a little bit of water being sprinkled by someone who shouldn't, it would matter little." Yet this was unfortunately not the case, he said, for all it took was such a splash of water from the hand of a servant for a squad of police to be sent to invade the home and remove the child from his family so that he could be educated as a Catholic. It was, he thundered, "the greatest outrage against the pure sentiments of nature, against the most elementary rules of morality, producing the most heinous oppression imaginable." At these words, rumblings of protest rose from the benches on the right, where sat the conservative members of parliament, defenders of the Church.

The deputy looked their way and continued: "To save my adversaries any more exertions, let me say right away that I have been informed of all this and provided with the relevant documents by my Jewish friends of Modena." Indeed, he said, "there is in Turin today a Jewish family that had to flee with their daughter from Modena out of terror that she would be taken from them because a young servant claimed to have baptized her."

The deputy concluded patriotically: "I have spoken out on this as a matter of conscience. I have spoken because such an outrage against the laws of nature and morality must, in this nineteenth century, at least be stigmatized in the only Italian parliament, in the only place in Italy that, thanks to the efforts of the People, and the loyalty of the Ruler, is still free." As he stepped down from the podium, he was met by cheers of "bravo" from the deputies to his left, epithets and mutterings from his right.[6]

In the days following Edgardo's departure, Bologna's small Jewish community—many of whom were in one way or another related to the boy— was mobilized, and through their networks, word of what happened began to spread to Jewish communities throughout Italy. The only Jew in Bologna not to hear the awful news was probably Edgardo's grandmother, Marianna's mother. No one had the heart to tell her. While the Pope, prime ministers, and even an emperor would be gripped by the drama of her grandson, she would find out about it only many months later.

Through the grapevine, the Mortaras heard rumors that Edgardo had been taken all the way to Rome. It was time to call for help from the leaders of Rome's ghetto, not only because they were the closest to Edgardo, but also because they were the only Italian Jews who had access to the Pope himself.

Momolo's relatives and friends first helped him prepare his own formal request to have his son returned to his family. Their task was made simpler by the fact that the Jewish communities of Reggio and Modena kept files of past pleas, prepared for similar cases. On July 4, ten days after Edgardo's abduction, letters were sent not only to Father Feletti, but to the Secretary of State of the Vatican, Cardinal Antonelli, and through him to Pope Pius IX himself.

The Mortaras' cover letter to the Secretary of State employed the customary flowery, reverential style:

> Most Eminent Prince—
>   Momolo Mortara, a Jewish native of Reggio, approaches your most Reverend Eminence with the deepest respect, finding himself in need of calling upon the inexhaustible goodness of His Holiness, Pope Pius IX, to beg, as a most desolate father and husband, his sovereign providence, and not knowing how to bring before his August Throne these most humble supplications, thought of directing them to the Supreme Ministry under your command.

In addition to being sent the long letter addressed to the Pope, Cardinal Antonelli was given a copy of the letter sent that same day to Father Feletti. Still ignorant of just who was supposed to have baptized Edgardo and when, the Mortaras could not contest the facts of the case. They resorted instead to more general arguments. They asked the Inquisitor to consider the value placed on paternal rights in canon law, in particular the right of *potestà paterna*, the father's legal right over his children. Even if Edgardo had been baptized, they argued, he should be allowed to remain with his parents until he reached the age of reason, at which time he could decide "whether to remain in his paternal religion, or embrace Christianity."

Their letter to the Pope, signed by Momolo alone, was much longer, for in addition to making a canonical argument for the return of their son, they recounted the painful scene of Edgardo's capture, hoping that if the good-hearted Pope only knew the cruelty they had suffered, he would come to their aid.

The letter began, following its humble expressions of respect, by describing the events of the night of June 23. We were "struck as if by a bolt of lightning," Momolo recalled. Marianna, racked by grief, had subsequently returned to her family in Modena, where she remained "gravely ill from anxiety." "The dumbfounded boy," Momolo's letter to the Pope continued, "was taken from his father's arms by the police and sent to the capital. It is inconceivable, for me, that a child can be taken away like this." Surely, he wrote, there must have been some misunderstanding, some mistake, behind it all. He concluded his letter by praising the Pope and expressing his faith, given the Pontiff's renowned kindness, that he would restore the child to his grieving parents.[7]

The written plea to Father Feletti had no effect; the Inquisitor informed the Mortaras that the matter was out of his hands. Their only hope lay in Rome, but there the matter was much more complicated. While Sabatino Scazzocchio, the secretary of the Jewish community of Rome, took on the task of coordinating efforts on behalf of the Mortaras with the Vatican, he urged them to do what they could in Bologna to get to the bottom of the matter. They had to discover the circumstances of the alleged baptism if they were to have any hope of preparing a successful appeal. Who had baptized Edgardo?

The attention of the Mortara family and that of the other Jews of Bologna fell inevitably on the Catholic women who had worked as domestic servants in the Mortara home. Italy's Jews, at least those with the modest resources that would permit them to have such domestic help, had long had an ambivalent relationship with the young women who worked for them. Jews looked outside their community to recruit these women, not only because that was where they were plentiful, but more importantly because one of the major services they could provide was to work on the Sabbath, when, beginning at sundown on Friday, Jews were forbidden by their religious law to light the lamps that gave them light, the flames that provided warmth or cooked their food. A family with no non-Jew to perform these and other tasks on the Sabbath lived uncomfortably. In Bologna in 1858, almost all the Jewish families had Catholic women working for them.

Yet Church authorities had never been happy about the practice of Christians working in Jewish homes. The Church's goal was to keep the faithful away from the Jews, who, it was thought, might undermine the faith and corrupt the beliefs of any Christians who got too close to them. Already in 417, the Christian rulers of the Roman Empire forbade Jews to acquire Christian servants. The history of papal pronouncements and inquisitorial manifestos dealing with the Jews is a history of the reiteration and repeated expansion of this ban.[8]

Typical was the "Edict on the Jews" issued in Bologna on June 6, 1733, a large manifesto attached to church doors throughout the diocese. Signed by Father de Andujar, the Dominican Inquisitor of Bologna, it listed dozens of restrictions on Jews, one of which was "that Jews cannot keep either male or female Christian servants." Eleven days later, the portals of Bologna were covered by a different version of the same edict, this one signed by Cardinal

Lambertini, Archbishop of Bologna and soon to become pope himself. The edicts specified that Jews were to remain in the ghetto every night, they could not read the Talmud or any other prohibited book, they must "wear the sign of yellow color, by which they are distinguished from others, and they must always wear it in every time and place, both within the Ghetto and outside it." The edict warned that "the Jews may not play, nor eat, nor drink, nor have any other familiarity or conversation with Christians." It dwelt at particular length on the evil of allowing Christians to work in the homes of Jews, and specified that any father who allowed his child to do so would be punished severely, and his child imprisoned.

All this attention to the Jews in Bologna in 1733 may seem odd, since they had been ejected from the city and its hinterland 140 years earlier. There was no longer any ghetto whose portals could be closed at night. But the edict was a product of the Holy Office of the Inquisition in Rome, and local archbishops and inquisitors throughout Italy were directed to disseminate their own versions, whether there were Jews or not. Such was the thoroughness, and the bureaucratic logic, of the Church.[9]

Following the restoration of papal rule in 1814–15, among the old restrictions reimposed on the Jews was the ban on Christian servants. It was a ban, however, that was by this time only sporadically enforced. Occasionally, an eager inquisitor or concerned bishop ordered an end to the backsliding, and action was taken. In Ancona in 1843, for example, the Inquisitor issued an edict ordering the Catholic women working as servants in the city's large ghetto to leave it immediately.[10] But typically, by midcentury, Church authorities turned a blind eye to the practice. This was certainly the case in Bologna, where the priest of San Gregorio, the parish in which the Mortaras and several other Jewish families resided, listed, year after year, in his annual census of the households under his care, the servants living in the Jewish households, with the note *"servente cattolica."*[11]

Yet it was not only the Church authorities who were concerned about the danger of allowing Catholic women to work in Jewish homes. Jews themselves, while reluctant to do without such help, long remained uneasy about it, an anxiety that only increased in the years of the Restoration. The problem was that Jews saw these Christian women in their midst as potential agents of disaster, for if the servants were otherwise in a subordinate position, they had one great power: they could, when the parents were not looking, baptize an unknowing baby and thereby bring about the family's ruin. But although Jewish men and women spoke endlessly of the danger they faced, there is little evidence that they ever of their own accord sought to do without their Catholic servants. The possibility of allowing Jews to perform the tasks forbidden on the Sabbath was, given their religious beliefs and the attitudes of their rabbis, literally inconceivable.

In 1817, papal police were sent to a Jewish home in the ghetto of Ferrara, just thirty miles northeast of Bologna. There they seized the family's 5-year-old daughter. The abduction was prompted by a young Christian woman's claim that, five years earlier, when she had been caring for the girl, then an infant, she had secretly baptized her. In the wake of this case, the Ferrara Jewish community sent a delegation to Rome to plead with the Pope for the child's return, but apparently to no effect. Ferrara's Jews, now terrified by the dangers posed by their Christian servants, began to require that, on leaving their service, they sign (with an X) a notarized statement that they had never baptized a child of the family. Their innovation spread to other ghettoes in the Papal States.[12]

If the Inquisitor had received a report that Edgardo had been baptized, clearly the first place to look for the secret baptizer was among the women who had worked in the Mortaras' home. After Anna Facchini, the Mortaras' current domestic servant, heatedly denied having had anything to do with it, the family began to look back among their former servants, asking everyone they knew if they had heard anything from any of these women about a secret baptism.

Suspicion soon fell on Anna Morisi. She had moved into their home when Edgardo was but a few months old and had left it only recently to work with another Bologna family. They learned that Anna had since gotten married and left the city altogether.

One day late in July, when Momolo was off in Modena, Marianna's brother Angelo stopped by her house for lunch. As they sat down to eat, an unexpected visitor arrived, Ginevra Scagliarini. Now married and living outside Bologna, Ginevra had for years worked as a servant for the family of Marianna's sister, Rosina, the one who had taken in Marianna's other children on the day of Edgardo's abduction. Rosina and her husband, Cesare De Angelis, had six children of their own, and Ginevra had been there when most of them were born. She felt a strong bond with the family and often dropped in to see Rosina and her sisters when she made the trip to Bologna.

During most of the time when Ginevra had been with Rosina, Anna Morisi had been working for Marianna. Moreover, Ginevra and Anna were both from San Giovanni in Persiceto. The two young women had become good friends, a fact that came to Angelo's mind as soon as Ginevra entered the house. With the thought that out of friendship Ginevra might try to protect Anna, Angelo decided to employ a small ruse. Pretending that he had already been told it was Anna Morisi who had baptized Edgardo, he said, in an ironical tone, "Some nice thing Nina did, eh?" He added, "She's just devastated this poor family."

Ginevra took the bait: "Yes, it's true," she said. "I found out about it from Monica, her sister. She said that it really was Anna who baptized Edgardo."

When Anna had first heard the news that Edgardo had been seized by the police as a result of what she had done, Ginevra reported, she was overwhelmed by the fear that the Mortaras would want revenge.

Later in the day, when Momolo returned, Angelo excitedly told him of his discovery and proposed that he and Cesare De Angelis, their brother-in-law and Ginevra's former employer, make the trip to San Giovanni in Persiceto to confront Anna Morisi and find out what had really happened.

Angelo and Cesare arrived in San Giovanni two days later. It was a Wednesday, market day in this large rural community, so their arrival went unnoticed amidst the bustle of merchants hawking their wares and marketgoers descending on the town from outlying hamlets.

The two men went first to Ginevra's home, where Ginevra and Monica, Anna Morisi's sister, were awaiting them. The two women led Angelo and Cesare to the building where Anna lived. They climbed the stairs to the third floor, where Anna and her husband occupied a single squalid room carved out of the home of another of Anna's sisters, Rosalia. It was 11 a.m.

Monica and Ginevra had warned Nina, as Anna was known, of the men's arrival just a few minutes before the stagecoach carrying them arrived in town. Angelo described the scene that met them:

> We found Nina bathed in tears and trembling with uncontrollable sobbing. Only when we were able to cheer her up, assuring her that we had not come to do her any harm, but only to discover the truth so that a remedy to the sad situation might be found, did she tell us about the baptism. She told us the following story:
>
> "A few years ago I was in Bologna, in the service of the Mortaras, when a son of theirs, named Edgardo, about a year old at the time, got sick. One day when he got much worse, and I thought he might die, I spoke to Signor Cesare Lepori [who ran the grocery store near the Mortara home] about it, saying how sad I was, especially since he was a handsome baby, and I was sorry to see him die.
>
> "Signor Lepori suggested that I baptize him, but saw that I was reluctant, especially since I didn't even know how to do it. So he taught me, and I went back to the house with a glass, filled with some water that I got out of the bucket, and, coming up to the sick boy, I threw some on him saying, 'I baptize you in the name of the Father, of the Son, and of the Holy Ghost,' adding a few other words as well that I can't remember right now. The boy got better, and I didn't think any more about it, because I figured that it wasn't of any importance since I had done it without really knowing what I was doing.
>
> "It was only last year that, when a son of the Mortaras named Aristide died, I was talking sadly about it one day with a certain Regina, the

servant of our neighbors, the Pancaldis, and she told me that I should've baptized him. I told her that was a suggestion I wouldn't want to follow, and I went on to tell her about the time in the past, when Edgardo was sick, when I'd thrown some water on him, but that it hadn't had any effect. Hearing that, Regina told me that I should have spoken about it with some priest, but I didn't.

"Last winter I was called to the Convent of San Domenico in Bologna, and there that Saint Inquisitor interrogated me about what I had done with Edgardo, forcing me to tell him everything. Crying, I told him, and his secretary wrote down what I said, and the Inquisitor made me swear on the Crucifix to say nothing. I figured at the time that I must have been summoned to that Convent because of Regina, given what slipped out of my mouth when I was talking with her.

"I was surprised again when Edgardo was carried off, and, figuring that it was all my fault, I was very unhappy, and still am. I just hope that the fact that I did what I did when I was only around 14 years old, and not really thinking, is some excuse."

Angelo Padovani, hearing Anna's tale, found that he was moved by it, despite himself: "She said no more, but her words, and her demeanor, and her tears before she could launch into her story, persuaded me that what she told me was all true."

Going through the minds of the brothers-in-law as they listened to Anna's story was the question of whether there was anything in what she said that might help persuade the papal authorities to let Edgardo go. If there was, they thought, it would do them little good unless they could get her account down in legal form. When Anna finished her recollections, Angelo asked if she would be willing to repeat her account in the presence of witnesses. They were relieved to hear her say that she would.

Angelo and Cesare then ran off to find the local notary, which took a bit of doing, but at two o'clock they returned with the notary and two witnesses. They found Anna's room deserted. In her sister's apartment, they were told that she had left town.

Anna had in fact not left San Giovanni, but following her dramatic encounter with the two men, her sisters, Rosalia and Monica, warned her not to say anything more about the matter to the two Jews. In order to convince her, they took her to see their parish priest. Don Luigi, when told of Anna's interrogation by the Inquisitor and of the subsequent events, ordered her to say nothing more.

Angelo and Cesare rode the coach back to Bologna empty-handed, in possession only of a story, a story in some ways new to them, in others all too familiar.

CHAPTER 5

The Mezuzah and the Cross—
Edgardo's Trip to Rome

C ENTURIES OF CONFINEMENT in ghettoes had led
Italy's Jews to cultivate special channels for dealing with state
authorities, a kind of Jewish diplomatic service. A Jew normally
approached state or Church power not directly or alone but through the
offices of the local corporate Jewish community, which, through its official
spokesmen (they were never women), would petition the ruler on behalf of
any Jew who came under its authority.

Bologna's Jews, given their small number, the recency of their arrival,
and, above all, their dubious legal status, had no official organization at all.
They had no synagogue and, having no rabbi, remained under the religious
authority of the rabbi of Cento, a small town midway between Bologna and
Ferrara that, because it lay in the Estensi domain at the time Pope Clement
VIII banished Jews from most of the Papal States, had been able to maintain a
small Jewish community.

In the absence of a formal organization in Bologna, efforts on behalf of
the Mortaras fell to a handful of influential Jewish men who were close to the
family. It was they who first alerted the other Jewish communities of Italy to
the disturbing news, they who kept Jews throughout Italy and beyond posted
on the latest developments, and they who organized the fund-raising drive to
pay the costs of the campaign to free Edgardo.

No strangers to crises of this kind, Italian Jews were masters at spreading
bad news. Marriages linking the Jews of the various ghettoes, the movement of

families from one ghetto to another, the skillful use of Jewish ties to promote commerce in the face of archaic customs barriers, and a total population in the peninsula that, at around thirty thousand, was barely that of a small city combined to create a thriving, nonlocalized community. Sharing a long history of subjection to the powers of a hostile Christian state and forbidden to develop ties with their Christian neighbors, the Jews were cast together by outside pressures. But they were also fortified by a belief in their basic oneness as the People of the Book, united—at least in theory—with Jews everywhere.[1]

News of the Mortaras' misfortune spread quickly through the old Jewish ghettos of Italy, to Ferrara, Ancona, Cento, and Rome, under papal rule, and to Modena and Reggio Emilia, where many of Momolo and Marianna's relatives still lived, under the Duke of Modena's rule. The news sped on to Florence and Livorno, under the somewhat more benign authority of the Grand Duke of Tuscany, and to Turin and the other recently emancipated Jewish communities of the kingdom of Sardinia.

For the Jews of Italy who lived as not entirely welcome guests in places where the Inquisition was still in force, the Mortaras' misfortune was their own. Having gotten a taste of equality during the French occupation, and aware of the recent emancipation of brethren in Piedmont, France, and Britain, they reacted to news of the Mortara affair not only with fear but also with rage. Yet the Jews of the Papal States remained—as unemancipated Jews had been over the centuries—muted in their public protests, fearful of stirring up the wrath of their rulers. In the Italian peninsula, public protest was limited to Piedmont, for only there did Jews have basic constitutional rights, and these had been granted only a decade before. But in France and Britain, not to mention the United States, Jews were free to organize politically. Just as important, the development of a relatively free press, intended for a mass audience, had by 1858 changed the dynamics of power in much of Western Europe. One part of this movement was the founding of Jewish newspapers. While some of these, clinging to a more traditional path, were limited to the narrow discussion of religious matters and remained under rabbinical control, others, with lay editors, charted a new course. Weighing in on larger social and political issues, they gave Jews a public voice that they had never before had.[2]

If the Mortara case became an international cause célèbre, it was in no small part due to the newly acquired ability of the Jews to make their grievances known publicly and to communicate and organize rapidly across national boundaries. The emancipated Jews profited not only from their newfound freedom of expression and freedom of the press, but from their increased political influence, as the Enlightenment ideology that citizens were entitled to enjoy certain basic rights was rapidly spreading. Europe's Jews had long shared a sense that they were all one people, but in the past they had found it difficult enough to influence the actions of their own civil rulers and had no hope of intervening on behalf of their brethren elsewhere. Now Jewish solidarity would have a political dimension as well.

Within days of Marshal Lucidi's visit to the Mortara home, emergency meetings of Jewish community leaders were being called throughout Italy. Jewish fathers told stories of similar cases that had befallen their community. Mothers looked at their own children with new anxiety, and at their servants with new dread.

At Rome's central synagogue, in the ghetto that had since the sixteenth century enclosed the ancient Jewish community on the bank of the Tiber, Sabatino Scazzocchio, the young secretary of the four-thousand-member community, officially known as the Università Israelitica, was soon bombarded with letters from his counterparts throughout Italy, urging him to act. One such plea came from Livorno, dated July 7, 1858, sent by Signor Alatri, a man well known to Scazzocchio, for he was related to one of the influential families of the Roman ghetto.

"I want to let you know," Alatri wrote, "the many urgent requests and recommendations I have had from the most respectable persons, both from Florence and from here, that you take this matter in hand." He went on to tell the Roman leaders what they should do, listing eight points they should make in their petition to the Vatican, ranging from arguing the supremacy of paternal rights over a child to demanding that the Church reveal the facts of the alleged baptism.

Momolo had learned, wrote Alatri, that canon law called for the corporal punishment of anyone who baptized Jewish children without their parents' permission. (Although this was true, what he did not mention was the difficulty of discovering any case where such punishment had actually been meted out.) Momolo asked that the law be applied in his own case, in order to dissuade the overly zealous from baptizing Jewish children in the future. Alatri further reported that, although others had suggested enlisting the aid of foreign governments, he thought this was not a good idea. It would be best if the matter were handled by the Jews in Rome, as had been done for centuries.[3]

Two days after the Livorno letter was penned, the Mortara family sent its first letter to the Jewish secretary of Rome. It was written by Marianna's uncle Angelo Padovani, whose diplomatic skills had so impressed Marshal Lucidi. In the early days following the abduction, the family turned to Angelo to coordinate their efforts.

Aware that Scazzocchio already knew about the abduction, Padovani wrote from Bologna to bring him up to date on what had already been done to try to get the child back. Since the family's plea to Bologna's Inquisitor had been rejected, he reported, their only hope remained in Rome. He continued:

While we have been busy here tracking down rulings found in the sacred books in order to gather material for another petition, some people have advised us instead to try going to Court. I have already told you that there has been a great commotion in the city [about the abduction], and I haven't exaggerated. I know that it has been, and still is, the subject of bitter comment in high society here. And I found out that the Marquise Zampieri, who just arrived here on Wednesday, said that the subject is the talk of the town in Rome and that it has been acutely felt by [the French] General Goyon, who, moreover, said that something like this, given that the honor and glory of the Church are at stake, merits the attention of the ministers of the Foreign Powers, to show that such persecution is incompatible with the times.

Padovani asked Scazzocchio whether he thought it might help if Momolo himself came to Rome. As Momolo was far from rich, he quickly added, he wondered what sort of support might be forthcoming from Rome's Jewish community. He concluded by asking if Scazzocchio could reassure the anxious parents by providing word of Edgardo's well-being, for the boy had by now been in Rome for several days.

The informal committee of Bologna Jews launched a frenetic search for an advisor expert in canon law, hoping to find the citations that would clinch their case and persuade the Pope to free Edgardo. Meanwhile, research was under way at the Roman synagogue as well, and Scazzocchio sent the committee the results of the initial investigation into Church doctrine on the baptism of Jewish children. Two weeks after his first letter to Scazzocchio, Padovani wrote again, reporting his mounting concern that the Church canons were, in fact, not in Momolo's favor, as well as the committee's anxiety at the lack of a response from the Secretary of State to Momolo's plea.

Padovani also wrote that they were preparing Momolo for his trip to Rome, planned for the end of July. To offset his expenses, they had already circulated a letter to Jewish communities throughout Italy, calling for a collection to be taken up to support the Mortara cause. They were also still hoping to find a legal advisor—and here they felt a Catholic lawyer would be best—to accompany Momolo and act as his representative in dealing with the papal authorities. Yet they had run into insuperable difficulties. No one willing to make the trip and represent the Jews could be found in Bologna, and their urgent requests to the Jews of Ancona and Ferrara, Pesaro and Florence, to locate such a person had gotten them nowhere.

Scazzocchio was not pleased with the letter from Bologna. It would be best, he thought, if he and his colleagues in Rome were left to handle the matter in their own way, using their own channels and their own methods. The prospect of Momolo arriving with his own legal advisor—and a Christian one at that—to make an independent approach to the Roman authorities was deeply troubling. Anything that might cause the Vatican to view the Jews as lacking in proper deference to the Church was to be avoided at all costs, for it would be the Jews of Rome who would suffer most from the resulting papal displeasure.

On July 29, Scazzocchio sent an urgent letter to Bologna to try to persuade Momolo to put off his trip. At this point, he wrote, the need for his presence in Rome was less pressing; the matter "having lost its primitive virginity, a large part of the hoped-for effect of having the paternal pain on display has already been lost."

At the bottom of his letter, Scazzocchio added a worried postscript, reflecting a development that had been taking on increasing importance in recent days. Defenders of the Church were beginning to spread their own account of what had happened. In their version, the boy had left his parents without protest and had gone happily with his police escort to Rome. Scazzocchio's postscript reads: "Write me immediately, today, a detailed account of the abduction." He wanted to know the exact words the boy had uttered as he was being taken away.

The question had become so urgent, in fact, that the impatient Scazzocchio also sent Padovani a telegram, despite his concern about the prying eyes of the papal police. Both sides took care to do what they could to disguise the subject of their communication. Padovani's reply arrived in Rome by return telegram the same day: "Individual speechless, crying convulsively, frightened. Torn away, wanted parental company."

The major development in Bologna, meanwhile, as Momolo tried to get his business affairs in order for what threatened to be a long stay in Rome, was the discovery, thanks to Anna Morisi's confession, of what lay behind the Inquisitor's order to seize Edgardo. Right after Momolo's brothers-in-law returned from their encounter with her, Angelo Padovani wrote to Rome to recount her story. Padovani chose to write to a relative of his in Rome, Jacob Alatri, rather than directly to Scazzocchio, in part because he was not entirely happy with the way Scazzocchio was handling the affair. The tone of his July 30 letter reflects the family's mounting frustration.

Padovani complained that neither he nor his Bologna brethren could understand why Scazzocchio refused to send new pleas to the papal authorities, as they had asked. As for all the material on Church law that Scazzocchio had been sending them, it was practically useless, since none of them knew Latin and they had been unable to find any lawyer in Bologna to help them. Although they had located two experts on relevant canon law, one, Padovani wrote, was mired in "exaggerated superstition," and the other was a friend of the Inquisitor.

He then came to Anna Morisi's tearful testimony, which his nephew had written down and which he enclosed:

> There is no need to comment on the woman's deposition. You see that, when she was just fourteen or fifteen, she threw some well water, taken from a bucket, on a child 12 or 14 months old, who was sick with the kind of infection children get but not in any danger of dying (we attach the doctor's statement). She had no idea of the importance of what she was doing, which, consequently, might not have had the characteristics demanded by the Church. She acted as a result of the suggestion, very possibly made in jest, of the grocer Lepori.

Recognizing that the authenticity of Morisi's account might be questioned, for it was neither notarized nor signed, Padovani suggested that efforts be made to have the young woman sent to Rome to testify. He relished the prospect of such a confrontation and what he took to be its likely result: "a Decree of Nullification, and the return of the son to his father, and, in addition, for the glory of the Church, in the interest of Public Morality, and for the tranquillity of all, a law that would call for the censuring and punishment of anyone who, by such underhanded means, tries to steal children from their parents." He concluded by voicing the hope that the first to be brought to justice under the new law would be "the instigator," Cesare Lepori.

By the time Momolo left Bologna for Rome, on July 31, relations between the Jews of Bologna and the leaders of the Roman ghetto had become tense. The last letter received from Scazzocchio had begun with the remark: "I was hoping to be able to tell you today about recent developments of the greatest importance, but I hope to do so next Monday." The response from the Bolognesi showed their exasperation: "You wrote on the 27th that you hoped soon to send an extremely important communication, which filled us with great hope, and we anxiously await the news, which it seems you are still not in a position to give us. We would be very grateful if you would let us know the present state of things, insofar as you can, and what steps are in progress."

Momolo set out. According to a friend, he was in a sad state, his spirit broken, his once boundless energy drained.

While Rome's Jewish leaders wanted to handle all dealings with the papal authorities in their own way, the Jews of Bologna favored a more aggressive approach. Their end-of-July letter proposed a multipronged strategy. The first involved Momolo's activities once he reached Rome. The second, they proposed, should be a unified effort by all the Jewish communities of the Papal States, calling on the Pope to act in order to "relieve thousands of the state's most peaceful and obedient subjects from anxieties that are worse than having to fear for their lives and their possessions." It was the third, however, that brought Momolo's Bolognese kin and friends into active conflict with Scaz-zocchio and his colleagues, for the letter called for mobilizing "the most eminent foreign Jews to interest European public opinion, nations, and governments in the case."

The same day that this letter was written, another was sent to Rome's Università Israelitica, this one from Crescenzo Bondi, a Roman Jew who happened to be on a business trip in Senigallia, a town of twenty-four thousand in the central Adriatic region of the Papal States. Bondi reported on a meeting held there the previous day, a gathering of representatives from all the major Jewish communities of the area—Ancona, Urbino, Pesaro, and Senigallia— who had come to meet with Angelo Moscato, Marianna's brother-in-law. Moscato briefed them on the latest events and urged them to join a fund-raising campaign for the Mortaras. Knowing that this news would be poorly received in Rome, Bondi asked his Roman brethren to be understanding of their friends from Bologna, who were gripped by a desperate need for action and had organized the fund-raising campaign "without first consulting our Community, as it was their duty to do."

Rome's Jewish community could boast of being Europe's oldest, for Jews had lived there continuously for two millennia. Its location at the center of power in the Papal States and, indeed, at the center of world Christendom gave it a certain pride of place among the Jews of Italy—an honor, however, that came at a high price. Rome's Jews keenly felt the might of the Pope and the Church hierarchy, and their very proximity to ecclesiastical power meant they came under greater scrutiny than Jews elsewhere.

Rome's Jews had their own unhappy memories, which the news from Bologna once more brought to mind. One of the most searing was a story told to them by their parents and grandparents, the story of the dramatic confrontation that took place on the evening of December 9, 1783, when the ghetto gate, already shut for the night, was unexpectedly opened. A coach, with a large police escort, rolled in. Residents rushed to put on their yellow hats, which by law they had to wear at all times, as the carriage rolled across the cobblestones and stopped in the center of the ghetto. Out from the coach came two government officials, who demanded to see the rabbis and lay leaders of the community.

When the surprised ghetto leaders made their way to the carriage, the reason for the visit was explained. The men were looking for two orphans, a boy aged 11 and his sister, aged 7, who lived with their grandmother. They were to be taken to the House of the Catechumens to be prepared for baptism.

Alarmed and indignant, the Jewish leaders demanded an explanation and were told what had happened. Decades earlier, a great-aunt of the children had left the ghetto, converted, and married a Catholic man. Her son, a cousin of the children's father, was now a grown man. He had decided that his long-lost kin should enjoy the benefits of conversion and had asked the authorities to arrange for their baptism.

The armed escort was ordered to locate the children and seize them. By that time, the family had received word of the uninvited visitors, and the children were nowhere to be found.

The efforts to squirrel them away, however, proved of little avail. The police were ordered to grab whatever children they could and to hold them as hostages until the two youngsters were relinquished. Scores of children were rounded up. There was little for the Jews to do but fetch the two siblings from their hiding place. The carriage carrying the befuddled youngsters rumbled back across the cobblestones, and the ghetto gate thudded shut behind them.

Nor was this the end of the matter. When the Roman police chief heard of the Jews' insolence, he ordered an armed force into the ghetto, and sixty young Jewish men were hauled off and thrown, in chains, into dungeons. It took more than four months for the Jewish community to come up with the payment demanded for the men's release. The two children, meanwhile, were baptized, never again to set foot in the ghetto.[4]

Such encounters had taught the leaders of Rome's ghetto to tread gingerly in dealing with the Church, especially when questions of doctrine were at stake. Nor were the memories of their vulnerability all so old. Only nine years before the Mortara abduction, in the wake of the retaking of Rome by French troops in 1849, the Jews were accused of having purchased holy objects stolen from Roman churches in the previous year of upheaval. Soldiers invaded the ghetto one evening, locked the Jews in their homes for three days and nights, and went house to house ransacking their belongings in search of the stolen goods. Frustrated at not finding any of the loot they were looking for, the soldiers carried off the Jews' own golden sacred objects to compensate them for their efforts.[5]

Despite such experiences, Rome's Jews felt grateful to Pope Pius IX for relieving them of some of the most irksome and degrading restrictions that had been imposed on them. Shortly after becoming pope, he had eliminated the *predica coatta*, the centuries-old requirement that Jews attend a Saturday sermon, given by a priest, aimed at demonstrating the evils of Judaism and the joys of conversion. Pius IX had also ordered the ghetto gates to be torn down, despite lively opposition from the Roman plebes.

Yet the Jews of Rome still lived almost entirely in the old ghetto and were still bound by many restrictions. Of all the major Jewish communities in Italy in 1858, Rome's was the poorest, and visitors to the ghetto were appalled by the conditions they found. A Spanish traveler, Emilio Castelar, no friend of papal rule himself, has left a graphic—although somewhat overdrawn—picture of the sight that met him when he visited the ghetto in the 1860s. He began by putting the place into context, for, he wrote, aside from the beautiful Saint Peter's Square, Rome "is a filthy city. . . . Mounds of garbage lie at every street corner. . . . The Tiber is truly an open sewer; its sickly yellow waters give the appearance of an immense vomit of bile."

But amidst the general squalor, Castelar reported, Rome's ghetto was in a category of its own. As one entered, "one's feet sink into a soft layer of excrement, which seems to be the droppings of a pig or a hippopotamus. Half-naked children, covered with scabs of filth which resemble a leper's gangrenous sores, slither everywhere. A few old people, with wrinkled, jaundiced skin, white hair, glassy eyes, emaciated, with sinister smiles, stand guard by the doors to the houses, which seem to be true rat holes. And from each of those dens wafts a fetid smell."[6]

Complaints that Rome's Jews lived in squalid conditions, and that the Church was to blame for this, were dismissed as rank anti-Catholic propaganda by Church defenders. In a typical apologia of the 1860s, a biographer of Pius IX argued that there was no place in the world where the Jews suffered less than in Rome. Now that the good pope had opened the ghetto gates, the only reason that the Jews still lived there, he wrote, was "their own spirit of exclusion and separation." He continued: "If the ghetto in the past was dirty and disgusting, if even today it is unhealthy, that is certainly not the fault of the popes." In this account and thousands of others, the Church fathers were portrayed as having done the Jews a great favor by putting them in the ghetto, for this was the only way to protect them from the people's ire. "The Jews lived happily and peacefully in Rome, their property, their safety, and their beliefs effectively protected."[7]

Viewing life through lenses so different that they saw entirely different worlds, the Church faithful and the Jews were ever perched on the brink of conflict. Where matters of Church religious teachings were in question, and where the most basic of all tenets—the superiority of Christianity and the divine protection enjoyed by the baptized—were at issue, the stage was set for a confrontation that, historically, the Jews could not win.

In the Mortara case, this clash of two realities meant the construction of two narratives, two stories. The Jewish narrative, embraced not only by the Jews but by other opponents of the temporal power of the Roman Church as well, told of a loving family brought to ruin by the papal regime's religious fanaticism. In this account, papal police tore a desperate little boy from his helpless father's arms, forcing the child, despite his heartbreaking pleas to be returned to his parents, to journey alone to an unknown fate. While the boy plays a major role in the drama, his parents play just as big a part, for they are the major victims of the piece.

When the first protests on behalf of the Mortara family began to make their way out of the ghetto, Church defenders sought to deflate the tale of the kidnapped child and stricken parents by offering a very different account of what had happened. In the Church narrative, the parents' role was secondary. The focus was entirely on Edgardo himself. The story was not one of kidnap, the classic tale of evil outsiders arriving in the night with overpowering force to abduct a child from his loving parents. It was, rather, a heartwarming story of redemption, an inspiring tale of the divinely ordained salvation of a boy who until then had been consigned to a life of error and a hereafter of eternal damnation. Plucked from the clutches of evil and granted the joys of eternal happiness, the child had been bestowed a place at the side of the most holy and revered leader in all the world, the Pope himself.

Yet, if Edgardo had been blessed by the miracle that was the hallmark of baptism, there should be some sign. It was, after all, 1858, the year in which the apparition of Mary first appeared at Lourdes. God would surely signal His pleasure.

When Scazzocchio asked the Mortaras in July to send details of how Edgardo had behaved when he was being taken away, it was in response to the first Church reports that God indeed had sent a sign, one so dramatic that it bordered on the miraculous. A preternatural change, it was said, had come over the little boy on his trip to Rome, a trip that quickly began to take on the mythic quality of a voyage from error to enlightenment. He left Bologna a Jew; he arrived in Rome a few days later a devout Catholic.

Although Scazzocchio was aware of these reports in July, the first accounts in the Catholic press did not appear until the fall. In a long story published in *L'osservatore bolognese*, the newspaper founded by Archbishop Viale-Prelà to defend the faith in the battle against the liberals, lavish attention was devoted to the boy's miraculous transformation en route. The article began by telling of Edgardo's capture: "We can assure our readers," the paper reported, "that in carrying out the orders received from Rome, no violence was employed, and it was all carried out with gentleness, solely through the use of persuasion." True, on first hearing the news that Edgardo was to be taken from them, his parents were upset, but his mother was finally convinced by her husband to leave her son, and Edgardo himself "got into the carriage that awaited him tranquilly and serenely."

The paper excitedly revealed "touching details" from eyewitnesses about the subsequent trip to Rome. Two devout women had accompanied the boy, and gave him a prayer book to read. "He read those prayers with great pleasure, and each time the subject of the Christian religion came up in conversation, he paid great attention. Indeed, he often asked questions on particular points of our faith, showing such great interest that it was clear how important it was to him to know the truths of our holy religion." Nor was this all.

"Whenever the carriage stopped in any town or city, the first thing that he asked was to be taken to the church, and when he entered he remained there at length, showing the greatest respect and the most moving devotion."[8]

Scazzocchio urged Momolo to provide him with some ammunition to counter the damage being done by these inspirational stories of a boy going contentedly with the papal police and finding divine enlightenment on the road to Rome. After finally meeting with his son in the House of the Catechumens in Rome in August, Momolo prepared his own account, which he sent to the Pope.

Momolo's short document recounts that when, in the presence of the Rector of the Catechumens, he spoke to his son about what had happened, Edgardo "recalled the surprise and the immense shock he felt when he heard that the carabinieri were looking for him in order to take him with them." And the Rector, reported Momolo, had learned from Edgardo that he feared the reason why the police wanted to take him away from his family was so that they could cut off his head.

Momolo also gave a very different account of his son's journey to Rome than the one being broadcast to the Church faithful. In the place of demands to visit churches were pleas for his mezuzah:

> Edgardo added that when he was led away he was sobbing and asked for his father and mother. All along the way he repeatedly asked the person accompanying him for his mezuzah, which he normally wore around his neck as a symbol of the Jewish religion. But in its place the man offered him a kind of medallion, to be used in the same way. Edgardo, though, refused it, until finally the man assured him that it was just the same as the object he had asked for. Throughout the trip, the man tried to calm him with the promise that his parents were but a short distance behind them. When he got to Rome and discovered this was not true, he changed the favorable opinion he had had of the man, an opinion based on the sweet and wheedling manner the man had used with him throughout the journey.[9]

The source for the Church's account of Edgardo's trip was Giuseppe Agostini, the police officer who had taken him from Bologna to Rome. When Cardinal Antonelli received Momolo Mortara's very different account, and learned that it was being distributed to sympathetic newspapers throughout Europe, he asked Brigadier Agostini to prepare his own written report.

Dated November 2, the document was written four months after the disputed journey. Agostini's description of the scene at the house when he and Lucidi arrived and announced their mission jibed with that of the Mortaras themselves. It was, he reported, an extremely moving scene, an excruciating sight of desolation. The boy's parents, and especially his mother, had been "consumed with tears, protesting." He wrote: "It looked as though they would not give him up regardless of the amount of force used."

The brigadier reported that the following day, during the twenty-four-hour reprieve, he had returned to San Domenico to get further instructions from the Inquisitor. There Father Feletti gave him two French medallions of the Blessed Immaculate Virgin, with images of Mary on one side and of Jesus on the cross on the other. Agostini was told that, if at all possible, he should place one of them around the neck of the "new Christian" once they were on their way to Rome.

Agostini did not report on the final scene at the Mortara home (the "house of the Jew," as the brigadier called it) but skips in his account to five days into his journey with Edgardo, in the small city of Fossombrone, when, early in the morning, as the boy was getting dressed, Agostini first showed him one of the medallions the Inquisitor had given him:

> I gently asked him to put it around his neck, and to kiss it, while I did the same with mine. At first, he showed repugnance, saying that his mother didn't want him to kiss the Cross. But, using all the tenderness I could, I told the child that he was now passing from blindness to the sight of Divine things, the true light, and that he was not an Unbeliever but part of the Christian Religion. Finally yielding, he kissed the medallion and put it around his neck.

Agostini took Edgardo by the hand and led the boy to the cathedral of Fossombrone, where, the brigadier reported, he kindly urged Edgardo to go in. "At first, he stubbornly refused," Agostini recalled, "but seeing the other gendarmes going in to Mass, he entered as well." It was then that the miracle occurred. No sooner was the child inside the church—the first time in his life he had been in one—when, "thanks to the Heavenly wonders, there was an instantaneous change. Getting down on his knees, he took part quietly in the Divine Sacrifice, listening with interest to the explanations" that Agostini gave him. The Brigadier's first thought was to teach the boy how to make the sign of the cross. Having accomplished this, he then taught him how to recite the Ave Maria.

The transformation was indeed a thing of wonder: "From that time he showed the strongest desire to visit the other churches there. After lunch, while visiting one of them, he couldn't take his eyes off a painting showing the passion of the Redeemer," and so Agostini explained it to him. From that moment, the brigadier claimed, Edgardo "forgot his parents, and as we continued on our journey, at every stop the first thing he asked was to visit the House of God, where he would make the sign of the cross with the holy water and recite the Ave Maria that he had just learned."

When they reached Spoleto, Agostini reported, he took Edgardo to a church, where, after having him genuflect, he had the boy recite the Paternoster. A priest at the church, learning of the boy's stirring story, took him to the vestry, where, with great kindness, he gave him a scapular of the Holy Mary and put it around his neck, making him kiss it repeatedly. For the rest of the trip, the visits to churches continued, until the moment when Edgardo, the neophyte, was delivered to the Catechumens in Rome.

For Brigadier Agostini, who had already been given a bonus payment by Father Feletti in gratitude for his excellent work and his inspiring story, the request that he prepare a report of his experiences for Cardinal Antonelli, the Secretary of State, was a once-in-a-lifetime opportunity to make his voice heard at the highest levels of Church and state. Agostini's report of his remarkable success undoubtedly made the Cardinal very happy, but just how much of it the Cardinal—known within Church circles for his lack of religious conviction—actually believed is hard to tell.

CHAPTER 6

The House of the Catechumens

OR BOTH the Church faithful and the Jews of Italy, the Casa dei Catecumeni, House of the Catechumens, was a place of the greatest significance. It straddled the border of the two worlds, and in its liminality lay its awesome power. A Jew could enter the Catechumens and come out a Catholic; in so doing he left one world and entered another. The convert was reborn, with a new identity and a new name. For the Church faithful, what went on in the Catechumens was the work of God, the conferring of the highest of spiritual gifts, bestowing supernatural blessing on a condemned people. For the Jews, by contrast, the Catechumens was a place of utmost horror.

While the earliest houses of Catechumens can be traced back to the third century, the history of the house to which Edgardo was taken had more recent origins. It was the first of the modern Houses of the Catechumens, established in 1540 by Ignazio of Loyola, founder of the Jesuit order, and aimed at the conversion of Jews and Muslims. Its example was soon followed elsewhere: Bologna opened one in 1568, Ferrara in 1584, Modena and Reggio Emilia around 1630. Wherever there were Jews, a House of the Catechumens was founded.[1]

The Church hierarchy followed cases of conversion in the Catechumens with the greatest interest. The baptism of an unbeliever, and especially of a Jew, redounded to the glory of God and helped fulfill one of the requirements in preparing the way for the Second Coming of the Messiah. The baptism of Jews, following their period of confinement in the Catechumens—typically set at forty days for adults, although often longer for children—was a cause for great celebration. In Rome, cardinals frequently presided over such rites, which were held in the major churches of the city before large and appreciative crowds. In cities having no cardinal, bishops administered the baptism, often in the cathedral itself.[2]

According to Church teachings, a person who helped save the soul of an unbeliever earned divine blessing, performing a deed that would be remembered at heaven's gate. As a result, noble families competed for the honor of acting as baptismal godparents for Jews, the trickle of converts being small compared with the robust ranks of the nobility. Among the roster of baptismal sponsors listed in the records of the various Catechumens are the most distinguished noble families in Italy. Such families bore some responsibility for the welfare of their spiritual wards, a fact that provided Jews with material incentive for conversion. The converts were also offered the nobles' own family names. As a result, Italians who today bear illustrious noble names are not necessarily the progeny of nobility but may be instead the descendants of poor Jews who sought a new life by passing through the doors of the Catechumens.

Of the 262 Jews baptized after a period of training in Modena's Catechumens between 1629 and 1701, for example, 115 were accompanied to the holy font by princes and princesses of the Estensi family itself. The ceremony was typically held at the cathedral and conducted by the archbishop, following a large procession that began at the Catechumens. The Jew, dressed entirely in white, marched to the cathedral amidst a gaggle of banner-hoisting confraternities singing inspirational hymns. On their return to the Catechumens, the men's voices harmonized as they sang "Benedictus Dominus Deus Israel."[3]

Inspiring stories of Jews' seeing the light and entering the House of the Catechumens despite their families' desperate attempts to stop them were regularly published in booklet form, together with loving descriptions of the magnificent baptismal rites that followed. The great pride with which the Church broadcast news of the baptism of Jews continued right up to the time of Edgardo's abduction.[4] The news column of the most influential of all Catholic journals of the time, *Civiltà Cattolica*, bubbled with enthusiasm in reporting news of the most recent conversions, wherever they occurred. The names changed, but the story stayed the same.

For example, on the Saturday before Easter 1853, a young Jewish woman from Galicia was baptized by a cardinal at the Lateran church in Rome, with her godmother, Princess Torlonia, at her side. When still a little girl, the convert-to-be had had a vision in which she saw two temples. One was adorned with beautiful towers, a place of magnificence; the other lay in ruins. The interpretation was clear, reported the Jesuit journal: the first was the Vatican, the second the Synagogue. The woman heard a voice invite her to worship in the splendid temple. Her mother, learning of this vision, did every-thing in her power to persuade the girl to put it out of her mind. Although a marriage was arranged for her and she had children, she could not forget her vision. Secretly, she began to learn all she could about Christianity.

When at last she could resist the spiritual pull of the Church no longer, the woman fled with her little son, making her way first to Constantinople and then toward Rome. After countless hardships and dangers, she finally approached the Holy City, where, miraculously, she saw before her an exact replica of the beautiful temple of her vision: it was St. Peter's basilica. After years of torment, the Jew had finally found peace.[5]

For Jewish women, the standard Church conversion narrative tells of an early supernatural visitation in which they discover their true Christian voca-tion, and their subsequent fear of paternal violence should their yearnings be discovered. Such was the case in an 1856 *Civiltà Cattolica* account occasioned by the baptism of two Jewish sisters, aged 20 and 22, performed by the Bishop of Ascoli in the city's cathedral. When the Bishop first heard of their desire to convert, the journal recounted, he examined them carefully and assured him-self of their sincerity. He took great care in arranging their transfer from home to the convent, for he was aware of the mortal dangers they faced if their family found out. After a heroic escape to the convent, the girls wrote their mother to tell her what had happened. A howl of protest arose in the Jewish community. Meanwhile, the priest who had first heard of the girls' secret desire to become Christian received a letter from their younger cousin, who confided her own "thirst for the baptismal water" and her despair that, in the wake of her cousins' escape, she was too carefully guarded to get away herself. But, it being God's will, the young woman found a way to escape her family's clutches and joined her cousins at the convent.

"The three Jewesses," the *Civiltà Cattolica* story reported, "had long prac-ticed acts of our religion in their homes, such as reciting the Paternoster, the Ave Maria, the Credo. They said the crown of the Virgin, and they made Novenas in preparation for the feasts honoring Mary." One day the father of one of the girls discovered her wearing a Carmine scapular around her neck and carrying a little book of Christian doctrine, prompting him to assault her with "blows and worse." When, finally, the day came and the Bishop adminis-tered the Eucharist to the three young women, not only were they weeping, but many among the large crowd of government officers, nobles, and others were moved to tears as well.[6]

While the predominant Church narrative of Jewish female conversion tells of supernatural visitations and spiritual awakenings, men were more likely to be moved by the brain than the heart. Typical of such accounts is one from 1856, told on the occasion of the baptism, in the chapel of the Rome

House of the Catechumens, of Alessandro Cagli, the son of a rabbi of the northeastern city of Udine. The young man's path toward conversion had begun six years earlier, when, as a result of his studies, he began to have doubts about the religion into which he had been born. The more he studied, the journal reported, the more he realized Judaism's many inadequacies, from its lack of a priesthood to its preoccupation with the quibblings of the rabbis rather than devotion to the laws of Moses. But what convinced him above all was the "inexplicable disdain, unless there had been a divine curse, for a people that has riches, that has brains, that has civil virtues." He left Udine and went to Padua to study mathematics at the university. There he began to attend mass and to speak out in defense of the truth of the Christian religion. Finally, he made his way to the House of the Catechumens in Rome and the road to salvation.[7]

If the dominant Catholic narrative of Jewish baptism was of a few inspired Jews seeing the light and bravely facing the most terrible threats and abuse in order to embrace the true religion, the Jewish narrative was quite another matter. In the ghetto dwellers' view, the adults who freely entered the House of the Catechumens were traitors, the unfortunate misfits and evil schemers who sadly afflict any community. Their motives, far from spiritual, were crassly material. The shower of jewels and fine clothes, the attention paid by cardinals and nobles, were seen, in this very different light, as a story not of spiritual uplift but of the most degraded spiritual prostitution. This narrative had the dual advantage of suggesting that only the most immoral and untrustworthy Jews would enter the Catechumens, and, further, that no Jew could truly believe Christianity to be superior to the faith of his ancestors.[8]

Directors of the Catechumens, and the bishops and cardinals who had responsibility over them, were well aware that such ulterior motives lurked in the minds of at least some of their Jewish candidates. At times, clergymen invested considerable energies in determining the sincerity of Jews seeking conversion, for the sincere desire to become Christian was a requirement for adult baptism.[9] Yet the Church's desire for Jewish converts was so great, the feeling of religious triumph in the conversion so glorious, and the superiority of Christianity over Judaism so self-evident, that there was considerable temptation to accept any Jew who came to the Catechumens door.

The Church did have remedies in the case of Jews who exploited its benevolence. In Bologna in 1624, Moses Israel, who came from Salonica, across the Adriatic, was baptized by the Archbishop and given a reward. A year later he returned to the Ottoman Empire, where he went back to his old ways, living once more as a Jew. Unhappy there, after twelve months he went to Rome, where he again presented himself for baptism, this time under a different name. Shortly thereafter, he and another convert made their way back to Ottoman territories, where both rejoined the Jewish community. When

Moses Israel later traveled to Vicenza, in northeast Italy, and was baptized a third time, his reward was a license to beg. Soon thereafter, in 1636—he was still only 40 years old—a fellow convert denounced him, and he was arrested. Moses said in his own defense that he had returned to Jewish communities only in order to put into practice what he had learned at the Catechumens and to do all he could to convert the Jews. As for his multiple conversions, he said that he had no idea there was anything wrong with receiving the blessings of baptism more than once. The authorities, however, took a dim view, and the thrice-baptized Jew was condemned to spend seven years in the galleys.[10]

One of the reasons for the intense revulsion felt by Italy's Jews toward their brethren who freely entered the House of the Catechumens was the use to which the Church put such converts. For who was better equipped than the convert, who had been raised in the ghetto and given a Jewish education, to show the Jews the error of their ways and to convince them of the proper path to salvation?

Among the measures instituted in the Counter-Reformation was the requirement that Jews attend sermons aimed at their conversion. There was no more hated practice in the ghettoes. In Rome, by the end of the sixteenth century, every Saturday afternoon, on a rotating basis, groups of the Holy City's Jews were required to march outside the walls of the ghetto to a nearby church or hall, amidst the taunts of the surrounding population. Papal police checked names off a list and punished those who failed to attend. When church authorities learned that the Jews were squeezing wax into their ears, and those of their children, in preparation for their Saturday-afternoon ordeal, the police were ordered to begin inspecting the Jews' ears as they passed through the church doors.[11]

The satanic mass is structured as an inversion of the Catholic mass; the *predica coatta* was likewise an inversion of the sacred rites of the Jews. On the Sabbath, the rabbi at the morning services would comment on the portion of the Holy Scriptures scheduled to be read that day. Following lunch, at 3 p.m., the Jews would be marched to the nearby church to hear a priest use the very same portion of the Torah as the basis for his own sermon, turning the rabbinical commentary upside down.

This is where the convert came in, particularly one who had a solid Jewish education, a man able to cite the sacred passages in the original Hebrew. The ghetto dwellers sat murmuring their disgust as the gesticulating former Jew, with great gusto, expostulated on the falsity of their religious beliefs and urged them to see the light. The less-than-appreciative audience was well aware that their former coreligionist's salary, as well as the costs of the police guard, was billed to the Jews of the ghetto, as were the costs of the House of the Catechumens.[12]

Cases of children brought to the Catechumens by force, as Edgardo was, made a great impact on the Jews of Italy, but most converts came on their own. The children who entered were, for the most part, merely following their parents. Jewish women were more resistant to the lure of conversion than were Jewish men, and in cases where husbands came to the Catechumens without their wives, conflicts over the fate of their children were common, although always resolved in favor of the man.

Like other pontiffs, Benedict XIV, a mid-eighteenth-century pope, and a former Archbishop of Bologna, paid special attention to the workings of Rome's Catechumens. The conversion of the Jews was a great good, but the process had to be carefully regulated. In particular, the widespread popular belief that spiritual rewards accrued to anyone who baptized a Jew led, he knew, to many abuses. One of these was brought to his attention in 1746.

A Catholic man, Antonio Viviani, made his way into Rome's ghetto and came upon the home of Perla Misani, whose three daughters, the eldest of whom was 9, and son, aged 12, were there alone. Viviani took some of the water he had brought with him and sprinkled it over the oldest girl's head while reciting the baptismal formula. He repeated the procedure with the two other girls but ran out of water before he got to the boy. The three girls were then taken to Rome's Catechumens, the mother left with but one child, her son.

Viviani's actions were unquestionably illegal, for Church policy was clear: Jewish children under the care of their parents should not be baptized without parental consent, unless there was clear evidence that they were about to die. The bishop who reported the matter to the Pope informed him of the measures that were taken to punish Viviani. Yet, however illicit the baptisms were, in the Church's view they were still valid. The three girls were now Christian and could not be returned to their Jewish mother in the ghetto.[13]

Jews who entered the Catechumens of their own free will and later changed their minds were allowed to leave before they were baptized. But the atmosphere of the Catechumens did not encourage such backsliding. The success of the operation depended on keeping kin and other Jews away from the neophyte, and the Church repeatedly issued orders prohibiting Jews from coming anywhere near the House of the Catechumens. A 1705 edict prescribed three lashes and a heavy fine for any Jew who approached within sixty yards of the building or who, even from a greater distance, attempted to catch the attention of someone looking out of a window. Such provisions were still in force in the mid-nineteenth century. Shortly before Edgardo entered Rome's Catechumens, a Jew standing outside the building was arrested while gazing at a new convert who was standing at a window.[14]

When Edgardo was deposited by Brigadier Agostini at the door of the Catechumens, he entered a world wholly new to him, a world mysterious to the Jews outside. Unlike the adults who were admitted there, he had not come to be prepared for baptism, for he had already been baptized. But, like those others, he was there to bridge the gap between two worlds, to enter as a Jew and leave as a Catholic. The Rector had the task of instructing the 6-year-old in his new religion and, in so doing, giving him a new identity. When Edgardo's presence in the Catechumens began drawing such unwelcome public attention, and the very right of the Church to claim him came under merciless attack, the Rector's work became all the more pressing.

A document from the mid-eighteenth century offers a rare glimpse into the inner workings of the House of the Catechumens, including some of the methods used to convert Jews. Written by Anna Del Monte, a young Jewish woman of the Roman ghetto, just after her release from the Catechumens, it tells of the twelve days she spent there.

Anna's ordeal began one Sunday afternoon, just after the end of Passover, when a squad of papal police burst into her home and marched her to a waiting wagon, which took her directly to the House of the Catechumens. There the Prioress met her and showed her to a small room, locking the door as she left.

Anna had been turned in by a recently baptized Jew, Sabbato Coen, who wanted to marry her. Sabbato had informed the Catechumens authorities that Anna was pledged to be his wife—a claim hotly denied by Anna and her family—and that she had confided in him a desire to follow his example and convert. This was enough for an order to be given to seize her. The law of the Inquisition allowed the director of the Catechumens twelve days in such circumstances to determine the true desires of a potential neophyte. At the end of the period, should they persist in their desire to remain Jews, they were allowed to leave, although it was considered a sad day for the Church.

During the twelve days of her confinement, Anna was kept isolated in her room, where she was visited by a succession of priests, recent converts, and nuns, who prayed for her soul and beseeched her to open her heart and see the true light. In all, thirty-eight different people came to plead with her, preaching a total of eighty hours at her side.

The Father Preacher, the man responsible for convincing her to accept baptism, was himself a Jewish convert, and Anna described the hours he spent with her as pure torment. Disheveled and poorly dressed, he had an unnatural glint in his eyes, a man transported to a higher realm. "He had," she wrote, "such an ugly and frightening appearance that he seemed a demon descended from Hell." When neither his ardent prayers nor his threats of keeping her locked up for good seemed to help, he began to flagellate himself while decrying the devil within her.

Anna Del Monte's narrative is a classic tale of passage through Hell, of crazed priests and powerless Jewish victims. Her account of her last night in the Catechumens has all the elements of a heroic drama, a testing of faith and a triumph of virtue. She had survived twelve days of intense pressure to convert, clinging proudly to her religion, but it appeared that all would be lost:

> At nine at night I again saw the Father Preacher come in with the Prioress, and when I saw him I began to shiver from head to toe. He launched into his speech: "My daughter, you see how many times I have come to visit you for the good of your body, and for the health of your soul. I had to go to tell the Cardinal of your stubbornness, and he asked me to return to you, because today is the twelfth day, the day on which your conversion is assured. If my own efforts are not enough to convince you to declare yourself a good Catholic, the Cardinal will come in person with the order of the Holy Pontiff himself to give you the Baptismal water."
>
> At these words my breath was taken away, but somehow, aided by His Divine Majesty, I replied that they could do what they wished, but I wanted to die as I was born. At these words he became as enraged as a lion and ordered the Prioress to go get the object they had talked about, and in fact she left, and in a little while came back carrying a large crucifix, which he put on my bed while he howled like a dog.
>
> And then, crying and shouting, he again took the water and sprinkled it on the bed, and on my face and my back, telling me: "The time has come when you must convert to our true faith; tonight you will see this cross come to you in your dreams, so I leave it with you in your bed." Then the Prioress told me: "If you are invited to embrace our Catholic faith tonight, as must be, remember that I will be sleeping just below you. All you have to do is bang your shoe or your slipper, whatever the hour, and I will come and embrace you like my daughter, such has been my love for you from the first day you arrived here. So, my daughter, don't disappoint me. I leave this Crucifix to keep you company, and I hope that you will unite with it and become Catholic as I am."
>
> At these words my heart burst and I began to cry, and I started to shout at her: "It will never be; you can leave me with this piece of wood and put it on top of me, but this is no way to convince me. If it's true that you love me like a daughter, you mustn't do this to me." Seeing me cry like that, out of God's mercy she took it away, and then the Preacher began yet again to sprinkle his usual water all over the place, the bed, my face, invoking endless names of saints. He said: "You will see that tonight the saints that I have named will appear here, and they will make you call the Prioress, who will see your spontaneous conversion." And after three hours or more of preaching he finally left, in bad humor, leaving me more dead than alive, and so full of fear that it seemed to me that the earth would open up and swallow me.

The following day Anna Del Monte was allowed to leave the Catechumens. In the ghetto it was a day for rejoicing.[15]

CHAPTER 7

An Old Father and a New

MOMOLO MORTARA was 41 years old when he journeyed to Rome. In the years since he and Marianna had moved to Bologna from Reggio, he had established a business in upholstery supplies, selling both wholesale and retail out of a storefront in his home in via Lame in the center of town. His circle of friends in Bologna was limited largely to other Jewish immigrants from nearby cities, families also involved in commerce, although he occasionally spent evenings in a neighborhood cafe, where he met other, non-Jewish men. A historian of the turn of the century, basing his comments on the testimony of Momolo's son Augusto, writes that all who knew Momolo were fond of him, that he enjoyed great popularity in the neighborhood.[1] But other evidence suggests that Momolo was a rather formal man. The year after his son was taken, one of Momolo's Jewish friends from Bologna described him as "a man very honest but rather ill at ease."[2]

As a child, Momolo had received a good Jewish education. He learned to write in Hebrew as well as Italian, and sprinkled his speech, at least when speaking with fellow Jews, with Hebrew terms. Yet he was clearly among the category of better-off Jews whose lives had been altered by the deep currents of the Risorgimento, a man who had happily left many of the old ways of the ghetto behind. Momolo was a youth of 15 in 1831 when the Carbonari-inspired revolt drove the Duke from his duchy and ushered in a brief, exhilarating, but also threatening time of new ideas of equality and individual rights. The cycles of emancipation of the Jews, followed by the reimposition of the old restrictions, shook the closed world in which Momolo's ancestors had dwelled, and led him and his friends to a much more secular worldview.[3]

Marianna's story is much the same. If anything, in Modena, capital of the

63

duchy, the repeated threats to the old regime and the old ways of thinking were felt more acutely. Her uncle Angelo had no sooner gotten to Bologna when he was swept up in the revolt against papal power and elected to the city council that took control when the Cardinal Legate fled. When the papal regime again fell a decade later, Angelo was once more a candidate to the city council, winning election not only in 1859 but repeatedly thereafter over the next fifteen years. And when the new government took power, it turned to him, as a banker, to help broker loans to pay its expenses. Clearly these were Jews leading very different lives from those of their ancestors, living in a city with neither a synagogue nor a rabbi, something that in the past would have been unthinkable.

An intriguing glimpse into Momolo and Marianna's embrace of the new secular era comes from the names they selected for their children. A trip to the historical archives of the Reggio Jewish community reveals the names chosen by the various Mortara families who lived in Reggio's ghetto in the years before Napoleon: Mazel-tov, Rachele, Isach, Giuditta, Abram, Salomone, Sara, Jacob. Momolo's own parents had given him the name Salomone David; Momolo was a later nickname. His brothers were named Moses Aaron and Abram. Is there any significance in the names that Momolo and Marianna chose for their own children: Riccardo, Erminia, Ernesta, Augusto, Arnoldo, Aristide, Edgardo, Ercole, and Imelda? Of the eight, not one was biblical, not one a traditional name for an Italian Jew.

Yet when Marshal Lucidi and Brigadier Agostini arrived at the Mortara home on the night of June 23, they had come because Momolo and Marianna were Jews. The Mortaras' attempts to blend in, to embrace the new universalistic ethic, had run up against the reality of an old regime that may have been on its last legs but was still standing. The effect of being treated as Jews was to turn them inward, to their family and their fellow Jews. Not only did the Jews of Bologna become their principal, in fact their only, local social support group, but their attempts to recapture Edgardo in Rome turned them to their fellow Jews in the capital city and to the Jewish network that stretched not only across the Papal States but well beyond.

It had taken Momolo over a month from the time Edgardo was seized to make the trip to Rome, a lapse that, as we saw from Scazzocchio's letter of late July, lessened the impact of the image that the Jews wanted to convey: that of a distraught father grievously wounded by the loss of his son.

Yet the delay was not due to any lack of desire to see his son, for Momolo would have done anything to get him back. Other obstacles had slowed him down. Not until early July did he learn where Edgardo had been taken, and he had labored through the first days of July drafting pleas to the Inquisitor, the Secretary of State, and the Pope. Preparing petitions to the latter two was not a simple matter, both because, as Momolo was advised, he had to cite relevant canon law and Church precedents if he was to have any chance of being successful, and because the right channels had to be used if the appeal was to be received at all. It had become clear to Momolo and his Bologna friends that, as Jews, to approach the Pope, they would have to go through Rome's Jewish community. Their contacts in the capital meanwhile urged them to work on the Bologna side of the case, gathering evidence to strengthen their appeal: from Edgardo's birth certificate to the discovery of just who it was who had baptized the boy. Momolo also had to cope with his traumatized family, including his wife, who, in the wake of her son's abduction, had returned to her kin in Modena.

Although overwhelmed and depressed by the misfortune that had befallen him, Momolo arrived in Rome hopeful. As he later testified, he had set out on his journey "in the firm belief that justice would be done to me." Since Jews were not allowed to fix their eyes on the House of the Catechumens, still less knock on its door and expect to be admitted, Momolo's first step was to see the Secretary of State, Cardinal Giacomo Antonelli. The Cardinal received him graciously, although Momolo, the small merchant from Reggio, a man conscious of rank and proper form, must have been intimidated by the magisterial surroundings.

Antonelli had, a few weeks before, received Momolo's request to bring the appeal to the Pope's attention. Initially, as in other cases of the kind over the centuries, the appeal from a bereaved Jewish family was given little attention, and indeed no effort was initially made even to respond to it. But as the European press began to seize on the case as an example of the barbaric nature of papal rule, the Secretary of State's attitude toward the case shifted. The matter could no longer be ignored, for any further weakening of the Papal States' diplomatic position could be calamitous. His meeting with Momolo was arranged through the offices of Rome's Jewish community, and by the time Momolo appeared, the Cardinal was well briefed on the affair. He promised Momolo that he would bring the matter up with the Pope but suggested that Momolo prepare an additional written document setting down all the facts of the case and the legal basis of his request that Edgardo should be returned to him.

The Cardinal granted Momolo's request that he be allowed to see his son regularly during his stay in Rome. Momolo may not have fully appreciated his good fortune. While a single visit by a family member and a representative of the Jewish community to the neophyte at the Catechumens was, by this time, often allowed, it was unheard of for a Jewish family member to be granted permission for regular visits. It was the first inkling that the case would have an impact on the Church that, in the past, would have been unimaginable.

The Cardinal was clearly more concerned with limiting the potential diplomatic damage to the Church than he was with upholding the long-standing rules sealing neophytes off from their families.

When Momolo left his meeting, he had reason to be pleased. The Secretary of State had treated him well, had explained to him what he could do to make his plea to the Pope more effective, had promised to convey the plea to the Pontiff, and had given him unprecedented access to his son.

The strength of Cardinal Antonelli's concern about the publicity given the case was evident in an episode that took place when Momolo returned for the third time to see Edgardo. At the Catechumens door, a nun heard Momolo's knock and came out to meet him. Seeing a Jew who was insisting on seeing his son, she chased him away, slamming the door. The following day, when Scazzocchio was working at the Jewish community office in the ghetto, he was startled to see two priests ushered in, one of whom he knew: Enrico Sarra, Rector of the Catechumens. The Rector had come to offer his apologies for the reception Momolo had received the previous day, explaining that the nun who had greeted him had just happened to be visiting the Catechumens and was unaware of the situation. Canon Sarra invited Momolo to return soon for another visit.

Scazzocchio had, by this time, become deeply enmeshed in the Mortara case. He seemed to have time for little else. When the Secretary of State advised that a fuller brief should be prepared to justify Edgardo's release, Scazzocchio felt that this was a task for him to undertake, for the Bologna Jews were clearly out of their league.

On August 11, shortly after the meeting with the Secretary of State but before Momolo's first meeting with Edgardo, Scazzocchio wrote to Angelo Padovani in Bologna, who, on behalf of his kin, had begged for news from Rome now that Momolo was there. While Momolo was in a hopeful mood at the time, Scazzocchio was alarmed by the news he was getting. "The obstacles to be overcome today," he wrote, "are two: the resistance shown by Edgardo, and the fact of the baptism that was conferred." As for the second point, Scazzocchio and the other experts in Rome knew that the Church rarely gave up a Jewish child who was baptized, even if it could be shown that the child should not have been baptized in the first place. The first point, though, was the more discomfiting. Insistent reports from Church sources claimed that Edgardo was happy to be in the Catechumens, that he wanted nothing more than to be a Catholic, and that he did not want to return to his Jewish parents.

In writing to Mortara relatives of this concern, the Roman Jewish Secretary sought to ease the pain a bit by adding that Edgardo's attitude "can be easily explained by the thoughtlessness of a child entranced by the idea of an entirely new life." Scazzocchio added his hope that the boy's "trance" would be broken upon his first encounter with his father, which was to take place in a few days' time. However, he was clearly nervous about the reunion, noting that it would take place under conditions adverse to the change in heart that they were all praying for.

Shortly after this letter was sent to Bologna, Momolo had his first meeting with Edgardo in the Catechumens. Momolo's nervousness at the prospect of seeing his son for the first time since he was taken from his home was great, all the more so because of the reports that Edgardo was pleased to be where he was. Sitting by Edgardo's side at the first meeting, as at all subsequent meetings, was the Rector. In addition, various other religious personnel of the Catechumens, including the Rector's own brother and sister, were often present as well.

What took place at these tense encounters is a matter of dispute. According to Momolo and to accounts published in the Jewish and the liberal press, Edgardo lovingly told his father that his most ardent wish was to return home, and he took comfort in Momolo's assurances that he would not leave Rome without him. Momolo also complained that Sarra and his ecclesiastical colleagues, who never left him alone with his son, intimidated Edgardo and made it impossible for the boy to say what he really felt. Nor did Momolo appreciate the conversionary sermons directed at himself, which would be a constant refrain in his visits to the Catechumens and in the later visits of his wife: There is an easy and blessed solution to your woes. If you become Catholics, you will have your beloved son once again, and share with him in the joys of eternal salvation.

For the Catholic press, and the faithful whose view of the events was shaped by it, Edgardo's early meetings with his father followed the traditional narrative form of the triumph of Christianity and righteousness. Having been graced by divine light on his way to Rome, Edgardo, although only six, was blessed with a spiritual strength well beyond his years. Indeed, the story was so inspiring that it continued to be told for many decades—with significant variations in detail, though always with the same basic outline.

In all versions of the story, Edgardo, on entering the Catechumens, eagerly sought to learn all he could about his new religion. Most accounts report the dramatic scene in which Edgardo's eyes fixed wonderingly on the painting of Our Lady of Sorrows as taking place during his trip to Rome. In others, this happens only after he arrives at the Catechumens. In one such version, Edgardo asks the Rector who the woman in the painting is and why she is crying. The Rector replies that she is the most holy Madonna, mother of Jesus Christ, and that she is crying for the Jews, who refuse to become Christians, and for all sinners.

"Then she is crying for me too," the boy responds.

"No," replies the Rector, "for you are Christian, and you will be good."

"Ah, then," he says, "she is crying for my father and my mother."⁴

Joseph Pelczar, a Polish bishop and turn-of-the-century biographer of Pope Pius IX, narrates the epic battle between father and son. Soon after the boy's arrival in Rome, Pelczar recounts, Edgardo's conversion was powerfully reinforced by his first visit to the Pope. "Clutching him affectionately to his breast," Pius IX "made the sacred sign of the Cross on his forehead." Spiritually fortified, the boy could now see his father without fear.

On first setting eyes on his son, according to the Bishop, Momolo "broke out into torrents of tears and, holding the boy tightly to his breast, kept repeating that everyone in his family would be unhappy until he returned home. The boy turned white, he could not stop his tears, but he stood firm. After a few moments, he told his father: 'Why do you cry? You see that I am fine here.'" Although his father kept trying to convince him otherwise, the boy would not yield. Indeed, by the time Momolo left, Edgardo felt hope that his father would see the light and convert too. In this, Pelczar added, "he was to remain disappointed."⁵

Pelczar's rendition of Edgardo's first encounter with his father bears uncanny, though hardly coincidental, resemblance to one New Testament tale of Jesus himself. In Luke (2:41–50), the 12-year-old Jesus leaves his parents and goes off to the Temple in Jerusalem, where, after three days spent searching all over for him, his parents find the boy engaged in learned theological discussion with legal scholars. His mother says: "My son, why have you behaved like this with us? Don't you see, your father and I have been looking for you and have been so worried about you?" To which Jesus replies: "Why are you looking for me so much? Didn't you know that I have to be in the house of my Father?" These words, according to Luke, Jesus' parents could not understand.⁶

French readers at the time were learning about Momolo's dramatic first meetings with his son in the pages of *L'Univers*, an outspoken voice of Catholic conservatism and upholder of the temporal power of the papacy, put out by that fiercest of all defenders of papal powers, Louis Veuillot, a layman, and a convert (from Protestantism) himself. Veuillot would eventually devote hundreds of pages to the Mortara case and, indeed, would himself soon get to meet the famous boy in Rome.

In 1858, the paper carried what purported to be an eyewitness account of Momolo's first visit to the Catechumens:

The first impression we have of this man seeing his son was most vivid. He momentarily lost the use of his reason altogether. But in a few moments he clutched the boy in his arms, he covered him with kisses, with caresses, and with tears, telling him of his desire, and that of his mother, to see him back in his own house, telling him that the whole family was, because of him, suffering the most painful desolation. By the end, such was the power of paternal love and pain that tears began to run down the boy's cheeks.7

In another Catholic account, someone asked the boy why he spoke so little when his father visited him. Edgardo replied that it was because whenever he tried to speak, his voice trembled and he began to cry, since he could see the doleful effect his words had on his father. The child saw the love his parents and siblings had for him, "but the desire to be a Christian won out over it."

One day, this same correspondent recounted, Scazzocchio accompanied Momolo to the Catechumens and, as they were leaving, leaned over to give Edgardo a kiss. Filled with revulsion by this unwanted attempt at intimacy, six-year-old Edgardo, with Scazzocchio already through the door, said: "If that man comes with my father again and wants to kiss me, I'll take out an image of the Madonna and tell him to kiss it instead!"8

In these narratives, whenever Momolo visited him in the Catechumens, Edgardo could think of nothing except how much he wished his father would convert. One of the most prominent Church-linked papers in Italy at the time, *L'armonia della religione colla civiltà*, published a story titled "News of the Young Christian Mortara." It described how Edgardo had gone off to the Catechumens "with extraordinary happiness." The boy's transformation was miraculous. He had entered the Catechumens with a single idea already "stamped on his forehead, and even more in his heart—the great benefit for him of being Christian, the singular grace that he had received through Baptism and, by contrast, the immense misfortune for his parents of being and wanting to remain Jews."

In this version of the redemption story, when Edgardo heard that he was about to see his father for the first time, he was delighted, because "he hoped to be able to convert his father and make him Christian just the same as he." But when the meeting took place and Edgardo discovered that despite his fervent pleadings his father remained obstinately attached to his religion, the boy broke into terrible sobbing.

L'armonia carried a report from an eyewitness at the Catechumens claiming that the little boy's miraculous transformation was continuing at breathtaking speed. "Within a few days he had learned the catechism to perfection, and he makes the fullest and most exact professions of faith. He always insists on telling the Rector and others he speaks with that the Jews have no altars, no Madonna, no Pope, and he wants everyone to know that the

Jews are not Christians. He declares that he wants to convert them, and he feels God's grace speaking eloquently through him."

The boy was a prodigy: "The Pope wanted to see him, and was enchanted by him. The child blesses the servant who baptized him, and who thus opened the door to the Catholic Church to him." When someone asked him if he knew who Jesus Christ was, his face turned red with shame—the shame of his ancestors—as he replied, "Jesus Christ is the Savior of mankind, whom the Jews crucified." The Catholic paper concluded by asking facetiously, "And they would like a boy so full of faith to be sent back into the Ghetto?"[9]

Reports of this kind, flooding out of Rome and reproduced by the Catholic press throughout Europe, came in response to the mounting movement being organized to win Edgardo's release. Had the boy really been so transformed? Momolo and Marianna angrily denounced the Catholic accounts as infamous lies, but some of their allies, including Scazzocchio, who had sat in on a few of the disputed meetings that Momolo had with Edgardo, were not so sure where the boy's loyalties now lay.

From the perspective of the liberals of Europe, the Church story had a fatal weakness: it was, on its face, absurd. A booklet published in Brussels in 1859, denouncing the Church for its kidnapping of Edgardo, first offers an account of what it says really happened, before then taking aim at the version of events that had been published in a Belgian Catholic newspaper:

"His father follows him to Rome, where he is permitted to see his child, who does not want to be separated from him any longer. The boy is afraid; he wants to see his mother and his sisters. He says that he will travel all through the night, if necessary, to see them. He wants to leave, but Church canons are against him." The Church then mounts its counterattack. "The comedy is launched, aimed at stifling the scandal: The child is said to feel an irresistible calling. He cries; no longer is he in his father's arms, no longer is he asking for his mother, but rather at the foot of a cross, calling for the sacred Virgin. He wants to be baptized again. He wants to baptize all the Jews. He will be a missionary so that he can convert them. All this at age six and a half!"

Which side was lying and which telling the truth was self-evident:

Between the miracle of a six-year-old apostle who wants to convert the Jews and the cry of a child who keeps asking for his mother and his little sisters, we don't hesitate for a moment. The nature of the truth is too obvious when set alongside the clear signs of deceit. When nature appears, when the heart speaks (and only the heart can speak at that age), the conviction is irresistible. There is not a person who loves their children, not a father, nor a mother, nor a brother, nor sister, who believes the account given in *L'Indépendance*.[10]

Defenders of the Church appeared not to realize that, to many, their account sounded too good to be true. The single most influential Church article on the taking of Edgardo, which appeared in *Civiltà Cattolica* in November 1858 and was subsequently excerpted in Catholic papers throughout Europe, recounted the miraculous transformation that came over the boy as soon as he set foot in the House of the Catechumens. The effects of the baptismal sacrament erupted in the child:

"He is mentally sharper and more perceptive than is usually to be found in a boy who is barely seven." On entering the Catechumens, "he showed a marvelous happiness. He declared that he did not want to be anything other than what he was, that is, a member of Christendom. . . . As for his attitude toward his parents, the change that came over him was practically instantaneous." He implored the Rector not to let his parents take him away: "He begged to be raised in a Christian home, to avoid those seductions and perhaps even the violence that, under the paternal roof, would most likely have met him."

The *Civiltà Cattolica* account sketched a central theme in the Catholic narrative: Edgardo had a new father—"I am baptized," he said, "I am baptized and my father is the Pope."[11] He had a new mother, the sacred Virgin Mary, and a new family, the *"grande famiglia cattolica."*

One day, according to yet another Catholic version of Edgardo's early encounters with his father at the Catechumens, "his father reminded him of the fourth of the Ten Commandments, that he should obey his parents and return home. 'I will do,' he responded, 'just exactly what the Holy Father says. Here he is,' and he points to the bust of the reigning Holy Pontiff." Later, seeing a nun's habit laid out, and knowing that it belonged to the mother of another boy who was a neophyte in the Catechumens, he was silent for a moment and then said wistfully: "Oh, if only my own mother were to wear a nun's habit!"[12]

If Edgardo in fact told his father that he did not want to return with him, that he now regarded the Pope as his true father and wanted to devote his life to converting the Jews, this message seems not to have registered with Momolo. Momolo's own impressions of his meetings with his son were very different from those reported in the Catholic press, and his concerns focused not on his son's loyalties or supposed conversion but on the obstacles he faced in getting Church authorities to release Edgardo from captivity.

In early September, after having seen Edgardo several times, Momolo got more bad news. The experts of the Rome Jewish community had prepared a brief for the Pope, bringing together citations from twenty different Church authorities, aimed at convincing the Pontiff to have Edgardo returned to his family. On September 7, a delegation from the Jewish community presented it to Cardinal Antonelli. To their surprise, even before reading the document, the Secretary of State told them not to expect a positive response. As one of the delegation wrote the next day to Baron de Rothschild in Paris, "His Eminence expressed himself in such a way as to remove any hope on the matter."[13]

A blow of a different kind came a few days later, when Momolo received an unsettling letter from Bologna jointly written by Marianna's brother Angelo Padovani and her brother-in-law, Angelo Moscato. They could hold off no longer, they wrote, for "if up to now we tried to spare you further unhappiness, we think it our duty to delay no further, since we see that only your presence here might repair things." His business, they told him, faced collapse as a result of his absence, and they warned that "if you do not return right away, you and your family may be ruined. Get back while there is still time, and get here without delay."

Nor was this all. Although, they wrote, it broke their hearts to have to add to his miseries, they felt duty-bound to report that Marianna,

> who, from the fatal moment when her son was torn from her, has always been in poor health, is now reduced to a truly pitiable state. When she was able to write, she always forced herself to write in a reassuring way so that you would not be alarmed on her account, and so that you would not feel so badly that it would detract from the energy you are in such great need of there. But we can no longer keep up this vain illusion, for if we did, when you do come back and see her in such a bad way, you would be doubly pained.
>
> You well know the one medicine that would bring her back to life! the news that you were bringing your son back with you to put in her arms! Ah, if you could only send a telegram with such news, you would without doubt find her in a very different state.

Knowing that Momolo had promised Edgardo that he wouldn't leave Rome without him, and knowing how much it would pain Momolo to break that promise, Padovani and Moscato added, "Assure your son that your absence will only be temporary, and that you will return soon to embrace him and to take him back to the bosom of his family." They added that Momolo could comfort Edgardo with assurances that, in his father's absence, other members of the Jewish community—such as Scazzocchio—would be allowed to visit him.[14]

The letter jolted Momolo, and he hurriedly made arrangements for the long return trip by coach to Bologna. He would have to leave Edgardo behind. On September 25, back in the city where it all began, Momolo wrote to Scazzocchio in Rome. The letter reveals a man buried beneath a cascade of miseries, yet neither bitter nor consumed by anger, a loving father and dedicated husband, still hopeful that the Pope would release his son.

Having left Rome with a broken heart, after a very pleasant trip I arrived in the bosom of my poor family. Unfortunately, I found them in a state of desolation, and my business in total disorder. I will do everything possible to repair the latter, but as for the sad state in which I found my wife, the possibility of a cure remains rather far off. She asks for nothing except news of our kidnapped son, she wants nothing other than him, and she will have neither peace nor health until he is returned to her. For that, I have unwavering faith in the unquestionable sense of justice of the High Pontiff, in the strength of the arguments we have already presented, and in the new documents that we will send in soon which, as they say, will cut the head from the bull. God willing, my presentiments will soon be borne out.

Momolo had another worry as well, for Marianna's distraught state had robbed her of her once plentiful milk, and little Imelda was suffering as a result. Even if they had not suffered the death of their baby boy the previous year, they would have been concerned about Imelda's health, for they lived at a time when a quarter of all children died before their first birthday, and when there was no good alternative to breast milk.

For now, I have the consolation that despite the fact that my wife has suffered so and suffers still, Heavenly Providence will not allow my little baby daughter to suffer and will, by some miracle, ensure that she grows normally. However, so that we don't lose our new one, the doctor thinks we should not further abuse her by continuing to feed her milk that has for too long been unhealthy. Within the week, despite what we would like, we have to wean her. We will have to wait and see what becomes of her then.

Job-like, Momolo added, "Ah! my dear Signor Secretary, unfortunately one misfortune brings with it a hundred others!"

"I fervently pray," he wrote, "that you go often to see my beloved son, shower him with kisses for me, comfort him all you can and assure him of my unceasing efforts to get him back, to bring him back to me and to his mother, his brothers, and his sisters."

CHAPTER 8

Pope Pius IX

E DGARDO'S NEW FATHER, Pius IX, may well be the most important pope in modern history. The fact that his reign, from 1846 to 1878, was the longest of any pope since Peter himself was merely a demographic achievement, a product of his relative youth at ascension to office and his longevity. But his reign marked a watershed, the uneasy transition from an outworn medieval papacy, uncomfortably combining the roles of temporal prince and spiritual head, to one presiding over no armies and no state. This transition to modernity, however, came not because of the Pope's efforts but despite them.

Born in 1792 in Senigallia, near Ancona, Giovanni Maria Mastai-Ferretti was the last of nine children, his father a count. It was common at the time for a younger son of a noble family to dedicate himself to a high clerical career, and in Mastai-Ferretti's case there were a number of signs that the fit might be a good one. Even as a youth he seemed to have a spiritual quality about him, and his family's inclination to place him in the Church was reinforced when, at age 15, he began to have his first epileptic seizures. Mastai-Ferretti was never much of a student, and the upheavals caused by the Napoleonic wars and occupation disrupted his studies. Even his sympathetic biographer Roger Aubert writes that the future pope's education was limited, and that "in history, canon law, and even in theology his notions would always be superficial."[1] In 1819, Mastai-Ferretti received ecclesiastical dispensation to become a priest despite his epileptic episodes, although with the restriction that he could not celebrate mass alone; he had to be assisted by a fellow clergyman.

Mastai-Ferretti's career in some ways paralleled that of Michele Viale-Prelà. Both men were born to elite families in the provinces, both were younger sons, and both had close family ties in the Church hierarchy. One of Mastai-Ferretti's uncles was a bishop, and another was a canon of Saint Peter's. The future Pius IX had been a priest for only a few years when he was assigned to the papal diplomatic corps and, in 1823, sent for two years to Chile. Unlike Viale-Prelà, however, he was not by temperament or ability particularly suited for a diplomatic career and was undoubtedly pleased when in 1827, at age 35, just eight years after becoming a priest, he was named Archbishop of Spoleto, in the Papal States. Five years later he became Bishop of Imola, not far from Bologna. In 1845, the year before becoming pope, Mastai-Ferretti, by now a cardinal, was called upon to fill in for his neighbor, the Archbishop of Ferrara, and, amidst great pomp, baptized a young Jewish man, Samuele Coen.[2]

When, on June 1, 1846, Pope Gregory XVI died, after a fifteen-year reign, hopes sprouted that the reactionary pope's successor might be someone better suited to come to terms with the new currents sweeping Europe, the movement away from the old regimes of autocrats and noblemen toward a system of nations based on constitutional rule and the separation of Church and state. Following brief deliberations, and barely two weeks after his predecessor's death, Giovanni Maria Cardinal Mastai-Ferretti, Bishop of Imola, was elected pope, taking the name of Pius to honor Pius VII, the pope who had befriended him in his youth in Rome and who, arrested and sent into exile by Napoleon in 1809, lived to return as ruler of the Papal States upon the Corsican's fall five years later.

People in the Papal States initially saw Pope Pius IX as the answer to their prayers. In a series of measures taken in the first eighteen months of his papacy, he set out on a reforming path. He pronounced an amnesty, releasing a thousand political prisoners; he named Pasquale Cardinal Gizzi, a noted liberal, as his first secretary of state; he named commissions to study economic, judicial, and welfare reforms; and he relaxed press censorship. In championing the introduction of gas street-lighting and the expansion of railways—two signs of modernity his predecessor had disdained—the Pope solidified his reputation. His reform movement extended to the Jews as well. He established a high-profile commission of inquiry into the conditions in the ghetto, and in response to its report, among other changes, he abolished the much-reviled forced sermons and allowed the better-off ghetto residents to petition for permission to move to homes outside the old ghetto walls.[3]

The reaction in Bologna was typical. In the aftermath of the papal pardon, large, enthusiastic crowds paraded through the streets of the city, carrying white banners and torches and shouting their praises to the new pope. Flowers and garlands adorned the copies of the papal edict of pardon that were posted on columns around the city, and crowns were placed atop effigies that appeared all over the city center.[4]

All this would soon change. In the face of the revolutionary movements sweeping Europe at the beginning of 1848, rulers throughout the continent faced the unappetizing choice of either granting constitutions—and hence turning their subjects into rights-holding citizens—or fleeing. Pius IX was a reformer in the sense that he viewed some aspects of the old system as corrupt and in need of change, but he was far from a democrat. Yet he, too, felt constrained to grant a constitution in Rome in March 1848 in the wake of the constitutions granted by the kings of Sardinia and the Two Sicilies the month before.

In Italy, the antiabsolutist uprisings embraced another goal: the ejection of the foreigners from the peninsula and the end of foreign rule. When, in March, revolution erupted in Vienna and Metternich fled, the time for driving the Austrians out and proclaiming Italy for the Italians seemed to be at hand. Giddy at the prospects of the dawning of a new age, many saw the Pope as the potential godfather of a new political union.

But on April 29, 1848, just twelve days after he had ordered the gates of Rome's ghetto torn down, Pius IX issued an allocution that condemned the Italian nationalists, rejected the Risorgimento, and declared that the Papal States could never join in the war to drive Austrian troops out of Italy. Those who had seen in Pius IX the liberal pope who would lead the people into a new age were stunned. All the ministers of the new Roman government resigned in protest, and the paralyzed moderate nationalists gave way to the Republican movement, whose enthusiasts had long viewed the temporal power of the papacy as an anachronism, unfit for the modern age of nations.

Although Pope Pius IX championed some reforms on his accession to the papacy, he was very much a product of the Catholic frame of mind of the time. Civilization was identified with Christianity and, in historian Giovanni Miccoli's phrase, "the only true civilization was that born and developed in medieval Europe." The Pope believed in the virtues of tradition, hierarchy, and order. He feared the unknown and was diffident toward the new. Like others of the Church hierarchy, Pius IX viewed the changes introduced into Europe with the Enlightenment, and especially with the French Revolution, as threatening the proper order of things—indeed, as the work of the devil. It was the Church's responsibility to block these moves toward secularization, to prevent the questioning of traditional authority.[5]

Following Pius IX's late April condemnation of the nationalists, the tide of popular opinion turned against him, and his hold on Rome and the Papal States beyond weakened precipitously. He had brief hopes that his appointment of the able Pellegrino Rossi as the new prime minister would lead to the reassertion of papal authority, but these were bloodily dashed when, on November 15, as Rossi was entering the parliament building, assassins slit his throat. With huge demonstrations demanding democratic reforms and war on Austria, the Pope, fearing for his life, donned the garb of a simple priest, tinted spectacles obscuring his well-known face, and fled the Holy City. It was the night of November 24. He crossed the border into the kingdom of the Two Sicilies, taking up residence in the fortress of Gaeta. It was not one of the Pope's finest hours. Even for those who later sought his canonization as a saint, the flight to Gaeta was "one of the saddest and least glorious moments of his papacy."[6]

The following month Garibaldi marched into Rome at the head of his volunteer army, and enthusiastic crowds gathered in the piazzas, abuzz with enthusiasm for the proclamation of a republic. As we have seen, in February 1849, disregarding Pius IX's January excommunication of all those who sought to overturn the Pope's secular rule, a Constitutional Assembly proclaimed the end of the Pope's temporal power and the establishment of a Roman Republic. Among the first articles of its constitution was the granting of equal rights to all. The Jews were once again liberated, although not for long.[7]

In response, the Pope called on the Catholic powers—Austria, France, Spain, and the kingdom of the Two Sicilies—to send their armies to restore papal rule. On July 3, French troops marched into Rome, defeated the forces of the short-lived Roman Republic, and retook the Holy City for the Pope. Meanwhile, Austrian troops marched through much of the rest of the peninsula, reestablishing the ancien régime. When, a year after the French reconquest of Rome, Pius IX thought it safe enough to return to Rome, he arrived to a cold reception. Whatever sympathy the Pope had earlier harbored for specific liberal reforms had by now vanished. The task he saw before him was that of reestablishing the prestige and power of the papacy. The reforms granted in 1848 were abolished, the experiment with limited constitutional government was ended, and, protected by French troops in Rome and Austrian troops elsewhere in the Papal States, he struggled to bring law and order back to his realm.

The battle involved not only police, soldiers, and courts; it was waged on ideological terrain as well. Proper Catholic values had to become better rooted in the population, and for this, Pius IX—whose example Cardinal Viale-Prelà would soon imitate in Bologna—turned to the Jesuits.

Championed by a young Neapolitan Jesuit, Father Carlo Curci, the idea of a Jesuit bimonthly journal in Italian, aimed at commenting on the issues of the day, appealed to the pope. In the past, the Church had no need for a publication directed at the laity, but now, with the spread of a critical popular press, there was need for a means of combating liberal propaganda and showing how proper Christian ideas were to be applied. Sweeping aside the protests of the head of the Jesuit order, who argued that the Jesuits' constitution forbade them from publishing a political journal, Pius IX gave Father Curci his enthusiastic support, and the first issue of *Civiltà Cattolica* was published in 1850. It soon became the unofficial organ of the Holy See.[8]

The Pope, a man of great religious faith, believed that the defeat of the Roman rebels by the French troops had been the work of God, a matter of divine retribution. He realized his own failings as an executive and a diplomat and so, in reestablishing his rule over the Papal States, turned to a man whose political and administrative abilities he had recently come to rely on, Cardinal Giacomo Antonelli. Indeed, for many residents of the Papal States, who refused to see in the oppressive return of absolutist rule the guiding hand of their beloved Pope, it was Antonelli—named secretary of state by Pius IX while they were in exile in Gaeta in 1849—who was blamed.

Antonelli's twenty-seven-year term of office was almost as remarkable as that of the Pope himself. It was marked not only by controversy over his policies, but—unlike the Pope, who might be regarded as irascible but certainly not corruptible—by the constant buzz of scandal that hung over him. That Cardinal Antonelli was able to hold on to power so long was seen by many—not only the masses of faithful unwilling to doubt the Pope's benevolence, but fellow cardinals as well—as evidence that the crafty and unscrupulous secretary of state had hoodwinked the credulous pope.

Giacomo Antonelli was born in 1806 to a wealthy family living in the southernmost part of the Papal States, near the border with the kingdom of the Two Sicilies. His father had made his fortune when Giacomo was a child, administering the properties of a large local landowner who, having been captured by brigands in 1807 and freed only after payment of a prodigious ransom, had taken a strong dislike to his old neighborhood and moved to Rome. Domenico Antonelli had five sons and three daughters. While his older sons were groomed to help him run the business, Giacomo was prepared for a clerical career. He had a meteoric rise in the Church hierarchy and was a cardinal by age forty. Yet Antonelli never became a priest. He was one of the last of a breed, men of wealthy or noble families who entered upon an ecclesiastical career predestined for high diplomatic office, but had little inclination for and little interest in religious or pastoral duties and were not required to be ordained as priests.[9]

The experiences of 1848–49 had a traumatic effect on Antonelli, as also on the Pope, and he concluded that papal rule could survive only if absolutist methods were reimposed and a close alliance was built with Austria, whose military forces would guarantee stability. Fending off a legion of critics, Antonelli succeeded in centralizing in his own hands all power over the Papal States' domestic administration and its diplomatic relations, preventing other government ministers from making decisions without his approval.

Together, Pius IX and his secretary of state were able to rebuild the papal regime. Unrest gradually died down, assassination attempts against Church officials became less common, and economic conditions began to improve. The period from 1851 to 1857 saw the Pope regain some of his lost popularity, and the cult of the saintly, good-humored leader once more gained ground.

Pius IX could show that he was made of stern stuff when he thought firmness was required. One day in June 1855, for example, as Cardinal Antonelli was descending the steps of the Vatican Palace, he noticed a young man waiting nervously on a landing. When he saw the man reach into his shirt, the Cardinal raced back up the stairs. The flustered would-be assassin, brandishing a large carving fork, was subdued by the papal police before he could reach his target. Identified as Antonio De Felici, a 35-year-old Roman hatmaker, he was already known to authorities as a frequenter of republican and Carbonari circles. De Felici was tried, convicted, and sentenced to death. Although the Secretary of State asked that the sentence be commuted to life in prison, the Pope decided that an example should be made of him, and on July 10 De Felici was decapitated.[10]

The hatred inspired by Antonelli is nicely captured by a secret report of Britain's representative at the Vatican, Odo Russell, written in January 1860. Russell noted that, despite Antonelli's responsibilities as head of Vatican diplomacy, the Cardinal had never traveled outside Italy and was only "very slightly acquainted with the affairs of other countries." But what he lacked in education, Russell observed, he more than made up for by "laborious habits, a logical mind, insinuating manners, animated conversation and the experience of diplomatic drawing rooms." Russell concluded with the observation that the Cardinal "has complete control over the amiable but weak mind of Pius IX."

According to the British diplomat, ever since Antonelli had returned with the Pope from exile in Gaeta, "he has been the object of general, bitter and unceasing hatred. . . . His youth irritates the venerable members of the Sacred College, his low origin annoys the patrician families, his firmness exasperates the liberal party, his commanding position excites the envy of all." In addition, tales of his love of money and his nepotistic ways were rampant. He had arranged for his brother to become head of the Pontifical Bank, and together, the British envoy reported, the two "have largely increased their private fortunes."[11]

Recent historians have been no kinder to the Secretary of State. Typical are the comments of J. Derek Holmes, who paints an appalling picture: "Antonelli lacked both principles and intelligence . . . while what he lacked in political or theological insight, he made up for in his acquisitive instincts and luxurious living. A greedy man, Antonelli used his position to accumulate a large personal fortune for himself and his relations." Nor was this all, for

Cardinal Antonelli was also widely rumored to keep a mistress. Following his death, in a case deeply embarrassing to the embattled Church, a woman filed suit in Italian court claiming, as Antonelli's illegitimate daughter, a portion of his substantial estate.[12] The fact that he left none of his fortune to the Church, not even to any of the religious orders for which he served as cardinal protector, only reinforced the popular view of his greed and impiety.[13]

The similarities between the common view of the time in Rome, which contrasted the good pope with the wicked secretary of state, and the view that subsequent historians have embraced, are striking. Holmes portrays a devout and deeply moral pope, who, although he had his weaknesses, including a hot temper, is described as "a man of deep and genuine piety who had a quiet confidence in God." Spending much time each day in prayer, he was "an attractive person, sympathetic and charming, intelligent and witty." As an example of the last-mentioned trait, Holmes cites the Pope's encounter with a group of Anglican clergymen at which he blessed them—in a variation on the blessing over incense at the Holy Mass—with the words: "May you be blessed by Him in whose honour you shall be burnt."[14]

A less generous Italian historian from earlier in the twentieth century attributed the Pope's gentle, benevolent image to the persistent trembling of his lip, due to his epilepsy, which caused a sweet smile to flash regularly across his face. However, by contrast with this historian's portrait of Antonelli, his view of the Pope was positively adulatory. The Secretary of State, he wrote, was "ugly in appearance, but frank . . . he never said mass, nor took confession. He was cold, egoistical, a schemer."[15]

The construction of the Cardinal as demon and the Pope as saint, while having a long pedigree, obscures more than it reveals about the two men and the historical roles they played. Even historians favorably disposed toward the Pope record some of his less attractive qualities. Roger Aubert, who has written something like an official Church biography of the Pontiff, characterizes Pius IX as, above all else, emotional and excitable, often betrayed by a tendency toward irritability and rapid mood swings. Sensitive to anything he took to be a slight, he was known for frightening visitors with angry outbursts, uttering words he would later regret. In recent years, one of the charges that proponents of his sainthood have had to face was Pius IX's tendency to ridicule people when he was annoyed with them, displaying a caustic wit that sometimes left a poor impression of the Holy Father.[16]

All that said, Aubert paints the picture of a firm and principled champion of the Church. Pius IX's only ambition, his biographer argues, was to serve the Church, a commitment rooted in a deep and unshakable faith. With his melodious voice, his kind smile, and his willingness to receive a long line of visitors day after day, giving each his complete attention, the Pope won a reputation as a deeply religious and caring man. Although he could be indecisive in dealing with affairs of state, when his role as pastor was at stake and when he saw Church dogma under attack—factors both very much at issue in the Mortara case—he was resolute and unbending.[17]

At the other end of the spectrum, August Hasler, a heterodox Swiss priest and scholar—in a more recent study of how, under Pius IX's direction, the doctrine of papal infallibility came to be officially established—gives short shrift to the idea of the Pope's amiable personality and rock-hard faith. Hasler paints an unflattering picture of a credulous, superstitious, and mean-spirited bigot. Nor does Hasler have kind words to say about the Pontiff's intelligence. He cites a letter written by Mastai-Ferretti to Pope Leo XII in which the future pope, then aged 33, complains that owing to his earlier bouts with epilepsy, he "had a very weak memory and could not concentrate on a subject for any length of time without having worry about his ideas getting terribly confused." Pius IX, Hasler maintains, was considered by those who knew him to be "impressionable, capricious, impulsive, and unpredictable."[18]

Whichever we choose, it is clear that Cardinal Antonelli's ability to get the Pope to do what he wanted had its limits. While much of papal administration and diplomacy held no interest for Pius IX, and in those arenas he gave his trusted secretary of state a free hand to do what he thought best, in matters that did interest him he had a strong will of his own. Many of the actions for which Pius IX is today remembered, and revered, by the Church are products of his uncompromising stand on matters of doctrine: the proclamation of the Immaculate Conception of Mary as dogma in 1854 and the First Vatican Council, with its proclamation of papal infallibility, in 1870 stand out especially. In the latter case, Antonelli had clear misgivings, accurately predicting the diplomatic damage that would be done throughout Europe by the pronouncement. Pius IX dismissed these concerns with the comment: "I have the Blessed Virgin on my side."[19]

The Pope continued to see himself as benevolently disposed toward the Jews, but it was a benevolence necessarily qualified by his strong belief in the superiority of Christianity, in the divine punishment meted out to the Jews for their historical role in the killing of Christ, and in the perniciousness of the Jews' own religious beliefs and practices. Events of 1848–49 only strengthened Pius IX's opposition to the idea of freedom of religion. He was committed to the principle of the Catholic state, one in which any other religion had to be viewed with suspicion and closely regulated, if not banned.[20] This principle extended not only to the Jews but to other Christian denominations as well. Indeed, the Pope was more favorably inclined toward the Jews, who represented no threat to the Holy Church, than toward the Protestants, who did. To the complaints of those who said that the Jews were poorly treated in the

Papal States, the Pope and his defenders could argue that, on the contrary, they were accorded privileged treatment, allowed to have their own synagogues and practice their religion undisturbed. By contrast, Protestants were not permitted such freedoms, and Rome itself had no real Protestant church, other than a converted granary outside town used by diplomatic personnel and other foreigners. Papal police stood guard at its doors to ensure that no native went inside.[21]

Not only did the Pope in the 1850s resist calls to give the Jews equal rights; he angrily denounced moves by other Italian states to do so. When the old regime of the Grand Duke was restored in Tuscany and the new constitution was nullified, the Pope was infuriated to learn that the constitutional provision giving Jews equal rights, including the right to attend the university, was to remain in force.[22] In an era when the absolutist state was giving way to notions of individual rights and religious freedom, Pius IX remained a true believer in the time-honored, divinely ordered way of the world, a world in which the Jews lived as guests, benefiting from the Church's charity, until such time as they would see the light and join the true faith.

CHAPTER 9

The Pope Denounced

T HE FUROR provoked by the Mortara affair surprised Pope
Pius IX. Although he had suffered all manner of verbal attack,
and even revolt, in the twelve years of his papacy, his dealings
with the Jews had occasioned no particular difficulties. At most, he had had
to cope with an occasional annoying letter from one of the Rothschilds,
complaining about the restrictions placed on the Jews in the Papal States. As
Pius IX saw it, he had been a great friend to the Jews.

The chain of events that led the boy to Rome's Catechumens began when
Father Feletti, Bologna's Inquisitor, heard reports that a Christian servant had
secretly baptized a Jewish child in the city. Following well-worn Inquisition
procedures, Feletti had written, on October 26, 1857, to the Commissioner of
the Holy Office of the Inquisition in Rome, Cardinal De Ferrari, for permission to proceed with an inquiry. On November 9, the Cardinal replied, in a
letter reporting the results of the session of the Holy Office at which the case
was discussed:

"Your letter of 26 October, relative to the baptism conferred on the young
Hebrew boy, has been taken into consideration today and your suggestion to
proceed with prudence has been approved. As we know that you have the
wisdom to carry out the required interrogation . . . you are therefore given
permission to proceed. It is with determination that I tell you to go ahead with
this matter."[1]

With this authorization from Rome, Father Feletti summoned Anna
Morisi to San Domenico. The written test of her interrogation, prepared by
his secretary, was then sent back to the Holy Office in Rome with a request to
proceed with the taking of the child. The Holy Office's letter of response to

Father Feletti, reporting its final recommendation, was apparently burned by the Inquisitor when, a year after Edgardo was seized, the Cardinal Legate was driven from Bologna and the papal regime was overthrown.

As pope, Pius IX was titular head of the Holy Office of the Inquisition and occasionally attended its meetings. In major cases, the Pope was consulted before a decision was reached. But at the time it came to the Holy Office, the Mortara case was likely viewed as little more than routine, the application of principles and procedures long enshrined in the workings of the Inquisition. Since the case involved a family living in the Papal States, there was no question about the Inquisitor's ability to carry out whatever action was deemed appropriate. If the Pope attended either of the meetings of the Holy Office where the Mortara case was discussed, or if he was informed about it in advance, we do not know.[2]

In the subsequent controversy, played out in the press throughout Europe, the question of whether the Pope had approved the initial decision was debated, as was the question of whether, if he had heard about it only after the fact, he thought that the Holy Office and Bologna's inquisitor had acted wisely. The matter was not merely one of idle speculation or curiosity: for the Mortaras and the other Jews championing their cause, their belief that the Pope had known nothing about the inquisitorial order, and was shocked when he learned of it, was central to their confidence that the child would be returned. Momolo Mortara was certainly of this opinion, at least in the first months after Edgardo was taken: the kindly pope, he believed, had surely been horrified to learn what had happened in Bologna and, once fully informed, would see that all was set right again.

The strongest evidence in support of Momolo's belief comes from a letter written by the Marquis of Villamarina, the kingdom of Sardinia's ambassador in Paris, to Count Cavour in Turin on November 21, 1858. The Marquis described the stormy audience that the French ambassador to the Holy See, the Duke de Gramont, had with the Pope a few weeks earlier. At that meeting, the Duke warned the Pope that his refusal to release Edgardo to his family would have dire diplomatic consequences. Villamarina reported, based on his sources, that the Pope "was very upset about the incident, which he greatly regretted and which for all the world he would have wished to avoid. It is the fault, he said, of the careless zeal of Cardinal Viale-Prelà." To this, the Pope, according to Villamarina, added, "but now there is nothing that can be done; I can only do what the institutions of the Church force me to."[3]

There are good reasons for doubting the accuracy of this account. Throughout the controversy over the abduction, the Pope never wavered in his belief in the righteousness of the cause he was championing. Everything we know about his worldview suggests that, unlike his Secretary of State, Pius IX saw the decision to take Edgardo from his Jewish family as a sacred obligation. In his meeting with the French ambassador, the Pope may have expressed a kind of generic regret that the incident had occurred, and Gramont could have interpreted this to mean the Pope would have acted differently had he known in advance of the inquisitional order to seize Edgardo. And the Pope may well have mentioned the rigor with which Cardinal Viale-Prelà was directing his new archdiocese, leading the French ambassador to make another faulty inference. But Viale-Prelà's missionizing efforts were fully in harmony with Pius IX's battle against liberalism.[4]

We get a better insight into the Pope's thinking from a letter he received almost the same day as his meeting with the French ambassador. The author respectfully asked the Pope to return Edgardo to his family. Pius IX scribbled his reaction at the bottom of the page: "aberrations of a Catholic . . . who doesn't know his catechism."[5]

Within a few weeks of Edgardo's abduction, the campaign organized by the Jews of Bologna was beginning to find a receptive audience beyond Italy's small and beleaguered Jewish community. In the past, neither governments nor non-Jews had shown any interest in the problems Jews of other countries faced as they dealt with the power of the Church.[6] But in 1858 the international situation was dramatically changed. The debate over the continuing temporal power of the papacy, and hence the wisdom of a theocratic state in the middle of Europe, was reaching a fevered pitch. A panoply of forces, from the conservative King Victor Emmanuel II and his prime minister, Count Cavour, in Piedmont to the revolutionary nationalist Giuseppe Mazzini, in exile in London, were doing all they could to undermine the credibility of papal rule. And the spread of Enlightenment ideas of freedom of religion and separation of church and state was increasingly swaying public opinion, albeit an opinion that was largely confined to a literate elite.

Yet these efforts on the part of Bologna's Jews to involve the governments of Europe and the United States in the affair, aimed at pressuring the Vatican to give the child up, made the leaders of Rome's Università Israelitica nervous. And the efforts to drum up public criticism of the Holy See in the popular press horrified them. While the Roman Jewish community leaders concentrated on preparing their respectful petition to the Vatican, elsewhere Mortara champions worked to ignite a conflagration of international indignation and protest aimed at forcing the Pope to release Edgardo.

One of the milestones in triggering an international protest movement came in early August, when an emergency meeting of representatives from all the Jewish communities of the kingdom of Sardinia was held in the city of Alessandria, in Piedmont. The delegates, enjoying the benefits of the 1848 statutes that had emancipated the Jews, were incensed by the conditions in which their brethren in the Papal States were still forced to live. Viewing the seizure of Edgardo as an affront to Jews everywhere, a symbol of degradation that they would tolerate no more, and having no faith that the Pope would return Edgardo on his own, they sought help not only from their own government but from others as well.

A letter they sent to the Jewish communities of England and France began by noting how appropriate it was that the call they were issuing came from the Jews of the kingdom of Sardinia, the only Jews in Italy who were free to speak their minds. It continued: "It is for this reason that all the main Jewish communities in the Sardinian states join together in protesting, through the press, against the barbarous act committed in Bologna." They called on their French and English brethren to "regard it as their sacred duty to appeal to their own respective governments" and expressed the hope that the resulting intervention would, once and for all, prevent "the authorities in Rome and in any other place from disturbing, without punishment, the well-being and peace of Jewish families, in the name of a religion that claims to be founded on the solid principles of humanity and fraternal charity."[7]

On receiving this letter, the organization of French Jewish communities prepared a plea to the Emperor, Napoleon III: "The Central Consistory of French Jews implores Your Majesty to come to the aid of a foreign family, victim of an odious violence which took place two months ago in the shadow of our glorious flag and before the eyes of our brave soldiers." Praising the Emperor as the champion of the oppressed and the weak, the French Jews called on him to act. Although the matter regarded foreigners, they argued, the fact that the boy was held in Rome, which was defended by French troops, meant that the Emperor himself was implicated.[8]

Napoleon III had, in fact, already received reports of the Mortara case from his cousin Marquis Gioacchino Pepoli, who lived in Bologna. Unbeknownst to the Jews of Bologna, Piedmont, or France, the kidnapping may have already had an impact on Napoleon III, and on the course of world events, that was beyond their imagination.

Two years earlier, at the Congress of Paris, Count Cavour had lobbied to extend the territory of the kingdom of Sardinia, partly at the expense of the Austrians and their allied duchies and partly at the expense of the Papal States. The kingdom of Sardinia could not itself annex any of these lands without outside help, both political and military. The French emperor was sympathetic to the Italian cause, although reluctant to take any bold action in its favor, not only because of his fear of the consequences of war with Austria, but because of the widespread support for the pope's temporal rule among his own Catholic population and members of the French parliament.

Napoleon III, repulsed by the anachronistic character of papal government, had unsuccessfully tried to persuade the Pope to modernize his state. News of the seizure of the Jewish child from Bologna, and of the boy's captivity in Rome, enraged him. It was especially galling because the Pope's ability to hold the child in Rome depended on the protection offered by French soldiers.

In the view of Roger Aubert, it was the Mortara affair that drove the Emperor over the brink, turning him against the pontifical state. Not only did it confirm his own belief in the anachronism of papal rule, but it weakened the French public's enthusiasm for the temporal power of the pope, giving him a freer hand to act. On July 21, 1858, less than a month after Edgardo's abduction, Napoleon III held a secret meeting in Plombières with Cavour. It was a fateful encounter. Together they hatched a plan to drive the Austrians out of Italy and, at the same time, to annex three-quarters of the Papal States, including Bologna and the rest of Romagna, to the kingdom of Sardinia.[9] In less than a year, the plan would be put into effect.

The hopes of the Mortara family, and of the Jews who anxiously followed the efforts made to win Edgardo's return, rested heavily on France and, in particular, on the French emperor. Not only did they see France as having special influence with the Vatican because of the role played by French troops, but they also thought the French, heirs to the Enlightenment and the Revolution, would be sympathetic to their argument of the superiority of natural law and paternal rights to religious authority.[10] The Piedmontese Jews who gathered in August in Alessandria also had faith that their own government, the kingdom of Sardinia, would be sympathetic to the Mortaras' plight. Yet they realized that their government had little influence on the Pope, who, indeed, viewed the designs of King Victor Emmanuel II and Count Cavour with the greatest suspicion. By contrast, Napoleon III was a man the Pope could ill afford to offend.

While Momolo Mortara was in Rome for his first visits with his son, Sabatino Scazzocchio and others of the Università Israelitica helped prepare a letter for him to sign to be sent to the Duke de Gramont, the French ambassador to the Holy See. The document is especially interesting because it represents an exception to the Roman Jews' general reluctance to involve foreign governments in Jewish affairs. However, it was in line with their commitment to quiet diplomacy—out of the public eye and, above all, out of the newspapers—and aimed at enlisting the help of a government friendly to the Vatican.

The letter to Gramont reported that, the previous day, September 7, the Jews had submitted a new brief to Cardinal Antonelli for transmission to Pius IX. It consisted of extracts of the opinions of prominent Church authorities of the past, adduced to support Edgardo's release. Accompanying the brief was a new request that the boy be freed. In the letter to the Duke, in which copies of both documents were enclosed, Momolo argued that the return of his son accorded with the rulings of past Church authorities. These rulings demonstrate, he claimed, that the "alleged baptism of my son should be declared void and he should be returned to his family, who for more than two months now have suffered a most cruel anguish."

Momolo's letter to the French ambassador marked a new phase in his efforts to get his son back. It came the day after Cardinal Antonelli had received the petition on which Momolo had pinned such great hopes, the capstone of the plan of action championed by Scazzocchio and Rome's Università Israelitica. The Cardinal's negative reaction on receiving the petitions, Momolo told the Ambassador, "has made me despair of the utility of my supplications. . . . Although he received the documents we presented with his accustomed kindness, His Eminence let it be known that nothing could change a decision that had already been delayed, nor annul an act that was considered valid." Knowing of the French interest in his case, and despairing at the failure of their direct supplications to the Vatican, Momolo wanted to bring the Ambassador up to date, hoping that the French could succeed where the Jews had failed.[11]

The Mortaras' drive to enlist foreign help not only was aimed at spurring governments to action but involved another, more traditional approach as well. When intercession with the Pope was needed, Italy's Jews were in the habit of turning to the Rothschild family for help. The Rothschilds, whose banking empire stretched throughout much of Europe and whose members oversaw operations in Austria, Germany, France, England, the kingdom of Naples, and beyond, were, for the Vatican, Jews of a special stripe. Long plagued by financial troubles, the Vatican had, over the years, often turned to the Jewish bankers for loans to keep the government afloat or to launch new projects. It was an arrangement that, while suiting both sides financially, was mutually embarrassing. For the leaders of world Catholicism to rely on Jewish bankers while preventing Jews in their own domain from owning property or engaging in professions was humiliating. And given the Catholic theology of God's punishment of the Jews and His coronation of the Roman Church, the Holy See's need to turn to Jews to stave off bankruptcy risked undermining the faith as well. For the Jewish bankers, the problem was different. By offering loans needed to keep the wheels of the ecclesiastical state turning, they appeared to be enriching themselves at the expense of their fellow Jews, propping up a regime that oppressed them.

By the mid-nineteenth century, the Rothschild family were justifying their loans to the Vatican by assuming the role of benevolent intercessors for the Jews with the Holy See. Michele Viale-Prelà, Bologna's archbishop, had himself been involved in such an episode back in February 1847 while serving as papal nuncio in Vienna. It was shortly after Pius IX had become pope. Baron Solomon Rothschild presented Viale-Prelà with a request for the new pontiff, listing in great detail the hardships faced by the Jews in Rome. Rothschild complained in particular about the confinement of the Jews in the ghetto, the ban on possession of property outside the ghetto, the prohibition on the exercise of the professions and of many other occupations, the annual carnival rites of degradation, the heavy annual special levies they were subjected to, their exclusion from Rome's hospitals, the obligation of attending forced conversionary sermons (by then just four times a year), and other such burdens. Viale-Prelà, requested by Rothschild to do all he could to win a favorable hearing from the Pope, confided in a letter to Cardinal Gizzi, the secretary of state of the Papal States at the time, his lack of sympathy for the request. However, he did send it on to Rome, and it apparently had some effect, for only a few days later Gizzi told Viale-Prelà that the Pope had decided to do away with the public carnival ritual for the Jews, and that a number of the other Rothschild requests, including the ending of the forced enclosure in the ghetto, would soon be granted.[12]

Three years later, following the rise and fall of the Roman Republic, the Vatican entered negotiations with James Rothschild, head of the French branch of the banking family, for a large loan. On that occasion as well, the Rothschilds took the opportunity to request improvements in the conditions in which the Pope's Jews lived. Pius IX, however, was no longer in a mood to hear of such concessions and took no action.[13]

Feeling otherwise powerless before the might of the Vatican, the Jews of the Papal States saw the Rothschilds as their champions before the Holy See. The Mortaras—along with Jews everywhere interested in their cause—looked anxiously to the Rothschild family to intercede for them.

They did not need to wait long. On July 17, barely three weeks after Edgardo was taken, James Rothschild wrote to Secretary of State Antonelli from Paris: "During my trip to Rome, I often had the opportunity to appreciate your sense of justice and kindness, so that today I have no fear in calling on them on behalf of Monsieur Mortara, a Jewish storekeeper who lives in Bologna." After briefly recounting to Antonelli how Momolo had seen his 6-year-old son taken from him by force "under the pretext that he had been baptized," Rothschild went on to tell of the failure of Momolo's efforts to gain his son's release, his despair, and "the illness of his wife, who has become practically insane as a result." Rothschild concluded by expressing his hope that Antonelli would support the "unhappy father" in his attempts to win back his son.[14]

A month later, on August 24, the English branch of the Rothschild family weighed in, as Lionel Rothschild wrote his own plea to Antonelli. Having just that year become the first Jew to serve in the British parliament, Lionel Rothschild was a man to be reckoned with.

Unlike James, Lionel Rothschild had never met Cardinal Antonelli. After recounting his somewhat confused understanding of what had happened, Rothschild wrote: "I am certain that this fact can only be an abuse of power or a miscalculated excess of zeal which was not known by the government of the Papal States, since Your Eminence's reputation for justice is, for me, a guarantee that a procedure such as this, which has thrown an entire family into despair, would not be tolerated." Rothschild called on Cardinal Antonelli to launch an investigation and then take appropriate action to redress the injustice.

In the last paragraph of his letter, Rothschild asked the Secretary of State's pardon for taking the liberty to write him on such a matter. He had decided to write, he explained, because he had "received various letters from different parts of the continent, in addition to communications from some of my most cherished friends," and as a result "felt the duty to make this appeal to Your Eminence to let you know how great the anxiety and interest are that have been caused by this fact."[15]

Shortly after receiving this letter, Antonelli prepared his guarded response. The facts of which Rothschild wrote, he replied, were "not unknown to me. . . . I would have truly wished, on my part, to be able to reciprocate the faith that you have placed in me, but, dealing as this does with a matter that does not regard my ministry, and that is in itself extremely delicate, I am not in a position to take an interest in the affair that is consonant with your desire." The Cardinal added, "Here it may be opportune to observe that, if the voice of nature is powerful, even more powerful are the sacred duties of religion."[16]

As word of the abduction of Edgardo spread farther through Europe and across the ocean to the United States, as committees of Jews throughout the West organized protests and raised funds, and as an increasing number of foreign governments made their disapproval known, the Pope stood firm. For Pius IX, it was a matter of principle.

Meanwhile, since their forays into ecclesiastical law and papal precedent had gotten them nowhere, Momolo and his friends in Bologna decided to try a different approach. If the Church would not concede that a baptized child could be returned to Jewish parents, what if it could be shown that the child had not, in fact, ever been baptized?

CHAPTER 10

A Servant's Sex Life

A FTER RECEIVING the panicked plea from his brothers-in-law in mid-September to hurry back to Bologna to rescue his business and his wife, Momolo made one last appeal to the Pope before departing. Its tone reveals his despair.

Dated September 19 and addressed directly to the Pope, it begins:

> Momolo Mortara, genuflecting before the feet of Your Holiness, declares that from the day in which his son was taken from him, he has seen nothing but one misery pile up upon another. The disorder in which he left his business in Bologna, increased frightfully by his long absence, has finally brought about its complete ruin. He has been urgently recalled there, not only because of his wife's failing health, but due to the above-mentioned business catastrophe. As he leaves the best part of himself [i.e., his son] in Rome and weeps in desolation, he dares to beg Your Holiness, with a wish from deep in his heart, that—given the great charity for which you are known—you relieve their great anguish even before he returns to the capital, and restore to those who have lost everything at least the sacred sweetness of family.[1]

Once he returned to Bologna and found that his wife was not in as bad shape as he had feared, Momolo tried to resuscitate his business but found it impossible to concentrate on anything other than getting Edgardo back. A series of Momolo's letters to Rome in the last days of September tells of his frenzied activity as he and his Jewish support group in Bologna orchestrated the drive to win the boy's release.

In a September 27 letter to Scazzocchio, Momolo spoke of how busy he had been getting various certificates and depositions needed to bolster his case. Having heard, to his distress, that Scazzocchio was being refused permission to visit Edgardo in his absence, Momolo appended a plea to be taken to Cardinal Antonelli, asking the Secretary of State to intervene so that he could continue to receive news of his son.

In his second letter of the day, Momolo reported that he would soon send Scazzocchio documents that would shed new light on Anna Morisi. Momolo also relayed word of a disturbing new development: he had received a letter from a Jew in Livorno reporting a conversation the man had had with a friend in Rome (such was the nature of Italy's Jewish network). According to the report, Momolo wrote, "a renewed baptism had just been administered to my beloved Edgardo." He urged Scazzocchio to investigate the report and, should it be true, to lodge a formal protest.

Momolo had more promising news to relate on the international front. He had just learned that forty of Germany's most prominent rabbis had sent a collective protest to the Pope in behalf of the Mortara family. Ten days earlier, in response to a request for more details from England, his Bologna friends had sent out a full account of the case. The world was taking an ever-greater interest in the Jewish boy from Bologna.

Momolo's letter concluded by reminding Scazzocchio to visit Edgardo regularly and to send him reports of how his son was doing. But in Rome, the Università Israelitica secretary was not having much luck. On September 29, Scazzocchio wrote a letter of protest to Enrico Sarra, Rector of the Catechumens, complaining of the humiliating treatment he had received and reporting the disturbing rumors that Edgardo had been recently baptized in the House of the Catechumens.

On the twenty-third of the month, Scazzocchio recalled, he had gone to the Catechumens, following Momolo's request, to see Edgardo. When he had knocked at the door, the Rector had come to the window and informed him that as a result of a new order he had received, he was not permitted to allow any Jew entrance. "I write to you," Scazzocchio informed the Rector, "not feeling that I deserve to suffer the humiliation of once again being turned away, a feeling reinforced by the fact that Signor Mortara, before returning home, reached an agreement with you that, in his absence, I would be able to come there to see his son and give him news of the boy from time to time."

Scazzocchio then turned to the other, even more troubling matter. "Signor Mortara writes me that he heard in Bologna that his son has recently been baptized according to the regular rite. As much as this report seems to me to be unbelievable, and as much as I was about to reply to that unhappy father to this effect, nonetheless, in order to carry out his request that I ask you directly, I beg you to give me confirmation of this so that I can relieve the poor soul from such painful doubt."[2] In fact, there seems not to have been any such baptism performed in these first few months in the Catechumens, despite the rumors that were flying around among Italy's Jews.

The certificates that Momolo was gathering, and in which he placed so much hope, were aimed at disputing the facts on which the Inquisitor and the other Church authorities based their case. At the center of the story was the servant Anna Morisi. She was the only witness to the baptism. It was on the basis of her account alone that Father Feletti had ordered Edgardo seized. Momolo now set about doing everything he could to undermine her credibility, investigating any parts of her story about the baptism that could be checked and trying to show that she was of such poor moral character that she could not be believed.

A key figure in Morisi's story was Cesare Lepori, the neighborhood grocer. It was he, she said, who had first suggested that she baptize the sick child and who had then told her how to do it. From his obscurity as a small-time grocer, Lepori suddenly found himself attracting unwelcome attention from far beyond Bologna. Indeed, throughout the Papal States, observers were blaming the whole disaster on him.[3]

In 1858, Cesare Lepori was 34 years old and lived near the Mortaras with his wife, their 4-year-old daughter, Maria, his 32-year-old unmarried brother, Raffaele, and his widowed father, Franco, age 72. All were born in Bologna, and they were well known in the area, running a family grocery store together with Cesare's older brother, Antonio, who lived nearby with his second wife and two children.[4]

When Momolo returned from Rome, he decided to confront Cesare Lepori. It must have been hard for Momolo to control his emotions when he entered the Lepori store, for at the time he too believed that the young grocer was responsible for the tragedy that had befallen him. When Lepori saw Momolo come in, three months after the police siege outside the Mortara home, he must have been tense himself, for by this time he knew that Anna Morisi had identified him as the instigator of the baptism.

The best account we have of what followed comes from an unexpected source: a retired judge, a Catholic, Carlo Maggi, who lived in the neighborhood. On October 6, Maggi appeared before a Bologna notary who had been hired by Momolo to transcribe and certify his account. The testimony was then submitted to Cardinal Antonelli for the Pope's consideration. Momolo had high hopes that once the Pontiff heard the true story, he would order Edgardo freed.

Maggi explained:

As I often stop by the café Genio in via San Felice, which is frequented by a number of Jews, including Signor Momolo Mortara, I have had various occasions to speak to him, especially about his little son. That was the boy who was taken from him a few months ago as a result of a governmental order, because he was baptized. I had also spoken with Mortara in this connection about the opinion that had taken hold as a result of the allegations made by a certain Nina [Nina being Anna Morisi's nickname], formerly his servant, about a certain Signor Cesare Lepori, a grocer with a store in Via Vetturini. She had said that he was the one who had urged her and taught her to administer the sacrament of baptism to his son, teaching her how to give it since she told Lepori that she did not know how to do it herself.

Our discussions had been left at this point when, on Tuesday, the fifth of this month, I stopped by the café in question at eight o'clock to have breakfast. Signor Mortara came in to tell me something like the following: "Haven't you heard? Last Saturday I went to Lepori's store. When Cesare saw me, after greeting me, he asked what was up with my servant Nina, and I told him that I'd rather not hear her name mentioned, and that it would be better for him as well, after she had so compromised him in public opinion by saying that he had gotten her to baptize the boy and taught her how to do it. At this, he replied that it was a lie, because never, ever had Lepori spoken to that young woman about it."

After hearing this account, I told Mortara that I found it hard to believe . . . that Lepori could so categorically deny something that was so widely known as a result of what Nina said.

To convince the retired jurist, Momolo invited him to accompany him to Lepori's store, to see for himself. Momolo was planning to go there anyway to pick up a written statement that Lepori had promised to prepare for him.

And so around 8:30 a.m., I went with Mortara to Lepori's store, where we found him with his father and their clerk, and I heard Mortara ask Cesare Lepori if he had prepared the letter that they had talked about the previous Saturday. But Lepori replied that, after getting some advice, he had decided not to write such a letter, because a private document like that would have no value. However, he added, he was ready to testify legally before any Authority, wherever he was called, and repeat all that he had told Mortara the previous Saturday. I heard him add these words: "I never spoke with Nina of your little boy, much less did I ever suggest baptizing him."

The grocer went on to add, Maggi recounted, that he was hardly in a position to teach the girl how to baptize someone, as he was not sure how to do it himself.

"What I told you Saturday [Lepori continued], I repeat now, and I'll repeat forever, because as a man of honor I can only tell the unvarnished truth. I'm sorry, Mortara, that I wasn't called earlier and interrogated about all this, as it seems only natural to me they should've done if Nina told them I was the one who urged her and taught her what she claimed, because if they'd talked to me, they'd have known long ago what I'm telling you now . . . in the presence of this Signore [here Lepori pointed to Maggi], and I'll testify to the same thing tomorrow. There's just one thing that surprises me, dear Mortara: If it's true that Nina said what they say she did, how come until now not a single official has come to look for me?"

The retired judge ended his account by saying that as he left the grocer behind, he realized that his earlier skepticism was unjustified; Lepori was telling the truth.[5]

Maggi's testimony was rushed to Rome, where, on October 11, Scazzocchio had it certified by a Roman notary before taking it to Cardinal Antonelli for presentation to the Pope. The cover letter, prepared on Momolo's behalf, urged Pius IX to read the brief, for it proved that Morisi had lied about the baptism.[6] But the attack on the young woman's credibility went well beyond this assault. She was portrayed not only as a liar but as a slut and a thief as well.

A few days before the Bologna notary welcomed the former judge to his office for deposition, his study was crowded with women less accustomed to such surroundings. The Mortaras and their allies in Bologna had heard titters and whisperings about Anna Morisi, insistent rumors about her sexual behavior, rumors that if true might discredit her in the eyes of the Church, or so the Jews hoped. As a result, members of the family and their friends began asking neighbors if they had seen or heard anything of Anna's secret sex life. They asked those who might be supposed to know the most, women who were part of the network of servants in the area, women who met each day in the hallways and in the streets on the way to the market, exchanging gossip about their bosses, their neighbors, and one another.

Momolo and Marianna themselves knew something about the subject, for after Anna had worked for them for three years, in early 1855, they discovered that she was pregnant. Such pregnancies of unmarried servants were far from uncommon in Bologna at the time; indeed, they were something of an occupational hazard. The young servants often found themselves alone in the city, their families at a distance in the hinterland, and they became the prey of an assortment of young and not-so-young men, the married and the unmarried, those who seduced them with promises of marriage and those who simply raped them. Among the common sources of pregnancy were the sexual advances of employers themselves or, often, their sons.

In Bologna, as throughout most of Italy, there was a remedy for the desperate situation in which such unmarried pregnant women found themselves: the local foundling home. Established several centuries earlier, and known to all as the "Bastardini," Bologna's foundling home took in the newborn children of unmarried women and thereby rescued the women's honor and saved their families from disgrace. Great secrecy surrounded the depositing of children at the *ospizio*, for only through such secrecy could a woman's honor be guarded. The babies were brought to the Bastardini not by their mothers, who were eager to hide their identities, but by the midwives who had delivered them.

Not only were unmarried women encouraged to abandon their babies at the foundling home in these years; they were required to do so. In the view of the officials of the Papal States, keeping such a child would both expose the woman's family to dishonor, and ensure the young woman herself a future life of sin. Nor were these the only unsavory consequences, for the sight of an unmarried woman with her baby would give rise to public scandal. The very thought of a child growing up in the home of an unmarried mother was indecent. And so once the babies were deposited at the foundling home, efforts were made to place them with wet nurses in the countryside.[7]

Like other young women in her position, Anna Morisi had been loath to return to her family in San Giovanni in Persiceto, where the suspicious eyes of neighbors would certainly look for the telltale belly bulging from her loose-fitting dress. She could not, of course, remain through the time of her delivery with the Mortara family, for the children could not be exposed to such a sight, nor would it be right for the neighbors to see the Mortaras keeping as a servant a woman of lost virtue.

Rather than simply firing her, as many other employers would have done, Momolo and Marianna arranged to have Anna sent to a midwife's home for the last four months of her pregnancy. They paid all the expenses for her lodging and the delivery itself. To protect her reputation—and their own, since they had promised to take her back once the baby was born and delivered to the foundling home—they told neighbors and friends that the girl had become ill and had returned to her parents to recuperate.

By September 1858, the Mortaras were no longer interested in protecting Anna's reputation—quite the contrary. They found they did not have to look far to find women eager to tell tales of the most scandalous behavior.

From September 30 to October 1, the Bologna notary recorded the statements of eight women and one man about Anna Morisi. Their reports were, like Maggi's, sent on to Scazzocchio in Rome, where they too were notarized once more and forwarded, with a cover letter, to Pope Pius IX. It is unlikely that the good Pope had ever before gotten his hands on such lurid descriptions of female sexuality.

The cover letter to the Pope got right to the point: "Momolo Mortara genuflects at the feet of the August Throne of Your Holiness, having just obtained documents . . . relative to Morisi's immoral behavior." He was sending this material, he wrote, so that the Pope could judge for himself "how much faith he should accord to the word of a woman who is so notoriously depraved." He concluded with the plea "Do not hesitate any longer, oh Holy Father, in issuing the judgment we have long yearned for, giving peace to the heartbroken family . . . relieving the fears of 10,000 Jews who are loyal and peaceful subjects of Your Holiness."[8]

The witnesses from Bologna were asked to address two points. One regarded the morality of Anna Morisi, the other the matter of just how sick Edgardo was at the time he was presumably baptized. The Mortaras were interested in the latter point because they had learned that, in the absence of parental consent, Catholics were permitted to baptize a Jewish child only if there was strong reason to believe that he was about to die. In such a case, canon law held, the importance of allowing a soul to go to heaven outweighed the customary commitment to parental (and especially paternal) authority over children. The Mortaras had already gotten an affidavit from their family doctor, Pasquale Saragoni, who had taken care of Edgardo during his illness, stating that the boy had never been in any danger of dying. Dated July 31, 1858, it characterized the illness the boy had when he was a year old as simply a run-of-the-mill childhood infection. The doctor's statement, too, was sent on to the Secretary of State and the Pope. Saragoni also testified that at the time that Anna Morisi said she performed the baptism of the sick child, she herself was very ill and confined to bed. The Mortaras sought to bolster this testimony through the use of other witnesses, aware that the word of Saragoni, a well-known anticleric and longtime opponent of papal rule, was not likely to weigh very heavily on the scales of justice of the Papal States.[9]

The testimony sent in to the Pope ranged widely, from vague secondhand reports to graphic firsthand descriptions. All the depositions were made by Catholics. No doubt these would carry more weight, and indeed testimony from Jews was not legally admissible against Christians in the Papal States.

Maria Capelli, a widow aged 44, was asked to testify about the severity of Edgardo's illness in 1852. That she was called at all reflects the Mortaras' desperation, for her knowledge was entirely secondhand, based on what she had been told by her mother, who had worked as a daytime servant for Marianna Mortara's parents. "I've known the Jewish couple Signor Momolo and Marianna very well for several years," she said.

I know that around six years ago, when the Mortaras lived in via Vetturini, one of their little sons, Edgardo if I'm not mistaken, had one of those childhood illnesses. My mother, who I lived with and who returned every night from the Padovani home to sleep at our place, told me about it. In the same way, I learned that the Mortaras' servant was quite sick at that time and had to stay in bed. In addition to hearing from my mother, who's now dead, that the Mortaras' son's illness wasn't serious, I never heard it said that he became any sicker, much less that he was ever in danger of death. In fact, his little illness ended within just a few days.

Following this testimony, another woman, who had known the Mortaras since Edgardo was a baby, told her story. Sixty-year-old Ippolita Zacchini began by saying that she, too, had known the Mortaras since they lived on via Vetturini. She was at the time working as the servant for the family of Solomon Ravenna, Jewish friends of the Mortaras who lived on the same street. In fact, Solomon, aged 57 in 1852 and practically a generation older than 33-year-old Marianna, had also recently moved to Bologna from Modena's ghetto, with his wife and 17-year-old son.

Because the two families were so friendly and lived so close together, Ippolita testified, she was constantly being sent on errands to the Mortara home. So it was not surprising, she said, when one summer day five or six years ago, the Ravennas told her to go over to the Mortara home and stay there for three or four days to help them out, since the Mortaras' servant, a certain Nina Morisi, was, for three or four days, so sick that she had to stay in bed. She continued:

I remember clearly that at the same time the Mortaras' little child, Edgardo, who was then about one or two years old, was also sick, with some kind of illness that children get, so that I had to help his mother take care of him. . . . But while the child's illness lasted four or five days, and his parents were distressed by it, because they were extremely loving of all their children, and they called some doctors, including, I recall, Dr. Saragoni, the child was never in any danger of dying. In fact, I remember Dr. Saragoni being asked about it by the boy's mother, and he laughed and told her it was nothing, just one of those things that children get.

Ippolita added, "Let me tell you, I've had eight children of my own, and I've seen and taken care of many more, and I remember very well that Edgardo Mortara never had any of those signs that you see in little children that show they're really sick and might die."

Following Ippolita's testimony, her 27-year-old daughter, Marianna, stepped into the notary's office to back up her mother's account. In 1852, when her mother worked as a servant for the Ravennas, Marianna also worked for them, as a maid. She recalled the time when her mother had filled in for Anna Morisi at the Mortaras for a few days, and her mother's comment at the time that one of their children had some mild childhood illness. Lastly, Giuseppina Borghi, a 41-year-old seamstress who had lived in the apartment below the Mortaras in 1852, was brought in. She recounted what was, by now, a familiar story, of a boy with a brief and slight illness, and a servant who was at the time much sicker herself and confined to bed.

Having done what they could to show that there was no time when Anna Morisi could have performed a Church-approved baptism, since Edgardo had never been at death's door, and having further cast doubt on whether Anna was even well enough to have gone out to the grocer at the critical time and done what she said she did, the Mortaras were now ready to speak to the young woman's credibility in the present. They first called on their 30-year-old business agent, Enrico Mattioli, who told of Anna's disturbing familiarity with Austrian soldiers who lived nearby, and of the young woman's tawdry reputation. She was viewed, he said, as "an unwholesome young woman, indeed of immoral and dishonest behavior."

But the lone male witness was but the warm-up for the steamy accounts to follow. First to testify was Elena Pignatti, a 22-year-old woman who, with her husband, Alessandro Santandrea, ran a grocery store not far from the Mortaras. They had hired Anna Morisi as their servant shortly after she left the Mortaras, in the early fall of 1857. Pignatti's testimony was short but disturbing:

"I knew Anna or Nina Morisi very well from the time last autumn when she came to work for me . . . and lived with me around three months. I couldn't keep her any longer because of her reprehensible behavior." Signora Pignatti gave some examples: "One of these occasions involved an evening when, having some suspicions, I crept up the stairs of my house in via San Mamolo . . . which is just above my store. When I got up there, I found the same Nina pushing an Austrian captain out of the house. When I scolded her for her scandalous behavior, she asked me to forgive her, admitting that she had invited him in there."

Signora Pignatti continued: "Around the same time she plotted with a stock boy in my store. The two were in cahoots: he stole the foodstuffs and she hid them. When I discovered what they were doing, I fired her right away. To have kept her on any longer would have only brought me further disgrace; her wicked nature was by then all too clear."

A similar tale was told by Anna Facchini, the young woman who had succeeded Anna Morisi as the Mortaras' servant, the one who had first answered Marshal Lucidi's knock at the door four months earlier.

Anna Facchini had begun work for the Mortaras while Anna Morisi was still living there. At the time, she came in only during the days. When Morisi left, her sister-in-law, Assunta Buongiovanni, came to replace her for two months, and it was by a coincidence linked to Assunta's arrival that Marianna Mortara came to know that Nina was a thief.

Facchini herself had observed Morisi in action on previous occasions. "More than once," she testified, "she asked me to help her steal wine from the Mortaras' cellar." But one day shortly after Nina had left, while Assunta was doing the wash, she was surprised to find a pair of socks just like one of hers. She mentioned this to Signora Mortara, and then went to get her pair to show her. These turned out to be socks that had been stolen from the Mortaras. When Assunta was asked where she had gotten them, she replied that before coming to the Mortaras she had lived briefly with Nina Morisi; in packing to leave for her new job, Assunta had mistaken a pair of her sister-in-law's socks for her own and had brought them with her. Signora Mortara told her servants that she was missing not only the pair of socks but assorted pieces of underwear as well. It then dawned on her that they had all been stolen by Nina.

Facchini went on to tell of something else that Nina was well known for: her couplings with Austrian officers. Here Morisi had profited from the fact that some Austrian officers boarded in the apartment adjacent to the Mortaras. Her penchant for sneaking soldiers into her home, the suspicion of which had led her subsequent employer to tiptoe up the stairs from her store to catch her red-handed, was well established when she worked for the Mortaras. Facchini told of seeing Nina lead Austrian officers into the Mortara home on several occasions, both when the Mortaras were in another part of the apartment and when they were out. "I warned her various times to show more modesty, to use better judgment and act less brazenly so as not to disgrace herself and not to disgust the Mortaras."

But the most graphic accounts of Nina's sexual escapades were offered by two middle-aged women.

Rosalba Pancaldi, a 44-year-old woman who ran a café next to the local parish church, was known by her friends as Rosina. She testified that she had known Nina Morisi for several years, for she had, until a few months earlier, lived in the apartment above the Mortaras with her husband and three children. She explained that next door to the Mortaras lived the Foschini family, whose boarders, Austrian officers, had the room immediately adjacent to the Mortaras. She had often seen Anna acting flirtatiously with the Austrian soldiers and had, indeed, heard it said that she did much more.

"One morning," the woman recalled, "the officer called Paja or Paolino brought Morisi into his room, from which, a little later, she came out shouting in that way she had, 'Oh! what a fuck I had, Signora Rosina, oh, what a fuck I had!' putting her hands over her face."

Rosina continued: "I remember, though it's a bit vague to me now, that one of the servants that I had back then, called Elena, told me she had seen these two in that same room, but I can't recall if she saw them through the keyhole or some other way." In any case, she went on, "after this encounter with Morisi, time and time again when she would see me she would repeat the words 'Oh! what a fuck I had!' while she laughed and winked."

Nor was this all. Pancaldi recounted that another of her servants, Maria, had told her of looking down from the terrace one night and seeing Nina "let some German officers into the Mortara apartment . . . by stepping across from their terrace to her window. I can't recall if they used a plank to walk across or just jumped." Signora Pancaldi concluded her testimony by aiming one final blow at what little remained of Anna Morisi's good name: "I know that this Morisi generally had a poor reputation due to her behavior with the German officers, and she even let them stroke her breasts while they stood at the window of the terrace I mentioned."

Lest this testimony be taken as the product of one woman's licentious imagination, the Mortaras arranged to have a final witness corroborate it. Geltrude Foschini, the 50-year-old woman who lived next door to the Mortaras with her husband and their Austrian boarders, told much the same story as her former neighbor, including Nina's use of the terrace to admit the soldiers into the Mortaras' apartment at night, and her furtive visits to the soldiers' rooms.

In fact, Foschini added a detail that Pancaldi had neglected to mention—namely, just who it was who was in the habit of spying on Nina's amorous adventures through the keyhole. One day, she recounted, Pancaldi had excitedly told her of having seen Nina, in broad daylight, go into the room of the Austrian officers, where Paja awaited her. "Moved by curiosity," Foschini continued, Signora Pancaldi "put her eye to the keyhole and saw the two in bed engaged in an obscene act. Just at that moment, she saw Signor Mortara coming up the stairs, so Pancaldi said in a loud voice, 'Nina, here comes Mortara.' And seconds later Morisi came out and said to Pancaldi, 'What a fuck I had!'—an expression that she would repeat from then on whenever she saw Pancaldi. In fact, I myself heard her repeat these words on many occasions, and I once asked Signora Pancaldi to explain it to me."

What the Pope made of all this when the notarized testimony arrived at the Vatican in early October, is hard to tell.

CHAPTER 11

Drama at Alatri

W
HILE MOMOLO was rounding up witnesses in Bologna, he and Marianna debated whether to stay in Bologna or go to Rome to see Edgardo and work there for his release. Arguing for staying in Bologna was the real danger that the family business would go bankrupt in Momolo's absence, leaving them with seven children to feed and no means to support them short of Jewish charity. Nor were the children, who had been shaken by their brother's capture, eager to see their parents leave, even though there was no lack of relatives to look after them. And a final doubt was raised by Marianna's health.

Just what her state of health was in the aftermath of Edgardo's departure is not easy to know. The problem is not any lack of sources, for month after month, newspapers published medical updates. Nor are these reports contradictory. For the most part, they all say the same thing. Yet they so closely resemble the tales told over the centuries by Jews about similar tragedies that we have some reason to wonder about them. We have seen this Jewish mother before.

News of Marianna's parlous health was broadcast throughout Europe within days of Edgardo's capture. Recall that James Rothschild, in his letter from Paris to Cardinal Antonelli, written July 17, spoke of the fact that, as a result of the kidnapping, Marianna had become sick, in fact, "*presque folle*"— she had practically gone crazy. Lionel Rothschild's letter to Cardinal Antonelli from London the following month contained a similar description.

As stories denouncing what the Church had done began to appear in the Jewish and liberal press throughout Europe, Marianna's failing health was a common theme. All could sympathize with a poor mother who had been driven out of her mind by despair at having her son torn from her. Indeed, reports suggested that her very life was in jeopardy. One of the first of these, published in *L'univers Israélite* in Paris, citing friends of the Mortara family in Bologna, described Marianna as "overwhelmed by sorrow." She had abandoned her numerous other young children and her home and fled to Modena. There she was being cared for by her relatives but had fallen "gravely ill from grief, and now there are strong fears for her life."[1]

The theme was a powerful one and apt to appear whenever the Jews appealed for support. When, after receiving the August letter from the Jews who had met in Piedmont, the Central Consistory of French Jews sent their plea to Napoleon III for his intercession, they wrote that Edgardo's mother had been "driven mad by the excess of pain." Their petition added that Momolo's untiring efforts to bring his wife back to her senses had been to no avail.[2] Around the same time, the letter sent by forty Prussian rabbis to the Vatican—written in French—likewise referred to the "poor mother" as having "almost gone insane."[3]

The tale of the distraught mother was pulling at the heartstrings of Europe and being wielded as a potent weapon in pressuring the Holy See to release the child. Only by letting Edgardo go could the Vatican remove the sorry sight of a mother—wanting only to hold her beloved child in her arms again—driven to madness while the Church kept him locked up under clerical guard.

The story was used to influence Edgardo as well. Given the fear that the boy's sympathies for his family were fast eroding in the face of the enticements of the Church, Momolo was urged to impress on him just how miserable his mother had become because he had been taken away from her. Indeed, Edgardo was told, if he did not return soon, she might die from the pain.

While Momolo was in Rome in August, Marianna sent a letter to her son via the Università Israelitica. After examining it, Scazzocchio and his colleagues persuaded Momolo not to deliver the letter to Edgardo. The problem, it seems, was that Marianna was too reassuring and sounded too much like herself. Scazzocchio explained their decision in a letter he drafted on August 25, addressed to the Mortara support group in Bologna: "Signora Marianna's letter will not be delivered because it does not correspond to what [Momolo] Mortara has already told the boy . . . We want him to think of her as a mother who is grievously suffering from moral and physical ills produced by the long and painful absence of her son." Edgardo must be convinced that his return home was "the only cure for her maternal bereavement."[4]

So alarming were the reports of the impact that the seizure of Edgardo had had on his mother that the Jewish press found itself having to reassure its readers that she was, in fact, still of sound mind and body. Two items in the

Archives Israélites of Paris in January 1859 are revealing. The first reported some good news. A letter had just arrived informing them "that the child's sainted mother has not become insane following the blow that she suffered. Her pain is great and mute; it is touching, it is immense, but she will bear up." Far from being beaten down, readers were told, the mother would, together with her husband, fight on for their child. "Edgardo Mortara's father and mother have assured one of our special correspondents that, whatever happens, they will not stop for even a minute of their lives to pursue the dearest object of their desires, the conquest of their son . . . nothing will stop them."[5]

Later in the same issue, the *Archives Israélites* printed a letter it had received from a friend of the Mortaras in Rome. He recalled that the family had been well respected in Bologna, known for their integrity and enjoying a flourishing business. Edgardo's abduction, however, had sadly altered their position. What was most alarming, the correspondent reported, was the emotional state to which the parents had been reduced, and it was the mother whose situation was most worrisome: "The father shows a great deal of courage, but the mother is having a hard time carrying on. Although she no longer cries when I see her, you can see the recent tracks of tears on her cheeks, and the self-control that she strains to keep up simply shows her pain and her affliction all the more. If the Holy Father had seen this woman as I saw her, he would not have the courage to keep her son another moment." Yet, the correspondent hastened to add, "the widespread rumor that she has gone mad is not true. She still has all of her wits."[6]

Just how eager Marianna was to make the trip to Rome is not clear. It would take her the farthest she had ever been from home and to a city that stood for everything she feared. It was for the men to deal with the powers of Church and state, not for women such as she. And although her physical health was not as fragile as so many of the family's supporters and the Church's detractors claimed, she was without doubt emotionally battered by her ordeal. The idea of leaving the solicitude of her relatives and friends, not to mention her children, was frightening. Yet the desire to see Edgardo again, fifteen weeks after kissing him good-bye in Bologna, was powerful as well.

If there was any doubt as to whether Marianna should make the trip, it was dispelled by the advice they received from Rome's Università Israelitica. Scazzocchio and his colleagues thought the time ripe for her appearance on the scene. Not only would the sight of the bereft mother put additional pressure on the Church to relent, but by embracing Edgardo she could, they hoped, help dispel their biggest nightmare: the signs Edgardo was showing of wanting to remain in the Catechumens and to become a Christian.

On October 10, Momolo informed Rome of their imminent departure: "I hasten . . . to advise you that, God willing, tomorrow evening, Monday, I will leave by stagecoach, together with the person whose coming was called for by those honorable men before my departure [from Rome]." They expected to arrive in Rome by Wednesday evening, the season being favorable for travel, and they asked that arrangements be made to have a room ready for them.7

When Enrico Sarra, rector of the House of the Catechumens, learned that Edgardo's mother was on her way to Rome to see her child, he panicked. The boy had held up well, he thought, against his father's entreaties, but the embrace of his weeping mother might be more than even Edgardo could resist.

Facing the unsettling prospect of Marianna Mortara's visit, the Rector turned to his family for help. When, the day after their arrival in Rome, having barely dusted themselves off from their long trip, Momolo and Marianna appeared at the Catechumens door, they were told that their child was no longer there. When Momolo then demanded to speak with the Rector, he was informed that he, too, had left.

Momolo soon discovered what had happened. Sarra had taken the boy into hiding in his hometown, Alatri, a small city of twenty thousand, fifty miles away in the hinterland of Lazio. The Mortaras hired a coach, and before setting out in pursuit, they got the name of a Jewish man in Alatri who would help them on their arrival.

Once in Alatri, thanks to their local contact, Momolo learned where the Sarra family lived and hurried there with his wife. Neither the Rector nor Edgardo was to be found there, but Momolo discovered that Sarra had been seen with a small boy earlier in the day going to a church nearby. Leaving Marianna at the Rector's home, he hastened to the church. He would not enter it, a disinclination made all the stronger by the fact that he could see that a mass was in progress. But, standing at the front door, he saw little Edgardo at the other end, assisting the priest who was saying the mass. Momolo decided to wait for the ceremonies to end for his encounter with his son and the Rector. He later told what happened:

"When I saw people begin to leave, I went over to the door near the Sacristy so that I could speak with the Rector and beg him to send Edgardo home so that my wife and I could see him. But hardly had I arrived at the door when a priest, whom I recognized as the Rector's brother, slammed the door in my face, so I returned to the street to wait for them to come out." Momolo kept up his anxious vigil for another half hour, when at last the Rector and his brother appeared at the church door, with Edgardo walking between them, each priest holding a hand. "Instead of turning toward where I was standing, that is, in the direction of their house, they turned the opposite way, picking up their pace. As I headed toward them, I saw the boy turn around so that he could see me, when all of a sudden I was stopped by another man, who said he was another brother of the Rector. He told me, on behalf of the Rector himself, to return to his home, where the Rector would meet me in a little while with my son."

Rather than follow Edgardo, who was being hustled off in the distance by the two priests, Momolo turned back and returned to the Rector's home, where he told Marianna what had happened and nervously awaited Edgardo's arrival. They waited and waited, but no one came. When they could stand it no more, they went outside to see what they could find out. As they began to walk down the street, Momolo realized that two policemen were following them. On their arrival at their hotel, where they had left their carriage, the policemen followed them in.

The marshal in charge asked to see the Mortaras' passports—Jews had to have special passports to travel within the Papal States—and, after confirming their identity, ordered the couple to follow him to see the Mayor. Momolo recalled the scene, which grew increasingly threatening, for word had been spread among the people of Alatri that the Jewish parents had come to murder their now Catholic son:

> We obeyed, and in crossing the piazza, we saw that a large number of people had gathered, looking at us angrily. We presented ourselves to the mayor, and he asked us what we were doing. We replied that we only wanted to embrace our son, but at that, he responded that it was impossible, because I had only been given permission to see him one time in Rome. I told him that the permission I had gotten was unlimited and, as proof, told him I had already seen my son many times, but I got nowhere with him. He gave me just one hour to leave town, and handed me back my passport with a visa for Rome.[8]

The Mayor had acted not on his own initiative but at the request of the Bishop of Alatri. On October 16, the day of the Mortaras' ill-fated trip to his diocese, the Bishop sent a report to the Secretary of State, Cardinal Antonelli:

> This morning at eight o'clock, the Jews Salomone Mortara and his wife Maria Anna, of Bologna, parents of the little Edgardo, now a Christian—about whom Your Most Reverend Eminence is already fully informed—arrived in this city. With the help of another Jew, whose name I do not know, they tried to get to speak with their son. Don Enrico Sarra, Rector of the House of the Neophytes, who has the boy in his custody, was surprised by the unexpected appearance of the above-mentioned couple in this city. Having learned, while he was in church with the boy, that the Jews had already entered his home, he thought it expedient to take refuge with Edgardo in this Episcope, and has implored us to take emergency measures.

The Bishop was alarmed by these developments, conscious as he was of the delicacy of the matter. His decision, he told the Secretary of State, was influenced by a stirring sight, the pleadings of a distressed child: "While considering this request I became aware that the boy had become extremely agitated, for he had learned that his mother was here, and he repeatedly begged me not to expose him, as he put it, 'to the torment.' "

Given this heart-rending plea, and his awareness of the importance of the case and the controversy swirling around it, the Bishop made his decision. He seized on the fact that the Mortaras had come to Alatri without any written authorization to speak with their son, and had them expelled from the city.[9]

Even before the Bishop's letter arrived, Antonelli knew about the Mortaras' abortive trip to the town, for no sooner had Momolo returned to Rome than he rushed to see the Cardinal. Conscious of how closely the ambassadors to the Holy See were following the Mortara saga, the Secretary of State wanted at all costs to appear judicious and decorous in handling the matter. Having the Catechumens rector fleeing from Rome with the child in tow, with bishops then finding hiding places for the pair, was hardly the image he was seeking.

On October 18, just after receiving the Bishop's letter, and having already seen Momolo, Cardinal Antonelli wrote back with faint praise: "While I thank you for your kindly involvement in the case, I must add that in my opinion it would be more opportune for the Rector, Don Enrico Sarra, to return to Rome with little Edgardo."[10] On receiving the letter, the Bishop found himself in an awkward position, because the Rector and his little ward had already moved out. He informed Cardinal Antonelli in his reply that the pair had started back to Rome but that Don Sarra had had second thoughts, fearing that someone might be lying in wait for them along the road, and so the Rector had decided to take the child to the archdiocesan office in Frosinone, to consult with Cardinal Cagiano. The Alatri bishop concluded by assuring Antonelli that he would get word to the Rector to bring Edgardo right back to Rome.[11]

Unbeknownst to the Bishop, Cardinal Cagiano had himself lost no time in seeking advice from the Secretary of State, writing to him on the very day Edgardo arrived on his doorstep. Don Sarra had told Cardinal Cagiano of his concern that a plan was afoot to steal Edgardo from them. "In telling me what had happened in Alatri, he expressed his fear of running into some surprise in taking the boy back to Rome, and he was extremely agitated." Agreeing that this fear was well founded, Cardinal Cagiano came up with a plan of his own: "The thought came to me of taking the child with me next week when I return to Frascati to participate in the reopening of the seminary, and placing him in that Holy Place, should Your Eminence find no problem with this solution, and should it please the providence of the Holy Father."[12]

Cardinal Cagiano's letter alarmed Antonelli. The continued flight of the Rector and the boy and the secreting of Edgardo in an obscure seminary would send all the wrong signals, signs of weakness and insecurity, and undignified to boot. The Secretary of State could see all too clearly what fun the anticlerical press—not to mention the newspaper artists who specialized in satirical drawings—would have with the story.

He replied immediately. Informing the Cardinal that the Bishop of Alatri had already sent him a report on the matter, Antonelli wrote that he wanted to remove "any further fear or apprehension from the soul of the one in whose care the young neophyte had been given." He had already sent an order to the Bishop of Alatri to have the boy returned immediately to Rome, "where his spiritual welfare can better be provided for and where any possible inconvenience can be avoided. It is difficult here," Antonelli added petulantly, "to understand the reasons that could have led to concern about some sort of surprise during the voyage." As for Cardinal Cagiano's plan, Antonelli wrote his fellow cardinal, "Your Eminence will therefore see how, given the present state of things, the idea of placing the neophyte in the seminary of Frascati may be less opportune, notwithstanding the charitable zeal by which your proposal is clearly driven."[13]

The Secretary of State had spoken, and Don Sarra and Edgardo were soon on their way back to Rome. Although the Rector looked nervously out his carriage window, no one disturbed them on their way home.

On October 20, while the Rector and Edgardo were still in hiding in Frosinone, Scazzocchio and his colleagues from the Università Israelitica sent a letter to all the Jewish communities in the Papal States, telling of Momolo and Marianna's arrival in Rome and their recent experiences in Alatri. Cardinal Antonelli is portrayed in glowing terms. Once he had been told by Momolo of the misadventures in Alatri, "the Most Eminent Secretary of State, clearly upset, promised that he would that very day send the requisite orders to have the boy returned to Rome." The Jewish officials also took the opportunity to reassure their brethren that Edgardo's mother was a real fighter, and had not been incapacitated by the loss of her son: "Signora Mortara has the timidity that women have, reinforced by the heartache that you can see in her face, but where the matter of her lost son is concerned, she becomes energetic and most courageous, and so pleads her case quite well." The news bulletin reported that the Pope had not yet pronounced his final decision in the case. Edgardo's parents still had hope.[14]

CHAPTER 12

Meeting Mother

FOUR MONTHS after tearfully bidding Edgardo good-bye at their home in Bologna, Marianna finally got to hold her child in her arms again. On Friday, October 22, she and Momolo were ushered into a room in Rome's Catechumens where their son nervously awaited them. Later the same day, Marianna wrote an account of the meeting in a letter to a friend in Bologna. The letter was distributed to sympathetic correspondents and published far and wide, although not in the Papal States, where such inflammatory material was banned.

"This morning," Marianna recalled,

> my husband and I made our way to the Catechumens, where we found that the Rector was just then arriving, returning with my dear son from Alatri. We went in and soon we had our beloved Edgardo in our arms. Sobbing and weeping, I kissed him and kept kissing him, and with great affection he returned our kisses and our hugs. He blushed deep red with emotion and cried, struggling between the fear he had for the man who controls him and his unchanged affection for his parents. The latter won out, and he repeatedly said, in a loud voice, that he wanted to go home with his parents and his brothers and his sisters. I told him that he was born a Jew like us and like us he must always remain one, and he replied: "*Si, mia cara mamma,* I will never forget to say the Shema[1] every day." When I told him that we had come to Rome to get him back, and that we'd not leave without him, the greatest joy and happiness came over him! The Rector and his brother and his sister were present for all of this, but they didn't know what to say.[2]

For the next forty days, through the end of November, Marianna and Momolo remained in Rome, regularly journeying from their lodgings to the Catechumens to visit Edgardo. Just what happened during these visits is a matter of controversy, for, once again, we find two very different stories.

In the Mortaras' account, the boy lived in constant fear of his clerical keepers, desperately longing to return home with his parents, yet intimidated by the priests who kept him under their remorseless control. The battle between his identity as a Jew and his identity as a Christian was, in this account, a contest pitting his loyalty to his parents against his loyalty to the priests who cared for him.

A little over a year later, at the trial of Bologna's Inquisitor, Marianna Mortara testified about these encounters. After describing her first visit, when, on seeing his mother, Edgardo threw himself in her arms and they both sobbed uncontrollably, she told how, over the next forty days, she saw her son often, always in the same room. "Although he was under the domination and the influence of the Rector, who was always present for our meetings, and who could intimidate him with just a look, Edgardo always showed his affection for me and his desire to return to his family and to his religion, and always recited his Jewish prayers with me, which he assured me he said every day when no one was watching." According to his mother, the boy was not looking well: "He had lost weight and had turned pale; his eyes were filled with terror."[3]

In mid-November, with hopes that the Pope would heed their pleas rapidly receding, the Università Israelitica of Rome prepared a French account of these meetings. The audience was the French Jewish community, who were eager for news of the boy.

> In Monsieur and Madame Mortara's most recent visits to see their son, who is under guard in the House of the Catechumens, the people there have begun to tell them, in an increasingly explicit way, that their efforts to get him back are hopeless. Since their return from Alatri, when the unhappy mother first saw her son again, and when, following her heart's impulse, she reminded her son of the religion in which he was born and raised, and his duty to remain forever faithful to it, the individuals in whose care he has been placed have complained about the negative effect that this call to return to the creed of his parents was having on the pressure they were exerting on his spirit. Consequently, they sought to reduce these inopportune visits insofar as possible.

The Catechumens officials, in this account, urged the Mortaras not to make any disparaging remarks to Edgardo about the Christian education that he was getting, but Momolo replied that he was only exercising his sacred rights as a father. He felt further justified by the fact that the child had confided in his mother that "the fear of displeasing the Rector, a fear reinforced by the man's reprimand following the parents' first visit, prevented him from declaring his desire to return to his paternal home." Momolo added that the Pope had placed no restrictions in giving them permission to see their son. When the Catechumens authorities responded by arranging for Edgardo to go out just at the hour when his parents were supposed to arrive, Momolo prepared a new complaint to the Rector, and the practice was stopped.

On one of the Mortaras' visits, as they were sitting with their son, the Rector's brother remarked that Edgardo was a very lucky boy, for the Holy Father himself had taken a great interest in him. He added that many people envied the Mortaras' good fortune, and went on to suggest that the Pontiff's solicitude for Edgardo might well extend to the parents themselves. "Because the kindly heart of Pius IX was saddened by the reversal of fortune suffered by the Mortara family," the Rector's brother told them, "he would like to do something to provide relief for the natural parents of his favorite son." Referring obliquely to the recent failure of Momolo's business, the priest went on to suggest that Momolo go to see the Pope, assuring him that he would find it to his advantage. This overture, according to the Università Israelitica account, wounded the Mortaras deeply. They firmly "rejected the idea of selling their approval of the Christian education of their child in exchange for financial help." No amount of money could begin to pay them back for the loss of their beloved son.

It is unclear whether the Pope was in fact inclined to provide any such financial reward to get the Mortaras to end their campaign. But one point that both sides agree on—although the two narratives treat it very differently—is that the Rector and his clerical colleagues did do all they could to convince Momolo and Marianna that a happy solution to their troubles was within their reach: They could follow their son into the House of the Catechumens and convert themselves.

The Università Israelitica document provides a glimpse of the Mortaras' state of mind during these visits, and of how, despite all the negative signs, they remained hopeful that their son would soon be released:

> Up until this moment, the direct relations with the Rector and his brother had stayed within the bounds of a certain politeness. The souls of Monsieur and Madame Mortara were torn between hope and fear. They awaited the decree that would produce either their consolation or their eternal sorrow. They could not resign themselves to the idea that, having traveled so far, having presented so many arguments in their favor,

having produced so many documents and cited so many authorities, they would not succeed in the end.

These hopes were very much on their minds as they held Edgardo in their arms on the morning of November 9. Across the room stood the Rector and his brother, with a few nuns at their side. The priests, talking loudly enough to be heard across the room, spoke of the airtight arguments being prepared by the Church authorities as the basis for what would be the Pope's final refusal of the request to let Edgardo return home. A dramatic encounter followed, as described in the Università Israelitica account:

> The poor parents begged the two speakers not to poison their conversation with such words, but rather than go along with this reasonable request, the two clerics exclaimed that it would be contrary to their duty, which was to exhort the parents to follow their child in his new faith. It was only by embracing Christianity that they would be permitted to see their son; if they converted, they would be treated with the greatest respect. They added that far from returning to the religion into which he was born, the new son of the Church was destined by God to become the apostle of Christianity to his family, dedicated to converting his parents and his siblings.

The three Jews clutched one another as—in an account eerily echoing the one that Anna Del Monte told about the same place a century before—both the priests and the nuns got down on their knees before an image of Jesus and began reciting heartfelt prayers for the conversion of the entire Mortara family. "The boy did not follow his teachers' example, although they would have liked to make him kneel down with them. He stayed by his parents' side. But Momolo and Marianna could not stand it any longer, and despite the enormous wound that they suffered, they were careful not to say a single word as they made their way out of the room."

As his parents were leaving, Edgardo threw himself in his mother's arms. The effect of the scene—the priests and nuns on their knees, begging Jesus to show them the light—was

> to redouble the tears, the kisses, and the sighs, while the poor mother pressed the boy to her breast until finally the Rector came to tear the boy away, saying, "That's enough."
>
> One can well imagine the state that Monsieur and Madame Mortara were in as they returned to their room, and how they were stunned and completely done in by the scene they had witnessed. The mother's pain exploded into atrocious convulsions, which lasted all day, and from that fatal moment she has not been able to get out of bed.[4]

As the moving accounts of the poor mother's torment circulated through Italy and beyond, a very different story began to appear in papers sympathetic to the Church. It tells of a child terrified of his mother, a woman who will not leave him in peace while all he seeks is the comfort of his new family, the Church. In the first of these stories in the stridently pro-Vatican newspaper *L'univers*, its French readers learned of Edgardo's horrified reaction when his mother told him to remain faithful to the religion of his ancestors. Edgardo told the Rector that if she returned, he would go and hide, for he could not bear to hear such awful words again.⁵

The most influential Catholic report of the mother's first meetings with her son appeared in the Jesuit *Civiltà Cattolica*. The long story in the November issue sketched out the main lines of counterattack to be used in the battle against all those forces—Jewish, liberal, anticlerical—that were, in the Catholic view, maligning the Pope and the Church over the Mortara case. The defense had two components. One, involving Church law and precedent, we will look at later. The other focused on Edgardo's actual behavior and on his attitude toward his parents and toward the Church. In the *Civiltà Cattolica* account, Edgardo had clearly made his choice.

Critics had accused the Church of flagrantly violating one of its own cardinal principles, indeed one of the Ten Commandments: a child should be taught to honor his father and his mother. *Civiltà Cattolica* responded that Edgardo's tutors had done nothing to compromise the boy's respect and love for his parents. The transformation that had come over him on entering the Catechumens, thanks to the miracle of the baptismal sacrament, was instantaneous, but the journal reported, "that did not detract one whit from his affection [for his parents], nor from his filial devotion." In fact, when, in his first few weeks at the Catechumens, he was taught the rudiments of reading and writing, the first little letter he asked to write was to his mother (this was before her first visit), and he signed it "your most affectionate little son."

This, of course, did not mean that he wanted to go home to be with his mother, for then he would have to live among Jews, which he did not want to do; indeed, he had reason to fear. "He begged to be brought up in a Christian home," the *Civiltà Cattolica* recounted, "to escape the seductions and perhaps too those acts of violence that, beneath the paternal roof, would more than likely have met him."

The choice of a new religion meant a choice of a new family, or perhaps it was the other way around. Escaping the threat of violence at the hands of his parents—Jews who would stop at nothing to keep their child from enjoying the spiritual liberation he had attained through baptism—Edgardo turned to his new father and his new family: " 'I have been baptized,' he said, with a wisdom and a precision far from childlike; 'I have been baptized, and my father is the Pope.' "

The Jesuit journal went on to report that the boy's sentiments were warmly reciprocated by the Pontiff, who indeed had come to view Edgardo as his new son: "Nor did His Holiness delay in responding with paternal solicitude to this new son that Providence, in such an unforeseeable way, had added to the great Catholic family." The Pope lost no time in calling the fortunate little boy to him; he embraced him warmly and, "with his august hand, made the holy sign of the cross on his forehead, and presented the boy to the distinguished priest taking care of him at the House of the Catechumens as someone who was most precious to him."

For the Jesuit journal, as for the Catholic press throughout Europe, the proof that the Church had acted properly lay in Edgardo's attitude toward his parents. More than that, his behavior demonstrated the truth of the Catholic religion. The child's firm desire to "persevere at any cost," his "calm wish to remain far from his own," could be explained only as the special workings of holy grace, divine testimony to the fact that he had indeed been baptized. The Church officials had paraded the little boy before a wide assortment of "important persons, clerical and lay, dignitaries, and diplomats," who had interrogated him. Moreover, the Church had let his parents visit him frequently. "In all these circumstances," the journal reported, "he never has wavered for a moment."

As for the behavior of Edgardo's parents, *Civiltà Cattolica* painted a very different picture from that found in the Jewish and the liberal press. Momolo and Marianna's anguish was the result not of losing a son but of their hostility toward the Church. Edgardo's fears about his parents, the journal reported, were well founded. "They act with such desperation not so much because one of their eight children has been temporarily taken away, for they still have seven left at home, but rather because it is the Catholic Church that has acquired him."

The Jesuit author told of speaking with Edgardo a few days after his first meeting with his mother at the Catechumens. The little boy told him a dramatic story of the encounter. As his mother embraced him, he reported, she noticed the medallion of the Blessed Virgin that was hanging from his neck. Enraged at the sight, she ripped it off. Edgardo was aghast but, out of respect for his mother, said nothing. Yet, he told his Jesuit visitor, "I kept repeating to myself: 'I am a Christian by the grace of God, and a Christian I want to die.'"

All this, the Jesuit journal reported, put the question of whether a child should obey his parents in an entirely different light. The real issue was this: "Should a Christian son be returned to a Jewish father?" And it asked, "Is it right to allow the father to freely abuse his paternal authority to make him become an apostate?" The author concluded: "Having posed the question in this way, it requires only common sense and a little faith in the supernatural to respond that one cannot, and one ought not. It would be inhuman cruelty to do so, especially when the son has the insight to see the danger himself, and himself begs for protection against it." If nature gives the father full responsibility for the care of his son, it is not so that the father can do as he pleases, but so that the son's interests can be protected. How can anyone think that such authority should be left to the father when "it is almost certain that it will be employed not for the son's good but rather for his supreme ruination? . . . Does not civil law provide that one should take a child away from a cruel and murderous father in order to protect his life? And why, then, should it be unjust to do for someone's eternal life that which seems so just when it concerns his temporal existence?"

The rest of the pro-Church press hammered away on the same theme. The image of the furious Jewish mother ripping the sacred medallion from her son's chest struck a deep chord. And the notion that what bothered the Jewish parents was not the loss of their son's company but the fact that he was being turned into a Christian redirected the attention of the readers from their feelings of commiseration as parents to their ancient anger at the perfidy of the Jews. In Bologna in December 1858, the weekly *Il vero amico* left nothing to its readers' imaginations. Further embellishing the story, the paper reported that Marianna, on seeing her son, was "filled with anger and ripped the medallion from his chest, saying scornfully, 'I'd rather see you dead than a Christian!' "[6]

Civiltà Cattolica brought all these themes together in concluding its counterattack, portraying a boy besieged by his cruel Jewish parents, a boy graced by God, begging the Church for its spiritual and physical protection.

"Now does it seem right and generous to abandon this poor, weak, solitary creature and cast him off into the middle of a Judaic family that, without making any bones about it, shows that it is disposed to employ any means of enticement, of persuasion, and perhaps even of violence to drive him to an easy victory for apostasy?" In a final appeal, the author asks, "Would it seem right and generous to place this innocent boy on this cross, subject him to these torments, to the torture that it would be to find himself day in and day out exposed to his mother's tenderness and his father's severity?" The author reported that when he talked to little Edgardo, the boy had bravely assured him that were he to face such torture, he would not give in but would "recite the Christian prayers from morning to night and persuade his little brothers and sisters to imitate him."[7]

These accounts of the divinely inspired Edgardo battling heroically against his infidel parents resonated profoundly among the faithful. The little boy became a martyr, ready to die for his newfound religion while standing up to (although unfailingly showing the proper respect for) his parents, who were prepared to murder him should their campaign of psychological terror fail.

Having spent practically six weeks in Rome, the Mortaras were now resigned to going home without their son. Marianna's promise to Edgardo would have to be broken. Around them swirled an international controversy as irate citizens gathered in protest meetings on both sides of the Atlantic and a chorus of voices, from Jewish ragpickers in Rome to international bankers, from Protestant ministers in England to the French emperor himself, urged that Edgardo be returned to his parents. Yet so far the Pope was standing firm.

The Mortaras' trip to Rome in October had been an easy one, and during their voyage they had been filled with an anxious hope. Their return to Bologna was another matter, and their coach mates might have been pardoned if they thought that they were traveling with Job himself.

When he reached Florence, two-thirds of the way to Bologna, in early December, Momolo wrote to Scazzocchio to tell of their misadventures: "Our voyage up to Siena was anything but good. Four miles out of Rome, Marianna suffered from a powerful fainting spell, which lasted until a stranger gave up his good seat so that she could lie down all the way to Viterbo, where we arrived at three." In Viterbo, they went to the home of a woman they knew, who kindly prepared Marianna's favorite dish, a chicken soup. But as the coach continued on its way, torrential rains fell, and the driver informed his passengers that the swollen streams made the road impassable. Although the already anxious Mortaras said nothing, other passengers argued with the driver, urging him to go on. Reluctantly, he continued through the downpour until the coach reached a stream that had turned into a rushing river, through which there was no hope of passing. Yet they could not turn back, for the streams behind them had come up as well.

They traveled two miles down the stream in search of roadmen who could help them, and eventually they located four workers. Offering to pay the men out of their own pockets, the passengers got them to return to the crossing and work on a washed-out bridge. "It was a horrendous night," Momolo wrote.

I leave to your imagination the hours of pain we passed there. Finally, at 4 a.m., one of the roadmen came to tell us that they had done what they could in the way of repairs, and that we could make an attempt to get through those dangerous, badly swollen streams, but that it would be best to take everything we could out of the coach to lighten the load. And so all of the men—there were six of us—got out, and the five women stayed in the coach. The coach then set off, passing through the streams with great difficulty, particularly the third, while we walked behind, fording through the water, not without a certain degree of danger. . . . God saved us, but I assure you that though it may seem romantic, it was a scene of great horror.[8]

The trip continued, but mishap piled on mishap. The horses became mired in the mud, and there was no new team to replace them, as there was supposed to be, along the way. Meanwhile, in Rome, things were looking no better.

CHAPTER 13

The International Protests
Spread

I N HIS November 21, 1858, entry, the diarist Giuseppe Massari,
who chronicled Italian events of the mid-nineteenth century, told
of running into his friend Boggio, from Piedmont. Boggio was
extremely upset. The previous Sunday he had been scheduled to serve as godfather for the baptism of a friend's child in the Piedmontese city of Ivrea. Just
before the ceremony, however, the Bishop of Ivrea informed him that he
would not be allowed to do so because he was a well-known liberal and opponent of the Papal States. Humiliated, Boggio told Massari he wanted to take
the Bishop to court for the affront. The diarist concluded the entry by noting,
drolly, "Boggio is jealous of the Mortara boy's fame."[1]

The case of the jilted godfather is revealing both for what it shows about
the relations between the Church and the liberals in Italy at the time and as a
reflection of just how deeply the Mortara case had entered public consciousness. The battle for Italian unification, the dream of Italian patriots for decades, was finally coming to a head. For the Church, stung badly by the revolts
of 1848, the liberal ideas of the Risorgimento were anathema, and their champions were condemned. For the liberals, on the other hand, the Church itself
was one of the principal obstacles to national unification and the construction
of a modern, constitutional state. The pope-king was a medieval vestige, a
national embarrassment. In Piedmont, where the state allowed them,
antipapal pamphlets abounded. For the opponents of papal rule, the taking of
the Mortara boy was manna from heaven, a publicist's dream.

No one was in a better position to make political capital out of the Mortara affair than Count Camillo Cavour, prime minister of the government of the kingdom of Sardinia and mastermind of the plan to unify Italy by the annexing of lands to the realm of King Victor Emmanuel II. Cavour saw in the Mortara case the perfect vehicle for demonstrating the anachronistic nature of the Papal States. The case could be used to undermine support for the Pope's temporal power among Catholics—at least among those who had been affected by the winds of modernity and the talk of equality and human rights—and to inflame the simmering antipapal sentiments of Protestants throughout Europe.

Cavour, in Turin, kept a close eye on developments in the Mortara case with the help of Count Dominico della Minerva, his emissary in Rome. On October 9, 1858, Minerva sent Cavour a copy of the appeal to the Pope prepared by the Università Israelitica in Rome the month before. The emissary went on to report the impact that the case was having: "This fact, which has so upset public opinion in France and which, justly, the periodical press has taken up, has recently become the object of great interest in the Capital of the Catholic world thanks to the lively interest that the French Ambassador has taken in it." So far, Minerva recounted, all the semiofficial channels that had been used to get the Church to release the child had proven useless. As a result, the Ambassador had decided to send Cardinal Antonelli an extremely strong note "in which he rightly stigmatized, in the harshest terms, a fact that is contrary to the first principles of natural right."

When the Duke de Gramont, the French ambassador, received no reply to his note, he went to see the Secretary of State personally to complain. Not only did the French government, given all it was doing for the Pope, deserve a response, he argued, but it was in the Holy See's own interest to provide a written account of its reasons for not returning the young Jew to his family. The exchange was far from friendly: "All this took place not without considerable animation and bitterness on both parts. But the French ambassador, unhappy at the indifference shown by the Cardinal to his pleas, took advantage of the prerogatives connected to his high rank and, a few days ago, without first asking either the Secretary of State or anyone else of the papal court, went directly to speak to His Holiness about the matter."

Count Minerva describes the Duke's difficult meeting with Pius IX, affording Cavour an excellent view of the Pope's attitude toward the Mortara case: "The Holy Father said that he was sorry about what had happened and was even more pained by the impossibility of ordering Mortara returned to his family, for to return the boy would be repugnant to his conscience. He was truly persuaded that the baptism was valid and that, given this fact, he could not permit a Christian to be raised in the Jewish religion." The Pope informed the Ambassador that he was having a document drafted which laid out the theological bases for the decision and that it would soon be available. Minerva concluded his report to Cavour by observing that the Mortara case had poisoned relations between France and the Vatican. The Pope's refusal to bend had been taken as a great affront by the French.[2]

On the same day, in a separate, confidential letter to Cavour, the Piedmontese emissary added a dramatic detail. He had spoken with Gramont following the duke's stormy session with Cardinal Antonelli and before he had seen the Pope. Gramont had made a startling suggestion: "The Duke de Gramont's irritation over the case of the Jew Mortara has reached the boiling point in the last few days. Walking with me, he asked me if, should the boy be put on a boat to Genoa, there would be any difficulty in accepting him there." Genoa was part of the kingdom of Sardinia. The plan was to seize Edgardo by force—not in itself a difficult matter for the Ambassador, given that it was French troops who patrolled the streets of Rome—and send him to the safety of the one part of Italy where Jews were free. Count Minerva, although surprised that Gramont would be considering such a move, assured him that arrangements could be made to receive the child in Genoa. The Ambassador said that after kidnapping Edgardo, he would have him put on a French steamship. "He urged me, however, to maintain the most absolute silence so that the element of surprise could be kept and thus play a bad trick on the priests." Minerva concluded his letter, "I don't know whether after his audience with the Pope he was still of the same idea."[3]

When, two weeks later, Minerva again encountered the French ambassador, the subject of the kidnapping came up, but the Duke had by then calmed down, his enthusiasm no doubt cooled by his government's alarm upon hearing of his plan. He told Minerva, however, that the reason he had abandoned it was that, while it would liberate the Jewish child, "it would not save the principle." Yet Gramont persisted in his belief that, given the Pope's obstinacy, the only way to get Edgardo back was to kidnap him. Indeed, in a conversation with Minerva in mid-November, the Duke criticized the "imbecility of the Jews," who, instead of going around complaining about the Mortara boy's situation and expecting someone else to help, should "at this very moment be arranging for him to escape." Cavour's emissary thought this unkind and unrealistic: "What could these poor unfortunates do unless the French police were willing to lend them a little help?"[4]

In fact, the idea of kidnapping Edgardo had occurred to the Jews as well, and various plans were hatched, at least in the safety of private conversations. Not long after the Duke de Gramont asked ruefully why the Jews themselves were not organizing a rescue party, one of his Jewish countrymen issued a call for the Jews to do just that. In the December 10 issue of *Archives Israélites*, a letter was published under the heading "*Moyen d'opérer la délivrance du jeune martyr*" (How to free the young martyr). "Let's promise," the take-charge author wrote, "a prize of twenty thousand francs to anyone who manages to abduct the Mortara boy and lead him to a safe place, whether in Piedmont, or in France, or any other country that has an honest government." He offered to start the fund with his own donation of twenty francs but added expansively that if the twenty-thousand-franc figure seemed too small, "let's double it!" His letter went into considerable detail as to how the fund would be administered (the Rothschild family would once again come to the Jews' aid), how it would be raised (not only by Jews worldwide but by outraged Catholics as well), and how the prize would be awarded. The only details it failed to explore were just who was going to do the kidnapping and how.[5]

Meanwhile, the benefit of the Mortara controversy for Cavour and the Italian unification movement was becoming even clearer. In a letter to Cavour sent from Paris on November 21, the Marquis of Villamarina, ambassador of the kingdom of Sardinia in France, reported how much indignation the incident had provoked there, turning French public opinion against the pontifical state. The French Emperor, Cavour was told, continued to take a great interest in the case and had branded the Church's action an outrageous violation of both civil and natural law.

In the Marquis's description of Gramont's tense meeting with the Pope, the link between the Mortara case and the events that were about to alter the political map of Italy was made clear. Gramont told Pius IX of the loud chorus of complaints in France aimed at the Holy See as a result of its handling of the affair. The Pope responded that he, too, had recently been hearing some disturbing reports regarding France. The Pontiff went on: "I would greatly appreciate it if you could help me, Monsieur l'Ambassadeur, to put to rest the rumors that are circulating in my states, rumors that have been accompanied, as well, by pieces of information that my agents have been picking up, in which all of Emperor Napoleon's intrigues in Italy have been exposed."

Just what those plans were the Pope then recounted to the discomfited Duke. The secret French goal, said the Pope, was "to chase the Austrians from Lombardy and Veneto and, through universal suffrage, let the people themselves select the institutions and the king of their choice. The Roman Legations would be joined to this new Kingdom of Italy." Pius IX accused the French of planning to go even further than this and annex other portions of the Papal States to Piedmont, including the kingdom of the Two Sicilies and the duchies—Tuscany, Modena, Parma—leaving the Pope to rule only the city of Rome.

"Monsieur de Gramont," the Sardinian ambassador wrote Cavour, "appeared astonished by this outburst by the Pope and sought to calm him down and assure him that there was not a single word of truth in the whole account." The Pope, skeptical of the Duke's assurances, directed him to convey his comments to the Emperor and to report back with Napoleon's response.[6]

Count Cavour's reply to Ambassador Villamarina in Paris similarly reflects the curious interweaving of concern over the Mortara affair with the momentous political events that were about to unfold in Italy. (Cavour, like Villamarina, wrote in French. Although he was the architect of Italian unification, the man responsible for expelling foreigners and creating an Italian nation, Cavour never felt entirely comfortable with the Italian language and, indeed, addressed his own parliament in French, not Italian. All this, to be sure, was natural enough in Piedmont, whose royal court and high society had until very recently seen France, rather than Italy, as their main cultural point of reference.)

"The news that you send me," he responded, "is of the utmost gravity." What Villamarina had written about what was going on in Rome, Cavour wrote, corresponded perfectly with what he had heard from other sources. Passing on to Villamarina news of Gramont's plan to kidnap Edgardo and smuggle him out to Piedmont, he wrote of the French ambassador: "He confided it to Minerva, to whom I gave the order to back it, although leaving to him the major part of the arrangements." Cavour, then, had approved the plan himself. "Gramont," he wrote, "later hesitated and has probably given up the idea, on orders from Paris."

Although Napoleon no doubt thought that his enraged ambassador in Rome had gone too far in cooking up the kidnapping plan, in Cavour's view, "the Emperor has been delighted by the Mortara affair, as he is with everything that can compromise the Pope in the eyes of Europe and among moderate Catholics." The case would give Napoleon a freer hand in whittling away the Papal States: "The more difficult it will be for the Pope to make his weight felt against him, the easier it will be for him to impose the sacrifices necessary for the reorganization of Italy."

Cavour spelled out for his ambassador to France the stance they should take with Napoleon III. They should remind him of the intransigence that the Pope showed in rejecting Gramont's pleas on behalf of the Mortara family "and conclude by arguing that the Pope's conduct shows the absolute impossibility of his conserving temporal power beyond the walls of Rome."[7]

As the liberal and anticlerical newspapers throughout Europe kept up the drumbeat of criticism aimed at the Vatican over the Mortara affair, and the French ambassador to Rome renewed his protests, Cardinal Antonelli's diplomatic pouch filled with updates by nuncios from all parts of the continent, reporting the troubling signs of a new wave of antipapal sentiment. In January

1859, the nuncio in Paris wrote Antonelli to report that the French emperor and his ministers were still unhappy about the Mortara affair, although, he added, "without the least reason."[8] A series of letters to the Secretary of State from the apostolic nuncio in Madrid likewise reported disturbing developments in Spain, a country that had virtually no Jewish population at all.

To a letter dated the first of December, 1858, the nuncio appended copies of recent Spanish newspaper stories on the Mortara case. Of particular concern was the fact that the *Diario Spagniol*, a paper close to the government, had published a piece that referred to the taking of the boy as "a kidnapping and a crime." The nuncio went directly to the Minister of State and to the Minister of Internal Affairs to protest the outrage, berating them for their "neglect in not preventing such scandalous abuses of the periodical press." He found the ministers agreeable, and they assured him that it would not happen again. But the nuncio did not stop there. He arranged for two Church-friendly newspapers to run stories lambasting the *Diario* for publishing the critical piece. The result of these efforts, he reported with considerable satisfaction, was publication of an apology by the paper in the previous day's edition. Unfortunately, the nuncio wrote, he had found no way of "repressing the impertinence of the other newspaper, *El Clamor*, which has always been less than devoted to the Holy See."[9]

In the Netherlands, the Vatican had to deal with a less cooperative government. On November 8, Count Du Chastel, the Dutch emissary to Rome, sent a letter to Cardinal Antonelli on behalf of his government. He wrote:

> The Mortara affair, which has created such a stir over the last several months in Europe, has not failed to make an equally distressing impression on the people of the Low Countries, where a substantial number of Jews live, distinguishing themselves by their private and civic virtues. The events of Bologna have greatly upset the High Commission of Dutch Jews, which, following the example of their counterparts in England, France, and Sardinia, petitioned the Dutch Government with the request that it interest itself in this affair and work, through its good offices, to obtain a favorable solution for the Mortara family.

Remarking that his government had no wish to become involved in the internal affairs of another state, the Count nonetheless wanted to let the pontifical government know how offended Dutch public opinion was. He concluded with the hope that "the Holy See, in its great wisdom, is able to prevent in the future the recurrence of similar actions, which, in strongly stirring popular passions, result in the growth of unfavorable impressions of the Holy See."[10]

The Secretary of State must have been especially concerned about this letter on behalf of the King of the Low Countries, for he wrote an unusually long reply. He complained that the Dutch were doing just what they themselves recognized that they had no right to do—namely, interfering in the internal affairs of another state. The matter, Antonelli informed them, involved "an essentially and exclusively religious fact, and therefore is naturally a matter to be handled by the Ecclesiastical Authority, which may not be interfered with by secular bodies." The plea was therefore improper: "As the nature of the case is entirely religious, involving the Sacrament of baptism administered to a child, with all the consequences that flow from it, so too are the reasons that prevent the Supreme Head of the Church from taking action of the kind requested by the Jewish parents of the baptized boy." As for the Count's argument that the case was making a bad impression on his countrymen, Antonelli responded: "Whatever the impression made on those who either do not want to or do not know how to see the case in its proper light, the Holy See remains confident that it has acted according to the unchanging maxims of the Catholic Church, from which no human reason would ever allow it to shrink."[11]

Across the Atlantic, the case was nourishing a new sense of national solidarity among the Jews of the United States. Although, at 150,000 strong, there were many more Jews in the U.S. than in Italy, France, or England, most American Jews were immigrants, and they had as yet little in the way of national organization. Even the three major English-language Jewish newspapers were local products, efforts of particularly influential rabbis in New York, Cincinnati, and Philadelphia.

Word of the Mortara affair came to American Jews indirectly, for neither the Università Israelitica of Rome nor the much more modest Jewish community of Bologna had direct links to their transatlantic brethren. A number of the leading American rabbis, however, were notified by a letter sent in September from Sir Moses Montefiore, head of the Board of Deputies of the British Jewish community. Interest quickly spread.

Only a minority of American Jews came from Roman Catholic countries, but the Mortara abduction represented for them all that was wrong with the Old World, a painful reminder of the oppression they had escaped. These sentiments were nourished not only by the American ideology of freedom and equality but by less salubrious forces as well. In the America of 1858, many took a dim view of Roman Catholicism. Catholic immigrants from Ireland and elsewhere were vilified and derided, and the Pope was painted as the devil incarnate. Ironically, the Jews, who shared much the same fate as the Catholic immigrants of the time at the hands of the overwhelmingly Protestant majority, were overjoyed to find such widespread popular support for their campaign against the Pope.

Beginning in mid-September, the major American Jewish papers carried story after story on the Mortara case. Rabbi Isaac Mayer Wise of Cincinnati—one of the founders of Reform Judaism in the United States and editor of one of the major Jewish newspapers—wrote in tones of which American anti-Catholics of the time could be proud:

> The facts are, Edgar Mortara never was baptized, the Pope and his numerous, soul-less lackeys never cared whether that boy is a Christian or a Jew. It was not nor is it now the object of the papal officers to make Edgar a Christian, in order that he be saved in the Romish style, or because a few drops of water were sprinkled on him and an unknown woman said a few words over the unconscious child. Some petty priest or schoolmaster of an illiterate Catholic congregation may believe such nonsense, and prompt his flock to subscribe to the doctrine. But the chief movers in all those things are not so foolish. . . . One must have grown up in the midst of the Catholic clergy to know how much they preach and how little they believe; how severe and strict they are in all religious matters before the illiterate, and how they make light of the whole concern when they find an intelligent and confidential man. Hence Rome's object is not and can not be the religion of a boy, not religion per se. . . . We may venture to say, if that nurse was brought before a court of justice in this country, any of our lawyers with a little cross-examination could make the woman tell, that she is the hired tool of some priest, who is himself the tool of his superior, and who again may be the blind tool of a Jesuit, who in his turn is the instrument of the inquisition, which sacred office is the handmaid of the Pope, who again is the subject of the Jesuits. . . .[12]

While the Jews living in the Papal States had to grovel before the terrifying power of the Pope, those in the United States clearly found no difficulty in going to the other extreme.

How much this scathing anti-Catholicism had roots in the European Jewish communities from which Wise and the other Jews came, and how much they picked up from their Protestant neighbors in the land of the free, is an intriguing question. Yet one of the ironies of Wise's diatribe is how closely it mirrors the image of the Jews found in the Catholic press. While the Pope's defenders viewed the motives of those calling for Edgardo's release as ignoble, and argued that the boy's parents themselves were moved by anti-Church rancor rather than parental devotion, in Wise's rendering, it is the Pope and his clerical colleagues who dissemble, driven not by any true religious belief but by the most corrupt and insincere of motives.

Throughout the country, Jewish communities organized meetings to decide what action to take, and from New York to San Francisco, public protest rallies were held. In Boston, where anti-Catholic sentiment flourished, two synagogues held a joint meeting to consider what to do, and a four-member committee read its resolution to much applause. Going a step beyond Rabbi Wise, they specifically appealed for solidarity with Protestants who shared their view of the "Prince of Darkness":

> We hear with astonishment and deep sorrow that the most odious act that ever emanated from the Prince of Darkness was recently perpetrated in the dominions of Pio Nono, the Pope of Rome. . . . This abominable outrage not only affects the Jew, but it equally concerns the Christian who is not of the Catholic creed, as what they (the Inquisition) dared in defiance of every principle of moral justice, inflict one day on the Jew, they may and *will* repeat on a future day to the detriment of the Protestants residing within the limits of their unprincipled power. The history of these incarnate fiends, written in the blood of millions of victims, fully justifies such conclusion.[13]

Not all of the protests in the United States leaned so heavily on the Know Nothing slogans that the Jews imbibed as part of their acculturation. In early December, at Mozart Hall in New York, a citywide gathering of Jews was called, the first in eighteen years, to protest the Mortara abduction. For hours more than two thousand New Yorkers heard speaker after speaker call for Edgardo's liberation. Anti-Catholic rhetoric in New York was more muted than in Boston. The most enthusiastically received speaker, Raphael De Cordova, a popular Jewish humorist, asked, irreverently: Could it be true that a Jewish baby baptized surreptitiously by a nurse was thereby made Catholic? What if, he ruminated, a band of Jews, armed with a razor, were to sneak into the Vatican, seize the Pope, and, while holding the protesting Pontiff down, perform a circumcision? "Surely," he concluded, to the chuckles of the appreciative audience, "that would not make the Pope a Jew, any more than the sprinkling of water made a child of a Jew a Christian."[14]

The rallies continued. In San Francisco, in January, more than three thousand people listened to the speeches of prominent Protestant clergymen, assorted other Christian community leaders, and the Jewish organizers themselves. Most of the speakers adopted a respectful attitude toward Catholicism, and some were deferential to the Pope as well. But others portrayed the Mortara case as but the last in a long line of outrages performed by a Church that was a menace to the rest of the world. F. P. Tracy, one of the Protestant speakers, recalled a visit to Rome in 1847 when, he said, he saw Cardinal Antonelli sitting beside Pius IX (which seems most unlikely, as Antonelli was not yet Secretary of State). "Like Mephistophiles, cold and unimpassioned,"

Antonelli—thundered Tracy—whispered instructions in the pliant pope's ear "and changed the character of him who otherwise might have been a kind and patriarchal ruler." Tracy warned his audience that they had to take matters into their own hands, since no decency could be expected from the Vatican: "The Pope would baptize every one of us, if he only had the power."[15]

The Mortara case had become a cause célèbre among non-Jews as well as Jews. In the month of December 1858 alone, *The New York Times* published more than twenty articles on the case; the *Baltimore American* published thirty-one major articles on Mortara from October 1858 through January of the following year; and the *Milwaukee Sentinel* ran twenty-three stories in November and December 1858. At the beginning of March 1859, when popular interest in the case in Europe had already subsided, the *New York Herald* claimed that American interest in the Mortara affair had reached "colossal dimensions."[16]

Flexing their still puny political muscles, the incensed American Jews, following the example of their European brethren, tried to get their government to speak out against the abduction and send a protest to the Vatican. They got nowhere. The American secretary of state replied to the cascade of letters by saying that it was the government's policy not to interfere in the internal affairs of other countries. Finally, the President himself, James Buchanan, thought it necessary to respond to the pleas personally, and on January 4, 1859, he wrote to a representative of the New York Jewish community: "I have long been convinced that it is neither the right nor the duty of this Government to express a moral censorship over the conduct of other independent governments and to rebuke them for acts which we may deem arbitrary and unjust towards their own citizens or subjects."[17]

For Buchanan, the matter was delicate, for the Jews' unhappiness was the least of his worries. The nation was on the verge of civil war over slavery, and abolitionists were calling on the enlightened powers of Europe to add their weight to the antislavery campaign. The President was hardly eager to set an example in the case of an Italian Jew that could later be used against him. And his own moral position was not very strong. How could he rail against a government that allowed a child to be forcibly separated from his parents when the same thing happened all the time in the slaveholding portions of his own country? As the President squirmed, the abolitionist newspapers became the unlikely ally of the American Catholic press as each, for its own reasons, attacked what it saw as the hypocrisy of the movement to free the Jewish child.

Catholic defenders of the Church published their own version of events, echoing the Catholic press in Europe. One pamphlet, published in New York in November 1858 under the pseudonym of "Fair Play," typical of these broad-

sides, branded the "alleged Mortara kidnapping case" a "windfall to the enemies of God's Church." Blaming the child's baptism on Momolo Mortara for
breaking the Papal States' law that prohibited Jews from having Christian servants, it argued that no one, not even a pope, could "unbaptize a Christian
child." Not only was it unthinkable that a Christian government "could leave
a Christian child to be brought up a Jew," but another principle, that of religious liberty, was also at stake, "the liberty of a child to be a Christian, and not
forced compulsorily to be a Jew." Edgardo (described as 11 years old, rather
than 7) was begging to remain a Christian: "To have surrendered him would
have been an eternal ignominy. To clamor for his surrender is an outrage
upon Christianity, and a shame to Christendom." And Fair Play concluded,
grandiosely, "The Holy Father's protection of the child, in the face of all the
ferocious fanaticism of infidelity and bigotry, is the grandest moral spectacle
which the world has seen for ages."[18]

CHAPTER 14

The Church Strikes Back

WITH PROTESTS mounting on both sides of the Atlantic, worried Church officials hastened to prepare their defense. For the members of the hierarchy, the abuse aimed at the Church was but the latest of a string of anti-Catholic outrages. Throughout its history the Church had treated its Jews in much the same manner as it had in the Mortara case, and no one—other than a handful of frightened Jews, on their knees—had ever said anything. In matters of Church dogma, this was as it should be. But now, with the forces of secularism, godlessness, and materialism sweeping Europe, respect for the word of God and His instrument on earth was rapidly eroding. True, the Church had been having to fight this battle in some form ever since the Reformation, when Church authority was first contested. But in the heartland of world Catholicism, the pontifical state itself, it was unthinkable that the Pope's spiritual authority should be challenged by such a motley assortment of schismatics and infidels.

The battle over the Mortara boy coincided with struggles within the Church over the extent to which all power should flow from the Pope. The modern low point of papal authority was reached in the latter decades of the eighteenth century. Civil rulers begrudged the Church its autonomy and opposed any practice that suggested that affairs in their own states were being decided by a foreign power, namely the pope and his representatives. Autocrats' desires to reign uncontested and unconstrained mixed with Enlightenment-generated ideas to create a movement against special privileges for the Church. The Jesuits, the embodiment of the Church as foreign power, and champions of an ideology in which the wishes of the secular rulers were subordinated to the word of God as interpreted by Rome, came in for special attack. They were chased from Portugal in 1759, from France in 1764, from Spain in 1767, and from Naples the following year. The anti-Jesuit outcry became so great that, in 1773, Pope Clement XIV abolished the Jesuit order altogether. In Vienna, in 1762, the publication of papal encyclicals was made contingent on prior approval from the Habsburg ruler. In the decades that followed, secular rulers throughout Catholic Europe wrested control over censorship from inquisitorial hands and barred the Church from putting their subjects on trial. The state claimed a monopoly on the power to arrest and try its subjects.

On his accession to the Austrian throne in 1780, Joseph II denounced the existing concordat and moved energetically to restrict the rights of the Church, seeking to build a modern, secular state. Ecclesiastical exemption from taxes was abolished, the Holy Office of the Inquisition suppressed, and the policy of closing monasteries and convents given new impetus. Through- out most of the lands in which Catholics lived, similar attacks on Church authority put the hierarchy on the defensive, and the prestige of the papacy suffered.

The Napoleonic conquests in Europe, and the years of French rule, accel- erated the decline in prestige and power of the centralized Church. But in the aftermath of Napoleon's fall, the attitude of most of Europe's secular rulers changed. While in intellectual circles the Enlightenment ideas of equality had spread, among the governors and the elites who supported them antagonism toward the Enlightenment and the notion of a society based on the use of reason brought about a strengthening of Church authority. In historian Stuart Woolf's words, "The only hope was to revert to an earlier, uncontaminated society, in which order and hierarchy were respected and the theocratic basis of monarchy consecrated by an infallible pope or divine revelations."[1] The result was the revival in the use of the Church as a bulwark of secular rule. Throughout Europe, the Jesuit order was restored and popular expressions of devotion—cults of apparitions and Marian worship, among others—were given new life. New concordats were eventually negotiated—Viale-Prelà's work as papal nuncio in Vienna constituted a part of this process—marking the harmony, once again, of Church and state.

The autonomy of national churches—championed in the past not only by secular rulers who were hostile to control from Rome but also by major sec- tors of the Catholic population and clergy in France, Austria, and elsewhere— was during this Restoration period increasingly challenged by the growth of the "ultramontane" movement. The ultramontanes argued that local churches everywhere should come under the strict control of the Holy See. They sought to bolster the power and the prestige of the Pope, and they championed the supremacy of Church law over secular legal principles. In all this, they fought not only the liberal movement but their opponents within the Church as well, those who, from the ultramontanes' perspective, were poisoned by Enlightenment ideas that were at odds with the Church's mission.

The Pope's refusal to return Edgardo to his family became a sacred cause for the ultramontane forces, involving the prestige and authority of the papacy as well as the supremacy of divine law over modern ideas of individual rights and religious equality. The campaign took various forms. Diplomatic efforts were under Cardinal Antonelli's control, but the counteroffensive among the general population was entrusted to the large European network of Catholic newspapers. Among these, two occupied an especially influential place: the Jesuit *Civiltà Cattolica*, advised directly by the Pope and regarded as speaking in his name, and the feisty *L'univers*, published by the greatest ultramontane champion of them all, the Frenchman Louis Veuillot.

Among the first Catholic newspapers outside Italy to comment on the Mortara affair was the Belgian *Journal de Bruxelles*. Its September 18 story is revealing, not only in sketching out the first lines of Church defense, but also in the embellishments that had crept into the Church narrative.

According to the Belgian paper, far from coming out of the blue, the decision to remove Edgardo from his parents was made only after rumors of the boy's baptism had become the talk of Bologna. The baptism was so well known that the Archbishop, Cardinal Viale-Prelà, had no choice but to see that basic canon law was applied "or else run the risk of an immense scandal in the eyes of the Catholics." The reluctant but principled archbishop, faced with this situation, repeatedly offered Momolo Mortara the chance to keep his son, as long as he would promise to see that he was raised as a Christian. "After repeated refusals, the Archbishop of Bologna simply did his duty," the paper reported. The boy was taken to the Catechumens in Rome, but his father was immediately invited to follow him to see for himself "that his son was not being sequestered, nor being made to break his natural ties, nor even being constrained by corporal or moral pressure to profess his faith." Rather, the boy was being kept in what amounted simply to a comfortable lodging so that he could be provided with "a religious education sufficient to afford him, if he chose, the grace of his baptism, since certainly, if he had continued to live in Bologna with his family, he would never have been able to know even what the sacrament was that had made him a child of God and of the Church." Indeed, the *Journal de Bruxelles* reported, the boy's father had recently visited him in Rome and "was able to see for himself that, far from being constrained by tyrannical and external influences to follow the grace that had been bestowed on him, his son obeyed with the most admirable spontaneity."[2]

The claim that Edgardo's parents, seeing how happy he was and how well he was being cared for in the Catechumens, were pleased to see him remain there was picked up by *L'armonia della religione colla civiltà*. Published in Turin by a priest, Giacomo Margotti, the paper fought the ultramontane battle in hostile territory, at the heart of the kingdom of Sardinia. Margotti's stream of stinging polemics against the liberal state and the liberal wing of the Church not only earned him frequent visits from government censors, who periodically shut the paper down, but, two years before the Mortara case, had led to a physical assault that almost killed him. Emotions ran high on both sides.

L'armonia ran its first Mortara article on August 17, 1858, and published a score more by the end of the year.[3] In its October 17 story, the newspaper reported news of Edgardo's family: "No one is posing the least opposition. The Mortara boy's parents themselves are now pleased that he is being educated in the Catechumens."[4]

None of these papers had as great an impact as *Civiltà Cattolica*. When the controversy first began to heat up, in August, both Church partisans and opponents began to look to the paper to see when the Vatican would make its position known and respond publicly to its growing army of critics. The Jesuit journal's reputation for being the mouthpiece of the Holy See was such that, Momolo later recounted, it was in reading their first article on the case, published on October 30, that he realized that the Pope had decided not to let Edgardo go.[5]

That article, as we have already seen, relied heavily on Edgardo's own miraculous transformation, and his consequent desire to stay where he was, in arguing that he should not be returned to his family. But other arguments were pursued as well.

In the article, sections of which were republished by Catholic papers throughout Europe, the journal assured its Catholic readers that the crucial question of whether the child had in fact ever been baptized had been thoroughly investigated. The Mortaras' lawyers had understandably focused much attention on this, the crucial issue, and had produced sworn statements from various people to discredit the servant's account. But, the journal reported, it took only a single witness to make a baptism valid, and that witness, Anna Morisi, had not changed her story. The widespread reports in the anticlerical press that there had been no baptism were preposterous: Isn't it strange, asked the author, that the rumormongers in France and Germany should be considered better informed about what had happened than Church authorities in Bologna and Rome, where an official investigation had been conducted? The parents had produced a doctor's statement that the child's illness at the time had not ever threatened his life. But this claim—suspicious itself in the hazy recollections of a physician six years after the fact—meant little. Even if the child had not been in danger of dying, he was baptized, and therefore a Christian.

Once the investigations had verified that Edgardo had been baptized, the Church had no choice but to take the action that it had. Here lay the heart of the matter. "Although the Voltairian unbelievers and the Jews claim to be scandalized and dumbfounded by it, for the true Christian no shadow of doubt is permitted. For, given that this seven-year-old child has been baptized, the question of whether he should be left with a Jewish father becomes another: Should someone who has been baptized become a Christian or a Jew? for in the end, the man will become what his upbringing makes him."[6]

Taking up another theme that was to be repeated in hundreds of Catholic articles on the Mortara case, the Jesuit journal asked whose fault it was that the Mortaras' son had been taken from them. It was their own fault, the author responded, for none of this would have happened if they had obeyed the law of the land in which they lived, which, to avoid uncomfortable situations such as this, forbade Jews to employ Christian servants. As residents of the Papal States, Jews such as the Mortaras tacitly accepted the laws under which they lived. If they found these too onerous, "they were fully free to move somewhere else." For the Jews to blame the Church for what had happened as a result of their flouting of the law was particularly galling. "If they and their fellow believers want to remain there, they show poor grace to pretend that the laws can be changed just to suit the Judaic people."[7]

As for why the Mortara case had occasioned such a commotion in the press throughout Europe, why the Church had become the victim of such abuse, the *Civiltà Cattolica* had an explanation: it was the power of the Jews. Since the members of the family of Jacob, the journal explained, "are extremely rich in Europe today, indeed in possession of the most powerful libertine newspapers in Germany, Belgium, and France, it is hardly surprising that these same papers band together in their defense, especially when they can at the same time assault the Pontiff and his government."[8]

Reports had reached Rome's Università Israelitica that the *Civiltà Cattolica* was planning a major statement on the Mortara case, and as a result, Scazzocchio and Samuele Alatri, head of the Jewish community, sent a letter to Father Carlo Curci, the Jesuit founder and director of the journal, pleading for favorable consideration. On October 30, the same day that the fateful issue of the journal went to press, Father Curci replied in a brief note, stating that "we desire only the truth and justice" and enclosing a statement on the Mortara case. "If you and the distinguished Signor Alatri remain unchanged in your opinion on the matter," Curci wrote, "that does not prevent me from expressing my sincere respect for both of you."

No sooner had they received this letter than Scazzocchio prepared a new plea to the Jesuit editor, accompanying it with various supporting documents. Curci's response, written on November 1, offers a glimpse into the mind of one of the Pope's most influential defenders. "I thank you for your kindness in sending me new clarifications on the noted affair," he wrote, adding that they had not altered his views, which they would find in the article that was currently in press in his journal. "You and your brethren might find that article to be rather severe," he continued, but he hoped that they would understand his situation. He was compelled to respond "to the wild invectives against the Catholic Church and its august head that so many newspapers in Europe have published on this affair."[9]

In Bologna, meanwhile, *L'osservatore bolognese* had already run three articles on the Mortara case in the course of the month. The last of these, in late October, began by responding to a recent attack aimed at it by the Parisian *Journal des Débats*. The Bologna Catholic paper disputed the *Journal's* report of a Church-induced climate of anti-Semitism in the city. The French paper had cited, among other episodes, a weekly puppet show in Bologna's central piazza in which the marionettes were regularly made to mouth "words of hate against the Jews."

Along with two other French papers, the *Journal* was also denounced for its relentless hostility toward the Pope and his authority. According to *L'osservatore bolognese*, the "chorus masters of modern rationalism" were nothing but a bunch of hypocrites who ignored the facts in order to wage their "disloyal and implacable war against truth and against Catholicism." The Mortaras were being used cynically: "Here we have the philanthropists, the humanitarians, who don't hesitate to exploit the anxieties of a mother and an entire family in order to wound, once more, that Church of which they claim with such hypocrisy to be the devoted and reverent sons."

For the Bologna Catholic paper, there was no room for debate or for criticism. It was a simple matter of facts and of knowing the divinely ordained laws of the Church, the laws of religion. The boy had been baptized, and "we hope that no one wants to deny the fact that baptism makes a person Christian." Admittedly, taking her child away might have been distressing for the poor mother, but all possible care had been taken to make the move as painless as possible. *L'osservatore bolognese* went on to report the "moving details" the paper had received about the trip, recounting yet another version of the miraculous conversion along the way. The story concluded: "From letters from Rome, we learn that now, as always, the boy is extremely pleased by his situation, and that he shows a lively intelligence and the most obedient and gentle temperament."Amidst this happiness, only one thought pained him, "the thought of seeing his parents and his siblings remain as Jews." "But I will pray to the Lord," the boy said, "that He shine His grace on them as well so that they too become Christians."[10]

Meanwhile, the other Bologna weekly close to the Church, *Il vero amico*, reiterated the argument that Momolo and Marianna were angry about their son's removal only because it meant seeing "one of their offspring pass from Judaism to the true human Religion of Christ." The paper also argued—taking up another *Civiltà Cattolica* theme—that if the journalists of France, Germany, and England were "raising their voices against the Pontiff, screaming injustice, kidnapping, and tyranny," this was hardly surprising, "since currently the newspapers of Europe are in good part in the hands of the Jews."[11]

An avalanche of articles in the Italian Catholic press defended the Pope and castigated the Church's enemies, who were accused of ignorance—probably willful—of the teachings of Jesus and the duties of religion. These denunciations grew out of a religious vision of the Jews that made the attacks on the Holy See on behalf of the Jewish family seem especially noisome. The advantage to the boy of being Catholic, rather than remaining Jewish, seemed so obvious—and the desire of any Christian to want to return him to the Jews so preposterous—that words could hardly express their outrage.

A good example is provided by the Genoa daily *Il Cattolico*, whose articles were written primarily by priests committed to defending the Pope's temporal power. Together with *L'armonia della religione colla civiltà*, *Il Cattolico* struggled mightily in the heart of the beast, for Genoa was part of the kingdom of Sardinia. From its first item on the Mortara case, in August 1858, through the end of that year, *Il Cattolico* devoted over a score of articles to the polemic.

Typical was a piece it published at the beginning of December. The correspondent pointed out that, by keeping Edgardo, the Pope was not only serving the boy's spiritual interest but benefiting him materially as well. Once the child had completed his education—all paid for by the Church—he could aspire to any of the careers and honors available in the Papal States, from which, he noted, Edgardo would as a Jew have been excluded. The article continued:

> Whoever among us gives a little serious thought to the matter, compares the condition of a Jew—without a true Church, without a King, and without a country, dispersed and always a foreigner wherever he lives on the face of the earth, and moreover, infamous for the ugly stain with which the killers of Christ are marked—[whoever]compares this reviled man with a Roman citizen, who has as his country the most civil nation in the world, Italy, and who can occupy the most splendid civil and ecclesiastical offices of the eternal city, will immediately understand how great is this temporal advantage that the Pope is obtaining for the Mortara boy.

It was clear to *Il Cattolico* that all the hand-wringing about the injustice done to the boy was but a smokescreen for what truly motivated the protests. How could the rabble-rousers be taken seriously when it was the wretched

Jews whom they were championing? "The libertines are making the devil of a noise, and have said, and keep repeating, with apparent seriousness, that all of the European Powers are sending strong letters of protest to the Pope to get him to give the Mortara boy back to his parents." This must be a joke: "Imagine, people! The European Powers taking so much trouble for a Jew, who doesn't matter one whit to them! This is a tale to tell children some winter night by the fire! Yet many of these rags have tried to pass it off as the absolute truth."[12]

Jews were beyond the pale of civilization, because civilization was based on Christianity. As outsiders, they were dangerous, for they did not feel bound to the laws of morality that governed Christians. They felt no obligations to anyone other than their fellow Jews, and they showed no pity for their Christian victims.

Charges of ritual murder in some ways epitomized the Catholic view of the Jews. Under the heading "The Horrendous Murder of a Child," *Il Cattolico* in January 1859 made no bones about the link between the commotion caused by the Mortara protests and their decision to run a breathless report of a new, terrifying example of Jewish villainy. "In the month of August," the Genoan paper began its report,

> while the libertine press was creating such an uproar against the Pope because of the case of the Mortara boy, the most horrendous assassination of a Christian boy was being committed by a Jew in Folkchany, a Moldo-Wallachian city [now in Romania]. So goes the world. The Pope arranges for a Jewish boy who had become a Christian to be brought up, with every possible care, in a Catholic boarding school, and they raise the roof. A Jew kills a Christian boy in the most horrible way, and the liberals, we are certain, will not have a single word to say about it.

One day in early August, according to the story, a woman from Folkchany set out on a trip with her 4-year-old son. As she was about to cross the nearby border into Moldavia, she saw that the child was tired and told him to go home, while she continued on her journey. When she returned, after dark, her little boy was nowhere to be found. Nervous and fearful, she told her husband, and the two of them searched without success, finally notifying the police. For five days they found no sign of the child.

Near the border crossing where the mother had last seen her son was a tavern run by a Jew. They suspected that it was he who had taken the child, eager to use the little Christian's blood to make matzah, the unleavened bread baked by Jews for Passover. (The belief that Jews used Christian blood to make their matzah was a centuries-old theme, linked to the recurring accusa-

849 - 280

tion that Judaism required the ritual murder of Christians.[13] In the case in question here, quite aside from the monstrous absurdity of the charge in general, the fact that Passover occurs in early spring, not August, apparently made no impression on the Jews' accusers.) The man denied ever having seen the boy, and initially they could find no proof that he had. But finally the police found the evidence they were looking for. Search dogs began scratching the ground not far from the tavern and soon uncovered the child's blood-soaked cadaver. He had been horribly mutilated. "They counted more than 120 wounds on the little body of the poor martyr, and they saw that thorns had been driven into his head and reeds thrust under his fingernails." Since the blood was still fresh, they realized that he had been tortured for five days. The signs were clear: "The type of torture was too much like that of Our Lord for them to be fooled about the intentions of the murderer or murderers."

When word of what had happened spread, the irate population of Folkchany rose up, and an angry crowd marched on the homes of the city's Jews to rid themselves once and for all of the evil in their midst. "From fifteen to twenty Jews were killed in this uprising, and it was only by the energetic intervention of the authorities that things didn't get further out of hand." The police arrested the Jews who looked most suspicious, and they began their investigations. But the Jews made sure that there would be no evidence against them: "All the Jews took the part of their coreligionists. In a few days they had raised 600,000 francs to be used to buy witnesses and to squelch suspicions. The Judaic gold produced its intended effect: it was declared that there was no sufficient proof." The imprisoned Jews were freed.[14]

The story was reported, in much the same form, in Catholic papers throughout Europe, including *L'Univers* in France. Two months later, the editor of the French *Archives Israélites* published a response. It was true, he wrote, that a little boy had been brutally murdered in the Moldavian town, and it was true that the population rose up, stirred by reports that the Jews had tortured and killed him for his blood, and sacked the Jewish homes of Folkchany, murdering a number of Jews before the police belatedly arrived. What *L'Univers* and the other papers failed to report, however, was that investigators had discovered that the boy had been killed by his uncle, who was currently awaiting trial in Bucharest.[15]

The notion that Jews regularly captured Christian children in order to drain their blood was widespread in Italy at the time and, while rejected by the small liberal elite, was firmly rooted in the general population, nourished by parish priests, Lenten sermons, and the Catholic press. Two years before Edgardo was taken from Bologna, for example, a Jewish merchant in a small northeastern Italian town was arrested, accused of abducting a 23-year-old Christian servant and of having drained much of her blood for religious purposes. Miraculously, the woman survived to report the crime in the most lurid detail. Indeed, the striking parallels between the story she told and the folk stories prevalent in Europe in the nineteenth century about Dracula-like vampires inevitably raise the question for us of the relation between the two myths. In this case, the Jew's trial revealed that the young woman—no doubt drawing on a combination of these legends—had invented the hair-raising story in order to divert suspicion after she had robbed her employers' home and fled with the loot.[16]

The Church's role in fostering the ritual-murder charge continued long after the Mortara affair. Thirty-five years after the *Civiltà Cattolica* published its influential defense of the taking of Edgardo, for example, it returned to the sanguinary theme in a series of articles about the Jews. "There is no point here in wasting time and words to make clear what everyone already knows—that is, that the Jews are always engaged in harrying and robbing the Christians. Rather, we intend to prove something that many people do not know, and that others find difficult to believe and even try to deny. We refer here to the mystery of the blood." The Jesuit journal went on at gory length to establish the irrefutable proof that the Jews had always made a practice of seizing unsuspecting Christians and taking their blood.[17]

The campaign against the Jews continued, in these later years of the nineteenth century, to be equated by the Church with its battle against liberalism. The liberals' defense of the Jews as having equal rights, and even worse, their doctrine that the state should recognize no religion as superior to another, directly contradicted Church dogma.

In an 1886 article, the *Civiltà Cattolica* took up this theme in characteristic fashion. Under the headline "On Jewish Persecution of Christianity," it set out to demonstrate that "Christians have never persecuted Jews, as the Jews and the Judaized liberals and Freemasons continue to assert falsely, but rather the Jews have always persecuted Christians."[18] A half-dozen years later, the Jesuit journal was still defending the Church's treatment of the Jews as a people in need of special surveillance and restrictions. "What," it asked, "have been the consequences of the emancipation of the Jews in all those countries that have given it? Two, both of them clear, palpable, and doleful: a remorseless, pitiless war against the Christian religion, and especially against Catholicism, and then an unbridled arrogance in usury, monopolies, and a series of thefts of all sorts, to the damage of the very people who gave them their civil liberty." The picture that *Civiltà Cattolica* painted of the Jews was not a pretty one: "For Judaism, brotherhood and peace were and are merely a pretext to be used to prepare—through the extermination of Christianity, if it were possible, and the enfeebling of the Christian nations—for their Messianic kingdom, the dream that the Talmud prophesies for them."[19]

To understand the Catholic reaction to criticism of the Church's treatment of Edgardo Mortara, one must keep in mind this basic attitude toward the Jews and its deep roots in Christian theology. When *L'armonia* ran its first article on the controversy, in August 1858, not only did the author try to link the protests to the antireligious, bomb-throwing revolutionaries—hence the title of the article, "The Jew of Bologna and the Bombs of Giuseppe Mazzini"—but he tapped into this view that it was the Jews who persecuted Christians, not the reverse. "Isn't it ridiculous in the extreme for an Italian and Catholic government [the Kingdom of Sardinia] to take up the cause of a Jew against the Government of the Head of the Church when it should instead be appealing to the foreign powers for aid against that wicked sect that, while trying to subvert the other governments, also continuously undermines the government that tolerates and nourishes it?"[20]

Six weeks later, the Turinese Catholic weekly, returning to the controversy over the Mortara case, defended the Church by arguing that from the most ancient times to the present, popes had always done all they could do to protect the Jews. Yet, the author pointed out, "We must not forget the great wrongs and the true infamies that have stained the Jews' reputation, and the disorders they have caused by the hatred that burns in them against Christianity."[21]

By the time Edgardo was taken to Rome, this centuries-old Church view of the Jews, although still influential, had not entirely withstood the onslaught of the new currents of thought sweeping Europe. One sign of this, of course, was Pius IX's own reforms at the beginning of his papacy, loosening the restrictions under which Rome's Jews lived. But by 1858, Church leaders saw defense of their traditional position on the Jews as an integral part of their more general fight against the liberal and revolutionary threat that faced them. The Jews, small in number as they were, represented a centerpiece of the ideological underpinnings of the Papal States: the need to protect the supremacy of the Church, and the folly of an ideology that treated all religions as equal and thus required a separation between Church and state.

Antonio Gramsci, no friend of the Church, writing from his Fascist jail cell in the 1930s, reflected on the use that the Church had made of the Jews in its battle against the liberal threat. He recounted how, in 1848, when a Jew who had participated in the protests in Turin returned to his hometown, reactionaries spread the tale that he had murdered a Christian child for ritual purposes, leading the peasants to march on the town's small ghetto and sack it. Gramsci concluded: "The reactionaries and the clerics wanted to make it seem as though the liberal innovations of 1848 were an invention of the Jews." To this observation, the imprisoned Communist leader added a note: "I must reconstruct the history of the Mortara boy, which had such a clamorous echo in the polemics against clericalism."[22]

If some in the Church in Italy thought that taking Edgardo and keeping him in the Catechumens were wrong, they kept their opinions to themselves. The Catholic press was unanimous in its support for the Vatican position and merciless in attacking those who criticized it. It was time to unite behind the Pope, not a time to show signs of weakness to the enemy.

Elsewhere in Catholic Europe, a few Church voices were raised in protest. The most significant was that of an obscure French monk, l'abbé Delacouture, whose letters denouncing what the Church had done were given wide circulation in the European press. His writings enraged the Pope's supporters, for he argued, as a priest, that the Vatican had violated the basic principles on which Catholicism rested.

Delacouture's writings on the Mortara case were published in late 1858 in a French pamphlet, and soon thereafter translated into Italian. What prompted him to speak out, he wrote, was the arrogance and presumption of the defenders of the pontifical government in arguing that no true Catholic could hold a contrary view. He would not, he said, allow the enemies of the Catholic faith to believe that the principles being espoused in support of the "kidnapping" of Edgardo were those of Catholicism. It was his task to show the contrary, for if the position of the Pope's supporters was allowed to stand, it would have grave consequences for the Church. "Is there anything in the world," asked Delacouture, "that could make so hateful a religion that is so holy and so beneficial, as does the fact of which we speak?"[23]

Delacouture's argument—a Catholic position clearly influenced by Enlightenment ideals—was based on the supremacy of natural law. Natural law came from the human capacity for reason, a capacity that God had given humankind. And one of the fundamental tenets of natural law, according to the abbot, was that a child belongs to his parents. Natural law has God as its author, and so is superior to all human laws and cannot be countermanded by them.

The abbot expressed another fear about the potential harm to come to the Catholic Church as a result of the position it embraced in the Mortara affair. If the Church claimed the right to seize baptized Jewish children in those lands under Catholic rule, would it not be encouraging those states where other religions were dominant to use force to convert their own Catholic citizens? What would happen to the Catholics living in the Muslim countries, or among the "schismatics" in Greece, or among the Lutherans in Switzerland?[24]

Behind the scenes, Delacouture's superiors tried unsuccessfully to silence him. In a letter of December 19, 1858, Carlo Sacconi, the papal nuncio in Paris, gave Cardinal Antonelli the disquieting news of the publication of Delacouture's booklet: "Having been prevented from having more of his letters on the Mortara affair appear in the *Journal des Débats*, since the Government has imposed silence on the press in dealing with this question or any other religious issue, he has adopted the expedient of publishing a booklet to expound his theses. This work has been placed on sale today." The nuncio enclosed a copy.

"This work of Delacouture," the nuncio reported, "is erroneous, defective, and baseless, just as his letters were. . . . But," he warned, "it may make an even greater impression than those letters did on people with little education, on those who are weak in religious matters." And then there was the question of ecclesiastical discipline, for the abbot had been specifically forbidden to publish anything more on the Mortara case. "With this publication, not only has Delacouture not paid any heed to the specific instructions and warnings given to him by the Curia of this archdiocese . . . but he has acted in clear violation of and disrespect for an order that remains in full effect . . . an order prescribed in keeping with the Laws of the Church, that no member of the clergy can publish a work bearing on ecclesiastical matters without having first given it to the Archbishop for him to censor."

In concluding his letter to Cardinal Antonelli, the nuncio expressed doubt that the local Church authorities "will have the courage to take severe measures against him." From the nuncio's point of view, the Parisian Church authorities were being overly indulgent.[25]

If the Archbishop of Paris was less than eager to impose sanctions on the rebellious abbot, he might well be forgiven. Less than two years earlier, his predecessor, Monsignor Sibour, approved of the disciplining of a priest for preaching against Church teachings (the renegade disputed the doctrine of the Immaculate Conception of Mary). On January 3, 1857, Father Vergès, believing that God was on his side, surprised the Archbishop as he was presiding over a ceremony in a Parisian church and planted a dagger in his heart. Monsignor Sibour died within minutes. When questioned, the clerical assassin explained that he was protesting the Archbishop's decision to silence him, although, he added, he meant "nothing personal" by his action.[26]

At the end of December, the Secretary of State sent his reply. After thanking the nuncio for sending him a copy of the "reprehensible booklet," he recommended action. Sharing Sacconi's concern that the Parisian Church hierarchy might be disposed to be too forgiving, Antonelli told him to give the Curia a push in the right direction. "Make them realize the unseemly and scandalous consequences that naturally follow when cases of such transgressions remain unpunished."[27]

Cardinal Antonelli could not have been pleased at the reply he received the following month. You must, Sacconi wrote, have already read with amazement "Abbot Delacouture's letter of the fourth of this month to the *Union* and reported in the *Presse* on the seventh, and in other newspapers." In his letter, the abbot declared "that the instructions he received from the ecclesiastical authorities regarding his publications on the Mortara affair did not address the substance of the matter but only whether his publications were opportune at this time ... Encouraged by the *significant*"—and here Archbishop Sacconi underlined "significant"—"silence of the ecclesiastical authorities, he even dared to send a new insolent letter, dated the twelfth, to the *Presse,* which was carried on the seventeenth."[28] It appears that Church authorities were at last able to silence the rebellious monk, but only after the damage had been done.

Fortunately for the Secretary of State, however, the abbot's voice was a lonely one. In Italy, Delacouture would be hard pressed to find a clerical soul mate.

CHAPTER 15

A Matter of Principle

MOMOLO MORTARA and those around him—both the Jews and the gentiles he knew, from the family doctor, Pasquale Saragoni, to his friend, the former judge Carlo Maggi—were all, to one extent or another, products of the Enlightenment. The influence of the French, who had occupied Emilia and Romagna for the better part of two decades, remained strong. To people in Momolo and Marianna's circle, belief in the power of reason, the inevitability of progress, and the equality of all citizens was nearly universal. The beliefs that tradition, rather than reason or the consent of the governed, formed the proper basis for authority; that the world, as God's creation, would not change until the millennium came; and that inequality was divinely ordained—these were part of the old, archaic worldview, a vestige of medieval times.

In the months following his son's forced departure, while angry denunciations and counterdenunciations filled the European press, Momolo himself avoided saying anything critical of the Church, the Pope, or the Secretary of State. His goal was clear, as were his methods. Edgardo's freedom would be won by marshaling evidence to prove that the Church had made a mistake in taking his son. Momolo had been assured early on by Cardinal Antonelli that any evidence he produced would be carefully considered and that the Church leaders were eager to ensure that justice was done. Momolo was also encouraged by the fact that the Secretary of State had received him and been so cordial. In the past, a simple Jewish storekeeper would never have merited such treatment.

The leaders of Rome's Università Israelitica reinforced this outlook. The Rome ghetto remained an island of traditional authority. When disaster befell a Jew as a result of the action of the Church or the pontifical state, the proper response was for the Jewish community to prepare a formal request for relief that would then be presented to Church authorities. The request should take a certain form: it should show respect and humility in the face of the Church's awesome power; it should cite Church doctrine and the time-honored writings of the foremost Church authorities; it should discuss precedents of Church decisions that supported the case; it should point out any particular features of the case at hand that put it in a more favorable light; it should proclaim the unshakable allegiance of the Jews to the papal government; and it should appeal to the charitable nature of the Catholic religion and the kindheartedness of the Pope.

This style was on display in all of the supplications made on the Mortaras' behalf, including the most important of these, the Pro-memoria and Syllabus delivered to Cardinal Antonelli at the beginning of September 1858, addressed to the Pope. Following a cover letter effusive in its praise of the Pontiff, the Pro-memoria recounted the facts of the case, facts which, the Mortaras and their supporters hoped, would show that the Church had erred in seizing Edgardo. A seven-page section written in Latin cited the works of various Church authorities in support of the case for freeing the boy. The Promemoria then returned to Italian, recalling various similar instances in which the Church had decided to allow baptized children to remain with their Jewish parents. Three appendices were included: Edgardo's birth certificate, Pasquale Saragoni's medical report certifying that Edgardo's illness was not life-threatening, and the text of a favorable 1639 Church decision in a case of forced baptism.

The Pro-memoria introduced the main document, the Syllabus, a fifty-page work in Latin, citing Church authorities to show why Church dogma dictated the boy's return to his family. This was the work that the Jews of Bologna had despaired of preparing. To persuade the Church to release Edgardo, they believed, it was necessary to show that ecclesiastical law and precedent were on their side, and this could be done only by experts in ecclesiastical law and Church history. Just who prepared the Latin document remains a mystery. In Scazzocchio's correspondence, he refers to their expert advisor with great circumspection, shielding his identity from the eyes of papal censors. The Pope himself later speculated that the Jews had had the help of some renegade priest, for who else could be so knowledgeable of canon law and Church precedent, and capable of writing a Latin text?

It is likely that the Jews did have such help, but we cannot take it for granted. Italy's Jews had become, by sad necessity, expert in canon law on matters affecting them, and especially on the question of forced baptism, the major communities regularly exchanged documents. As a result, the archives of these communities throughout the peninsula overflowed with lengthy extracts from relevant ecclesiastical legal sources and detailed descriptions of previous cases of forced baptism, Jewish protest, and Church response. Indeed, one of the first actions Scazzocchio had taken on behalf of the Mortaras, earlier in the summer, was to write to the representatives of the major Jewish communities in the Papal States, asking them to dig through their files and send him copies of any documents from forced-baptism cases that might prove useful in preparing the Syllabus.

The Syllabus began with a presentation of rulings of various popes in support of the Jews' position, beginning with Pope Clement III in the twelfth century. It next extracted passages from the writings of various other Church authorities over the centuries and then used these to argue that the Church had long opposed the baptism of small children without their parents' consent, that such baptisms were therefore invalid, and that even when Jewish children were deemed to have received a valid baptism, there was ample precedent for allowing them to be raised by their parents.[1]

The star witness in the Syllabus was Thomas Aquinas, who argued that a son should be considered a part of his father and under his authority. Saint Thomas addressed the issue of forced baptisms of Jewish children directly, saying that the Church had always opposed the practice. Among the reasons he cited for this opposition was the danger of apostasy, because baptized children, in such circumstances, would naturally feel sympathy for their parents and so continue to cling to Judaism.

But though the Church could be shown to oppose these forced baptisms, does it necessarily follow that no baptismal ceremony performed on Edgardo could have been valid? Here the question was more complicated. The Syllabus covered various bases, first arguing that forced baptisms were ipso facto invalid, but then giving ecclesiastical grounds for believing that the particular circumstances of Edgardo's baptism rendered it invalid. For a baptism to be valid, the Syllabus argued, the person baptized must give consent, must want to be baptized. In the case of the small child, where the age of reason had not yet been reached, this consent was the sole property of the father. If the father did not consent, then it was as if the child did not consent. Various Church authorities were cited in support of the further argument that, even in the case of small children at death's door, the father's consent was required for a valid baptism. And should Edgardo not, in fact, have been in imminent danger of death, the Syllabus argued, canon law provided that only a priest could perform a valid baptism, for it was only in the case of the urgent need to baptize a person who was dying that the laity were permitted to take the priest's place.

Finally, the Syllabus cited numerous cases to show that even when Jewish children were baptized, their parents did not lose their right to raise them.

Here, a number of precedents were mentioned, beginning with a case from 1547 and ending with one that was potentially the most important, both because it was so recent and because it had occurred in the Papal States. The case involved a baby born near Rome in 1840 to a French Jewish couple named Montel. Although the infant had been secretly baptized, the parents, following an investigation by the Church, had been allowed to keep her.

The Pope was not impressed by the Jews' argument. The very idea that Jews would try to tell him what the fathers of the Church had to say, and instruct him in the basics of canon law and ecclesiastical precedent, was deeply offensive to him. He directed his legal advisors to prepare a response to the petition, one that would demolish the Jews' case and demonstrate that Church law and, more important, the word of Jesus himself would not permit him to release Edgardo.

The resulting Church document was not aimed primarily at furnishing the Mortara family and the Jews of the Papal States with a response to their plea. There was no need to go to such trouble. But given the building international controversy and the uncomfortable pressures being directed at the Pope to change his mind, Cardinal Antonelli thought the Holy See needed to lay out the bases for its position, and the Pope himself was eager to show the fallacy of the arguments being made by his critics. Friends of the Church throughout Europe were pressing the Vatican for just such a document to help them mount a more effective defense.

The result, in mid–October, was a thirty-four-page document titled *Brevi cenni . . .* , "A brief explanation and reflections on the pro-memoria and syllabus humbly presented to His Holiness, Pope Pius IX, concerning the baptism conferred in Bologna on the child Edgardo, son of the Jews Salomone and Marianna Mortara." Bound with the Mortaras' Pro-memoria and Syllabus, it was distributed by Cardinal Antonelli on October 23 to papal nuncios and representatives throughout Europe, as well as in Brazil, Panama, Bogotá, and Mexico. Antonelli's cover letter explained that the document provided a refutation of the arguments found in the Jews' Pro-memoria and Syllabus. He expressed confidence that, with *Brevi cenni* in hand, the nuncios would be "in a position to speak when necessary with the full possession of the material needed to correct the ideas others have of a fact about which those who are in the habit of looking for every occasion for spreading hatred toward the Holy See have caused such an unpleasant and harmful uproar."[2] The Church document was subsequently made available to Catholic newspapers throughout Europe, to employ in their own counteroffensive.[3]

The Vatican response began by explaining the nature of the case. Its choice of phrasing did not bode well for the Mortaras' side: "The parents of a child who was singularly granted Divine Grace, which, having removed him from the blind Judaic obstinacy, made him by chance a son of the Church, have petitioned and brought action all the way to the august throne of the Holy Father in order to get back their son, who has already been placed in the bosom of the Church." The document continued: "What is more, these parents make their plea not simply with the usual appearance of humble supplicants, but with the outspokenness of those who believe themselves oppressed by an arbitrary act, asking that they receive justice, and that the object of which they think they have been unlawfully deprived be returned to them." Especially outrageous, in the authors' view, were the Jews' attempts "to prove with authorities and arguments deriving from [canon] law that the Mortara couple have been the victims of an offense against them." Examination of the works of the authorities cited in the Mortaras' brief would reveal that they supported no such conclusion.

It is indeed true, *Brevi cenni* stated, that the Church had always opposed baptizing the children of infidels against their parents' wishes. However, Church theologians and canon law had long recognized certain exceptions to this general principle, and one of them was operative in the case at hand, for "it is permissible to baptize those children who find themselves near death."[4]

As for the Church opposition to the baptism of Jewish children in the absence of consent, the Mortara plea was based on a misunderstanding. The fact that a baptized Jewish child who remained with his parents would be in grave danger of apostasy was, it is true, an argument against performing such baptisms. But the implication of this argument was precisely the opposite of that drawn by the Jews: it was just because of this danger that baptized children could not be allowed to remain with their Jewish parents. Recognizing that force would be required to remove such children from their parents, the Church had tried to prevent such baptism; nonetheless, once it has been conferred on an infidel child, "the Church recognizes it as valid, enters in control of its new son, and adopts every means, every care to distance him from the faithlessness of his parents and to nourish him and raise him in the grace of Jesus Christ."[5] The Vatican brief continued: "In fact, the Canonists and Theologians are in full agreement with this truth: that in no case should a baptized child be returned to infidel parents." Between the two competing authorities—that of God and that of the parents—God's must prevail, for was He not the author of the natural rights that parents enjoyed? The right "acquired by the Church over the baptized infant is of a superior and more noble order" than that of the parents.[6]

Since a baptized child could not remain with Jewish parents, the only question was whether Edgardo had been properly baptized. "Nothing more is required for the validity of the baptism than that the rite be performed according to the proper form with a suitable subject, such as even a newborn child can be, and it may be performed by anybody as long as he intends to do what the Church intends." Moreover, "The parents' approval has never been required for children who have not yet reached the age of reason for the rite to be valid."[7]

The Mortaras' other attempts to throw doubt on the validity of Edgardo's baptism were likewise dismissed. The notion that, to demonstrate that a valid baptism had been performed, it was necessary to have a witness other than the baptizer had no support in canon law. "That even a woman can be the single witness whose testimony demonstrates that a Jewish child has been baptized, especially in the case of imminent death, has been the unanimous opinion of all the Theologians and Canonists."[8]

The document made known, for the first time, how it was that news of the baptism had first reached the Inquisitor. In July, Anna Morisi had told the Mortara brothers-in-law that she had not reported what she had done to any priest or nun. It came as a shock to her, she said, when she received the summons to appear at the Inquisitor's court. The only person she had told, she claimed, was a friend, an older servant named Regina. If the Inquisitor found out, it must be because Regina had told him.

According to *Brevi cenni*, the matter came to the Church's attention through the report of a different woman: "In fact, there is in the official record a formal statement by Marianna Bajesi, an unmarried Bolognese woman forty years old, who, out of conscience, testified that she had heard from a number of individuals, whom she names, that a certain woman named Regina, aged seventy, had suggested to Anna Morisi, the servant of the Jewish family Mortara, that she baptize a boy of that family, who was in danger of death (and who in fact died)." To this suggestion, Anna "responded that she would not want to do it again, because in a situation of similar danger [of death] she had once baptized another son of the Mortaras, who it turns out did not die, and who, now around seven years old, was indeed still alive." In short, it seems that Anna had told Regina, who then had gossiped about the case of the baptized boy with friends and neighbors, one of whom was Marianna Bajesi.[9]

Having received this report, Bologna's inquisitor informed the Holy Office of the Inquisition in Rome, which ordered an investigation. Summoned to testify, Anna Morisi, after taking a solemn oath, told the whole story, stating that when she sprinkled the water over Edgardo's head, "SHE INTENDED TO BAPTIZE HIM ACCORDING TO THE CUSTOM OF THE CHURCH in order to restore a soul to God, and that she did it out of fear that his soul would be lost." After carefully examining the testimony, Church authorities had determined that it had "all the earmarks of the truth without leaving the least doubt about the reality and the validity of the baptism she performed."[10]

All these considerations of Church law, ecclesiastical precedent, and the facts of the case led to the Vatican's conclusions. "In the whole affair surrounding Edgardo, baptized son of Salomone Mortara, the Holy See has not in the least way violated the paternal rights of the Jews who are his parents." Five conclusions, corresponding to the five points on which the Mortara appeal had been based, were then listed.

First, "the Church has always prohibited the baptism of Jewish children in the absence of parental consent." This policy was designed to protect the parents' natural right to care for their children, and to avoid exposing the individual baptized, once he or she became an adult, to apostasy.

Second, if, despite this policy, it happened that a Jewish infant was baptized in the absence of parental consent, "the baptism is valid, and in some cases licit as well." It was valid if the proper form was used and if the person performing the baptism had the intention of doing what the Church intends to do in baptism. For young children who are baptized, "no intention [on their part] is necessary."

Third, "God has given the Church the power and the right to take possession of the baptized children of infidels in order to protect in them the sanctity of what they have received, and to nourish them for eternal life."

Fourth, in the specific case of Edgardo Mortara, the Holy See was fully justified in taking possession of the child, and in doing so had done no damage to paternal rights, "which must give way and be subordinated to that of the Church."

The fifth and final point regarded Edgardo's own behavior: "What finally proves the reality and the validity of the baptism that was conferred is that Edgardo Mortara has become son of redemption and of grace, son of the Church, son of the Supreme Father of the Faithful Pius IX, for, as Edgardo himself has expressed it: 'I AM BAPTIZED—MY FATHER IS THE POPE' "[11]

The Vatican's response to the weighty brief prepared by Rome's Jews, with its compendium of Church authorities and its Latin text, ended then with an argument not from law but from God Himself, speaking through the boy: "These words that the supreme light of the baptismal Faith and divine Grace placed on the innocent and sanctified lips of young Edgardo were not vain nor sterile. . . . This young boy was thus illuminated by the Faith infused on his forehead and lit up by the charity of Jesus Christ that seeps into his heart. He is now fully realizing the spiritual benefit received by his baptismal regeneration." Having passed his seventh birthday—celebrated two months after he had been taken from his parents' home—meant that Edgardo was in possession of his own powers of reason, for the seventh birthday had long been established in canon law as the point at which a child acquired this faculty. This power allowed him "to confirm how much Divine Mercy had already operated on him with the Sacrament of regeneration. He declares that he wants to be and to remain a Christian."

The Church authorities drew the obvious conclusion. "It would work against all notions of fairness and personal justice, against all natural and Divine right, if this son of grace were to be returned to the power of his infidel parents and thereby consigned to the next opportunity for his perversion and his death. Ah, yes! such unjust and cruel sentiments can be found only in the hearts of those lacking in faith and charity!"[12]

Two specific cases of forced baptism cited in the Mortaras' brief prompted vigorous rebuttals from the Vatican. The first came from Ferrara in 1785. The second was the case of the French baby born near Rome in 1840. Both are revealing of Church attitudes on the baptism of Jewish children.

In November 1785, the Archbishop of Ferrara received a report that a woman of the city's ghetto, Regina Bianchini, had been secretly baptized many years before. This was a rather delicate case for the Archbishop, because Regina was the wife of one of the most prosperous and influential Jews in a city known for its large and flourishing ghetto. She was reported to have been only three years old when, over two decades before, she had been baptized. The alleged baptizer was at the time only six years old herself.

Francesca Vandelli, whose tale of precocious baptism had come to the Archbishop's attention, was summoned to his court to testify and told the following story: One day, when she was just six years old, she happened to be at a neighbor's home where an infant lay dying. Seeing that the boy had little time left, the doctor sprinkled water over him, pronouncing the baptismal formula. He explained to little Francesca that by baptizing the boy, he was sending him to heaven. Soon thereafter, Francesca was outside playing with her 3-year-old friend Regina. Knowing that Regina was a Jew and that Jews were not baptized, she told her that since she had not been baptized, she would not go to heaven. Upset, Regina responded that she wanted to go to heaven too. Francesca replied that she would first have to learn what Christians had to know, and she then proceeded, as best she could, to teach her little playmate to recite the Mystery of the Holy Trinity. Once Regina repeated this to her satisfaction, Francesca sprinkled some water over her head and repeated the words she had heard the doctor say over the dying boy.

When asked why, after all these years, she had come forward to tell her tale, Francesca said that the memory of what she had done that day had been tormenting her for years. She decided as a matter of conscience to do her duty and report it. Cardinal Alessandro Mattei, Archbishop of Ferrara, was impressed by the woman's account but also troubled, not knowing how much to credit the decades-later recollection about an action she supposedly performed as a 6-year-old. He decided to ask some local theological experts for advice and to begin some fact-finding efforts of his own. Once he had collected all the information he could, he would contact the Holy Office in Rome.

On November 24, the Cardinal sent his chancellor into the ghetto to summon Regina and her husband, Leone. On the Bianchinis' arrival at his palace, Cardinal Mattei told Leone that his wife would have to remain there for a few days while a certain matter was cleared up. Leone protested that Regina was pregnant and due to give birth before long. The Archbishop assured him that his wife would be well taken care of, and he was sent off.

Cardinal Mattei then informed Regina of why she had been called to appear. Alarmed and indignant, she replied that she did not want to stay at the palace; she wanted to go home. She had been born a Jew and had no desire to be anything else. Hardly surprised by her reaction, the Archbishop told her that there was nothing to be done, and gave the orders to prepare a separate apartment for her, making it as comfortable as possible.[13]

While Regina remained at the palace, her testimony and that of her putative baptizer were sent to the Holy Office of the Inquisition in Rome. From the Archbishop's perspective, the case was ticklish, turning on two questions. First of all, did the 6-year-old Francesca follow the proper baptismal form? The Church tolerated no deviation from the approved rite. Second, did she have the proper intent? Could a 6-year-old be said to have intent, properly speaking, at all?

There was a considerable body of Church writing that employed the seventh birthday as the point when a child could be said to acquire the use of reason. Yet the evidence that the Archbishop had gathered led him to wonder whether this criterion might not be overly arbitrary. After all, at the time of the baptism, Francesca had been near her seventh birthday, and reports suggested that she had been an especially lively little girl. Moreover, it was known that girls were normally more serious than boys and more obedient. They were also more prone to be good, and the faculty of reason and use of good judgment developed earlier in them. Wasn't this recognized by both Church and civil law in allowing girls to marry at age 12 while setting the minimum age for boys at 14? All in all, if boys could be said to have the use of reason by their seventh birthday, was it implausible that a girl might reach this level of judgment a few months earlier? Moreover, since the judgment in question concerned the ability of the person performing the baptism to have the proper intent, didn't Francesca's testimony offer convincing evidence that her intent was exactly that of the Church: her desire to see her Jewish playmate saved by becoming Christian, allowing her soul to enjoy eternal blessings?

On December 6, 1785, the Congregation of the Holy Office met in Rome to discuss the case. There was no firm ground for dismissing the possibility that Regina had been baptized. If she had, and should she return to her life as a Jew, she would be committing apostasy, a grave form of heresy with appalling consequences.

The cardinals came to a decision: the evidence was inconclusive. They were not prepared to rule that the 6-year-old had been incapable of administering a valid baptism. On the other hand, there was some reason for doubt as to whether she had performed the rite as required, in precisely the correct way. Signora Bianchini should, therefore, be returned home.[14]

The Bianchini case was cited in the Mortaras' brief to the Pope to show that reports that a Jewish child had been baptized, when made years after the fact, were not necessarily to be believed. In its response, the Vatican argued that the brief had misrepresented the case, for the Bianchini decision was simply based on a finding that, in this particular instance, there was strong reason to doubt the accuracy of the alleged baptizer's story. *Brevi cenni* reported that the archives of the Holy Office revealed something the Jews apparently did not know: shortly before coming forward with her account, Francesca Vandelli had suffered from mental illness, and one of her symptoms had been frequent delusions. Had the woman been of sound mind, and her account therefore been credible, the Church would have taken very different action.[15]

The single most important case cited in the Mortaras' brief, however, involved the French family who had been traveling near Rome when their baby was born. The Montel case was used to argue that it was not against Church law to return baptized children to their Jewish parents. What made it so weighty, in the Jews' eyes, was not only its recentness, but the fact that it had been decided by Pius IX's immediate predecessor, Gregory XVI, a pontiff famous for his religious orthodoxy and not noted for great sympathy for the Jews.

According to *Brevi cenni*, however, the Jews had gotten the Montel case all wrong. The Vatican told a very different story: the tale of a Jewish baby, a meddling chambermaid, a French count, the Secretary of State, and the Pope himself.

In June 1840, the Jewish couple, Daniele Montel of Nîmes and his wife, Miette Cremieux, landed at the harbor of Fiumicino. No sooner had they disembarked than Miette felt the first pangs of labor, an unwelcome surprise, since she had not expected to give birth until they reached Malta, their destination. They found a hotel room, where a midwife delivered a baby girl. A chambermaid, fearing that the baby might not survive—or so she said, for no evidence in support of her claim was ever produced—entered the room and, when no one was looking, baptized the girl. Unaware of what had happened, the Montels decided not to reboard, a fateful decision, and took their child to Rome instead. The baptism soon came to the attention of a Fiumicino priest, triggering an ecclesiastical investigation. "Orders were given to have the baptized girl's parents placed under surveillance," *Brevi cenni* recounted, "for the girl's personal safety." There was no telling what the distraught Jews—having discovered what was afoot—might do to their little girl. On July 1, the Holy Office issued its decision: a valid baptism had been performed. The order was given to seize the baby and place her in Rome's House of the Catechumens.

The French couple had by this time already sought help from the French embassy in Rome, pleading that Roman officials had no right to take their child because they were French subjects. The French representative to the Holy See, Count de Rayneval, "argued this point strenuously with Pope Gregory XVI but was able to obtain nothing for the Jewish parents, for the Pontiff's Sacred Duty would not allow it." The Pope had a higher obligation, for he was bound by God to care for "the eternal welfare of that soul which had been regenerated by divine grace." The French chargé d'affaires, however, "assured the Holy See, with an official act in the name of His Royal Government, that, were the Montel-Cremieux girl to be entrusted to his Government, of which she was a subject, the government would pledge to raise her in the Catholic religion and become responsible before God for doing so. Thus, under these express conditions, the Holy Father ordered the baptized girl given to the same Signor Representative and never returned to her Jewish parents." The proper lesson to be drawn from the handling of the Montel affair, according to *Brevi cenni*, was quite the opposite of what the Jews had argued. The case provided "new proof to conclude that the Holy See has never tolerated that the children of Jews, once baptized, remain in their parents' power."[16]

Was it true that the Montels never got to see their daughter again? Although the *Brevi cenni* account was never contested by the Mortaras or their supporters in Rome, it turns out that in some crucial respects it was misleading. Fortunately, the diplomatic correspondence between Count Alphonse de Rayneval, the young French chargé d'affaires to the Holy See, and Louis-Adolphe Thiers, president of the Council of Ministers in Paris, has been preserved. It offers a very different view of the case.

As *Brevi cenni* reported, in early June the Montels had disembarked at Fiumicino, where Miette soon gave birth to a daughter. A few days later they went to Rome. There, on the evening of June 17, a police officer, with a group of carabinieri in tow, appeared at their door and ordered Montel to hand over his daughter, "on the pretext that she had been baptized and, as a result, she could not remain in the hands of persons who were not of the Catholic religion."[17] Montel, horrified, insisted that his daughter had never been baptized and at last persuaded the police not to take the infant without first verifying their report. The officer left, but—and here images of the police visit to the Mortara home eighteen years later are hard to avoid—two carabinieri were left behind to make sure that the parents did not try to flee with their baby.

Montel rushed immediately to the French embassy, where he was received by Count de Rayneval. Alarmed at what he heard, the Count turned to his old friend Monsignor Capaccini, formerly a papal nuncio to various European countries but now based in Rome. Capaccini, whom Rayneval knew to be a levelheaded and sophisticated man, looked into the matter and reported back that a Vatican investigation into the alleged baptism was under way. "If it turns out that the sacrament was administered correctly," he informed the French diplomat, "it would be impossible, following canon laws, to allow a Christian child to remain with its Jewish parents."[18]

Having learned this much, Rayneval wrote to the Secretary of State, Cardinal Lambruschini, pleading the Montels' case. The Count's main argument was not likely to have been to the reactionary Cardinal's liking. For the French government, Rayneval wrote, all citizens were equal before the law, regardless of their religion; consequently, he could only view Montel "as a French citizen whose most sacred rights were being injured."

The Cardinal, in his reply, expressed regret over the Count's discomfort and reported that he had discussed the matter with the Pope himself. He assured the Count that a thorough inquiry would be made and that the woman who baptized the baby would be arrested and punished, unless she could produce a convincing reason to justify what she had done. She would also be interrogated as to just how she had performed the rite. A report of the interrogation would be sent to the Holy Office, which would then decide if the baptism was valid. Should the Holy Office find that it had not been properly performed, the child would be free to remain with her parents. However, should they determine that the woman had administered a valid baptism, the Cardinal reported, "the child will be raised, until she reaches the age of reason, far from her parents in Rome."[19]

Rayneval told Minister Thiers in his report to Paris that he had tried everything to persuade the Cardinal to change his mind but could not get him to budge. Meanwhile, Montel had gone to consult with the chief rabbi in Rome, but the rabbi's words were discouraging. The situation looked bleak, and the French chargé d'affaires sought guidance from Paris.

On July 8, the Minister sent his reply: "The conduct of the Holy See toward Monsieur Montel wounds the principles of international law no less than those of freedom of conscience." The Pope, the letter continued, was ignoring "the inviolable laws of nature and of equality, the sacred rights of man and the rights of a father. . . . Monsieur Montel is not, strictly speaking, a Jew for us, but a French citizen who should be treated in the Papal States as the equal of his fellow citizens." Therefore, the Minister concluded, France could not accept the rationale provided to the Count by the Secretary of State. Rayneval was directed to make immediate arrangements to have the Montels and their daughter sent directly back to France and to address a letter to the pontifical government demanding that the child be allowed to return to the *patrie.*[20]

On July 17, Count de Rayneval wrote back to Minister Thiers, letting him know that the Holy Office had, indeed, declared the baptism of the Montel girl to be valid. All his pleas had been rebuffed, and the Count had begun to despair of persuading the Holy See to change its mind. However, he reported, by redoubling his efforts, and with the considerable assistance of the enlightened Monsignor Capaccini, he was able to make the Secretary of State realize how much political damage would be caused by keeping the French child, and a way out of the impasse had been devised.

"The Cardinal Secretary of State has informed me that the Holy Father could not in good conscience return a child who had become Christian to her infidel parents." Yet the Pope recognized the strength of French feelings on the matter. "Wishing to give the King's government proof of its confidence," the Count reported, the Pope "will put the child at my disposition as long as I give a vow that she will be raised in the Catholic religion, thus discharging the duties of his conscience." Rayneval informed the French minister that because this solution would allow him to send the child and her parents wherever he pleased, he had accepted the Cardinal's offer.

That the Holy See must have known what would happen to the child, should she be permitted to return to France, was evident to the Count, who wrote that he had on many occasions told them that "the King's government does not have the power to make a Frenchman raise a child in a religion different from his own." The assurances he had to give would merely allow the Church to observe proper form, for "it was clear that the Holy See was looking for a way to protect its conscience behind words. I thus agreed to respond as they asked me to."

Before he could get the ministry's reactions, Rayneval had to act. Receiving the July 18 letter from Cardinal Lambruschini setting out the Church's terms for the agreement, the young Count, on July 21, sent his carefully worded reply: "I have no doubt that the King's government will take care that it will be thus, and I am persuaded that it will employ, toward that end, all possible means. I dare to hope that, as a result, you will soon go ahead with the conciliatory intentions that you expressed to me and which the King's government will certainly view as new testimony of the sentiments of His Holiness."[21]

Count de Rayneval was uncomfortable about what he had done, for it seemed to go against the instructions he had received and might be perceived by his superiors in Paris as not properly upholding the honor of the French government. He thus concluded his letter somewhat defensively: "I believe

that this solution, given the ideas that they have that it is an absolute obligation for the Holy See to ensure a Catholic education for the child, is the best
that one could reasonably hope for, and I ardently hope that it receives Your
Excellency's approval."[22]

On July 27, the Count wrote his last report to the French ministry on the
case. The pontifical government had released the infant to him, and he had
immediately returned her to her mother. On the twenty-fourth, mother and
baby boarded a boat for Malta, where Montel was waiting for them.

To this report Rayneval appended the text of Cardinal Lambruschini's
letter of July 18, in which the findings of the Holy Office investigation into the
baptism and the agreement reached with the French representative were set
out. The Holy Office had decided that the child should be removed from her
parents and placed in the House of the Catechumens. However, because the
case involved subjects of the French king, the Pope, "wanting to demonstrate
to His Majesty and to the royal Minister his full confidence in the loyalty of
the French government, is disposed to release this girl, now baptized, to Your
Lordship, provided that in the name of your government you will assure the
Holy See that the said government commits itself to raising her in the Catholic
religion." The Secretary of State's letter went on to emphasize that "the matter
is of such great importance to the Holy Father's conscience that, without this
condition, he would not be able to allow the release of this child."[23]

In taking stock of the whole affair, Rayneval recalled that he had had two
goals: "to return the child to her parents, and to avoid creating any serious
conflict between the two governments." It had not been easy. The French
chargé d'affaires, a member of a diplomatic and aristocratic family—his father
had been French ambassador to Spain—was only 27 years old. Cardinal Lambruschini, famous for his intransigent faith, held out against any compromise.
It had taken ten long meetings between Monsignor Capaccini and the Secretary of State, in addition to the Count's own meetings, to convince the Cardinal. The Secretary of State was concerned about the precedent that might be
set; for him the Church's right and indeed obligation to keep baptized Jewish
children away from their parents was absolute. "I have to observe, apropos of
this affair," the Count concluded, "that the hatred and contempt for the
Jewish race, even on the part of the most enlightened souls here, remain in full
force."[24]

The actual outcome of the Montel case was, then, the reunification of a
baptized baby with her Jewish parents. But even if those who prepared the
brief for Rome's Università Israelitica in 1858 had known all the details, it
would have done them little good. If the child had been returned to her parents, the Vatican could rightly argue, it had been despite the Holy See's
explicit instructions to the contrary. If there had been any slippage, it was the
fault not of the Church but of the untrustworthy French.

Those who met with Pius IX to discuss the Mortara case were struck by how animated he became when the subject came up, and reported his lament that in the matter he was being vilified for doing what was right, for doing his sacred duty. One of the stories that raced through political circles in Rome following the Duke de Gramont's stormy audience with the Pope on the Mortara affair, described a pained pope pointing to the image of Jesus on a crucifix on the wall behind him and saying, "That one there will defend me."[25] And to the ambassador from the kingdom of the Two Sicilies—an unlikely Mortara protester, since the kingdom had banished Jews entirely three centuries before—Pius IX is said to have replied, "I know what my duty is in the matter, and God willing, I will let them cut off my hand rather than be found wanting."[26]

The Pope was not above a conspiratorial view of the forces lined up against him. No organized opposition to papal rule was permitted in the Papal States, and so he had some grounds to worry about conspiracies, which from the time the Restoration began had plagued the papacy. Those opposed to the temporal power of the pope were not only branded agents of the devil but cast together in one large, godless cabal run by the Freemasons. A *Civiltà Cattolica* article illustrates the Pope's thinking. The minister of a great power, the journal reported, had come to plead for Edgardo Mortara's return to his parents "in the name of the needs of modern society." "What you call modern society," the Pope replied, "is simply Freemasonry."[27]

In this struggle between good and evil, Pius IX's principled stand in opposing Edgardo's release fed the adulatory cult that developed around him, a cult that would continue to grow despite—or perhaps because of—the many political reverses that the Pope and the Church suffered in the years ahead. A typical hagiographical biography, written by a Frenchman a decade after the Mortara affair, depicts an embattled leader, unbending in his commitment to the eternal truths of the Catholic faith, waging war against the devil's forces. The Mortara case is cited in this context as one of the triumphal examples of the Pope's commitment to principle over expediency: "To the strongest outbursts of evil against him, Pius IX never stopped showing an unshakable confidence in the promises of the divine Founder of the Church. One day he told Monsieur de Gramont, the French ambassador, pointing to the ivory crucifix on his work table, 'I rely only on the One there.'" And the biographer continued: "During the affair of the young Mortara, he told a French priest: 'Many men with good intentions but with little faith have written to console me. They tell me that I must be really frightened and terribly unhappy.' Then, he adds, with a sweet smile [referring to himself in the third person]: *Ipse vero dormiebat* (Yet he slept well)." And his biographer concluded: "The Pope understood how his divine Master had been able to go peacefully to sleep in the middle of the storm that tossed the boat of the apostles."[28]

Louis Veuillot, publisher of the Catholic newspaper *L'Univers*, painted a similar picture of the heroic, embattled pope. On February 23, 1859, during his visit to Rome, Veuillot met with the Pope, who wanted to talk about the dangers that the Church faced. "He said that he felt calm and had no fear, but that all he could see were all the blows being aimed at him, from England, Italy, Germany, and even Russia." Pius IX told the French journalist that he would risk his life to defend the papacy's temporal rule, "because temporal power is necessary for the Church's full freedom, and the full freedom of the Church is necessary for all Catholic society and for all humankind." Painfully aware of the superior political strength of the forces lining up against him, the Pope ruminated: "Undoubtedly, order will one day be restored. But after how much time? and at the cost of what catastrophes!"

It was then that the subject of Edgardo Mortara came up. The Pontiff, Veuillot reported, recalled "that during all the hubbub raised on that occasion by the freethinkers, the disciples of Rousseau and Malthus, we steadfastly sustained the cause and the right of the Church." He went on about the deplorable ignorance that was revealed among many Christians, "who seemed no longer to know the character, obligations, and divine privileges that came with baptism. . . . Many lies were propagated, many mistaken facts and erroneous doctrines. The ministers of various powers were hardly any better than the journalists. They stated a number of useless propositions which simply betrayed the ignorance of those who advanced them."

Rather than seeing Edgardo's capture and the decision to hold on to him as demonstrating the Church's continued ability to bring the powers of coercion to bear in the substantial lands under its control, the Pope drew the opposite conclusion. The case showed the triumph of spiritual principle over those who held the power of arms. He used a parable to explain his thinking: "If a very powerful sovereign came and told the Pope, 'Pay me millions!' the Pope, to avoid greater misfortunes, would go along, asking God not to demand later too severe a reckoning for the plunderer. But when someone tells the Pope, 'Give me a soul!' all the force in the world could not make him consent. There is no danger so great that it would make him give in, because the Vicar of Jesus Christ has nothing more precious than the souls who belong to Jesus Christ." What was being demanded, in Pius IX's eyes, was the soul of a little Jewish boy from Bologna. He would not give in, though the costs, he knew, would be high.[29]

Each year, shortly after New Year's, it was the Pope's custom to receive a delegation from the Roman Jewish community, the officers of the Università Israelitica. It was a tradition that went back centuries, with roots in the annual homage paid by the Jews to the emperor of Rome. The first recorded meeting between Rome's Jews and a pope dates from 1119, but the practice had long been in abeyance before Pope Leo XII resuscitated it in 1827.[30]

The Jews who went to see Pius IX each year had learned that the nature of their encounter depended entirely on the Pope's mood. The delegation that came to see him on February 2, 1859, no doubt did so with some trepidation, for in the wake of the international storm of protest over the Mortara case, Pius IX was not likely to be kindly disposed. If that was their expectation, it proved to be only too accurate.

Sabatino Scazzocchio, the young secretary of the Università Israelitica, felt it his duty, in the brief opening report that was customary on these occasions, to make a plea on behalf of the Mortaras, couching it in the accustomed phrases of reverence, respect, and appreciation for the good Pope. But at once Pius IX flared up in anger: "Oh, certainly, certainly, you have given a wonderful display of your loyalty this past year, stirring up a storm all over Europe about this Mortara case!" Scazzocchio tried to defend himself, denying that Rome's Jews had had a hand in the attacks against the Pope, but Pius IX was not to be placated so easily: "You, yes, you have thrown oil on the fire, you have stoked the conflagration. . . . But this doesn't surprise me," he continued. "You lack the experience, you don't yet have the gray hair that these gentlemen here do," and here he pointed to the secretary's older colleagues. "You are crazy, crazy, not to say a scoundrel. You bragged that the Mortara couple would not be able to see me without you! Crazy! Who are you? What power do you have? What authority do you have that would feed such boastfulness?"

The Pope was just warming up, his animus against Scazzocchio—who represented for him the height of gall, a Jew who would try to get the Pope to do his bidding—now exploding. "But that wasn't enough for you. You went to the editors of the newspapers, you even went to the editorial office of *Civiltà Cattolica* to protest and to distort the facts. You even tried to play theologian [referring to the Pro-memoria and Syllabus Scazzocchio had submitted on the Mortaras' behalf], but here someone must have helped you because certainly you know absolutely nothing about theology. The newspapers can write all they want. I couldn't care less about what the world thinks!"

The Pope then turned to the rest of the Jewish delegation, and briefly made them, too, feel the weight of his wrath. "I suppose these are the thanks I get for all the benefits you have received from me! Take care, for I could have done you harm, a great deal of harm. I could have made you go back into your hole." At this point, the Pope began to calm down, and he added: "But don't worry, my goodness is so great, and so strong is the pity I have for you, that I pardon you, indeed, I must pardon you."

It was the delegates' turn to speak again. Giacobbe Tagliacozzo, a leader of the Università Israelitica who had been corresponding with Momolo Mortara over the previous few months, addressed the Pope: "We are very upset to see that Your Holiness seems to want to blame us for the polemics in the newspapers. But in fact we had absolutely no part in it. On the contrary, we profoundly deplore the way the newspapers have exploited a case that we ourselves have spoken of without ever trespassing the limits of moderation that befit our humble devotion to you." Tagliacozzo, carried away in his urgent attempt to placate the Pope, spoke in ever louder tones. The Pope interrupted him, saying, "Lower your voice. Do you forget before whom you are speaking?" Tagliacozzo quickly asked the Pope's pardon, explaining, "It must be knowing our innocence that pushes me despite myself to go beyond the proper bounds." He continued: "A clear proof of everything I have said is that not a single newspaper account of the Mortara case has ever reported its exact and true circumstances, while they would certainly have done so if they had had any help from us." And he concluded, "Sanctity, let me repeat, we have never in this case strayed from the long and proven devotion that we have always maintained, even in those times when maintaining it was risky for us." He added, lest the Pope miss his point, "I refer here to the period of the revolutionary upheavals." In short, even when under pressure to join in the revolt against papal power in 1848, Rome's Jews had remained loyal to the Pope.

But the Pope was not impressed by this argument, responding: "Oh, certainly, it was easy enough to predict that those uprisings would be brought to an end. We are not in Africa, where the cannibals can take control. Fortunately, we are in Europe."

The conversation then returned to the Mortara case. With the Pope now more calm, Tagliacozzo ventured one last attempt to get him to change his mind, arguing that given Anna Morisi's dubious morals, her account of having baptized the child should not be given too much credence. To this the Pope responded that although the woman might be of poor moral character, she had no reason to make the story up. Tagliacozzo countered by speculating that Morisi had acted out of spite, seeking revenge against the family who had fired her. The Pope replied: "In any case, it is the boy himself who wants to become Christian. Do you think I should have driven him away? I know that someone might say that he was influenced by his environment, but let me tell you that in fact he made his decision freely." And he added: "If Mortara hadn't taken a Catholic girl into his service, he would have nothing to complain about today."

Scazzocchio had by now built up the nerve to speak again, and was eager to defend himself. Another demonstration, he told the Pope, that fomenting press campaigns against the Pontiff was totally alien to them was the following: Various foreigners had recently come to him as word had spread that, in response to the Mortara affair, the papal police were rounding up Christian servants and chasing them out of the ghetto. Although the journalists had pressed him for confirmation, they had had to leave empty-handed, because the Jewish community of Rome wanted to avoid any clamor in the press. The Pope again was not impressed. Why, he asked, had they not told the journalists that the police were simply enforcing the law of the land, which prohibited Jews from having Christian servants?

This was the last straw for the wobbly Scazzocchio, and, to his embarrassment, he began to cry. Yes, he sobbed, perhaps he was a maniac from an insane asylum as the Pope seemed to think, but he had never done anything to deserve such a bad reputation. It was true that he had gone to the editorial office of *Civiltà Cattolica*, but only because he had heard that the journal was interested in the Mortara case, and he had merely wanted to make sure that they knew what the facts were. He had felt that it was his responsibility, as secretary of the Jewish community and as someone well informed on the case, to do what he could to defend the unfortunate Mortara family. As for the charge that he had bragged that the Mortara couple would never be able to get to the Pope's throne without him, the lachrymose secretary continued, this was absolutely false. Not only had he never made such a boast; such a thought had never even crossed his mind.

Somewhat mollified, the Pope observed that he had heard that Momolo himself had denounced the harsh criticisms of the Church carried in the newspapers, thinking that they served only to damage his cause, and, the Pope added, "he was not mistaken." To this, the Jewish secretary replied, "Holiness, we too were displeased along with him about the poisonous polemics, which we viewed as purely the product of political passion."

The Jews were ushered out. The whole roller-coaster session had lasted less than half an hour. Scazzocchio was so humiliated by the tongue-lashing he had received that, it is said, he suffered a nervous breakdown. Apparently Pius IX heard about this and in later years, at the annual meeting with the Roman Jewish delegation, the Pope went out of his way to be kind to him.[31]

As the polemics over the case continued, the Pope drew comfort from his regular visits with Edgardo, viewing the boy's evident attachment to the Church as a sign of God's blessing of the Pope's work and the righteousness of his cause. At one of their meetings, he told the boy, "My son . . . you have cost me dearly, and I have suffered a great deal because of you." And, turning to the others present, he added, "Both the powerful and the powerless tried to steal this boy from me, and accused me of being barbarous and pitiless. They cried for his parents, but they failed to recognize that I, too, am his father."[32]

CHAPTER 16

Sir Moses Goes to Rome

O N   H I S   A R R I V A L   in Bologna early in December, following
the harrowing trip back from Rome, Momolo remained in an
oddly optimistic mood. On December 3, he wrote to Scazzocchio to assure him "of our most happy arrival here, although only at four in
the morning . . . after a most tiring journey. Nonetheless, Marianna's health is
quite good and I am just fine, as are my children here." He ended by asking
the Roman Jewish secretary to send him "some news of my dear one there."[1]

Scazzocchio's reply is revealing: "As for Edgardo, I repeat what Signor S.
Alatri [president of the Università Israelitica of Rome] and all of us have said a
thousand times: that is, that the indiscreet chatter of so many newspapers,
which take advantage of whatever event excites the political passions that they
represent, has poisoned the matter. If they had only left it up to us to take care
of our own affairs, the policy of legal conduct that we have always had as our
motto might have allowed us to obtain our most desired goal, given the
benign and charitable nature of the one who sits on high." Only the lack of
capitalization in the last phrase makes it clear that the Jewish secretary is referring here not to the God of Abraham, Isaac, and Jacob but to Pope Pius IX.

"It is certainly not in these recriminations against journalism that you can
find comfort from your immense pain," the Roman Jewish secretary wrote,
"but can I not express the words that weigh on my soul, making it drink of
bitterness and anger?"[2] This is indeed a remarkable letter. The bitterness and
anger of Scazzocchio, and perhaps that of the other leaders of the Roman
Jewish community as well, were directed not against the Pope or his secretary
of state but at the liberal press that had championed the Mortara cause. Those
who so loudly criticized the Church for taking Edgardo were denounced as

self-seeking opportunists, more interested in making their own political points than in winning the child's release and the family's happiness. While these critics cast their stones at the Vatican from a safe distance, Rome's Jews were left to bear the consequences of an irate pontiff and his seething supporters.

At the time Scazzocchio was writing to Momolo, a new development was attracting the attention of the Jews throughout Europe who were following the Mortara case. Word reached Rome, and Bologna, that one of the most famous Jews of all, the renowned Sir Moses Montefiore—a British Jew who had been knighted, no less—was planning a trip to the Vatican to appeal to the Pope for Edgardo's release.

This would not be Montefiore's first such voyage as the champion of the Jews in the palaces of the world's rulers. By the time of Edgardo's abduction, Sir Moses had developed a reputation as the court of last resort for Jews around the world who suffered from persecution, a man willing to travel to all corners of the world on behalf of his less fortunate brethren. For Italian Jews, there was special cause for pride, for Montefiore's ancestors were from Livorno; his paternal grandparents had emigrated to England in the mid-eighteenth century. Indeed, he himself had been born in Livorno in 1784, while his parents were visiting the city.[3]

An observant Jew and no friend of those religious reformers then trying to alter Jewish rites to better fit with modern times, Montefiore was part of the elite of Britain's small Jewish community, a network of families linked by marriage who controlled major banks and businesses. His wife's sister, for example, was married to Nathan Mayer Rothschild, and Lionel Rothschild, who became the head of the Rothschild family in Britain, was their son, and Moses' nephew. With Montefiore's wealth, his connections, his talents, and his kin relations, he represented an ascension of Jews to the halls of power that excited marvel among his coreligionists throughout Europe. Montefiore was able to retire as a wealthy man at the age of 40, and devoted the remaining decades of his long life to philanthropy. In 1835, he agreed to become president of the Board of Deputies of British Jews, the central organization of Jews in Britain, a post he held for the next forty years. Two years after becoming president, he was knighted, in one of the first ceremonies that Victoria performed as queen.[4]

The event that first triggered Montefiore's philanthropic wanderlust—and that was to establish his international reputation as protector of the Jewish oppressed—took place in 1840. On February 5 of that year, Friar Tommaso, a Capuchin monk of Italian origin living in Damascus, disappeared along with his Muslim servant. The city, capital of Syria, and since 1832 under Egyptian control, was divided into separate sections of Muslims, Christians, and Jews.

When Tommaso disappeared, his fellow monks spread the story that he and his servant had been captured by Jews, who wanted to drain their blood to use in making matzah. Sixty-three Jewish children were seized and thrown into a dungeon as a means of forcing their parents to tell what they knew about the whereabouts of the missing men and to reveal what the Jews had done with their blood. Jewish homes were torn apart to find evidence—and to vent rage—and in a sewer in the Jewish quarter, suspicious bones were found. These were proclaimed to be the remains of the unfortunate monk and were buried in a tomb, on the grounds of the Capuchin convent. The tomb bore the words: "Here rest the bones of Father Tommaso of Sardinia, Capuchin missionary, murdered by the Hebrews on February 5th 1840." By the end of April, 129 Jews were being held in prison, four others had already died from torture, and ten men had been found guilty of murder and awaited execution. Most of the rest of the Jewish population of Damascus had fled.

When word of all this reached Britain, the Board of Deputies approved Sir Moses's plan that he lead a mission to Damascus to intervene on the Jews' behalf. He left England on July 7. Two weeks later he reached Livorno—"my native city," as he called it in his diary—where a delegation from the Jewish community met him. They warned him that he should not get off the boat when it came to port in Civitavecchia, near Rome, as there had been some recent disturbances aimed at Jews who passed through there, the product of the fulminations of "a priest called Meyer, a converted Jew." He also learned of the unpleasant experiences of some other Jewish travelers who, but a few weeks before, had gotten off their boat not far from Civitavecchia, a French couple named Montel.

Of even greater concern to Montefiore were reports he received from Rome that, as he wrote in his diary while still off the Italian coast, "both the Pope and his Government were extremely against the Jews and had expressed a belief in the murder of Father Tomassio [sic]. The Pope had refused to confirm the two Bulls issued by former Pontiffs when similar charges were brought against the Jews."

The ruler of the Egyptian-controlled lands, Muhammad Ali, was based in Alexandria, and so it was there that Sir Moses went. Presenting himself as having the authority of the British government behind him, Montefiore demanded that he be given permission to sail on to Damascus and launch an inquiry, and he called for the immediate release of all Jews being held in the Syrian prison. Three weeks after his first meeting with Muhammad Ali, an agreement was struck: the Jews would be freed from jail, Damascus's Jews could return to their homes, and the Pasha would condemn the tales of Jewish ritual murder. In exchange, Sir Moses would forgo his demand—made credible by the strong diplomatic support he enjoyed from the British government—that he be allowed to go to Damascus and mount an investigation. For

Montefiore, it was a great victory, and for the Jews in Europe and the United States—where protest meetings had been called for the first time on behalf of Jews abroad—it marked the birth of a new champion, the Jewish knight.

On his way back home, Sir Moses stopped in Italy, hoping to persuade Church officials to remove the offending tombstone at the Capuchin convent in Damascus, but he had no luck. It was reported to him that the Pope, and the others in the Vatican and in the Capuchin order, remained convinced that Tommaso had indeed been ritually murdered by the Jews. The tombstone stood for two decades as a continuing reproach to the Jews' perfidy, before being destroyed in 1860 when a Druze raid laid waste to the Christian outpost.[5]

On landing in Livorno on his way back to England in January 1841, Montefiore wrote to several Italian Jewish communities, reporting the outcome of his expedition. Among these was a letter he sent to the deputies of the Università Israelitica of Reggio Emilia. "Knowing of your religious zeal and noble humanitarian sentiments," he began, "it is my pleasure to send you the documents relative to the Damascus affair." He went on to inform them of Muhammad Ali's official proclamation of the Jews' innocence, and of the Sultan's decision to grant full rights to the Jews who lived in the Ottoman Empire, which Montefiore obtained during a stop in Constantinople. He appended both documents. Receiving such a letter from the Jewish hero surely created a stir among Reggio's Jews, among whom lived Momolo Mortara, aged 23.[6]

In 1846, after finishing a stint as sheriff of London, Montefiore journeyed through the Russian winter to reach Saint Petersburg in order to meet with the Czar and enlist his help in ending a wave of Jewish persecution. That same year, Pius IX became pope, and Sir Moses presided over a Board of Deputies meeting in which a letter was prepared expressing the board's appreciation to the new pontiff for his efforts to improve the conditions of the Papal States' Jews.[7]

In August 1858 Montefiore, as president of the Board of Deputies, received the plea prepared by the Jewish representatives of Piedmont seeking aid in winning Edgardo Mortara's release. The board responded immediately, forming a special committee on the case that was headed by Montefiore himself.

Three and a half months later, in December, Sir Moses gave the committee's final report. Montefiore had fed materials received from the Piedmont Jews to the British press, and then sent copies of the story that had run in the London *Times* to every member of the Catholic clergy in the United Kingdom, eighteen hundred in all. He reported the committee's pleasure at the solidarity expressed by Britain's Protestant community; the Evangelical

Alliance had taken an especially vigorous role in the protest. Although the British government had expressed its full support for their efforts, the Foreign Minister had noted that Britain's diplomatic relations with the Vatican were already strained, so that an official government protest could not be contemplated, nor, the Minister had added, would it do any good.

Sir Moses reported that the committee members, following a thorough investigation, "have strong grounds for believing that the alleged baptism never took place." Even if it did, he added, the circumstances of the alleged baptism "appear to render it invalid, even by the Roman canonical laws." Rejecting accounts being spread in the Catholic press that "Edgar Mortara rejoices in his adoption into the Catholic Faith (a statement which, considering the still tender age of the child is manifestly absurd)," Montefiore reported that the child "yearns incessantly for the restoration to its home." And he concluded: "The civilised world will indeed be wanting in energy and wisdom if it permits the nineteenth century to be disgraced by the retention of the child in contravention of the laws of nature, morality and religion, and most especially it behooves the Jewish community to exert itself to the utmost."[8]

In receiving the report, the board not only decided to send a petition to the Pope, urging him to free Edgardo, but called on Sir Moses to make the trip to Rome to present it personally. Curiously, Sir Culling Eardley, head of the Protestant Evangelical Alliance of Britain, who had taken on the campaign to free Edgardo as his own, had strongly urged Montefiore to another path. In a series of five letters to the Jewish board's committee, he had called on them to organize a delegation to plead not with the Pope—whom Eardley no doubt believed to be unsympathetic to such an appeal—but to the French emperor. When informed by Montefiore of the board's finding that "a deputation from the Jewish community to the Emperor of the French would be of no utility," the Protestant head expressed his disappointment in a letter to Sir Moses, which was published in the *Times*. Eardley explained:

> Had your attention been directed to Paris our arrangements were made to help you. The Lord Mayor of London and the Lord Provost of Edinburgh had agreed to accompany a deputation from the British branch of the alliance to the Emperor. The secretaries were instructed to request the Lord Mayor (elect) of Dublin to do the same. . . . It was felt that such an appeal to the Emperor in support of a similar one from the Jews of Europe, would be gratifying to the French nation. We were also assured that the Emperor would appreciate it.[9]

In preparing for his trip to Rome, Sir Moses met with Lord Malmesbury, the British foreign secretary, who offered to do what he could to help, which included letters of introduction to various British diplomats in Italy. After prayers for the success of the Mortara mission were recited in synagogues throughout London, Montefiore and his party set off. It was March 3, 1859, more than eight months since Edgardo had been taken.[10]

The party took its time en route, partly as a result of Lady Montefiore's illness, and did not arrive in Rome until April 5. None of the diplomats Sir Moses spoke to were encouraging about his prospects. His ability to persuade the Pasha, the Sultan, and the Czar were one thing; his power to move the Pope was quite another.

Indeed, it soon looked as though he might not get to see the Pope at all. Montefiore enlisted the aid of members of the British diplomatic community in Rome, who were supportive but pessimistic. He relied particularly on Odo Russell, the British military attaché, who went to see Cardinal Antonelli on his behalf. Russell reported back to Montefiore: "It is with deep regret that I have to inform you that all my exertions in the interest of your cause have failed. Cardinal Antonelli declined to enter upon the subject, saying, 'It was a closed question.' " The Secretary of State referred Russell to the papal chamberlain, Monsignor Pacca, to try to arrange a meeting for Montefiore with the Pope. Although the matter seemed hopeless, Sir Moses hurriedly prepared a letter to Monsignor Pacca and delivered it personally at the Vatican.

The situation in Rome was tense. Rumors circulated of an impending drive by Piedmontese troops down into the Papal States and a war against the Austrian forces in Italy. In February, a secret accord had been signed between France and the Kingdom of Sardinia pledging French military assistance for the creation of an enlarged Italian kingdom running from the north of Italy— with the Austrians evicted from Lombardy and Veneto—down through the Legations of the Papal States. Members of the National Society in Tuscany and in the Legations had received secret instructions to prepare the partisans of Italian unification for an uprising.

On Friday evening, April 15, at the beginning of the Jewish Sabbath, a phalanx of police entered the Roman ghetto and searched the synagogue, rummaging among the sacred scrolls of the Torah and scouring through the nooks and crannies of the basement. An angry crowd meantime began to gather outside, accusing the Jews of kidnapping two Christian children so that they could use their blood to make Passover matzah. Late in the night, the last of the crowd dispersed, but the next morning fear hung over the ghetto.

The following day, the newspaper *Il vero amico del popolo* ran a piece reporting that a Catholic man had recently been murdered in Smyrna by Jews who sought his blood for matzah, and dredging up the accusations of the Jews' murder of Father Tommaso in Damascus. Among Rome's Jews, the suspicion began to grow that the timing of these attacks was significant. Montefiore's visit was apparently not welcome in some quarters.

When leaders of the Jewish community reported their suspicions to Sir Moses as he prepared for the Passover seder, he grew depressed. But his spirits recovered when the British representative to the Vatican dropped by to tell him that he had spoken with Cardinal Antonelli on his behalf and that the Cardinal was willing to meet with him. Wasting no time, Montefiore had his carriage take him to the Vatican, where the Cardinal had his rooms on the floor directly above those of the Pope. "I had to ascend 190 steps"—wrote the 74-year-old Sir Moses—"a most splendid marble staircase"; but Antonelli was not there to receive him. He left his card for the Secretary of State and then did the same at the residence of the French ambassador, the Duke de Gramont, whom he wanted to thank for his impassioned efforts to win Edgardo's release.

That evening, Signor Tagliacozzo—who two months before had been part of the Jewish delegation that met with the Pope—came to see Montefiore, reporting the latest news from the ghetto. In two different synagogues the Jews had found Catholic children hiding, apparently placed there by people who hoped that they would be closed in at night, allowing the rabble-rousers to whip up anti-Jewish fury. In one case, just as a synagogue was about to be locked up following Friday evening services, a small child was found asleep in a corner, under a seat, and was put out. An hour later, a crowd of women, children, and some men, accompanied by police officers, descended on the ghetto and made their way to the synagogue, where they charged that the Jews had concealed a Christian child to prepare him for sacrifice. The next morning, many of the Jews who worked outside the old ghetto stayed home, having recently become targets of verbal abuse—and, in some cases, stones— aimed at them from passersby.

Finally, on April 28, Sir Moses, escorted by Odo Russell, had his appointment with Cardinal Antonelli. The day before, although no one at the Vatican yet knew it, Austrian troops had crossed into Piedmont in an attempt to defeat the Piedmontese troops before their French allies could arrive. On the very day that Sir Moses was again climbing the 190 steps to the Secretary of State's office, Grand Duke Leopold II—facing popular demonstrations for the annexation of Tuscany to the Piedmontese kingdom, as well as a rebellion among his own troops—fled Florence. The battle for unification, and for the dismantling of the centuries-old temporal reign of the popes, was under way.

Montefiore told the Secretary of State why he had come to Rome, and expressed his disappointment at being unable to see the Pope to make his case. He asked the Cardinal to present the British Board of Deputies' written plea to the Pope for him, lest he not be able to do so himself, and added that he would wait in Rome another week for the Pope's reply. Antonelli received the elderly Jew with great courtesy, shaking his hand vigorously and insisting that Montefiore sit beside him on the sofa in his office. However, as for the question at hand, he could not have been less encouraging. Once a child has been baptized, he informed Sir Moses, "the laws of the Church prevented its being given back to the parents." However, on reaching adulthood—about age eighteen—Edgardo would be free to do as he pleased. In the meantime, the Cardinal promised that the boy's parents would be able to visit him regularly. "On my expressing a hope to receive a reply to the address [of the Board of Deputies] from the Pope," Montefiore wrote, the Secretary of State said simply: "No reply had been given to similar memorials from Holland, Germany, and France."

Chastened, Montefiore returned to his quarters and sent a telegram reporting the disheartening news to London. It was addressed to the Board of Deputies, the Lord Mayor, the Chief Rabbi, Baron Rothschild, and Sir Culling Eardley, head of the Protestant Evangelical Alliance.

Two days later, news of the battle between Austrian and Piedmontese troops, and the grand duke's flight from Tuscany, reached Rome, and members of the English community in the Holy City, fearing the spread of disorder—if not the arrival of hostile troops—hurriedly packed their bags. It was no longer certain that the French troops who protected papal rule in Rome would remain.

Montefiore would not leave, however, until the week was up, clinging to the hope that the Pope would respond. Finding a berth on a boat was not easy, for people were streaming out of the city, but by paying double fare, the Montefiores were able to get tickets and left Rome on May 10. Sir Moses wrote in his diary: "This journey and mission has been, on many accounts, a painful and sad trial of patience . . . but our God is in Heaven, and no doubt He has permitted that which will prove a disappointment to our friends, &c., and is a grief to us, for the best and wisest purposes. Blessed be His name!"

On his return, Montefiore stopped in Paris, where he met with the French minister of foreign affairs to thank him personally for the efforts made by the French ambassador, the Duke de Gramont, to win the Mortara boy's release. The British newspapers were filled with news of Montefiore's abortive mission, and an ad hoc committee was formed in London to lodge a protest to the Pope on behalf of the British Christian community. A statement was drawn up and signed by two thousand members of the British upper crust, branding the Vatican's actions a "dishonour to Christianity" and "repulsive to the instincts of humanity."[11]

Reactions in the British Jewish press combined praise for Sir Moses with harsh words for the Catholic Church. Two weeks after Montefiore's departure from Rome, London's *Jewish Chronicle* reported that the mission was a success in showing the Pope "that the Jewish people no longer intend tamely to submit to outrages on human nature." Yet, sadly, "degenerate modern Rome has by the weapons of brutal force obtained and maintained a momentary advantage. It refuses at the entreaty of an outraged community, at the bidding of insulted religion and down-trodden morality, to make the only adequate, acceptable reparation for the atrocity committed, by restoring to the robbed parents their kidnapped child."[12]

Meanwhile, in France, Sir Moses did not receive such uniformly adulatory reviews, even in the Jewish press. A number of French Jewish leaders were offended at the treatment they had received from the peripatetic crusader. He had gone off on his own, thinking that the backing of the British government would be sufficient to repeat his Damascus success, even though everyone knew that it was the French, and not the British, who had influence with the Vatican. Although he had traveled through France to get to Rome, he had not bothered to stop off to confer with leaders of the French Jewish community.

In its July 1859 issue, the *Archives Israélites* reported the failure of the Montefiore mission. "At the time of his departure," the editor recalled, "we had expressed our regret that he did not come to Paris to find support for the cause that he went to defend before Cardinal Antonelli. . . . In Rome, he wasn't even able to get an audience with the Pope."[13]

The article, written a year after Edgardo entered the Catechumens, reported with great satisfaction that the boy, "according to well-informed persons, has not capitulated. . . . Neither threats, nor promises, nor gifts, nor amusements, nothing has shaken this young soul, and so nothing should lessen our perseverance."[14] At about the same time, another French paper, the *Journal des Débats*, reported the news that on June 14, in a solemn ceremony held at Rome's famous church of San Pietro in Vincoli, Edgardo had been confirmed.[15] The paper—no friend of the Vatican—had the details wrong, for in fact the ceremonies had been held the month before, presided over by Gabriele Cardinal Ferretti—nephew of Pope Pius IX—in a private chapel. The rites had been performed three days after Montefiore's departure from Rome, and apparently the Church was not eager to make the ceremony public, given the rebellions that had broken out in the north and the fear that the French might move their troops out of Rome.[16]

It was true, however, that Edgardo was now being educated at San Pietro in Vincoli and no longer at the Catechumens. In a letter Scazzocchio wrote on February 1, just before his debilitating audience with the Pope, he reported this news, which the Rector of the Catechumens had given him, to the Mortaras.[17] Once Edgardo had received his initial Catholic education, there was no point keeping him in the Catechumens. He was ready to be send off to a *collegio*, to study religion and other subjects together with other boys.

The decision as to where Edgardo should go was made by the Pope himself, for the boy from Bologna was no run-of-the-mill neophyte. Pius IX had initially favored entrusting him to the Jesuits' care, with the hope that he might one day become a Jesuit himself. What could be more appropriate? Not only had the founder of the Jesuit order, Loyola, been the founder of Rome's Catechumens, but the Jesuit journal, *Civiltà Cattolica*, had taken the lead in defending the Church decision to keep Edgardo. But on further reflection, and perhaps on the advice of his more politically savvy secretary of state, the Pope changed his mind. The Jesuits were all too exposed to the displeasure of foreign governments as it was. It might not be doing them any favor to put them in the limelight again.[18]

The *collegio* at San Pietro in Vincoli was run by the order of the Lateran Canons Regular. Perched atop Rome's highest hill, no more than a half-hour walk from the ghetto, the church was one of the oldest and most famous in the Eternal City. The name of the church, Saint Peter in Chains, derived from a reliquary containing what was thought to be the chains in which Nero had bound Saint Peter. At the time Edgardo arrived there, it was believed that the chains had been brought to the church in Rome directly from Jerusalem in the fifth century.[19] In another reliquary were bones that were thought to be the remains of the heroic Maccabees from the Holy Land. The *collegio*'s quarters, situated beside the glorious church—with Saint Peter's chains, beautifully painted ceilings, majestic pillared architecture, and Michelangelo's famed statue of Moses—and with a magnificent view of the city, offered dazzling surroundings for the seven-year-old son of a storekeeper.

Shortly after Scazzocchio's letter reporting Edgardo's move to San Pietro in Vincoli reached the Mortaras, the boy and his fellow students went on a trip to Saint Peter's. Coincidentally, Louis Veuillot and his sister were just then touring the Vatican. The French Catholic editor spied the group of boys, dressed in the same habit as their teacher, as they were being led into the church. Veuillot's guide, a French bishop, pointed to one of the smallest of their number and exclaimed: "Voilà! There is the famous celebrity who has so much occupied all of Europe, us included. Let me introduce you to the little Mortara." The bishop then pulled aside the monk who was leading the group and explained who Veuillot was.

Veuillot provides the following account of the encounter: "Since the time I arrived, I had always hoped to see the famous little Mortara. I was delighted to meet him at the foot of St. Peter's chair. On his superior's order, he kissed my hand." The sense of satisfaction, of triumph, that *L'Univers*'s editor felt directed his thoughts to his enemies, the editors of the secular French press, who had vilified the Pope over the Mortara affair. "What a sight for Monsieur Plée of the *Siècle*, if only he could have seen it!" Veuillot took the boy into his arms and hugged him. Edgardo, Veuillot reported, was in good health, had a trusting and "spiritual" face and "the most beautiful eyes in the world," and "responds to questions without embarrassment, just like a well-raised child." Veuillot was told that of all the students his age, Edgardo knew the catechism best.

The French editor arranged to visit Edgardo at San Pietro in Vincoli one day soon thereafter. On his arrival, he first stopped to kiss the reliquary containing Saint Peter's chains, and then met with the neophyte. "I found again the same open and lively manner, the same big, intelligent eyes." Ever eager to gather material to support his cause, Veuillot asked the boy about his family. "He tells me that he loves his father and his mother, and that he will go to live with them when he is older and has been educated, so that he can speak to them of Saint Peter, of God, and of the most Holy Mary." After further conversation along these lines, Veuillot recounted, it was time for Edgardo to return to his class. The Frenchman concluded, with his accustomed sarcasm, "He doesn't seem to be aware of all the horror of his fate, but that, Monsieur Plée would say, is the height of the horror."[20]

CHAPTER 17

Uprising in Bologna

C OULD THE STORY of an illiterate servant girl, a grocer, and a little Jewish child from Bologna have altered the course of Italian and Church history? The question is not nearly as far-fetched as it appears. A case can be made that Anna Morisi—sexually compromised, dirt-poor, and unable to write her own name—made a greater contribution to Italian unification than many of the Risorgimento heroes whose statues preside over Italian town piazzas today.

National sensibilities encourage Italians to view unification as the product of Italian nationalist sentiments, embodied by the cerebral (and driven) Giuseppe Mazzini; Italian military bravery, embodied by the swashbuckling Giuseppe Garibaldi; Italian diplomatic savvy, embodied by Count Cavour; and the dedication of Italian royalty, in the person of Victor Emmanuel II. But what most effectively precipitated Italian unification, which began in 1859, was the decision of the French government—and of Emperor Napoleon III in particular—to commit troops to join the Kingdom of Sardinia in driving Austrian forces from northern Italy, and to approve the annexation to the kingdom not only of the Austrian-ruled lands but of all those protected by Austrian troops, lands that encompassed much of the Papal States.

This is not the place to examine the life and times of Napoleon III. He had been an enthusiast for Italian unification earlier in his life, and indeed took part in the Carbonari-inspired revolts in Italy in 1831. On the other hand, in order to win Catholic support in his bid to solidify power at home in 1849, he had ordered French troops into Rome to defeat the Republic and reinstall the old regime. His fear of antagonizing Catholics in France led him to keep French soldiers in Rome, but his distaste for the idea of a state ruled, under Church law, by the Pontiff made him a fainthearted supporter at best of papal power.

In the words of a Bolognese journalist, looking back on the case a half century later, the taking of Edgardo Mortara constituted the coup de grâce for the pontifical government. In fine patriotic fashion, the journalist attributes this not to the impact that the case had on the French but to its effects on liberals and Freemasons in Italy itself, for whom papal rule was already largely discredited.[1] French journalists, on the other hand, who portrayed the Mortara case as the straw that broke the back of papal rule, focused on its impact on French public opinion. An article in *L'Espérance* published in the wake of the fall of the Legations, at the dawn of 1860, reported, no doubt hyperbolically, that there was not a single French soldier who, returning to his natal village, did not tell the tale of the little Jewish boy who had been stolen from his parents.[2]

Nor is this view of the impact of the Mortara case limited to journalists or boosters of Italy's minuscule Jewish community. Arturo Carlo Jemolo, the foremost historian of Church-state relations in Italy, cites Pope Pius IX's actions in the Mortara affair as among the most significant of his papacy, a papacy that was one of the most consequential in Church history. Jemolo lists the Mortara case alongside the Pope's 1864 proclamation of the *Syllabus of Errors*, the Church's famed rejection of modernity, and his convening of the First Vatican Council in 1869–70, at which papal infallibility was made Church dogma, as the principal actions that signaled the Pope's philosophy to the wider world. It was a philosophy that fatefully undermined the inclination of constitutional Catholic governments to come to the aid of the Holy See.[3]

Pius IX's principal biographers similarly make the connection between his handling of the Mortara affair in 1858 and his loss of most of his earthly kingdom the following year. "In a broader historical perspective," writes Giacomo Martina, the Pope's most distinguished Italian biographer, "the Mortara case shows Pius IX's profound zeal, his firmness in doing what he took to be his precise duty, even at the cost of losing his popularity, his still largely intact prestige, and, above all, French support for his temporal power."[4]

The premonition that major changes were on the way had kept the people of Bologna in a state of anxious excitement for months. The city was no stranger to revolts against papal rule, nor to the realization that battles waged farther north might decide their own fate. Although Bologna's famous university was under pontifical rule, its students remained a potentially seditious lot.

In mid-April 1859, when a lecture on Napoleon Bonaparte was scheduled, a great crowd of students packed the hall, excited by the prospect that Bonaparte's nephew might soon be leading the way toward Italian unification. Appalled by the sight, authorities advised the lecturer—a priest—not to hold the class, and a squad of papal police, their swords drawn, descended on the assembled students to disperse them. Bologna's liberal diarist Enrico Bottrigari describes the encounter: " 'Get out of here, you ugly swine! Out, dogs!' These were the words uttered by these brutal soldiers, who, not satisfied with their insults, began to beat and wound these unarmed youths with the blades and the tips of their swords." As the students fled the hall, they found two more columns of gendarmes waiting for them, under the command of the mastermind of the operation, Colonel De Dominicis.[5]

On the night of June 12, 1859, at 3 a.m., Austrian troops, having been stationed continuously in Bologna ever since they put down the revolt of 1848–49, marched out of the city. A group of local notables—identified with the National Society that sought Bologna's annexation to the kingdom of Sardinia—met in the middle of the night with the Cardinal Legate. Cardinal Milesi was still hoping somehow to hold on to power, although he must have realized that the cause was, at least in the short term, lost. Embarrassingly, in the city ruled for more than two and a half centuries by papal authorities, absolutely no one tried to prevent the overthrow of the pontifical regime.

At 6 a.m., Piazza Maggiore, outside the Palazzo Comunale, began to fill up and, urged on by members of the National Society, the people waved tricolored banners and took up the chant: Viva l'Italia! Viva Vittorio Emanuele! Viva the War of Independence! Viva Napoleone III! Viva la France! Cavour! Garibaldi! The city band hurriedly assembled, pumping out stirring war songs and patriotic hymns. From the windows looking out onto the piazza, women waved white kerchiefs and hung the national colors from their sills. A group of men climbed the face of the Palazzo Comunale and, to the crowd's delight, tore down the papal insignia, substituting the Italian flag imprinted with the cross of the House of Savoy. Papal rule had fallen. But it had fallen other times in recent memory. No one could be sure it would not rise again.

Cardinal Milesi, whom Edgardo's uncles had so desperately sought out the previous year, finally recognized that he would have to go. At 9 a.m., guarded by a squad of papal soldiers, he was allowed to leave the Palazzo Comunale unmolested. Just before departing, he issued a proclamation, his last: "Bolognesi. The Austrian garrison has left this city. This does not, however, mean the end of the solemn agreements by which the Sovereignty of the Holy Father is guaranteed by both of the Catholic Emperors who are now belligerents [i.e., Austria and France]." The Legate concluded: "I appeal to the good sense of this city and province. All those who love order join me to maintain and defend it. And it will be maintained, if the first and most sacred of rights—that of the Prince, the Holy Father—is respected."[6]

In response to this appeal, members of the hastily assembled provisional government of Bologna proclaimed the city's adherence to the "War of

Independence" and their desire to have Bologna annexed to the Kingdom of Sardinia. That night, homes throughout the city were ablaze with candles and gaslights celebrating the end of papal rule, and huge crowds gathered, caught up in the festivities. The city band marched through the streets, trailed by a line of men holding flaming torches aloft to light the way, with the chords of popular tunes rumbling through the air.[7]

The day of the Austrians' departure was the Sunday of Pentecost, the day of Confirmation. Notwithstanding the mayhem, the city's children who were scheduled to be confirmed that year, dressed in white, gathered in Bologna's cathedral. The children saw a strange, almost surreal sight, as one such child recalled years later.

Alberto Dallolio first noticed that something odd was happening when he and his grandfather, hand in hand, passed near the central piazza on their way to the cathedral. A rowdy procession was moving toward them, shouting—in obvious joy—muffled words whose meaning the boy could not make out. A boisterous man led them, waving a large flag and heading toward the piazza. When they passed, one of the men stopped Alberto's grandfather and pulled something out of a box he carried. It was a little, brightly colored ribbon, which the man attached to the buttonhole of the grandfather's jacket. He then turned to the boy and fastened the tricolored cockade to him as well. Wearing the cockade on his confirmation suit, Alberto entered San Pietro cathedral. Who knows, he later wrote, what a disagreeable impression he must have made on Cardinal Viale-Prelà as he did so.[8]

The Archbishop indeed found himself in an impossible position, one that was deeply galling. Although the Cardinal Legate might flee, he could not. He was pastor of the flock, responsible for the souls of all those in his diocese. He was urgently needed where he was, to defend a Church and a Pope under merciless attack.

On the very day of the Austrian departure, a delegation of noblemen and others from the provisional government met with the Archbishop to assure him that he would not be harmed, nor would he be prevented from exercising his religious duties. But Cardinal Viale-Prelà was not won over. The new governors were illegitimate usurpers of papal authority, and he could not recognize their right to rule. The Cardinal's newspaper, *L'osservatore bolognese,* centerpiece of his campaign for religious renewal, was closed down by the new government, charged with subversion.[9]

The Archbishop's first acts of defiance were fueled by the deep repugnance he felt toward the rebels and the sacrilege they were committing against the Church. But his efforts were sustained as well by the hope that a day of reckoning might soon come when the proper order would be restored and the rebels would receive their just deserts. In Rome, as news of one setback after another came in, Cardinal Antonelli continued to place events of 1859 in the mold that had been established for him by the revolt of a decade before. A month after the fall of Bologna, the British military attaché, Odo Russell, reported in a letter to London:

> The Cardinal Secretary of State, who is also Minister of War, told me yesterday that at the beginning of the year the Papal army numbered about 8000 men: 2500 had deserted to join the Piedmontese army so that the army of His Holiness was now reduced to about 5500 men. His Eminence was organizing new regiments and recruitment was carried on with great energy so as to bring the Papal army to its normal condition which was 14,000 men.
>
> This was to be effected by the end of the year and Cardinal Antonelli assured me that he sincerely hoped he could by that time insist on the withdrawal of the French army of occupation from Rome and Civitavecchia—a measure he now had more than ever at heart. The French Government had obtained from King Victor Emmanuel the recall of Marquis d'Azeglio from Bologna. The next step, he hoped, would be the withdrawal of the Piedmontese troops from the Legations, and once they were free, His Eminence foresaw no difficulty in attacking and reconquering those rebellious provinces. At the request of the Emperor he had given up the idea of breaking off diplomatic relations with Sardinia and in return he expected France would keep order on this side of the Apennines while the Papal troops effected the submission of the Legations.
>
> Cardinal Antonelli seemed very sanguine as to success of these measures. Perhaps His Eminence is not aware that the Emperor's positive orders to General Goyon at the commencement of the war were to maintain order in and about Rome, but in no way to interfere in any other portion of the Papal States.[10]

In fact, the arrival of Massimo d'Azeglio, sent to Romagna as emissary of the Kingdom of Sardinia, had triggered a new confrontation with Cardinal Viale-Prelà, for he viewed it as the first step toward annexation, recognition by King Victor Emmanuel II that Bologna and all Romagna were part of his expanded kingdom. Two years after crowds had lined the streets leading into the city to catch an eager glimpse of the Pope's triumphal entry, they reappeared to welcome D'Azeglio. His horse-drawn carriage made its slow way through the flag-draped city streets as a shower of flowers and garlands rained down from the windows. By the time the carriage had reached Piazza Maggiore, it was so covered with flowers that the Marquis could barely be seen. Behind him marched a long line of militiamen—many mustered as quickly into the new service as they had been unceremoniously mustered out of the old—followed by officials of the new provisional government, trailed by hundreds of carriages carrying Bologna's elite, paying tribute to the new rulers.

Repeating Pius IX's gesture of two years before, the Marquis entered the Palazzo Comunale and climbed to the window overlooking the throbbing piazza. To the right, he saw the majestic facade of San Petronio, lit by six huge candelabra and adorned with banners and wreaths. To his left was the medieval Palazzo del Podestà, washed in shadowy light by the flickering flames that burned in a huge pot on its roof. Amidst those flames stood eight placards, each bearing the name of a recent victorious battle waged by the allies along with the insignia of the House of Savoy. On the far side of the piazza, the banners of Bologna and of Savoy hung together, alongside the Italian and French flags, while in the middle of the piazza stood a bust of the King—pathetically small, given the grandeur of the piazza and the splendor of the occasion, but the best that the patriotic artist could come up with on such short notice. The aroused multitude, viscerally moved by the spectacle of so much light after nightfall and by the sounds of the four military bands and the cheers of their delirious compatriots, shouted for D'Azeglio to come out and address them. The Marquis, amazed at the sight, walked onto the balcony and waved to the crowd.

Amidst the lights of the city, one large palazzo, that of the Archbishop, remained conspicuously dark. The gesture did not go unnoticed. Angry crowds made their way to his courtyard, hurling insults and muttering profanities. When at last they were driven out by the police, they left behind a grove of candles to illuminate the buildings.[11]

Accustomed to reading *L'osservatore bolognese*, *Il vero amico*, and other papers reporting local news through ecclesiastical eyes, the people of Bologna soon found themselves getting a very different picture. New papers sprang up, singing the virtues of the Savoyard king and praising the courageous soldiers of national unification. Anticlerical sentiment—indigenous to Bologna and Romagna, where the Church had long been identified with autocratic rule— was overnight transformed from furtive mutterings into black-and-white, official-looking declarations.

On August 17, for example, Bologna's new *Gazzetta del popolo* addressed the rural peasants, who, it was feared, were especially susceptible to the clergy's cries of alarm. "Your Priests have deceived themselves, and they deceive and hurt you immensely by speaking constantly against the new government. . . . Did the Pope's government ever make you happy?" asked the correspondent. He continued: The Pope, in an attempt to hold on to his kingdom, and the priests, out of ignorance, claimed that papal rule was necessary for the Pontiff's free exercise of his spiritual duties. "But we can ask, just how is it that a sovereign is free in his rule when he relies on some other power to keep him on the throne?" And wasn't it Jesus himself who said, "My reign is not of this earth? . . . Perhaps our religion isn't exercised freely in Piedmont? The Priests say it isn't. But how dare they utter such a lie? In Piedmont there are more priests than there are here, and more beautiful churches, and everyone goes to mass when they like." Warming to the theme, and styling himself as the true defender of the message of Christ, the indignant correspondent concluded: "How dare the representative of Jesus Christ tell such lies so that he can continue to hold wealth and lands, and what is worse, wealth and lands that are not his. How dare he excommunicate people because they have taken from him that which he has no right to have. . . . Shame! Shame! don't you see that the Pope is deceiving you?"[12]

Just a week earlier, in one of his first official acts, the new governor general of Romagna proclaimed freedom of religion and the equality of all citizens before the law. Jews were now, for the first time since Christianity became the official faith of the Roman Empire—with the brief exception of the Napoleonic period—to enjoy the same rights as Christians. In November 1859, just seventeen months after the Inquisitor had ordered Edgardo seized, Luigi Carlo Farini, dictator of the former duchies of Modena and Parma, and Governor of Romagna, issued a declaration abolishing the Inquisition. Denouncing the inquisitorial court as "incompatible both with civilization and with the most basic principles of public and civil rights," it noted that civilized nations everywhere had already done away with such courts, and that only in the Papal States did they remain.[13]

The Archbishop lost no time doing what he could to protect his diocese from the influence of all the anticlerical writings that appeared in the wake of the Austrians' departure. At the end of August he issued a notice, printed on large sheets of paper and posted on churches throughout the diocese, warning people of the "grave danger" that these publications posed. "We are distressed to see insults and profanities hurled at the Sacred Person of the one who, possessing the supreme authority of the Church, should be the object of our veneration and our love." After condemning, as well, the alarming upsurge in offensive theatrical performances, Viale-Prelà concluded: "We strongly recommend that you follow the example of the faithful of the primitive Church, of those of whom we read in the Acts of the Apostles, who threw evil books into the flames."[14]

The problem persisted, and so the Cardinal issued yet another ecclesiastical warning a few months later, in early December, alerting his flock to the "pernicious and reprehensible means being employed to destroy your faith . . . and to drag the unwary and the ignorant into the deadly abyss of heresy. . . . Toward this end," the Archbishop continued, "ungodly little books are being offered and sold to you at low cost, heaping hatred and mockery on the saintly

Catholic Church, trampling its authority, and ridiculing its doctrine." Viale-Prelà concluded his new appeal, as he had the last, with the fervent hope that the faithful would treat these publications as they deserved, "throwing them in the flames, as we know some of you have already done."[15]

The battle was joined, fought on the one side through ecclesiastical proclamations and ritual sanctions and on the other by popular demonstrations and a spate of journalistic attacks. Enrico Bottrigari, in September, offered the patriots' view of Cardinal Viale-Prelà's battle against the new regime: "Our Archbishop, as could be expected, remains hostile to the new order of things and publishes Notifications full of lies, trying to make people believe that pious acts and sacred functions are being opposed or prevented." Some priests, Bottrigari reported, had cooperated with the new rulers, but the Archbishop had moved quickly to suspend them from their ecclesiastical offices.[16]

The ritual struggle was a two-way affair. Far from being a Church monopoly, ritual served as the primary means by which the new rulers constructed their regime, covering themselves with the mantle of legitimacy, instructing people in their ideology, and rousing them to a state of excitement.[17] Most galling of all for Bologna's embattled Archbishop was the constant stream of requests from the usurpers to involve priests in the counter-rites of the new state, in a brazen attempt to use the Church to legitimize the new regime.

Bologna's patriotic elite needed to demonstrate to the rest of the world that the people of Romagna fully supported the new regime and wanted to be part of the kingdom of Sardinia. The elite also faced the problem of instructing the overwhelmingly illiterate population in just what the new state consisted of, making them feel part of it, and convincing them that they were happy about it. Publishing newspapers that sang the praises of the new state and attacked the Pope was all well and good, but only a small portion of the population could read them. And reading an article that claimed that the people of Bologna were enthusiastic about the new government was considerably less convincing, and less emotionally engaging, than participating with thousands of others in mass rites in which the sacred symbols of the new order were trotted out and the new sacred songs sung.

In the early days following the flight of the Cardinal Legate from Bologna, when the old regime had been battered but it was not yet clear that it would not return, public ritual filled a pressing need for order, for definition of political reality amidst chaos, and for reaffirming bonds of fellowship at a time of potential fratricide. For Bologna's new rulers, the main task was getting people to shift their allegiances from the Church and Rome to the King and Italy. Just as the succession of leaders of the French Revolution devoted great energies to crafting public rites to help define and legitimize the new political order for the aroused but confused masses, so too did Bologna's leaders put together an exhausting—but hopefully exalting—series of new patriotic rites.[18]

When the newly formed Assembly of Romagna held its first meeting, in Bologna, on the first of September, 1859, delegates unanimously approved two resolutions. With echoes of the American Declaration of Independence, they proclaimed: "We, the representatives of the people of Romagna, convened in general assembly, swearing the righteousness of our intentions to God, do declare: (1) That the peoples of Romagna ... no longer want pontifical, temporal government; (2) That the peoples of Romagna want annexation to the constitutional Kingdom of Sardinia, under the scepter of Victor Emmanuel II."[19]

The Assembly sent representatives to present these resolutions to the King. Their return from Turin, with a friendly message from Victor Emmanuel II in hand, was taken as a proper occasion for ritually marking the link between the people of Romagna and their not-quite-yet monarch. The Bologna City Council was the first to take the initiative, proclaiming a day of popular festivity to give thanks to the Almighty. Given the historical connotations of San Petronio—the massive church on Piazza Maggiore where Charles had been crowned emperor of the Holy Roman Empire in 1530—it was there that the Christian part of the ritual would have to take place. Following a Te Deum sung in the church, a ceremony would be held placing the glorious coat of arms of the House of Savoy above the main gate of the Palazzo Comunale. And, in a further symbolic transubstantiation, Piazza Maggiore itself would be rechristened: the sacred center of Bologna would take the new name of Piazza Victor Emmanuel. To mark the occasion, finally, a marble plaque would be put up on the front of the palace, recording the great day for prosperity.

The rites that October day went largely according to plan; the cavernous San Petronio released its huge crowd at the end of the Te Deum to mingle with the multitudes already gathered in the piazza. Amidst great enthusiasm and the stirring music of patriotic bands, the Savoyard coat of arms was raised, artillery was sounded, and church bells were rung. Yet something was missing. The Archbishop had instructed the priests of San Petronio not to take part in the event. Since it was inconceivable to have such a rite without the clergy, chaplains from the local military regiment—who were not under the Archbishop's authority—were brought in to do the honors. Cardinal Viale-Prelà himself arranged to be out of town on the day of the celebrations, saying mass instead in one of the rural parishes of his diocese. He was no longer a well man—indeed, although not old, he did not have much longer to live—and as he raised the host in preparation for offering communion that day, he fell to the ground in a faint. Commenting on this juxtaposition, the uncharitable Bottrigari wrote: "Political events are giving the Cardinal severe indigestion!"[20]

The patriotic rites enacted in Bologna were repeated in communities throughout Romagna, tying the people to the new government and demonstrating their new Savoyard loyalties to the rest of the world, especially to the Catholic powers who needed to be convinced that it was the people themselves who wanted to shift their political allegiance from the Pope to the King. In community after community the same ritual battle was joined, as parish priests, under orders from the Archbishop, refused to preside over the sacrilegious ceremonies and did what they could to keep the secular celebrants out of their churches altogether.

In San Lazzaro di Savena, just outside Bologna, the ceremonies were scheduled for a Sunday in late October. At the conclusion of the morning's first mass, the parish priest announced that the second mass was canceled. He then locked the church door and left. When the local dignitaries arrived at the church for the patriotic ceremonies, scheduled to coincide with the second mass of the day, they were chagrined to discover it locked and ordered the police to force the door open. They then rustled up a military chaplain, who presided as a solemn Te Deum was sung, thanking God for the deliverance of Romagna to the Savoyard kingdom.

Unamused at the parish priest's rebuff, the civil authorities immediately ordered him, along with a clerical colleague deemed to be his co-conspirator, sent into exile in Piedmont. When Cardinal Viale-Prelà heard what had happened, he lodged a protest with the Governor of Romagna—the same man who, two months before, had proclaimed religious freedom in the newly liberated territory—arguing that in beating down the doors of the San Lazzaro church the government had violated a sacred place and trampled on the rights of members of the clergy. The Archbishop demanded that the two priests be returned to their parishes immediately. Leonetto Cipriani, Romagna's first governor—recently returned from exile in California—replied that the two priests had been sent away for their own good, to protect them from the patriotic wrath of their own parishioners. The Governor promised to permit the priests to return just as soon as popular anger had subsided. Not long thereafter, under Romagna's new governor, Luigi Farini, the clergymen were in fact allowed back. Their case was hardly an isolated one. In the summer of 1859 alone, six priests of the Bologna diocese were exiled, five jailed, and twenty-four given official warnings.[21]

Luigi Carlo Farini, who became governor of Romagna in November, had not always been an antagonist of the Church, and had even served as a minister in the short-lived constitutional government of the Papal States in 1848, before Pius IX was routed from Rome. However, by 1859 he had changed his loyalties, and he wanted to move quickly to solidify the new regime. In mid-November, Farini proclaimed that the laws of the Kingdom of Sardinia would be extended to the areas under his control; later in the month, he announced the end to the separate governments of Romagna and the former duchies of Modena and Parma. The result was a single entity that would serve as the basis for the region of Emilia-Romagna, with its capital in Bologna, a territory that remains today one of Italy's twenty regions. To link this new government to the Kingdom of Sardinia, Farini proclaimed that from January 1, 1860, the region would bear the name of the *Royal* Provinces of Emilia, and coins would be minted bearing the likeness of the King.

Heading a government that claimed lands taken from two dukes and the Pope, Farini knew who the enemy was and what had to be done to hold on to power. At the end of November 1859, he wrote: "I will fortify Bologna as necessary. Good soldiers and good cannons against all those who want to fight annexation. This is my policy. And I don't give a damn about scruples. Without hanging me and burning down Parma, Modena, and Bologna, God knows that neither dukes nor priests will be returning here."[22]

In Rome, the Pope and his Secretary of State refused to believe that Romagna was lost for good. On December 10, Odo Russell, in a confidential memo to the Foreign Office in London, reported that since September the Pontiff had become extremely irritable, venting his rage "indiscriminately before those who approach his presence in acrimonious invectives against the Emperor Napoleon and his Ambassador in Rome."[23] For the Pope and the Church, however, even greater ignominy lay ahead.

CHAPTER 18

The Inquisitor's Arrest

F ATHER FELETTI HAD SEEN the Cardinal Legate flee, angry mobs gather outside the Archbishop's gate, the new rulers perform their sacrileges in the basilica of San Petronio, parish priests warned, arrested, and exiled, and, most close to home, the Inquisition denounced as a barbaric vestige of the Middle Ages, intolerable in a civilized society. He had little reason to feel confident that the new rulers would leave him alone.

The topsy-turvy political developments that so pained Father Feletti appeared to the Mortara family as providential, offering a new ray of hope that their son would soon be freed. The Pope had made it plain that he would never willingly give up Edgardo, but his ability to keep the boy depended on the continuation of his temporal reign. Once he lost control of the police, all the ecclesiastical law and Church precedent cited by the Pope's learned advisors would not avail him. Edgardo would be returned to his parents.

The family had moved out of Bologna shortly after Marianna and Momolo returned from Rome to find that little was left of his once-flourishing business. Marianna did not want to remain in the city that, for her, conjured up only wretched memories. Fortunately, the Rothschild family had offered the Mortaras enough money to pay off their debts and establish a home elsewhere. Their choice of destination seemed natural at the time: they moved to Turin, where Jews were free, where the Inquisition had long since been abolished, where their children would be safe. They would join the Jewish community that had championed their cause and that would help Momolo start up his new business.[1]

Papal power had fallen in Bologna, but Edgardo was in Rome, where the

Pope still ruled. Although Momolo saw no point in returning to Bologna, the crumbling of papal power there did give him hope that the rest of the Pope's temporal kingdom would soon fall as well. Short of that, Momolo hoped that, given Pius IX's parlous situation, the European powers could make him yield Edgardo as part of the price to be paid for continuing to rule Rome. The people whom Momolo most needed to influence, then, were to be found not only in Turin but in Paris and London, and so it was that he spent the last months of 1859 and January of 1860 in the French and British capitals, aided by funds raised by Jews not only in Italy but in France as well.

Luigi Carlo Farini's dramatic entry in the old duchy of Modena as the champion of the people against the retrograde powers of the Church made an impression on another Mortara, Momolo's father, Simon, who lived in Reggio. If the new ruler was promising to right the wrongs of papal rule, would he not do everything he could to undo the damage done to the Mortara family? On October 30, Simon called on the Dictator to have his grandson returned to him, and Farini obliged by ordering the newly formed Justice Department to launch an inquiry. A few days later, Farini added the role of Governor of Romagna to that of Dictator of Modena and Parma, and among his first actions, taken November 14, was the abolition of the Inquisition in all the lands under his control.

On December 30, writing from his home in Reggio, Simon pressed his plea to Farini. "My son, Momolo," he wrote, "devastated by having his son Edgardo abducted by the Pontifical Government of Rome, is currently in London seeking the support of that Power to demand the restitution of our beloved Edgardo." Having thus explained why it was he, rather than the boy's father, who was making the appeal, Simon continued: "Independent of the steps that my son is able to take, and knowing of the loyalty, justice, and humanity of Your Excellency, I make so bold as to call on you and beg you with this note, in my son's name as well, to make use of your powerful inter-vention to bring about the longed for return of my most beloved grandson Edgardo, for since the day he was taken from his family, we have had neither peace nor solace."

Farini was a busy man, facing the daunting tasks of constructing a new government, maintaining public order, and warding off the much-feared counterattack of the armies of the ancien régime. But he gave immediate attention to Simon Mortara's plea, and on December 31 ordered the Justice Minister to go after the "authors of the kidnapping."[2] Shortly thereafter, newspapers throughout Europe reported the arrest of the Inquisitor on the request of Edgardo's grandfather, but they did not have it quite right. What Simon Mortara had asked Farini for was the return of his grandson, not the Inquisitor's arrest. Unfortunately for the despondent grandfather, neither

Edgardo nor those who kept him came under Farini's power. Father Feletti, however, did.

When, on New Year's Eve, the order was given to proceed with the case against the Inquisitor, the man put in charge was 41-year-old Filippo Curletti, a trusted agent of Count Cavour, and director general of police for Romagna, who had been sent from Piedmont to assist Farini.[3] Knowing how strongly Farini felt about the Mortara case—viewing it as the incarnation of all that was wrong with the old order of justice, and hence offering potent symbolism for demonstrating the virtues of the new—Curletti gave it top priority. Early in the morning of January 2, 1860, he left the city and took the road down the Po Valley to the town of Cento, twenty miles away. He was in search of a key witness, Second Lieutenant (formerly Brigadier) Giuseppe Agostini, the man who had taken Edgardo to Rome and whose accounts of the miracle en route had inspired Catholics across the continent.

In a second-floor room of Cento's government palace, Curletti interviewed the 53-year-old police officer. After describing the painful siege at the Mortara home, Agostini told of the journey to Rome but made no mention of any miraculous visitations, saying simply: "Arriving in Rome in the first days of July, I took the boy to the House of the Catechumens, where the superior of that institution received him, telling me that he had already had a communication from Father Inquisitor Feletti about it." Agostini ended his account by saying that, after leaving the boy off, he had gone directly back to his post in Lojano. But suspecting that the policeman was leaving something out, Curletti asked him if, following his return, he hadn't spoken with Father Feletti and, indeed, received some kind of reward from him. Yes, the Second Lieutenant admitted, he had gone to see the Inquisitor at San Domenico subsequently, but only because he was ordered to do so by Colonel De Dominicis. At the convent, "after I told him I had brought my assignment to a happy conclusion, he showed great satisfaction, and as I was leaving he gave me a gift of four scudi [coins], wrapped in paper."[4]

It was late in the day when Curletti finally got back to the police offices on the third floor of Bologna's Palazzo Comunale, but despite the hour, two Bologna-based carabinieri awaited him there. Both men had recently passed smoothly from their jobs with the pontifical police to the police force of the newly organized state.[5] Curletti had called them in to verify, through duly sworn legal declarations, who had ordered that Edgardo Mortara be forcibly removed from his home on June 24, 1858. Curletti was in a hurry. It was after midnight when the first of the men, Placido Vizzardelli, aged 59, Lieutenant Colonel of the carabinieri, began his testimony.

Vizzardelli recalled that one day, when he was at work at the Bologna carabinieri headquarters, his boss, Colonel De Dominicis, post commander,

told him to send a message to Brigadier Agostini ordering him to come immediately to Bologna. Agostini soon appeared, as ordered, and was directed by
De Dominicis to go to the home of the Mortara boy and to take him to Rome.
Vizzardelli volunteered, further, that the order had come to De Dominicis
from the Dominican Father Feletti, the Inquisitor. "The ones who could give
you more information on this disgusting fact," he added, "are Agostini,
whom I mentioned, and Marshal Caroli, both of whom are now under my
command."

Indeed, the other man waiting his turn to testify that night was Pietro
Caroli. Aged 38, Caroli had in 1858 been vice-brigadier in the pontifical carabinieri, in charge of keeping Bologna police records. One day in June 1858, he
recounted, he processed a letter in which Feletti directed De Dominicis "to go
to the home of the Israelite Mortara in this city in order to take his son, who,
as I well recall, was named Edgardo, and to put the boy at his disposition."
Caroli continued: "I know that this task was carried out by Pietro Lucidi, Marshal of the carabinieri, and, if I recall correctly, aided by Brigadier Giuseppe
Agostini . . . and that the boy was taken to Rome to the House of the Catechumens by Agostini." Caroli remembered, further, that Father Feletti's letter
warned them to be sure not to confuse Edgardo with one of his brothers.

For the police chief, Curletti, as later for the prosecutor, one of the key
bits of legal evidence in fixing responsibility for the order to seize the child was
the letter that Caroli had described, in which the Inquisitor ordered De
Dominicis to take Edgardo. Its whereabouts interested the investigator a great
deal, and it was to this topic that the interrogation of the former police record-
keeper turned. Caroli informed Curletti, to his dismay, that Feletti's letter and
De Dominicis's subsequent orders for seizing Edgardo were no longer to be
found: "When the Turin newspapers began to speak of this fact, Signor De
Dominicis removed the papers, which were in my hands, and from that time
on, I never saw them again." Nor were related orders to be found, for when
the end of papal rule in Bologna was approaching in June 1859, Lieutenant
Colonel Vizzardelli ordered the records of the pontifical police destroyed.

Marshal Caroli, perhaps feeling that he was not making the best impression on the newly appointed chief of all police in Romagna, added that shortly
after the Mortara boy was taken, Father Feletti had written a letter to Agostini
praising him for the happy outcome of the operation. The Inquisitor, he
added, had remarked to Caroli himself how satisfied he was at the way things
had gone. On the other hand, Caroli volunteered, he later heard Marshal
Lucidi, who had carried out the operation, "complain about the difficulties
they ran into, and protest that, should a similar case appear, he would for-
mally refuse to take part."[6]

Father Feletti was far from the first inquisitor to find his authority contested by the secular rulers. Indeed, the history of the Inquisition in Italy is that of a struggle for power—the power to sit in judgment of the population, from pauper to prince, infidel to bishop—pitting the centralized Church against a panoply of other contenders, both civil and religious.

From its beginnings, the Inquisition had been closely identified with the Dominicans, the Church's foremost experts on matters of theology and law. From the thirteenth century, when the first Inquisition went after here- tics, most inquisitors were Dominicans. While this initial inquisitorial effort petered out, the battle against the Protestant Reformation brought a revival and reorganization of the Inquisition in Italy in the sixteenth century as the struggle against heresy took on new urgency. In 1542, Pope Paul III established the Congregation of the Holy Office, composed of cardinals, to oversee the Inquisition. This centralized in Rome the battle against heresy and unortho- doxy in all their forms, from offensive profanity to satanism, from ridiculing the clergy to having sex with the devil, from reading proscribed books to founding new religions. Alongside this modern Italian, or Roman, Inquisition were two quite separate institutions: the notorious—at least among Jews— Spanish Inquisition, established in 1478 by King Ferdinand V and Queen Isabella, directed initially against Jews and Muslims—and the Portuguese In- quisition, begun in 1531. While both the Spanish and the Portuguese inquisi- tions had been abolished earlier in the nineteenth century, the Italian Inquisition remained alive.[7]

For the Church, the Inquisition was no minor matter. The cardinals who made up the Holy Office were among the most powerful in Rome, and its head, who sometimes chaired its sessions, was the Pope himself.[8]

Every inquisitor in Bologna—from the first, in 1273, to the last, Father Feletti—was a Dominican and lived in special quarters at the convent of San Domenico. One of Father Feletti's rooms there housed the huge wooden cabi- nets in which the most precious of all his possessions were kept: the inquisito- rial records, containing the texts of interrogations and correspondence with the Holy Office in Rome. A second room, above the first, had in the past been dedicated to the torture used to encourage confessions, although it was no longer employed for this purpose in the nineteenth century. A third room served for more traditional interrogations, and this is where Anna Morisi had been brought for her tête-à-tête with Father Feletti. It contained a leather- covered table, a leather armchair, a rush-seated chair, and a wooden bench on which sat the scribe who recorded the interrogations. Adjacent to this chamber was a little room, well insulated from the rest of the convent, which had in the past been used for difficult interrogations that were likely to be loud and unpleasant, although not requiring the special features of the torture chamber. Below was the schoolroom, where the younger Dominican brothers studied proper legal procedure so that they, too, might one day become inquisitors. In the past, there had also been jail cells, a perennial headache for the inquisitors, both because there were not enough of them and because they were not as secure as they should be. Escape was far from unknown.[9]

Throughout most of its history in Bologna, the modern Inquisition focused on stamping out Protestant heresy, a task made more demanding by the fact that the city's famed university attracted students and teachers from lands where the virus of Lutheranism and Calvinism was widespread. In the half century between its establishment and the expulsion of the Jews from Bologna, however, Bologna's inquisitors had on numerous occasions to deal with the special problems posed by the Jews.

On August 12, 1553, the Holy Office in Rome ordered inquisitors throughout the land to collect and burn all copies of the Talmud found in Jewish homes and synagogues; four years later, it forbade Jews to own any Hebrew books other than the Old Testament.[10] Just months before the Jews were expelled from Bologna and began their two centuries of exile, a Jew was arrested and charged with having destroyed a number of sacred Christian images at roadside shrines in the city. Allegro, son of Jacob, from the ghetto of Modena, was arrested together with a Christian friend, Ottavio Bargellini. Although they were found innocent of the sacrilege, the interrogations revealed their guilt of another crime against God and religion: sodomy. To that charge was added, for Bargellini, accusations of having been "Judaized" through his contact with Allegro. The two men were condemned to death.

On May 22, the day set for his execution, Allegro—no doubt hoping to win a reprieve—declared his desire to become a Christian and, indeed, was baptized at eight o'clock that very morning. But the sentence stood, and the two men were promptly led off to the special platform set up in Piazza Maggiore, where without further ado they were decapitated. Yet even under these sanguinary circumstances, the baptism of a Jew was cause for celebration. While his Christian companion's body was unceremoniously tossed in a hole and covered, Allegro's was laid out in San Petronio, his head placed atop his neck. That afternoon, amidst great pomp and the enthusiastic participation of large numbers of Bolognesi, his bipartite cadaver was transported to the church of San Domenico for burial. He was buried with his new name, Paolo Orsini, bestowed on him that day by his proud baptismal godfather, Lodovico Orsini. It was nine days after notices had appeared on the streets of Bologna ordering all Jews out of the city.[11]

The Inquisition's heyday had passed by the beginning of the eighteenth century—no longer were heretics publicly immolated, nor were suspects hoisted off the ground by their wrists, bound behind their lower back.[12] But it was only with the French invasion of Italy in the last years of the century that the Inquisition was first declared at an end. Not only was Bologna's inquisitor out of a job; he no longer had a home, for the Dominican convent was dismantled and the inquisitorial archives were seized. The Inquisition returned in Bologna, as in the rest of the Papal States, only in the aftermath of the fall of the French in 1814.

Among the Holy Office's major responsibilities in the Restoration years was oversight of the Jews of the Papal States. In addition to adjudicating individual cases of Jews who had run amok, it issued edicts reminding the population of the restrictions that had been reimposed on the Jews. In 1843, the Holy Office distributed a complete list: Jews were prohibited from providing Christians with lodging or food, nor could they have Christians work for them. Jews were not permitted to own land or buildings. Jews could not spend the night outside of their ghetto, nor could they have "friendly relations with Christians." Jews were prohibited from conducting any ceremonies in connection with burying their dead. The Inquisitor General concluded the edict: "Those who violate these dispositions will be punished by the Holy Inquisition," adding, "these provisions will be communicated to the Ghettoes and published in the Synagogues."[13]

At the time that Father Feletti first wrote to the Holy Office in Rome asking how to proceed in the Mortara case, he, like his Bologna predecessors, had had little practice in dealing with Jews. He knew, however, that the Holy Office had had a great deal of experience. The twelve cardinals who made up the Congregation of the Holy Office, with their expert staff, met each Monday to decide just such cases as he had sent before it.

By contrast, the newly assembled team in charge of criminal justice for the Royal Government of the Provinces of Emilia, an entity that had come into existence only the day before, had had little experience at all. In prosecuting the first criminal case under the new regime, they faced a political and legal morass; it was far from clear just what laws should be applied. But for the moment, they were more concerned about the outrage of an inquisitor ordering a child seized from his parents than they were about the niceties of applying a new legal system retroactively to the actions of the old.

Once Curletti completed his late-night interrogations of the two carabinieri, he decided, with Farini's encouragement, to arrest the Inquisitor. He assembled an imposing group for the mission, for Father Feletti was no ordinary criminal. Accompanying Curletti to San Domenico were several top officers of the Bologna police, plus Francesco Carboni, the prosecuting magistrate, and a large number of other police. Just before 3 a.m. they arrived at San Domenico, barely a two-minute ride from the Palazzo Comunale. Father Feletti himself later described the scene of his arrest:

> On the morning of the second of this month, at around 2:30, I was surprised in my bed by various police officers, and by a large number of

other policemen, who announced that I had to get dressed and prepare for a search of the premises. Putting my clothes on as quickly as I could, I was taken from my bedroom to the other room of my residence, where I was told by a police inspector—who was not Bolognese [Curletti's accent giving him away]—that I was under arrest. After that they began to interrogate me, declaring that I was guilty of an assault on public tranquillity for having ordered, as they said, the taking of the boy Edgardo Mortara, son of the Jew Momolo.[14]

Two worlds collided that night as the police officers invaded the Inquisitor's quarters with their accusations of kidnapping and their impatience with the Dominican brother who stubbornly refused to recognize their right to judge him. The tables turned as Father Feletti, in his own quarters in San Domenico, faced his inquisitors.

"My name is Father Pier Gaetano Feletti, of the Order of Dominicans," he told them. "My father, now deceased, was Filippo. I was born in Comacchio [near Ferrara]; I live in this convent. I never before this moment have had any encounter with the Law, nor have I ever been arrested or tried." Asked whether he knew why he had been placed under arrest, he replied that he did not but added: "In this regard I must declare the following: I view this arrest as the act of an incompetent authority, for I am a priest, and, indeed, I was once charged by the Holy Pontiff with overseeing the Inquisition in Bologna."

"Are you aware," the police chief asked, "of the kidnapping of the boy Edgardo Mortara, which took place in this city, at the hands of the Pontifical gendarmes, on June 24, 1858?"

On that subject, Father Feletti responded, "I can say nothing."

But the police inspector persisted: Did you write a letter to Colonel De Dominicis, in your capacity as Father Inquisitor, ordering him to arrange the boy's abduction?

"If I wrote official letters to anyone I would not deny it, but neither can I say anything about it."

Curletti, infuriated by the monk's reserve, repeated the question, but the Inquisitor simply responded: "I am prevented by a sacred oath from revealing anything that is the property of the Tribunal of the Catholic Faith."

Phrasing the question a bit differently, Curletti asked whether it wasn't, in fact, the Inquisitor's order that had led Brigadier Agostini to take the boy to the Catechumens in Rome. After brushing this off, too, by invoking his oath of secrecy, Father Feletti added: "Since I hear the name of a certain boy, Edgardo Mortara, mentioned, I must say that I am filled with consolation knowing that I have in that innocent creature another guardian Angel who will pray for Divine mercy for me to save my soul."

After a series of other questions failed to elicit a useful reply, Curletti ordered the monk to hand over all his files dealing with the Mortara case.

"I have nothing here having to do with the affairs of the Holy Office," he responded. He had burned all of the Mortara documents. But when asked to specify when he had committed them to the flames and how he had gone about it, Father Feletti repeated that on matters concerning the Holy Office he could say nothing.

Curletti made one last attempt to loosen the Inquisitor's tongue: "The kidnapping of the Mortara boy undermined public order and family tranquillity. So let me once again urge you to give more satisfactory responses, since whatever office a man occupies, and especially for someone like the Father Inquisitor, he should be prepared to give an explanation of the orders he has given."

"As far as the activities that I carried out as Inquisitor of the Holy Office of Bologna," Father Feletti replied, "I am obliged to explain myself to one forum only, to the Supreme Sacred Congregation in Rome, whose Prefect is His Holiness Pope Pius IX, and to no one else."

As was the custom, the transcript of the interrogation was then read to Father Feletti for his signature, but he refused to put his name on it. The document was signed by the other eight men present: the police chief, Curletti, the prosecutor, Carboni, four police officers, and two others brought in as witnesses.

Despite the monk's protests, Curletti ordered the police to search the convent for the inquisitorial records dealing with the Mortara case. They explored every cranny of Feletti's quarters, as well as the cabinets that had housed the inquisitorial archives, and the convent library. Finding nothing, and with sunrise fast approaching, Curletti gave up. The Dominican priest, his flowing white robes dragging along the stone courtyard outside San Domenico, was escorted into the police wagon. The procession galloped back to police headquarters, stopping on the way to deposit the Inquisitor at his new home in the notorious Torrone prison.[15]

Of all the episodes in the heavily mythologized Mortara story, the arrest of Father Feletti at San Domenico stands out for the speed with which it acquired mythic dimensions. Despite his central role in the case, the priest had not previously gotten much popular attention. The other personalities on the Church side were too well known. When anyone in Bologna was blamed for the affair, it was always Cardinal Viale-Prelà, whose fame was continent-wide and who conveniently incarnated, in the public eye, the zeal for religious orthodoxy. Story after story had assigned the Cardinal the role of organizing and overseeing Edgardo's seizure, despite the lack of any supporting evidence. And, in any case, with the main battle having long since moved to Rome, where Edgardo was being held, attention centered on Cardinal Antonelli and

Pope Pius IX. It was only with the arrival of Curletti and his police compan-
ions at San Domenico that Father Feletti, belatedly, earned his rightful place at
the center of attention.

Dramatic as his arrest actually was, the scene at San Domenico was greatly
embellished in the European press. The liberal papers treated the news with
great excitement, their accounts reporting details (largely invented) that fed
the image of him as a religious fanatic—sincere in his beliefs perhaps, but
fanatic nonetheless.

Most widely quoted was the story carried in the *Times* of London, which
had the police arriving in the nick of time, catching the monk just as he was
boarding a carriage to flee. As the hand of the law came down on him, the
monk fell to his knees in the street "to thank Heaven for having chosen him to
be the martyr for the holy cause." Turning his attention back to earth, the
Times account continued, Father Feletti then hurled curses and threats of excommunication at his captors, to which they responded with derision.[16] Bottrigari, in his Bologna chronicle, added that although Feletti had claimed that,
on the orders of his superiors, he had burned all the inquisitorial records, a
careful search by the police had yielded "a pack of papers that are thought to
have some importance."[17] This rumor, too, gained wide distribution, although
in fact the police had found nothing.

The Catholic press greeted news of the Inquisitor's arrest with outrage,
yet, curiously, some of its own inventions neatly paralleled those of the liberal
press. Just how the two narratives dovetailed can be seen in the decision by the
ultramontane *Il Cattolico* to reproduce, in lieu of its own account of the arrest,
the version published by Milan's newly founded liberal paper, *La perseveranza*. In this account,

> When the police arrived at the convent and knocked on the front gate,
> although it was 3 a.m., it was promptly opened, because the porter was
> expecting a monk who was still out. Obeying the police agents' orders,
> the porter took them to Father Feletti's rooms. . . . No sooner had they
> rung than a lay brother opened the door for them. When the police
> entered the Inquisitor's rooms and ordered him to get up, he did so, but
> then he immediately got down on his knees and said, "I give thanks
> to the Lord for your visit; blessed are those whom He visits in their
> suffering."

What to the liberal *La perseveranza* was evidence of fanatical folly was, for
the pious editors of *Il Cattolico*, an inspiring account of faith and the triumph
of Christianity against the brutality of its adversaries. That the event in question happened only in their imaginations made little difference.

For the Jews of the former lands of the Papal States that now came under

Farini's control, news of the Inquisitor's arrest was greeted with joy and deep satisfaction. On January 17, one Leone Ravenna wrote to the *Archives Israélites* from Ferrara to say that the government gazette had just confirmed Father Feletti's arrest. For Ravenna, the order to arrest and try the Inquisitor was additional grounds for praising the new government, "a government free to act to redress all wrongs, to see, above all, justice and reason triumph." Farini, he wrote, realized what the Mortara case represented. "The whole world applauds him, and the Jews of all nations will pray to the Almighty God for the final victory of this cause that is Italy, that is the cause of Jewry, the cause of civilization and freedom."[18]

At the same time, Joseph Pavia, a Jew from Bologna, also wrote to the French paper to report the exciting news. He added an unflattering portrait of Father Feletti, describing him as a "well-educated and very cunning man. He well knew the Roman government's bad faith and the mess it has made but, because he was eager for power and money, he attached himself to it with all his force and became its most devoted agent." Although Pavia shows a marked lack of sympathy for—or understanding of—the Inquisitor, he does raise a concern that was beginning to trouble even some of those who were happiest to see the proud Dominican jailed: "The question arises as to whether his arrest is legal or if, rather, it is no more than an act of reprisal against the papal government." Pavia got to the heart of the problem that the Bologna criminal court would soon face: "If, in effect, he played no role other than that of a gendarme, I don't know how they can find him guilty." Pavia entered this doubt parenthetically, for, he wrote, "regardless, this arrest is a great demonstration against the intolerance of the government of Rome." He expressed doubt that the Inquisitor's arrest would prompt the Vatican to release Edgardo but concluded his letter by reporting that the news of the arrest had been "met everywhere with great joy, as always happens when oppressors or their lackeys are punished for their tyranny."[19]

CHAPTER 19

The Case Against
the Inquisitor

FATHER FELETTI'S NEW HOME was a frigid, window-less cell in the tower that still today forms one corner of the massive municipal complex in the center of the city. Known for centuries simply as *il torrone*, "the tower," it had a notorious history, specializing in political prisoners. When it was built, in 1352, prisons were designed primarily for people awaiting trial. The notion of keeping a person locked in a cell after sentence had little appeal when better options—public penance, torture, exile, consignment to the galleys, and execution—were available and were swifter, cheaper, and more educational. In 1365, a fortification was built around the emerging government palace, and *il torrone* began its long history as the northwestern corner of the palisaded center of power in Bologna. Massively walled, but of modest dimensions—about eight meters square—the tower loomed over via Vetturini, where the Mortaras had lived when, according to Anna Morisi, she baptized Edgardo.[1]

In the first days following Father Feletti's arrest, his case remained in the hands of the police chief, Curletti. While the monk got accustomed to his new quarters, Curletti, in his office in another part of the government complex, saw a parade of witnesses as he reconstructed what had happened on those two days in June 1858. The Mortaras' Jewish friend Giuseppe Vitta testified about the scene when Edgardo was finally taken from Momolo's arms and put into the police carriage. Marianna Mortara's brother and her uncle then testified, the first telling how the crying Riccardo had told him the terrible news at the cafe and pleaded with him to rush to his family's aid, the latter recounting how he had convinced the Inquisitor to grant a delay and how he had taken the Inquisitor's slip of paper and presented it to Marshal Lucidi. He also recalled his fruitless trip the next morning in search of the Cardinal Legate and the Archbishop. Bonajuto Sanguinetti, the 73-year-old Jewish banker who had lived next door to the Mortaras, remembered peering out of his window and seeing five or six carabinieri milling outside, and then recounted the ghastly scene he had witnessed on his arrival that night at the Mortara home.

On January 18, full authority for the prosecution of the case was turned over to Francesco Carboni, the magistrate who had been present at Father Feletti's arrest and who had witnessed his defiant testimony at San Domenico. Carboni first had to draw up the official charge. It was a significant moment, for neither the decision of whom to include in the charge nor that of what to charge them with was a simple one. Clearly they would charge Father Feletti, who had ordered the child seized, but what of those who had actually carried out the abduction? Colonel De Dominicis had overseen and organized the operation, Marshal Lucidi had been in charge of carrying it out, and Brigadier Agostini had taken the boy from his home to Rome. And what about Father Feletti's own superiors in Rome, those who had presumably authorized him to have the child seized? The implications of following that path had to give the magistrate pause, for he could quickly end up—in the first major criminal case tried by the new government of Emilia—bringing charges against the Pope himself.

No less thorny was the problem of what to charge them with. Did Farini's prosecutors and courts have any jurisdiction over what had happened in Bologna a year before the new regime emerged? Could they put on trial an inquisitor who had, at the time, been legally invested with the power to enforce the faith? In short, could legal principles of the new state be applied retroactively? Or would the courts have to judge those charged according to the laws of the ancien régime, able to find them guilty only insofar as they were determined to have disobeyed the laws then in effect?

Dated January 18, 1860, and embossed with the name of the Royal Government of the Provinces of Emilia, Civil and Criminal Lower Court in Bologna, Carboni's indictment read as follows:

Charge

Of the violent separation of the boy Edgardo Mortara from his own Jewish family on the grounds of presumed baptism, occurring in Bologna the evening of June 24, 1858, and followed by his reclusion in the House of the Catechumens in Rome.

Against

The monk Pier Gaetano Feletti of the Order of Preachers, and former Inquisitor of the Holy Office, arrested January 2, 1860. Lieutenant Colonel Luigi De Dominicis of the Pontifical Police, who has fled to the Dominions of the Holy Faith.

The charge, then, was abduction. In addition to Father Feletti, De Dominicis was charged, but not Lucidi or Agostini. The logic employed was that De Dominicis, as the head of the Bologna police, was responsible for determining whether the order given him by the Inquisitor was legal, whereas those under his command could not be held responsible for obeying a direct order from their superior. More to the point, perhaps, was De Dominicis's status as a symbol of the abuses of papal power and craven collaboration with the Austrian occupiers. Memories of his recent cowardly assault on unarmed students at the university were still vivid. The police chief, no doubt recognizing the risks of remaining in Bologna after the fall of papal power, had fled along with the Cardinal Legate, seeking safety in what remained of the Papal States.

On January 23, three weeks after Father Feletti's arrest, he had his first visitor, the prosecuting magistrate Carboni, who had come to the monk's cell to hear his story. "He seems to be aged 65," Carboni wrote in his report of their meeting, "of average height, his hair is gray, as are his eyelashes and eyebrows, with a large forehead, dark eyes, big nose, evenly proportioned mouth, round chin, and oval face." Carboni asked him to identify himself:

> I am Father Pier Gaetano Feletti, aged 62, born in Comacchio, resident in Bologna, member of the religious family of the order of Dominicans. I have been in this city since I was sent here by the Holy Pontiff in 1838 to serve as the chief Inquisitor of the Holy Office. I always exercised that office with a prudent moderation which the whole city could count on, and operated in conformity with the orders of the Supreme Sacred Congregation of the Holy Office in Rome, on which I depended. . . .
>
> In responding to your interrogations, I do not intend to renounce that Canon privilege that the Church gives me not to be tried by an incompetent court. I believe that it is my duty to say this if I am to avoid running the risk of incurring ecclesiastical censure myself.

Father Feletti's claim of ecclesiastical privilege made no impression on Carboni, who warned the prisoner that he was obligated to tell the truth, to answer the questions that the magistrate would put to him. The privilege of which he spoke, Carboni informed him, had been abolished by the government's recent proclamations. Now all citizens were equal before the law.

Asked to describe his arrest, Father Feletti told of being roused from his sleep, getting hurriedly dressed, being informed of the charge against him, and refusing to answer the questions put to him because to do so would violate his sacred oath of silence. "How can they charge me with a crime against public tranquillity for something that took place two years ago by order of the Government that was then in office? How," the Inquisitor added, "could they proceed with such severity against a functionary of the Holy See simply because he did his duty and obeyed the commands of the Head of the Catholic Church?" Yet the monk expressed his deep faith: "I bow my head before the decisions made in Heaven, I put myself in God's hands alone, trusting in His mercy."

In the three weeks that Father Feletti had spent pondering his predicament since his arrest, he had decided that there were some things about the Mortara case that he could say without violating his oath, and he was eager to say them. Since certain aspects of the episode had become public knowledge, he told Carboni, there was no harm in trying to set these straight.

Despite this preface, what Feletti first had to say was anything but public knowledge, for it regarded his communication with the Holy Office in Rome. The point would turn out to be a critical one, for as the trial evolved, a key issue became whether the Inquisitor had acted on his own or had simply been following orders from on high. "Having learned that the boy Edgardo Mortara had been baptized while in danger of death," he told the magistrate, "the Supreme Sacred Congregation ordered that this child be taken to Rome to the House of Catechumens, and I was given responsibility for [the order's] execution."

Lest the prosecutor miss his point, Father Feletti reiterated that in having the child taken from his family and sent to Rome, he had done nothing other than "carry out the orders that were given me by the Supreme Tribunal of the Holy Office in Rome, which never promulgates any decree without the consent of the Roman Pontiff, the Supreme Head of the Catholic Church."

In seeing that the order was carried out, Father Feletti hastened to add, he had taken every possible precaution to ensure that only the gentlest means of persuasion were employed. He had, in particular, been at pains to persuade Edgardo's mother to give her son up "spontaneously," and he had even granted a twenty-four-hour stay toward this end. This had had the desired effect. When Momolo visited him on the afternoon of June 24, the monk reported, the two of them agreed on a plan "to induce his wife to let her son go, and in fact the mother, in complete tranquillity, left her son."

Where the Inquisitor drew the line was in answering any questions on the sources of his information, on how he first heard that Edgardo had been baptized, or what he had done to see if the rumors were true. The frustrated magistrate asked Father Feletti to give him at least the names of people who could verify his claim that the child had been baptized. "The Tribunal of the Supreme Sacred Inquisition in Rome," responded the former inquisitor, "the Prefect of which is the Vicar of Jesus Christ, Pope Pius IX, is the one best informed of the matters you are asking me about."

"You say that the order to take the Mortara child from his family came from the Supreme Sacred Congregation of the Holy Office in Rome," the magistrate countered. "Do you have any means of supporting that claim?"

"The proof that I can adduce . . . is the faith that the Roman Pontiff placed in me, although I am but his miserable and humble servant. And another proof," Father Feletti added, "comes from the good people of the city of Bologna, who have always regarded me kindly, believing me incapable of abusing the office that the Roman Pontiff has entrusted to me."

Under questioning from Carboni, Father Feletti went on to describe the orders he had given to Colonel De Dominicis, his preparation of the list of names of the Mortara children, and his warning to Marshal Lucidi to keep a close watch on the Mortara home during the daylong vigil, given the danger that the Jews might decide to sacrifice their son rather than give him up to the Church.

It was getting late, and Carboni told the Inquisitor that he had to go. But the monk who, three weeks earlier, had refused to respond to any questions had more now that he wanted to say. He had not yet had the chance to tell of Edgardo's trip to Rome, nor of the boy's wish to become a Christian and leave his parents behind. It was a tale that, in the monk's eyes, provided proof enough that his actions had been not only legal but providential, guided by the hand of God.

He got to tell Carboni his story the next day, beginning with the very moment when, on the evening of June 23, 1858, the Mortara family first learned that Edgardo had been baptized and would be taken away. While "his brothers and sisters all cried at this news," said Father Feletti, "Edgardo remained quiet and tranquil. And then on the evening of June 24, when he had to get ready to leave, he let the carabinieri help him get dressed. His spirit was serene, and he was completely at ease and happy." And then on the voyage to Rome, "when it was time to stop to let the horses cool off and to get something to eat, Edgardo often asked the marshal to take him to church."

In Rome, the boy's inspiring saga continued:

Seeing so much happiness in the boy for having become Christian, the Holy Pontiff, in his wisdom, always guided as he is by the Holy Spirit . . . arranged to have the boy's father and mother called to Rome. He put two seats in a stagecoach at their disposition so that they themselves could judge their son Edgardo's desire to remain in the Christian religion. . . .

In fact, once they got to Rome, Edgardo's parents were given permission to speak with their son together with the Rabbi of Rome. These three did all they could, using all the arguments they knew, to persuade the boy to return with them. But he, all by himself, a child of about nine years [sic], knew how to protect himself from his father's, his mother's, and the Rabbi's temptations. He told them that he was a Christian, and he wanted to live and die as a Christian.

Moreover, he added that he would "pray to God for the conversion of his father, his mother, and his brothers and sisters." Said Father Feletti, "I do not know whether it was just once, or more often, that the two parents spoke with their son. But I do know that the boy had a number of meetings with the Rabbi of Rome, and that he always remained firm in his desire to remain a Christian."

Father Feletti then gave his version of the encounter in Alatri: "At the time the Mortara parents were staying in Rome, which was in the month of October, or thereabouts, the Rector of the Catechumens took Edgardo on a holiday for a few days. Having learned about it, the Mortaras went to that same place. Waiting for the chance that would present itself when the Rector went to say mass and Edgardo was assisting him . . . they entered the church and approached the boy." Fortunately, Edgardo was alert to the danger. "Seeing his mother, who, perhaps, was thinking of kidnapping him, he clung to the Rector's habit and shouted as loudly as he could: 'Mamma wants to take me away!' Those around him were thus warned, and, realizing that they were unprotected, they left the church. The boy remained with the Rector, and they returned right to the Catechumens in Rome."

Learning of the narrow escape, the Pope "decided to move the boy to the College of the Lateran Canons in San Pietro in Vincoli, where he can still be found today, doing very well, and studying in such a way as to promise much success." Indeed, Father Feletti concluded, one day the boy will prove to be "his family's support and pride, since baptism does not annul the ties of blood but, rather, reinforces respect for them, and so Edgardo will have more love for his parents than do his other brothers and sisters."

The Magistrate, hearing this amazing story of the little boy who suddenly saw the light, rejected the religion in which he had been raised, embraced Christianity with all his soul, and clung to the priest's robes to protect him from his mother, was skeptical. "Do you have any means of proving the facts you have stated?"

"As for what happened in Bologna," the monk responded, "I can only point to Agostini and Marshal Lucidi. For what happened along the voyage, there is only Agostini. As for the facts in Rome, I received my information, through letters, from individuals deserving of full faith, but I cannot give you their names."[2]

Father Feletti had now said what he wanted to say. Carboni left. The warden turned the key to his cell as the magistrate left the monk to his prayers and his thoughts.

Having heard from the Inquisitor, Carboni was now eager to hear from the victims, from Momolo and Marianna. This turned out to be difficult, for the Mortaras were not easy to locate, as they no longer lived in Bologna. Carboni requested, and received, authorization to petition the authorities of the Kingdom of Sardinia to summon Momolo to testify, but he learned that Momolo happened to be in Florence on business. Carboni discovered that Marianna's uncle Angelo Padovani, the banker, who was still living in Bologna, was in touch with him. On February 1, Padovani was called in to the prosecutor's offices and given a written request to pass on to Momolo as soon as possible, asking him to report to the Bologna prosecutor. Five days later Momolo appeared in Bologna to testify.

Carboni invited Momolo to tell about his son's kidnapping. Once he got started, it was hard to stop him. He told of the appearance at his home on the evening of June 23 of Marshal Lucidi and Agostini, his horror on learning of their mission, and the desperate attempts over the next twenty-four hours to keep them from taking Edgardo.

When Momolo's torrent of pained recollections ceased, Carboni seized on the points that were of most interest to him.

"Did Marshal Lucidi ever show you any written order that the boy be taken?"

"No."

"Do you know for a fact, as you have said, that the order in question came from Rome, and that the proof of the baptism was undertaken by that Tribunal?"

"I was never able to learn anything about it."

"Do you have any complaints about the behavior of the police in the way that they carried out their order?"

"No, I can't complain. The Marshal kissed me many times, and many of his men were clearly moved by our tears and our desolation."

"Didn't the Father Inquisitor attempt to persuade you to give up your son voluntarily, to avoid having to separate you by force?"

"I was so beside myself that I can't recall if the Father Inquisitor tried to persuade me to give him up spontaneously. The fact is, though, that I gave him up only because of force. Without that, they would never have gotten my son."

"And yet, the Father Inquisitor . . . has said that, having assured you that your child would be brought up and educated in those sciences for which he had most inclination, so that he would one day be able to support you, he was able to persuade you, so that you left quietly, and you went home to persuade the boy's mother to leave her son behind. Isn't that true?"

"It's false! Father Feletti may have used those arguments to try to convince me, but I wasn't persuaded in the least, nor did I go home to persuade my wife."

In fact, Momolo told the magistrate, at the time he went to see the Inquisitor, his wife had already gone to the Vitta home.

"And the boy, Edgardo, how did he feel about being taken from you and from your family?"

"The boy remained in bed until one o'clock in the afternoon, and though he may have realized to some extent that the police had come for him, we tried to hide it from him so as not to injure his health. Then it was all so sudden when they took him from my arms, and took him away, that I couldn't tell you whether he shouted or what he said, especially since at that moment I was practically in a daze myself. I have heard people say, though, that on his trip he kept asking for his parents and for his Mezuzah, which is a kind of medallion of our religion."

"And how did your son behave during the visits that you and your wife had with him in Rome?"

"Although he was frightened, and intimidated by the Rector's presence, he openly declared his desire to return home with us."

Perhaps Carboni felt that, for all its peculiarities, the Mortara case was not unlike many other criminal trials he had known. Accuser and accused had entirely different accounts of what had happened. The task of the Magistrate was to provoke his witnesses in such a way that the truth would come out:

"You should know," Carboni told Momolo, "that Father Feletti has said that from the moment you and your wife were told . . . that . . . Edgardo, having been baptized, had to be turned over to the Church, the boy . . . remained unperturbed, and that while the other brothers and sisters all cried, he remained quiet and tranquil. That the next evening he let the police help him get dressed, showing the same lack of concern and happiness." And then, on his way to Rome, Edgardo constantly asked to be taken to church. Carboni continued his paraphrase of Father Feletti's testimony, leading Momolo to believe that he found it convincing.

The Inquisitor's story, replied Momolo, was but a litany of lies.

When the police arrived, and for several hours afterward, Edgardo slept soundly. When he finally woke up and saw the police, he was seized by convulsive trembling, which lasted until full sunrise. And when we offered him some food to give him strength, he refused to eat before having said our morning prayer, for it is prohibited to eat before reciting it. In fact, he then recited the prayer with the prayer book open, as the police can attest, but even so he could eat very little the whole day because his system was upset. He got up late, and he got dressed without anyone's help, other than the usual assistance from his mother, who had him put on his usual clothes, along with a cap, something that doesn't bother him at all, because all his other brothers wear one when they go out of the house.

No Jewish boy should leave his head uncovered.

At the meetings with Edgardo in Rome, no rabbi had ever been present—as the Inquisitor had claimed—but, rather, once or twice Signor Scazzocchio, the secretary of the Jewish community, had accompanied him. And the Inquisitor's claim that it was the Pope who had invited Momolo and Marianna to Rome, much less paid their way, was *"falsissima."* As for the boy's alleged fright at being accosted by his mother in the church at Alatri, Marianna had never come anywhere near the church, remaining at the Rector's home while Momolo went in search of their son.

The Magistrate then turned his attention to the question of the baptism itself, for if there had been no valid baptism, the Inquisitor would have had no legal right to order Edgardo taken from his parents. Anna Morisi took center stage.

"How long was Morisi working for you?"

"About six years, with some interruptions of a few months here and there, and she left for good five or six months before our son was taken from us. She quit after having some words with my wife. She had worked for us for so long, she seemed to think that she should be the boss and do things her own way."

Had she gone away angry? asked Carboni. Was there reason to fear a vendetta?

"For some time there was less than perfect harmony between her and us, though we bore it with more good nature and patience than we should have. But there weren't any bad feelings of a sort that would reasonably lead to any fear of a vendetta."

"Who took care of little Edgardo at the time he was sick and was said to have been baptized by Morisi? Did she ever have him in her care by herself?"

"She never cared for him alone, not even at the time of that illness. . . . At night we kept him in a cradle beside our bed and during the day in a bedroom where his mother watched over him."

Carboni concluded the interrogation by asking about Anna Morisi's religious observance.

"We sent her to do her duties, but whether she did them or not I couldn't say. One thing is certain: she was no religious fanatic."[3]

CHAPTER 20

The Inquisitor's Trial

A NNA MORISI WAS NOT eager to be found by the Bologna authorities. She did not know what they might do to her. After all, were it not for her, Edgardo would never have been taken from his parents. Although she knew little about the new government beyond the fact that it was a foe of the old, she had heard her priest in Persiceto say that the new rulers were anti-Catholic, godless enemies of the Pope. If they thought nothing about barging into a convent in the middle of the night and hustling off the redoubtable Dominican monk, what chance had she in the face of their displeasure?

For Magistrate Carboni, back in Bologna, the time had come to see what he could learn from the Mortaras' former servant. On February 9, he and his assistant set off in a carriage bound for Persiceto. On their arrival, they were escorted by the chief local magistrate to a sunlit corner room on the second floor of the town hall, which he had readied for them. A policeman went to get Anna Morisi, and she soon appeared.

The Bologna magistrate led the young woman through the preliminaries: "I'm Anna Morisi, daughter of Giovanni, who's no longer living. I'm 23 years old. I was born in Persiceto and I live here, near the church of San Lorenzo. I work as a cotton spinner, and I'm married to Giuseppe Buongiovanni. I've got just one son, and I'm Catholic."

Anna was actually 26 years old, but she had never been too clear on how old she was. Her exact age would ordinarily have made little difference, but the unexpected attention paid to her otherwise obscure life had turned her age into a topic of discussion from Rome to London, Munich to San Francisco. She herself had said that she was just 14 years old when she baptized Edgardo, and her youth was picked up by the Mortara-friendly press as further evidence of why the reported baptism should not be taken seriously. In fact, at the time that, by her account, she baptized Edgardo, she was nearing her nineteenth birthday.[1]

Asked if she knew why they had called her in, she replied: "I guess it's because of the boy of my old employers, the Mortaras, Jews who live in Bologna, who I baptized, and who because of that was taken from his family by order of the Inquisitor, Father Feletti. I assume that's the reason because I heard that this monk was recently put in jail."

Anna was then asked to tell her story. Although she had hoped to avoid this encounter with the magistrate, now that she had the chance to give her own version of what had happened, she did so eagerly. Anna told of Edgardo's sickness, which, as she recalled, took place in the winter of 1851 or 1852, when he was about 4 months old. (As Doctor Saragoni's records would later reveal, Edgardo had taken ill at the end of August 1852, when he was just over a year old.) She told of the Mortaras' apparent fear for his life. "One morning," she recalled, "I saw them sitting, sad and crying, at a little table next to Edgardo's crib, reading from a book in Hebrew that the Jews read when one of them is about to die."

This scene made a big impression on her, she said, and so, a little later, when she was sent to buy some oil from Cesare Lepori's grocery nearby, she couldn't help telling him about the boy's illness. Hearing the story, Anna recollected, "Lepori suggested that I baptize him, so that when he died he would go to heaven. But I told him I didn't know how to baptize someone. I was only 14 or 15 years old, and didn't have much education about Christianity, since I was raised so roughly." The grocer, she said, assured her it was easy. All you had to do was say " 'I baptize you in the name of the Father, the Son, and the Holy Ghost,' take some water from a well, and sprinkle a few drops on the boy's head."

> When I got back to the house, I saw that the parents were watching over their sick son, so I had to wait for about an hour. They finally left the room, which was the living room, and went to their bedroom; I don't know why. I quickly drew a little water from the well, went over to the boy's crib, and repeated the words that I'd been taught, with the fixed idea of sending a soul to heaven. I put the fingers of my right hand in the glass of water, sprinkled a few drops on the boy's head, and in a moment it was all done, without anyone noticing.

To Anna's surprise, shortly after the furtive ceremony Edgardo got better, and, she said, she gave no more thought to what she had done. But years later, just three months in fact before she left the Mortara home for good, another

Mortara baby, Aristide, who was a little over a year old, also got sick. Two days before he died, Anna, on her way to the storage room upstairs, ran into another servant she knew, whose name was Regina—Anna could not recall her last name—a woman who worked for their neighbors, the Pancaldis. Regina asked her what the problem was with the Mortaras' baby, for she had heard him screaming all night long. Anna told her what she heard the doctors say: the boy had something they called the "sacred flame" and would surely die.

"Regina then asked me," said Anna, " 'Why don't you baptize him?' I said: 'Not me. I already baptized another one of them, and I wouldn't want him to live, like the other one did, and I told her the exact details about the baptism I gave Edgardo."

About two months after she left the Mortaras and began to work for the Santandrea family—above five months in all after her conversation with Regina—a man appeared, delivering a printed summons for Anna to appear before the Father Inquisitor at San Domenico. Signora Santandrea read it to her.

"I obeyed the call and was brought into that convent, into a room where Father Feletti and another Dominican father were. Father Feletti had a book open and made me touch it on a page where I could see a little cross printed, and he told me that it was the Gospel, and he said that it was a kind of oath, which bound me not to say anything about what he'd question me about." Father Feletti had then begun his investigation of the baptism:

"I innocently told him everything that I later told to those men [the Mortara brothers-in-law], and that other monk . . . wrote down everything I said, but they didn't read it back to me, and I didn't sign my cross to it, at least I don't remember it. When he finally dismissed me, he told me again not to say anything about it."

Her interrogation had taken place on a Saturday, around Christmastime, she said. Just a month later she returned to her hometown, San Giovanni in Persiceto, for she was soon to marry, and her groom was a local man. A few months later she heard rumors that the police, by order of the Holy Office, had taken Edgardo away, news "that surprised me and made me unhappy." She then told of the visit by the two Mortara brothers-in-law, her initial conversation with them, and then the decision not to talk to them anymore: "In fact, our parish priest made me keep quiet and wouldn't let me see the Jews again."

Carboni asked whether she had told anyone other than Regina about the baptism. "At first," she replied, "I didn't say anything about it to anyone else, not even to the Confessor. But after I got to Persiceto, I told my sisters about it."

After Anna repeated that it was Lepori who had told her to baptize Edgardo so he could go to heaven, Carboni asked:

"And when you later saw him get better, didn't the idea of seeing him grow up ignorant of the Catholic religion and being educated in that of the Jews make you want to get advice from your Confessor about what you had done?"

"No. It never occurred to me."

"How could it be that you never thought of it?"

"Well, sometimes I did think about it, because ... when the boy walked with me in front of one of our churches he would tip his cap, seeing that I bowed my head. But I never said anything, not even to my Confessor, named Luigi, who was one of the Fathers of the Madonna on via Galliera, because I was afraid of how angry my employers would be. They had forbidden me to take the children into our churches."

"But you really believed that you had made Edgardo a Christian after what you had done?"

"Yes, I believed it."

"But the Jews Angelo Padovani and Cesare De Angelis, who have been questioned about this matter, claim that you said that, once the boy got better, you didn't give any more thought to what you had done, that you said you didn't think it was significant because you did it without really knowing what you were doing. Is that right?"

"I can't remember what I said to the Jews because I was crying and I was all confused."

The magistrate moved on to the grocer's role in the baptism. If Cesare Lepori had, in fact, given her detailed instructions for baptizing Edgardo, as she said, it seemed obvious that when the grocer next saw her, he would have asked her whether she had gone through with it. Hadn't she said something to him about it after the baptism?

"I didn't tell him anything, and he never asked me anything about it."

"Can you prove that he advised and instructed you to baptize Edgardo?"

"There were only the two of us, so I couldn't give you any proof."

"And what did the Inquisitor say about what you had done? Did he praise you or blame you?"

"He told me that if I understood correctly that he was in bad shape, I acted excellently in baptizing the boy, because that way, if he died, he'd go to heaven."

"Were you given any payment, any gift for your deposition?"

"No, sir."

At the end of her testimony, Anna put her cross to the document. Although she had forgotten it, it was a cross that she had also scrawled at the bottom of the testimony she had given a little over two years earlier at the Dominican convent in Bologna. As in that earlier interrogation, Anna received a warning before leaving. The authorities reserved the right to initiate proceedings against her should they decide that they had the grounds to do so. If she was lying, she was in trouble. Magistrate Carboni, meanwhile, prepared to return to Bologna, where, the next day, he would send a summons for a key witness. He was eager to interview the man who, according to Anna Morisi, was responsible for Edgardo being a Christian.[2]

On February 11, Cesare Lepori sat before Carboni in the Bologna interrogation room. He said that he knew Momolo Mortara, who had occasionally dropped off a list of groceries at his store, but that he had never met Marianna Mortara. He was familiar with their children because they had sometimes accompanied the family servant, who had shopped at his store. And, he added, he had heard rumors in 1858 about a police raid on their home, aimed at taking away one of their children who had been baptized.

Lepori was aware that the Inquisitor was in jail and that Anna Morisi had blamed him for the whole affair. When asked what he knew about the baptism, he was ready:

"I don't know anything about it. In fact, a little after they took his son away, Signor Momolo Mortara came to find me at my store, along with someone I didn't know. He asked me if it wasn't true that a few years earlier I'd advised one of his servants, named Anna, to baptize the son in question. But I had to tell him, just as I'm telling you now, what's the whole truth: that it just never happened." When told by Momolo that Anna had said it was he who had told her what to do, Lepori recalled, "I was surprised and angry. I told him that if it was true that I'd gotten her to baptize the boy, given that she continued to come to my store to shop for various years after that, she would've told me that she'd given the Sacrament. But I only found out that the boy had become a Christian when he was taken from his parents."

"Do you recall Anna, the person Mortara spoke to you about?"

"No, I can't remember her, but if I saw her again I might be able to recognize her."

"You don't even remember that a woman named Annina came in the past to shop in your store as the servant of the Mortara household?"

"No. I just remember that various women came to shop in my store for the Mortaras."

Did he not recall that in 1852 the Mortaras had a child who was sick? "No," he answered.

"Nor that they had a nursing child named Edgardo?"

"I don't remember."

But, the magistrate insisted, Anna Morisi's testimony was clear. One morning that year, when she came to buy some oil at his store, she had told him about Edgardo's illness, and he had suggested baptizing the boy and given her detailed instructions on how to do it. "Isn't that all true?"

> "It's not true at all, and I don't know anything about those things that this woman has accused me of."
>
> "Tell the truth, because Morisi, after having already told this to many different people, who found her story to be entirely believable, has repeated it for this court. How can you explain why she would want to accuse you, both in court and outside it, of something that she just dreamed up?"
>
> "Having baptized the boy, she probably wanted to make excuses for herself by blaming me for having told her to do it. But I tell you, and I'm ready to say it to her face, she lied, both in court and out of it."

Carboni had his doubts about the grocer. Lepori, like Morisi, was warned on his way out that the magistrate reserved the right to charge him should he find the grounds to do so.[3]

Other than the Inquisitor himself, Anna Morisi had cited only two people who could serve as useful witnesses to verify her story. One was Cesare Lepori, who had called her a liar. The other was Regina, the woman who had worked for the Mortaras' neighbors, the Pancaldis. According to Morisi, Regina was the only one she had told of Edgardo's baptism before getting the Inquisitor's summons. Carboni was eager to track her down.

She was not easily found. Regina Bussolari no longer lived with the Pancaldis. A 60-year-old childless widow, she was now living at her nephew's home in the center of the city, a ten-minute walk from where the Mortaras had lived. On February 18, she came to testify.

Yes, she said, she knew the Mortaras. She had gotten to know them in the summer of 1857, because she had spent three months working for Signora Rosina Pancaldi, who lived next door.

> "Do you know [asked Carboni] that, some time after the period you mentioned, the Mortaras suffered a serious misfortune because of one of their children?"
>
> "Some time after I'd left the Pancaldi home, rumors spread through Bologna that one of the Mortara children, whose name I don't know, though I do recall it was a boy, was ordered separated from his family by the Holy Office because he'd been baptized. I never heard any of the details of the case, and even today I'm totally in the dark about it."

"But didn't you know before the abduction that he was baptized?"

"I didn't know anything, because no one told me a word about it."

On Carboni's prompting, Regina admitted that she did know a girl who had worked as a servant for the Mortaras, a girl from San Giovanni in Persiceto, but she didn't recall her name.

Hadn't you ever talked with her, Carboni asked, about the baptism she performed on the boy who was later taken away by the police?

"I think I only spoke with that servant once or twice, when she was going up to the storage room to get something, because to get to the stairs that led up to it, you had to pass by the front door of Signora Pancaldi's house. But she never said anything to me about that boy, much less that he'd been baptized." Nor, she said, responding to another question, had she ever talked to Anna Morisi about Aristide, the Mortara child who had died.

Yet, Carboni responded, Anna had said that she had run into Regina as she was climbing up to the storage room and that, after talking about Aristide, the Mortaras' dying child, she had told Regina of Edgardo's baptism. "You admit that in the same circumstances you had a talk with Morisi. Isn't it also true that the subject you discussed was what Morisi says it was?"

"I say Morisi's a liar. I didn't even know that the boy, that Aristide who you've been talking about, was sick. I only found out about it when I saw the casket, and someone told me—I don't remember who—that one of the Mortaras' children had died."

Asked if she had ever spoken with the Inquisitor, Father Feletti, Regina responded no, she had not.[4]

As she penned her cross to the transcript of her testimony, Regina, like Cesare Lepori and Anna Morisi herself, was warned that the court reserved the right to proceed against her. Either Anna Morisi was a talented spinner of yarns, thought Carboni, or both Lepori and Bussolari were liars.

The magistrate prepared a request to the head of the Bologna police, sent on February 20, for a police investigation to be launched into the records of Morisi, Lepori, and Bussolari. That same day, he called in Bussolari's old employer to help him determine whether Regina could be believed. Signora Pancaldi verified that the notarized testimony she had given, at Momolo Mortara's request, back in the fall of 1858 was accurate, complete with Anna Morisi's giggling boast about her sexual encounter with her Austrian neighbor. In contrast to her steamy portrait of the seductress Morisi, she characterized Regina Bussolari as "a good woman, and very religious." Regina "went to Church often, even too often."[5]

As the magistrate was aware, this evidence of Bussolari's religiosity cut two ways. As testimony to her upright and moral character—particularly in contrast to the growing evidence about Anna Morisi's penchant not only for illicit sex but for petty larceny as well—it weighed heavily in favor of crediting her account over that of the Mortaras' former servant. On the other hand, Bussolari's reputation for spending a lot of time with the priests gave rise to the suspicion that, having heard from Anna Morisi about Edgardo's baptism, she might have passed it on to one of her clerical confidants, with the report ultimately making its way to the Inquisitor.

But a week later a very different picture began to emerge when the first reports, based on a check of the police records, arrived on the magistrate's desk. No police records involving Morisi or Lepori had been found, but something disturbing had turned up on Regina Bussolari, a native, like Anna Morisi, of San Giovanni in Persiceto.

Back in 1838, Regina had been interrogated by the police, following a charge that she had slandered and indeed threatened two of her neighbors. The case was later dismissed.[6] The incident had occurred many years before, and the charge had never been proven, but the magistrate's flickering hopes of rescuing Regina Bussolari's reputation were soon extinguished. A quite different explanation for her penchant for fraternizing with the priests of Bologna came to his attention when, at the beginning of March, the full police reports arrived.

The police chief of San Giovanni in Persiceto reported that Anna Morisi's behavior had never given his department reason for concern, and the director of Bologna's police force reported that their investigations had revealed nothing against either Morisi or Cesare Lepori. On the other hand, reports on Regina Bussolari were disturbing. "From the information we have received, it turns out that she is a procuress, and her house is frequented by all types of people, indeed even priests, for relations with women."[7]

On February 22, the magistrate brought in Elena Pignatti, the woman who had employed Anna Morisi after she left the Mortaras in 1857. Elena was among the women whose notarized testimony on Morisi's moral failings had become part of the Mortaras' petition to the Holy See. In her earlier testimony, Pignatti had spoken of Anna's sexual misdeeds and larcenous tendencies. It now turned out that she had much more direct evidence to give as well. She was the same age as Anna Morisi, and the two women had known each other for many years. Indeed, Elena Pignatti knew the Mortaras as well, for in the early 1850s she had herself been working as a maid for the De Angelises, the family of Marianna Mortara's sister.

Anna had gone to work for Pignatti in the fall of 1857, a couple of months after she left the Mortaras. It was said "that she left them because she was pregnant and went somewhere else to have her baby."

I remember very well that seven or eight years ago, when I was with the De Angelises ... a son of the Mortaras, whose name I don't know, became sick, and it was said that he was going to die. Around then, one morning, as I was taking some of the De Angelises' little children to school in via Gambruti, I ran into Morisi. Among the other things we talked about, she—without mentioning that child's illness—asked me, "I've heard that if you baptize a Jewish child who's about to die he goes to heaven and gets indulgence; isn't that right?" I don't remember what I told her, but when the Mortara boy was kidnapped by order of the Dominican Father, I was sure that he must have been the one who was sick when I was working for the De Angelises, and baptized by Morisi.

Elena remembered having herself seen Edgardo once when he was sick that time. "I saw him in a crib that wasn't in a bedroom, but in another room where his mother was watching him. He was little; he seemed to me to be about a year old."

"Did you think," asked the magistrate, "that the boy was in danger of dying?"

"Since his mother was crying, and despaired for his life, I thought he was dying, also because of his appearance: his eyes were closed, and he was hardly moving."

Elena also had something to add about events during the three months in late 1857 when Anna had worked in her home. Anna had never said a word to her about having baptized one of the Mortara children, but "four or five times she went to the Convent of San Domenico, summoned by a man from that church." Elena, her curiosity aroused, asked Anna what they wanted with her. She responded that "the Father Inquisitor had promised her a dowry." Following the last of these visits, Elena added, "she led me to believe that she'd been made to swear, and promise, never to live with Jews again."[8]

Three days later, the magistrate called in Second Lieutenant Agostini. It was the first time Carboni met the man who had taken Edgardo to Rome. In the records of Agostini's testimony with Police Chief Curletti, taken right before the Inquisitor's arrest, little had been said about the behavior of the boy himself. Father Feletti, in giving his account of Edgardo's placid departure from home and pious pilgrimage to Rome, had claimed that Agostini would confirm his story. Carboni was eager to hear what the policeman would say.

Agostini seemed ill at ease in the Bologna interrogation room. He had already testified about the matter in Cento, he said, and had told them all that he knew. But the magistrate asked him to tell how Edgardo had reacted to being taken from home on that June evening.

"He was pretty unhappy about it," Agostini responded. "After Sorcinelli [a fellow policeman] put him in the carriage, a Jew, whose last name, I think, is Vitta, came up to the window and told him that he would be following in another carriage with his mother and father. On the other hand, the Father

Inquisitor had provided me with a good supply of sweets and toys so that I could calm the boy down during the trip when he asked for his parents."

"The boy never cried?" asked Carboni.

"Never."

Carboni had just taken testimony from Antonio Facchini, the passerby who had witnessed the scene of Edgardo's removal from his home. It was Facchini who had ruefully wished that he could have led an expedition of his friends to intercept the departing police wagon and rescue the boy. He had clearly recalled that as Edgardo was being forced into the police carriage he had begun to scream, and that a policeman had put his hand over the boy's mouth. The magistrate asked Agostini if this was not, in fact, true.

"I know that his father was shouting," Agostini replied, "and I could hear him while I was in the carriage, since the door was open. But from the time I got the boy, right up through Rome, he never cried."

Carboni was eager to check the Inquisitor's account of the six-year-old's penchant for visiting churches on the way. "During the trip and during the various rest stops you made," he inquired, "did the boy ever ask to be taken anywhere in particular?"

In Fossombrone [recalled Agostini] we spent the night at the police barracks, and the next day was San Pietro's Day. Seeing the policemen going off to mass, the boy expressed the desire to follow them, since I myself had to go to mass. I took him to the mass with me. From Fossombrone until Rome we had two rather devout women from Fossombrone in our carriage. Having learned the boy's unusual story from me, they gave him a lot of attention, and taught him the Ave Maria on the way, and read to him from books of devotion. . . . So that during the various other stops on the way to Rome, he'd ask me to take him to church, and either I, or those women, did so.

Thinking, no doubt, of Momolo's portrait of a boy crying for his parents while begging the officer for his mezuzah, Carboni asked, "And didn't the boy ever refer in any way to the religion he was born in?"

"Never," Agostini replied.

"He never asked for any object from his religion?"

"No."

"Yet it is said that throughout the trip he asked continually for his parents, and for his 'mezuzah,' a kind of Jewish medallion. Isn't that right?"

"No, that's not true at all."

How, the magistrate asked, could Agostini account for the boy's desire to keep going to church?

"I'd say it was a matter of simple curiosity and also the effect, maybe, of those two women's influence."⁹

That same day, Magistrate Carboni received news that he had been eagerly awaiting. Although he had been able to interview Momolo Mortara, he had not yet heard from the other injured party, Marianna Mortara. Momolo, in his testimony, had said that his wife, bedridden for the past three months as a result of the continued trauma she had suffered from her son's abduction, could not come to Bologna. The only way to get her to testify was to have the Turin police question her. Although Bologna was still a few weeks away from joining the kingdom of Sardinia, relations between the courts of Bologna and Turin were good and cooperation was to be expected.

Yet it seemed doubtful at first that the authorities would ever get her testimony. In response to the Turin court's request that she appear, her doctor sent a letter painting a disturbing picture:

> The serious illness that afflicts Signora Marianna Mortara of Bologna . . . has had extremely dangerous phases that have at various points put her life in danger. And these phases occur just at the times when particular circumstances recall to her mind the disaster that struck her family (the cruel abduction of her son). As a result, as her doctor, and having had occasion to get to know the anguish that torments her, and the great sensitivity and weakness that this leaves her in, I recommend [you to . . .] touch as little as possible on all that regards that which lies at the origin of her past misfortunes, and to do so only with the greatest care, if you do not want to exacerbate a fatal disease.¹⁰

Thus warned, two magistrates of the Turin court set off the next day to find Edgardo's stricken mother, hoping she would be able to testify from her sickbed. They had been briefed by Carboni, who sent them a detailed account of the testimony he had received to date, and the points on which Marianna's testimony would be most valuable.

Arriving at the Mortara home around 3 p.m. on February 18, 1860, the Turin magistrates found that, although Marianna was momentarily out of bed, she was in poor shape. "When we told her why we had come, on recalling the event in question, she almost fainted and, after a long time, recovering a bit, said that she was not at the moment able to bear any examination, having just today gotten out of bed for the first time, following four months of being ill following childbirth." Marianna asked them to give her another day, and the men left.

They returned the next day. Although in bed, Marianna said that she was now prepared to answer their questions.

Marianna recalled for them that night in June, and then how, at noon the next day, "at which point I had practically fainted away, I was put into the carriage of our friend Giuseppe Vitta and taken to his house." There, she said, "I was overcome by my pain, and as a consequence I wasn't able to see just how the police tore my son away from my husband."

It was late, and the magistrate thought that Marianna had had about all she could take for the day. They told her that they would return the next afternoon.

The following day, the magistrates, once again at Marianna's bedside, asked whether she knew anything about Edgardo's behavior during his trip to Rome. She replied: "He did nothing but cry. He wanted to go back to his parents. He kept asking what he had done wrong to be taken away. He kept asking for his mezuzah. He rejected the other medallions that they wanted to give him, and he didn't eat. The boy himself," she said, "told me all this in Rome, with the Rector of the Catechumens right there. In fact . . . the Rector told me that the boy must have a lot of guts to have survived·such suffering."

The magistrates then turned to the question of the presumed baptism itself, asking Marianna about Edgardo's illness. She denied that it had been anything serious and insisted that she would never have left Anna alone with the baby. Indeed, on the days that Edgardo had been sickest, she said, Anna herself had been very ill and confined to bed. Marianna remembered it well, because the Sabbath was approaching and, since as Jews they could not kindle a fire or a light on Friday evening or Saturday, they arranged to have a friend's servant spend those days with them to help out.

Asked about Anna's behavior during her years of service with them, Marianna painted a less than flattering picture: "Her behavior was like all servants. She had her defects, which I bore but was unable to change: I saw that she was a liar, an oath breaker, and a thief. But it seemed to me that she was fond of all my children, and so I put up with her. I came to realize, though, that because Edgardo was so lively, she often hit him."

It was the end of Marianna's interrogation. Momolo stood by her side as she signed the transcript.[11]

Back in Bologna, Carboni heard from other witnesses. Dr. Saragoni, the Mortara family physician, vigorously denied that Edgardo's illness had ever been life-threatening, saying that he had made as many house calls as he had only to calm the boy's parents, who were nervous types. He had also examined Anna Morisi when she was pregnant in the mid-1850s, but Anna's baby was delivered not by him but by the midwife in whose house she was staying, at the Mortaras' expense. Meanwhile, the Bologna magistrate discovered that he would not be able to interview either Marshal Lucidi or Officer Sorcinelli, the man who had placed Edgardo in the police carriage outside the house, for both had retreated, along with Colonel De Dominicis, with the forces remaining in the papal police.

Carboni decided that he needed to talk to Anna Morisi again, this time ordering her to appear before him in Bologna. He had more questions to ask. As far as he could tell, Father Feletti had never looked into Anna's background, nor had he summoned any witnesses to check her story. If the Inquisitor were to be judged according to the law in effect at the time that he had ordered Edgardo taken, his failure to conduct an adequate investigation into Anna's claim might allow the magistrate to find grounds for his conviction.

On February 29, Carboni received a certificate from the town doctor of San Giovanni in Persiceto. It stated that, "having a nursing baby, and having no one to leave him with, nor means to procure transportation," Anna "cannot now go to Bologna." To this another town official added a certificate attesting to Morisi's "*stato di miserabilità.*" She was destitute and had no way of buying a ticket on the coach to the city.[12]

Carboni had no desire to make another trip to Persiceto, yet needed to talk to her, so he arranged for a seat on the coach to be provided for the young mother and ordered her to appear. On March 6, she showed up at his office, the last witness—other than the defendant himself—to come before him.

The Magistrate's first question got right to the point: "Is it really true that, as you said in your earlier examination, you baptized the boy Edgardo Mortara when, around the time he was eight months old, you believed he was in danger of dying?"

"It's the Gospel truth."

Carboni informed Anna of the doctor's testimony that he had never told her or anyone else that Edgardo's illness was serious, and of the Mortaras' testimony that they had never spent the whole night awake by Edgardo's side and had never read prayers from a Hebrew book while standing over him, as she had claimed. And anyway, the magistrate added, "what would you know about a book like that? You are illiterate!"

Dr. Saragoni had, Anna insisted, told her that Edgardo was very sick, and the Mortaras had spent two or three nights by Edgardo's side. One morning, she said she saw Momolo

"reading the book of the dying. I learned from my sister Monica, who worked as a servant for the Mortaras for four years before me, that when a Jew was about to die, they stood over him and read a book in Hebrew."

"We have also determined [the Magistrate cut back in] that Edgardo was born on August 27, 1851, and that he had the illness of which you speak at the end of August 1852, when he was in his thirteenth month, which we confirmed . . . by inspecting Dr. Saragoni's records."

"But I began to serve at the Mortaras when the boy was four months old," Anna responded, "while the snow was still on the ground. And he became sick soon after that, and I remember anyway that it was the cold season, because they still kept the fire burning in the room where the boy was."

Carboni proceeded to reconstruct the dates of Edgardo's illness, Anna's own illness—during which, she had herself testified, she didn't notice anything because she was so sick that "I felt like I was going to die"—and the arrival of the substitute servant. The timing, Carboni told her, proved that the baptism could not have taken place the way she claimed it had. He then got her to admit that the Mortaras had never given her any responsibility for caring for the sick child, over whom they kept a constant vigil. "It is for this very reason," proclaimed the magistrate, "that the parents deduce that it was impossible for you to have baptized him."

"But didn't the Mortaras say that in the morning I was talking about they left the boy's crib to go into the bedroom?"

"No, they didn't. And it is hard to believe that, when they left the crib and went into a nearby room, you would have dared, practically under their eyes, to baptize Edgardo, at the risk of being surprised in the act that they without doubt would have abhorred, since it was contrary to their religion."

"I dared do it because even if they had surprised me they would've just found me with a glass of water in my hand, and they probably wouldn't have understood what I was doing, or what I meant to do."

And what of the fact, the magistrate asked, that Cesare Lepori had, under oath, denied that he had ever spoken to her about baptizing Edgardo, much less instructed her how to do it?

"He may not remember," Anna responded, "but it's a fact."

The final subject that Carboni wanted to explore with Anna involved the defendant, Father Feletti, more directly. If Anna had not told Regina Bussolari about the baptism, how had the Inquisitor heard about it? Might Anna not have invented the whole story of baptizing Edgardo in a fit of pique at the way the Jews had treated her? Might she have thought that this was just the kind of story the Dominicans—and especially the Inquisitor—would want to hear? And might she have thought that she could get a reward for telling such a story, allowing her, after so many years working away from home as a servant, to return to Persiceto, get married, and set up a household of her own?

After leaving the Mortaras in 1857, Carboni observed, Anna had gone to work for Elena Pignatti, whose home was near the San Domenico church. Where, he asked, had she gone to take confession while she was at Signora Pignatti's house?

"I went to the Fathers of the Madonna on Galliera," she replied.

"Tell the truth," warned the magistrate. "Didn't you once go to San Domenico to confess? The church is, after all, closer."

Carboni must have been excited by Anna's reply:

> Since I was involved in negotiations to get married and they told me that Father Feletti had dowries to give out, I went to find him and told him what I wanted. He told me that I should return on a certain day and he'd give me a reply when I took confession. And so I did, but I didn't actually confess. I kneeled at the confessional, and Father Feletti told me that the dowry didn't depend on him but on the Brothers of the Annunciation. I wasn't able to get any, though, and I had to get married without a dowry.

Did you know, Carboni asked, that your neighbor in the Mortaras' building, Geltrude Laghi, testified that "she had gone to visit you during the last days you spent at Elena Pignatti's house, when you were about to get married, and you confided in her that you had gone to confess at San Domenico?"

> "Well, I might have told her what I just told you about the dowry that I asked Father Feletti for."
>
> "Tell the truth, because Geltrude Laghi has testified that, in confiding in her, you told her that after you took confession at San Domenico, the monks took you into another room, where you were seized by a great fear, and they put you through an interrogation. What were they asking you about?"
>
> "Geltrude told you a lie. I never told her that."

"I am warning you again to tell the truth," said the Magistrate. He told Anna that he had also called in Regina Bussolari, and that she had denied that Anna ever told her anything about baptizing Edgardo. "Since you yourself claim that you never told anyone else about the baptism, I ask you how could Father Feletti have come to know about it, and have you called to the Holy Office to interrogate you?" He continued: "You have admitted implicitly that it was you yourself who told them and, from what you said to Laghi, you told them as part of the confession you made at San Domenico. What do you say to that?"

"I didn't report anything to them, either in the confessional or anywhere else, because in the confessional I only spoke to Father Feletti about my dowry."

"And your conversation about your dowry took place around the same time as you were called in to be interrogated by the Holy Office about Edgardo's baptism?"

"It was three or four days after I was called to be interrogated when I heard that Father Feletti had dowries to give, and I went to ask him for one."

"How many times did you have occasion to go to San Domenico, and to speak with Father Feletti?"

"There were three times. Once to ask for the dowry, another to hear his answer at the confessional, and the third to respond to the interrogation on Edgardo's baptism."

"Aha! You see that even the way you give the order of your visits to San Domenico shows that first you went to the confessional, and only later to the interrogation."

In addition, the magistrate added, Elena Pignatti had testified that, being curious about the four or five messages sent to Anna from San Domenico, she had asked her what they were all about.

"You told her that the Father Inquisitor had promised you a dowry, and in your last visit you led her to believe that you had been made to give a solemn oath never again to live with Jews, and not to speak of it with Elena or anyone on pain of excommunication."

"No, I had the interrogation first, and only then asked for the dowry. And I was called to San Domenico only once by that man, and not four or five times."

"And how was it that, on your return to Persiceto, you told your sisters about the baptism you had given Edgardo?"

"It was when we happened to be talking about Jews, and I told them about what I'd done to Edgardo."

Their conversation had taken place, she added, sometime before she first heard the news about Edgardo's abduction.

"So having had a vow of silence imposed on you by the Holy Office, you talked about it with your sisters? How is it that you find it so easy to break your oath?"

"I told my sisters about it, but I was sure they would never tell anyone else."

The magistrate had one final question to ask. Anna had earlier testified that her only break in service to the Mortaras was when she left on her own initiative to work in another household. Hadn't there been another time? Carboni asked.

"There was one other time I went away, about four months, to a midwife's house, because at that time there was a boarder living at the Mortaras' house, and I'd gotten in trouble." Here, the transcript of Anna's final testimony ends with the note: "She began to cry."[13]

CHAPTER 21

Defending the Inquisitor

T HE POLICE RAID on San Domenico and the arrest of the former inquisitor alarmed Bologna's archbishop and others in the Church hierarchy. It was, for them, yet another clear sign of the new rulers' intention of violating Church law, judging ecclesiastical activities by the secular laws of a godless government and humiliating the clergy. In the months since the new government had come to power in Bologna, it had fought a series of battles with the clergy, but never before had someone of Father Feletti's rank been dealt with so brutally.

Shortly after the Inquisitor's arrest, Cardinal Viale-Prelà sent a protest to the Governor, Luigi Carlo Farini, delivered personally by the Archbishop's assistant, demanding the monk's immediate release. Farini agreed to speak with the emissary and, according to the latter's report, suggested that Father Feletti would be freed if he could prove that he had simply acted on higher orders. The Archbishop was unsure of what, in the terrible uncertainty of the new, chaotic situation, it was proper for the Inquisitor to say—indeed, whether it was permissible for him to say anything. He knew that Father Feletti was refusing to answer any questions about the workings of the Holy Office. Seeking instructions, the Archbishop wrote to Cardinal Giacinto De Ferrari, the Dominican who served as the Commissioner of the Holy Office of the Inquisition in Rome.

Cardinal De Ferrari was well informed about the Mortara case, for it was to him that Father Feletti had written, on October 26, 1857, to report the first rumors that a Jewish boy had been baptized in Bologna. Feletti had requested authorization to proceed with an inquiry, and it was De Ferrari who, on November 9, writing from the central office of the Inquisition

222

in the Vatican, had sent the Bologna inquisitor the fateful instructions to proceed. Of all this, the Bologna court and the magistrate, Carboni, knew nothing.[1]

Now, little more than two years later, Father Feletti was languishing in prison. On February 11, the Commissioner of the Holy Office responded to Cardinal Viale-Prelà's letter:

> I have been asked whether the prisoner may respond that he was carrying out *Superior Orders from Rome*, etc. The immediate answer is that there is no difficulty in giving this answer, although he should add what Saint Peter said: *Obbedire oportet Deo magis quam hominibus* [Obey God before man]. Now fearing that that letter [authorizing Father Feletti to have Edgardo taken] has been lost, we thought it most prudent to refer the matter to Your Most Reverend Eminence to do the best you can.

Ten days later, the Archbishop wrote again to the Commissioner with word of a disturbing new development. It no longer looked as though getting the monk out of jail would be as simple as they had thought:

> I had sent my Pro-Vicar to Signor Farini to speak on behalf of Father Feletti, and he responded that to free him nothing more would be necessary than affirming, as I said, that he had merely carried out *superior orders*. But now, it seems, they no longer consider such a declaration to be sufficient. We have written Signor Farini to remind him of his assurances and to bring the matter to a close, and I await his reply. I will not fail to do everything possible for the prisoner.[2]

After his second interview with Anna Morisi, Magistrate Carboni was almost ready to prepare his brief for the prosecution. But before doing so, he wanted to make one last attempt to get the Inquisitor to talk. On March 6, Carboni entered the Torrone prison and was escorted to Father Feletti's cell.

The monk seemed happy to have the company but began on a peevish note, for there was something he had been mulling over. If they were so concerned with illegal acts committed in connection with the case before them, why, he wondered, had they not gone after "the Jew Momolo Mortara, who broke the laws promulgated by the Church forbidding him from keeping any Christian in his service, laws designed to prevent just such a situation as this." But the monk's irritation soon subsided, and he returned to higher ground, recalling the Holy Office instructions he had received via the Archbishop: "The judgments of the Church should certainly not be subject to any other authority that is inferior to it, for Catholic doctrine teaches me that the Faith of Peter cannot be subject to the judgment of any other. It is not right for anyone to sit in judgment over the decisions that emanate from the Apostolic Faith in matters of Faith and conduct."

It was now time for the magistrate to begin his final interrogation. Carboni realized that his best chance of getting a conviction was proving that the former inquisitor had broken the laws that were in effect at the time of Edgardo's abduction. If Father Feletti proved able to demonstrate that, in ordering the boy seized, he was simply following higher orders that were legally formulated, he could be found guilty only by the retroactive application of the new law of the land, and there were many both in the courts and in the government who would not want to set such a precedent.

"Do you persist even today," Carboni began, "in maintaining that, in ordering Lieutenant Colonel De Dominicis to seize the Mortara child, you were executing an order received from the Sacred Congregation of the Holy Office?"

"Yes, sir. I was only the loyal executor of the orders received from the Supreme Sacred Congregation of the Holy Office in Rome."

Yet, the magistrate responded, neither Marshal Caroli, the carabiniere officer who processed the order that the Inquisitor had sent the police, nor Brigadier Agostini, who had been shown the letter by De Dominicis, recalled its saying anything about his acting on orders received from Rome. Unless you show me the letter you received from Rome or other such proof, warned Carboni, I will have to conclude that the abduction was your idea.

In sending an order to the police, responded Father Feletti, there was no need to cite any authority higher than his own. As for the proof that he had acted on orders from Rome, it was sufficient to note that "the boy was received by the Rector of the Catechumens in Rome, and that the Holy Father was kind enough to want to see this boy himself, bless him, and act as his father in all senses of the term." For Father Feletti, the suggestion that he would have acted on his own in such a matter, without instructions from the Holy Office of the Inquisition in Rome, was insulting: "It is a mortification that I accept from the hand of God, and it comforts me that no one who knows me would think so poorly of me."

Why, then, asked Carboni, would he not show them the order he claims he received from Rome?

In all those things I could discuss without breaking my oath to the Holy Office, responded the monk, I have. "But when it involves things that I am not allowed to talk about, I don't believe I am remaining silent to be discourteous, for on the contrary, it would be in my own interest to speak. But my conscience absolutely forbids me to give you any response."

But, the magistrate asked Father Feletti, why, if he was simply following orders he received from the Holy Office, had he given Agostini four scudi as a special reward for his services?

"I just paid Agostini for the expenses that he and the boy incurred on their trip. I gave him the four scudi purely as a tip, for his inconvenience, as he himself is the father of a family."

The magistrate turned next to the question of the baptism itself. When Momolo Mortara had first come to see the Inquisitor, while the police were stationed by his son's side back at the house, he had asked him why he believed that Edgardo had been baptized. Why had the Inquisitor offered no explanation?

"I told the Jew Mortara that his son had been baptized, but I could not give him any explanation because of the oath by which I am bound."

"Well," Carboni demanded, "at least now explain and justify how, when, and by whom the boy was baptized, how news of it got to the Holy Office, and what efforts were made to verify it before ordering the separation of a Christian boy from his Jewish family."

"The Supreme Sacred Congregation, having recognized the boy's baptism to be valid, ordered me to have him sent to Rome to the College of the Catechumens. The Supreme Sacred Congregation is aware of every act, every bit of investigation that was believed to be necessary for this purpose, and it alone may provide you with the details on that investigation."

Carboni was annoyed:

"Enough, Reverend Father, of this evasive way of responding, which not only precludes you from any useful means of defense, but may give rise to some interpretations that are unfavorable to you."

"I am truly sorry you think I am being evasive in answering the questions about the investigation undertaken into the Mortara boy's baptism. When I have been interrogated about things I can talk about, I have responded straightforwardly with what clarity I can. But about the things you are now asking me I cannot respond at all without permission from the Supreme Sacred Congregation in Rome."

"Since you do not want to or you cannot produce the records that we have asked you for, at least tell me who it was who reported Edgardo's baptism, and which persons were interviewed to verify it."

"The oath that one takes calls God as witness of that truth or act that is being asserted, and the violation of this oath brings divine punishment. I am more concerned about the salvation of my soul than about any punishment inflicted in this world simply as a result of my obeying the orders that were given me by the Head of the Catholic Church by means of the Sacred Congregation. I do not wish to incur divine punishment by violating the oath of secrecy that I gave with regard to the acts of the Holy Office."

But, the Magistrate asserted, you can rightly say that you did not voluntarily break your oath but were compelled to do so in order to defend yourself in a criminal trial.

"I leave my defense in God alone, in the Most Holy Virgin Mother of Mercy, who is the refuge of all sinners, and in the intercession of the prayers that the child Edgardo Mortara raises before God for me, which I learned about many months ago from someone in Rome who works for the Pope."

Since you have refused to offer any proof of what you say, Carboni told the monk, this court has had to do everything it could to discover the truth. We have interviewed Anna Morisi and heard her story of having baptized Edgardo. "But," he added, "aside from her statement, we have not been able to obtain any other confirmation. Indeed, her assertion not only was found to be exaggerated, because at the time of that illness the boy was never in danger of dying, but it was denied by the very people who were cited to prove it." And none of these witnesses, said Carboni, reported ever being summoned by the Inquisitor so that their testimony could be heard. "I call on you once and for all," the magistrate implored, "to abandon your stubborn silence and tell me that you did not order the Mortara child taken away simply on Anna Morisi's assertion alone."

"I have already said that when I am asked about acts regarding the Holy Office I cannot respond. Let me only say that the order for taking the Mortara boy came to me from the Supreme Sacred Congregation, which certainly had the proof necessary to reach such a finding."

Carboni was not to be put off. The timing of Anna Morisi's testimony about the baptism, he said, should have led you to view it with suspicion. She had just left the Mortaras' service following a heated argument and was likely to be angry and bitter toward them, ripe for a vendetta. Adding to such suspicion, said Carboni, was the proof that he had collected from many sources of the young woman's dishonesty and lack of loyalty. In the light of all this, asked the magistrate, do you still remain silent about the efforts you made to establish the truth of the alleged baptism?

"I reply once more that I cannot give you any response."

The end was near. Carboni had prepared a draft of his findings, which would soon be sent to the court for the final phase of the trial. Before leaving Father Feletti after this, their last duel, he read it to the monk. He pointed to the lack of any evidence to support the monk's claim that he had acted on higher orders. Moreover, the Inquisitor had done nothing to verify Anna Morisi's story about having baptized the child years earlier, despite ample reasons for doubting it. The magistrate added that the taking of the child had upset the whole city and aroused the condemnation of the press; he described the scene of a mother wailing, of a father tearing out his hair, and of policemen who were themselves moved to tears by the inhumane task the Inquisitor had given them. Do you contest the fact that by this course of conduct you have made yourself liable for punishment? asked Carboni.

Father Feletti had his last chance to respond to the magistrate before the case went to the judges.

> To your narration of the facts I have nothing to oppose, except to note that I gave the orders best designed to lessen the pain of the boy's mother and father. But I don't know by what law you can proceed against me for having carried out an order that I received from the Supreme Sacred Congregation of Rome two years ago under a government that was legally recognized by all the Powers of Europe. . . .
>
> It isn't true that this action upset the whole city, because when people learned that the Mortara boy was taken away because he had been baptized, no one talked about it anymore. As for the newspapers, there were other papers that were moderate and full of good sense. They spoke of the case with those fair and just ideas that are required in dealing with a religious matter.
>
> I commiserate with the Mortara parents for their painful separation from their son, but I hope that the prayers of the innocent soul succeed in having God reunite them all in the Christian religion.
>
> As for my order to De Dominicis to take the boy, I gave it in writing in the name of the supreme authority, and I told him to show it to the Mortaras themselves just so that they would not think that it was simply my own personal order.

Finally, after insisting that Edgardo might well have been at risk of dying from his illness—for it did not take much to kill a baby—the former inquisitor concluded: "As for my punishment, not only do I place myself in the Lord's hands, but I would argue that any government would recognize the legitimacy of my action."[3] The magistrate had had enough. He passed the transcript of the interrogation to the jailed monk and was no doubt surprised when Father Feletti signed it.

The following day, March 7, Carboni sent his preliminary findings to the court, charging Father Pier Gaetano Feletti, arrested on January 2, and Colonel Luigi De Dominicis, who had fled to the dominions of the Holy See, with the "violent separation of the boy Edgardo Mortara from his own Jewish family." The Magistrate sought to show that the order to seize the boy was illegal according to the law in effect at the time, on two grounds: First, Father Feletti had given no good evidence that he was acting on behalf of the properly constituted authorities in Rome, that is, the Holy Office. Second, he had in any case provided no evidence that he had adequately investigated Anna

Morisi's claim that she had baptized the boy, and there was a great deal of evidence that cast doubt on her story.[4]

There was just one loose end that Carboni wanted to tie up. Father Feletti had claimed that the Pope himself had been involved in the decision to take Edgardo, and knew that the boy was happy to have been taken from his family and delivered to the Church. As evidence, he had argued that the Pope had invited Momolo and Marianna to come to Rome to see for themselves, arranging free passage for them. Carboni wrote to the stagecoach office in Bologna, asking them to review their records to see if any such arrangements had ever been made. On March 17, the answered had arrived. They had checked through all their records for the period July 1 to December 31, 1858. No evidence of a request from Rome for a free trip for the Mortaras was found.[5]

On March 20, Carboni's assistant was sent to see the prisoner:

I went to the Political Prisons and passed on to the secret room used by Father Gaetano Feletti. I advised him that the trial had now been opened . . . and thus he needed to name a Defender. He refused to do so, saying he was placing his defense entirely in the hands of God and the most Holy Blessed Virgin, because they know he is innocent. He continued to persist in this position, so I informed him that a defense attorney would be appointed for him by the Court.

Six days later, the judge presiding over the trial appointed Francesco Jussi to defend the monk.[6]

Jussi was a well-known figure in Bologna legal and social circles. More than a decade earlier, he had been satirized by an amateur poet as a man who was "rich, haughty, and ignorant," a verse read to much hilarity in a room full of the city's elite—Jussi, no doubt, included.[7] In appointing Jussi to defend the former inquisitor, the judge signaled the importance of the case and his desire for a vigorous defense. Indeed, the published version of Jussi's closing argument would soon be circulated among Church defenders throughout Europe. For the proud Jussi, this was the case of a lifetime.

Although for the previous six years, Jussi had taken court-appointed assignments on behalf of criminal defendants, this was the first time he had a client who refused to speak to him. More commonly, the men he defended (we have no record of any female defendants) were impoverished peasants. Indeed, just a few months before Father Feletti ordered Edgardo seized, Jussi defended a sharecropper who had murdered his eight-months-pregnant wife with an ax.[8]

Jussi had little time to prepare for the former inquisitor's trial. On

April 10, 1860, two weeks after the judge appointed him, he learned that the final hearing was scheduled for Monday morning, April 16. Three others were notified of the trial date that same day—the defendant, Father Feletti, and the two injured parties, Momolo and Marianna Mortara. None of the three attended the trial. In the Mortaras' case, the notice was delivered to them in their Turin home only two days beforehand, and Marianna had to sign for her husband, who was away from home. It would have been practically impossible for them to attend, even if they wanted to do so, and there is no sign that they did.

The Inquisitor's case was different. He was ordered to appear to respond to the charge of "violent separation of the child Edgardo Mortara from his family." Later that day, Jussi submitted a plea on Father Feletti's behalf asking that the monk be released from the obligation of appearing in court, for he wanted "to renounce this benefit that the law gives him." Bologna's ex-inquisitor, in short, would not appear in court for his own trial, for to do so would be to recognize the right of the new state to sit in judgment over him.[9] The court consented and, on the morning of April 16, when the six-judge panel, headed by Judge Calcedonio Ferrari, called the session to order, Father Feletti remained in his cell.

Neither the prosecution nor the defense had any witnesses to call. The prosecution had already furnished the court with a copy of all the testimony that Curletti and Carboni had gathered. The only prosecution witnesses who hadn't testified were those, such as Marshal Lucidi, who had fled to the lands still under pontifical control. Jussi faced a different situation, a rather ticklish one. He was representing a man who, on principle, did not want to defend himself. What particularly tied the lawyer's hands was that many of the central facts to be established involved just those questions that, from the Inquisitor's point of view, should not be revealed to the court. Not only could he not call Anna Morisi to the stand to discuss her interrogation at San Domenico, but how could he call other central witnesses, such as Cesare Lepori and Regina Bussolari, without raising the issue of whom the Inquisitor had interviewed and whom he hadn't? And how could he even think of calling the witnesses who could refute the charge that his client had acted without orders from higher authorities? None of them would agree to testify in this court, nor would Father Feletti or his defenders appreciate efforts by Jussi to try to summon them. In short, with less than three weeks to prepare his case, and without the benefit of discussing it with Father Feletti or cross-examining the witnesses interviewed by the prosecution, Jussi would have to rely on his considerable oratorical powers alone, leaving everything to his closing argument. He had only one advantage: the prosecution would go first. Jussi would have the last word.

Following standard court procedure, a special prosecutor, the *procuratore fiscale*, and not the investigating magistrate, presented the prosecution's case to the court. Radamisto Valentini had been appointed to be the prosecutor attached to Bologna's trial court in January. This was his first big case.

To get a conviction, the prosecutor realized, he would have to prove that the Inquisitor broke the laws in effect at the time Edgardo was taken. To accuse him of acting contrary to the new criminal code—in which the role of the Inquisitor was not recognized—conflicted not only with international norms but with the new government's desire to pacify the Italian population and win the favor of foreign governments.

When Valentini got up to address the court, he followed the path suggested by Carboni, focusing on two grounds for the Dominican monk's guilt. Their first claim was that Father Feletti had acted on his own, seizing Edgardo without first receiving instructions from Rome to do so. Valentini cited a variety of evidence to support this claim. Giuseppe Agostini, who had been shown the letter in which Father Feletti had ordered the operation, recalled no mention of higher authorities in it. And why would Colonel De Dominicis have been so eager to filch the letter from the police files as soon as the international cascade of protests about the case began if he were not worried that the order had been improper? Otherwise, it was this very document that would protect De Dominicis and the rest of his officers, justifying what they had done. As for the Inquisitor's claim that he must have had authorization from Rome in advance, since the Rector of Rome's Catechumens was waiting to take the boy in, Valentini pointed to a subtle point in Agostini's testimony. According to Edgardo's escort, when he arrived at the Catechumens with the boy, the Rector told him that he was expecting their arrival, because Father Feletti had already notified him. Although Father Feletti claimed that he had never been in direct contact with the Rector, and that the Rector must have been informed of Edgardo's impending arrival by the Holy Office in Rome, this showed, the prosecutor charged, that the Inquisitor had arranged the whole affair by himself.

The Inquisitor had also lied, Valentini argued, about the Pope's knowing about the order to take the boy, as demonstrated by his lie about the Pope sending tickets for the boy's parents to come to Rome. And, the prosecutor asked, if the Inquisitor's orders had come from the Holy Office, why had the Church authorities not come to his aid? "Why would they, by their silence, let an innocent man suffer in prison if he had been following their orders? . . . Why don't they contribute to God's glory by the triumph of the truth, the discovery of innocence, by making known a fact that reveals nothing that ought to be secret?"

Valentini did all he could to make the case that the monk had acted on his own, but Carboni, who had gotten to know the prisoner well, had little confidence in this argument. He knew what kind of man Feletti was. He might, in certain respects—such as his attitudes toward the Jews—be considered a fanatic, at least from a liberal's point of view, but he took the responsibilities of his office seriously, and the operations of the Holy Office of the Inquisition were nothing if not hierarchical. That Father Feletti would have flouted proper procedure—launched an unauthorized investigation and then, without checking with his superiors, ordered police to abduct a boy from a Jewish family—seemed implausible. That he would have then sent the boy to Rome and thereby broadcast news of what he had done seemed even more far-fetched. Father Feletti was no maverick, nor was he stupid.

The prosecution's strong point was its second claim. As Valentini put it, "Let us admit, for the moment, that the Inquisitor received the order to proceed with the abduction of the boy Edgardo Mortara from the Sacred Congregation of the Holy Office in Rome. Who was it who would have told them about the alleged baptism given to the boy? . . . If the Sacred Congregation of the Holy Office in Rome was informed before the abduction that the Mortara boy had been baptized, it could only have been from Father Inquisitor Feletti." This is a point that the Inquisitor had never denied.

If the cardinals of the Holy Office had ordered Edgardo seized, then it could only have been based on the Inquisitor's investigation. But how, the prosecutor asked, had the Inquisitor established that Edgardo had really been baptized? Father Feletti relied on the word of one woman alone, and had made no effort to check with any other witness who could have helped verify her story, or who could have helped him determine how much faith could be put in her words. Instead, thanks to Father Feletti, "a tender young child was torn from his beloved parents' arms on the simple sworn statement of a woman." Valentini added: "And we shall soon see just what kind of woman she was."

It is one of the ironies of Italian unification, and of the fall of papal power in the Legations, that this first major trial in the new Italian region of Emilia—which had been annexed to the new kingdom only the month before—turned on a dispute over what constituted a valid baptism. The case was fought less on the ground of secular law than on the proper interpretation of ecclesiastical law. Valentini went over Anna Morisi's account of the baptism in great detail, arguing that she did not, in fact, do it correctly if, indeed, she had done it at all. Hence it could have had no effect. For example, she had not pronounced the words at the same time she sprinkled the water on the boy's head. If the Holy Office had known this, "they would never have claimed that he was baptized" and never have ordered Edgardo taken from his parents.

Here the prosecutor could not resist a flight of rhetoric. Speaking of the illiterate girl's approximation of a baptism, he said:

And for this bit of silliness, was it worth upsetting and saddening a most noble city with the sudden, clamorous, violent abduction of a child by so many policemen? Was it worth throwing a quiet, honorable, industrious family . . . into desperate tears of pain, and ruining their health and their wealth? Was it worth putting such a strange, mean, wicked kidnapping on the lips of both friends and enemies of the Catholic Church throughout Europe and in the rancorous pens of journalists in two hemispheres?

Yet Valentini would not admit that Anna Morisi had performed even the flawed rite that she had described. During Edgardo's illness, his parents had never left him unattended, and at the time he was sickest, Anna herself was confined to bed. In her account, the baptism occurred in the middle of winter, yet the doctor's records provide irrefutable proof that the child's illness took place in the summer.

"Morisi," the Prosecutor pronounced, "was at the time a peasant girl: foolish, boorish, and a chatterbox, according to the witnesses. . . . She wasn't good at taking care of the children, and she didn't even know what *pancotto* [a dessert] was." In short, Valentini concluded, "she had a poor background, which is to say, she had little instruction in Christian doctrine, and she herself says she didn't know how to administer a baptism."

This led the prosecutor to a crucial witness: Cesare Lepori. It was only through Lepori's assistance that Anna could have baptized Edgardo, as she herself admitted. But Cesare Lepori had, under oath, sworn that he had never spoken with Anna about baptizing anyone. Moreover, he had said the same thing to witnesses in 1858, when the pontifical authorities were still in power, so this was not a matter of trying to cover up his behavior now that the papal regime had fallen.

And what of the ignorant, silly peasant girl of 1852? Had she, over the years, matured into a woman of character, one meriting our trust in her probity? "Corrupted by the foul breath and touch of foreign soldiers who were then sullying these unhappy lands, she rolled over without shame with them and then, showing that she had the dirtiest of minds, she bragged about it." Unbeknownst to her employers, she had blithely turned their homes, day and night, into houses of prostitution, and "twice, before she got married, those soldiers made her a mother." Her word, in short, meant nothing.

"Will Father Inquisitor Feletti's deed go unpunished?" asked the Prosecutor. "No one thinks it will. He has already suffered the condemnation pronounced by public opinion, not only in Bologna, nor just in Italy or Europe, but throughout the entire civilized world."

But why did the Inquisitor do what he had done? What moved him to believe Anna Morisi's story without checking it, or worse, to act on it without ever fully believing the shameless servant's tale of sudden heroic piety? The Prosecutor thought he had an answer. Father Feletti had been driven by his "obsessive zeal, his mania for fame, for power, and, finally, from an Inquisitor's hatred of Judaism."

As Valentini neared the end of his closing argument, he issued a call of conscience, a call of the new order against the old, the new secular state against the old regime. There is no more terrible hatred among men, he said, than that motivated by religion. "A private citizen who, to satisfy his whim, abducted a boy . . . would be liable for punishment. Are we to believe that a high magistrate—because he induces fear, because he is inquisitor of the Holy Office, because he can take advantage of secrecy, because he can be certain not only of impunity but, indeed, of praise and reward—that he should be let free?"

The prosecutor concluded: for arbitrarily ordering the violent abduction of the little boy, Edgardo Mortara, carried out in Bologna on June 24, 1858, under the pretext of his having been baptized, and for sending him to be confined in the House of the Catechumens in Rome, Father Pier Gaetano Feletti stands charged under the legal codes that were then in force. He violated the laws directed at magistrates who abuse their power and "against those who arrest others arbitrarily and keep them imprisoned." Valentini asked for a sentence of three years of public service, reimbursement of court costs, and payment of damages to Edgardo's parents.[10]

It was now time for the flamboyant Francesco Jussi, sitting alone at the defense table. He rose to confront the six black-robed judges.

"Oh, most excellent judges!" Jussi began. "Who does not know what happened to the Mortara family . . . how a child was taken from them, and how this child was then taken to Rome? The fact is too well known, sirs, and thinking of the pain expressed in that poor mother's tears tells us the story even before words do so." Yet, nonetheless, he added, the man who stands accused of a crime for this deed has no real need for a defense, for the simple facts demonstrate his innocence.

What crime did Father Feletti commit? He testified that when the Sacred Congregation learned that Edgardo Mortara had been baptized, it ordered him to take the boy and send him to the House of the Catechumens in Rome. The Inquisitor also declared that he had sent an order to this effect to Lieutenant Colonel De Dominicis. "Where is the prosecutor's proof that this assertion is false?" If the prosecutor has no copy of the letter to De Dominicis, this is certainly not Father Feletti's fault. And he could not expect Father Feletti to show him the letter he received from Rome, for the Inquisitor had taken a sacred oath not to reveal the secret acts of the Holy Inquisition.

And in any case, Jussi continued, the facts speak for themselves. Father Feletti sent the boy off to Rome without ever even seeing him. "The real decision could only have been made by the bishops who compose the Sacred Congregation, whose head is the Roman Pontiff himself." As further proof, Jussi cited an authority whom none of the judges would dispute: Marquis Gioacchino Pepoli, one of the leaders of unification forces in Bologna and cousin of the French emperor. Pepoli, describing the Mortara affair, had written: "To those who appealed to him about the taking of the little Mortara, Pius IX replied, '*Non possumus,*' the last word is this, he could not offer any other." But, argued Jussi, "if the Holy Pontiff responded '*Non possumus*' to those who asked about the boy, he must have known that he had given that order, or at least that, as President of the Sacred Congregation, he had approved it."

Even if the Inquisitor had in fact acted on his own, asked Jussi, what right would this court have to try him for it? "Was Father Feletti the Inquisitor of the Holy Office at the time or wasn't he? Was there or wasn't there this tribunal in Bologna?" Indeed, Jussi added, it had taken two acts of the new government to abolish it: the declaration that all citizens were to receive equal treatment before the law, and, later, Farini's proclamation explicitly abolishing the inquisitorial court. "How, then, can you proceed against a magistrate for enforcing a law that it was his responsibility to enforce at a time when that office still existed?" He continued: "The new government that replaces the old can cancel the law if it doesn't like it, but it may never proceed against those who enforced it solely out of hatred for that law or that office."

Having thus dispensed with the first issue, Jussi turned to the charge that Father Feletti had done his job poorly, that he had deceived the Sacred Congregation, telling its members that he had determined that a valid baptism had taken place when in fact it had not. On this point, the lawyer argued, Church law was clear: Inquisitor Father Feletti's work could be judged only by the Holy Office and the Pope, not by any secular court such as this.

"But let us suppose for a moment that it could be; what would such a trial show? Would it show that there had never been a baptism? Would it show that it was invalid? that it was not given to a person who was dying? Quite the contrary, sirs, and I believe that even the most superficial and rapid reading of the trial record is enough to convince all of you that the fact is just the opposite of this claim. . . ."

"I call as witnesses," said Jussi, "the Jews Padovani and De Angelis, who, as they recounted, around the end of July 1858, went to Persiceto to see Morisi to find out from her how it all happened." Jussi quoted at length from Angelo Padovani's recollection of Anna Morisi's tearful account of her baptism of Edgardo, concluding with Padovani's own testimony: "From her words, her behavior, and her tears, I was convinced that she had told me the truth."

Anna's story, Jussi said, had the undeniable ring of truth. What could be more natural than for a simple servant girl, when off shopping at the grocer's, to gossip about her employers? And isn't it the custom of grocers to try to find out all they can about what is going on in their neighbors' houses? Jussi also made note of a police report on Lepori in the trial record, which referred to him as "an intimate friend" of the local parish priest, Don Pini, an "Austrian-loving Jesuit."[11] Lepori was clearly someone "who must have known very well how to baptize a child." Jussi might have added, had he but known, that for years one of Lepori's major customers was the Convent of San Domenico itself, a fact all the more striking because his was by no means the closest grocery.[12]

As for how the Inquisitor came to hear about the baptism, what could be more believable than the story that Anna Morisi had told of running into a neighbor's servant and talking about the boy who was then dying in the Mortaras' home? Or the other woman, Regina Bussolari, urging her to baptize the dying boy, and Anna's refusal and her story of what she had done five years earlier when Edgardo was sick. Regina then went off, Jussi reconstructed, and "recounts it to someone else, and this other woman tells a third, until it comes to the inquisitor's ear.

"And here too," Jussi argued, we have in Bussolari

> a woman who herself was on friendly terms with the priests, for she is described as overly devoted, and a bigot. Indeed, the police commissioner, Meloni, would have her as something more, charging her with having had an affair with a priest who is now dead. But lacking any information in the trial beyond what the commissioner said, we would rather choose to believe Signora Pancaldi, who tells us in her sworn testimony that Bussolari was a good and very religious woman, and that she went often, perhaps even too often, to church.

But then why, Jussi asked, would both Lepori and Bussolari deny Morisi's account? The answer was simple: they were both afraid to tell the truth. They lied to try to save themselves.

Lepori's behavior, Jussi argued, shows this from the beginning. He had first told Momolo Mortara that he would give him a signed statement refuting Morisi's account, but then he refused to do so. What possible motive, Jussi asked, could Lepori have had for refusing to sign such a statement if it were accurate? Nor did Lepori's later testimony have the ring of truth. Is it credible that he had no memory of the girl the Mortaras sent every day in 1852 to shop in his store?

And what about Regina Bussolari? Isn't it a little suspicious that the police had such a difficult time tracking her down?

It was about three months ago, exactly at the time that Father Feletti was taken to prison—what strange coincidence!—that she abandoned her poor home in the San Lorenzo district in order to move in with her nephew Giuseppe Rossi in via Galliera. Was it merely by chance? Was it out of love for her kin? Or was it only from fear of being called in to testify? Bussolari admits all the circumstances regarding the place and time of that discussion [with Anna Morisi], and denies only that part that could expose her to legal action.

Jussi next turned his attention to Anna Morisi herself, for she was admittedly the only witness to the baptism, and Father Feletti's action was based on taking her at her word. Anna Morisi's life was not, Jussi admitted, above reproach. "On the contrary, she had been involved in illicit loves and had known the liveliest sensual pleasures. But if we are unwilling to believe anyone who has fallen prey to human weakness," asked Jussi, "whom would we be able to believe in this world?" And, he continued, Morisi must have some good qualities, or why would the Mortaras have gone to the expense to have her cared for when she was pregnant, and then taken her back after she left her baby in the foundling home?

As for the prosecutor's claim that Edgardo was not in any danger of dying at the time of the baptism, even if true, it would do nothing to negate the validity of the baptism and hence the need for the Inquisitor to act as he did. And how credible was the prosecutor's claim anyway? Didn't Dr. Saragoni's records show that he had made twelve house calls in seven days to check on the boy?

Jussi was now ready to sum up: Father Feletti had gotten word of Edgardo's baptism, he had heard Anna's story, a story that the Jews Padovani and De Angelis had themselves heard and found convincing. What had the Inquisitor done? He had merely done what his office demanded that he do. "And this is to be called a crime?" Jussi asked. And just what crime was it? The prosecution first "called it an attack on public tranquillity, then a kidnapping, then a violent separation, and then an abuse of power. But it is not any of those things; it is no crime at all." He went on: "It was not a crime when it happened because there was no law that prohibited it. On the contrary, there was one that expressly required it."

The lawyer then spoke of his long-suffering client.

Father Feletti has not thought of himself when it came to preparing his defense, for he did not want to incur ecclesiastical censure, nor would he break the oaths that he swore when he accepted his office. In his long hours of solitude, in the anguish of being in jail, in the total silence in which he finds himself, he feels inspired to give glory to the maker of the universe, whose grace he sees infused in that young child, in the boy's tranquillity when he first saw the police and when he was separated from his family, for his miraculous tranquillity . . . and for what I would call his evident pleasure during the journey, which Marshal Agostini confirms.

Compelled by his oath and his office to have the child removed from his Jewish parents so that he could be raised as a Catholic, Father Feletti had only done his duty. Yet he did all he could to make the separation as painless as possible. He had asked De Dominicis "to select the most humane soldiers in his militia, and to tell them to show every possible consideration, as in fact everyone in that family, including the boy's mother herself, has said they did. And when," Jussi asserted, "the boy's father[13] and brother-in-law went to see him to obtain more time for the separation, he welcomed them with kind words and granted them twenty-four hours, if not to persuade the mother, at least to make her son's sudden departure less harsh and less painful. . . . What more," asked Jussi, "could he have done that was compatible with his duty?"

Jussi carefully chose the final image he would leave with the six judges, and with the thousands of the faithful who would soon read his defense. It was an image of a martyred man of God, inspired by the divine light that shone through a little boy: "Suddenly assailed by this misfortune, he followed his conscience not to violate those oaths to which he was bound by his office. Then in his mind's eye he saw the grace with which the Lord had infused Edgardo and, absorbed in this idea, decided to leave himself to the fate that the heavens had for him, disdaining any human defense, content to offer his tears to God and not to men."[14]

CHAPTER 22

The Rites of Rulers

MUCH HAD HAPPENED outside the walls of Father
Feletti's prison in the fifteen weeks he had been locked up.
Farini's efforts to solidify the new regime in Emilia were
moving ahead, while the old grand duchy of Tuscany was likewise hurtling
toward annexation with the kingdom of Sardinia. The Risorgimento goal of a
unified Italian state appeared to be a pipe dream no more.

The white-robed Dominican monk in Bologna's prison tower was not the
only churchman to feel besieged and persecuted. As the papal territories
shrank, the victim of popular revolt and military intrigue, Pope Pius IX saw
the devil himself at work. One week after Father Feletti's arrest, the Pope
replied to King Victor Emmanuel II's request that he accept the loss of
Romagna and cede effective political control over the central Italian regions of
Umbria and the Marches. The Pope angrily rejected the proposal, asking the
king "to reflect on my position, on my sacred character, and on the duty I
have to the dignity and the rights of this Holy See, which are the rights not of a
dynasty but of all Catholics." On January 19, 1860, Pius IX issued the encyclical
Nullis certe, denouncing the seizure of Romagna and calling for its immediate
restitution.[1]

In Bologna, relations between the Church and the new state were tense.
On the very day of the ex-Inquisitor's arrest, the government of the province
of Bologna published a warning, delivered to all town offices. It threatened a
penalty of jail and fines for those priests "who, in the exercise of their ministry
or by means of their public speeches or writings, or by other public means,
censure the institutions and the laws of the state, or provoke disobedience
toward those laws or to other public authorities."[2]

The new rulers were moving quickly toward the annexation of Romagna, Modena, Parma, and Tuscany to the kingdom of Sardinia, which was being steadily transformed into a kingdom of Italy. While Father Feletti reflected on his fate and God's will in prison, Bologna was preparing for a plebiscite on annexation. The government that had replaced the papal regime had long since proclaimed its desire to become part of Victor Emmanuel's kingdom, but international diplomatic considerations argued for a demonstration that the end of papal rule and the embracing of the Savoyard king were the product of irresistible popular demand. The plebiscite would show that it was the Pope's erstwhile subjects themselves who had rejected his rule.[3]

Not that the wording of the plebiscite Farini prepared for Emilia and Romagna gave much room for diehard defenders of the Papal States. The question put to a vote on March 11–12 asked the citizens to cast their preference for "annexation to the constitutional monarchy of King Victor Emmanuel, or for a separate kingdom." The ritual nature of the exercise was evident from the result: 426,000 votes for annexation to 756 against. A week later, Farini took the implausible tally to Victor Emmanuel, who, the very same day, issued a royal decree proclaiming the annexation of the provinces of Emilia to the kingdom of Sardinia.[4]

Each such milestone on the path away from papal rule turned into a battleground between the new state and its sworn enemy, the Church. Were the walls of his cell not so thick, or had he had more than a small window, Father Feletti would have heard the bands playing and the crowds streaming toward the nearby central piazza on March 21. A special mass was being celebrated in San Petronio, a Te Deum of thanks sung, a heavenly blessing sought for the Bolognesi's new monarch. The grand chapel orchestra played as a host of dignitaries basked in the sacred glow of this, Bologna's holiest place. Among those in the first row was the provincial intendant who had issued the stern warning to the clergy three months earlier, surrounded by members of the provincial and city councils. And alongside them sat the dignitaries of Bologna's judiciary—including, no doubt, the judges who would, less than a month later, decide Father Feletti's fate. All too embarrassingly missing, by contrast, were San Petronio's priests. The Archbishop, Cardinal Viale-Prelà, had again forbidden them to take part, and so the usual military chaplains had been pressed into service.[5]

Four days later, Pius IX gave his own response to the loss of Bologna and Romagna: an edict excommunicating all those involved in the "evil rebellion" in those provinces. They were to lose all the privileges of the Church and could receive absolution only if and when they "publicly retracted all that, in whatever way, they had done," and restored the lands to their former political condition.[6] The judges of Bologna's court were, in this way, forewarned of what would happen to them if they were to convict the jailed monk. Farini, who had brought about Father Feletti's arrest, and Curletti, who as police chief had seized the monk from his convent, were already beyond the pale. The judges' position was more ambiguous.

The judges were far from revolutionaries, for the elite of the new regime in Bologna hardly differed from the old. What had been cast off in the revolt was not the previous order of social and economic privilege, but a political regime that had become increasingly anachronistic for Europe's elite. It was not a revolt led by proponents of a new social or economic order; still less was it the product of any peasant or protoproletarian uprising. And just as Bologna's new political leadership came disproportionately from the old claque of nobles and notables—Napoleon's cousin Gioacchino Pepoli among them—so too did the city's judiciary. The head of the six-judge panel in the ex-inquisitor's trial, Calcedonio Ferrari, was a count, as was a fellow judge, Achille Masi. A third member of the panel, Carlo Mazzolani, was a baron.

The concluding session of Father Feletti's trial began on April 16 with Count Ferrari, in his chair as president of the court, reciting a prayer. The day proceeded with the prosecutor's closing arguments, followed by Francesco Jussi's stirring brief for the defense. The judges then filed out of the court-room for their deliberations. Their discussion of the case was brief. Upon their return to the courtroom, Count Ferrari read their decision:

> The Court, responding to the questions put to it by its Head, invoking the most holy name of God, declares it determined that on the evening of 24 June 1858, the police took from the Jewish couple Salomone, alias Momolo, Mortara and Marianna Padovani their son Edgardo, and that this action was authorized by the government.
>
> Therefore there were not, and are not, grounds for proceeding crim-inally against the executors of the above-mentioned action, and thus against the defendant Pier Gaetano Feletti of the Order of Preachers, for-merly Inquisitor of the Holy Office in Bologna. Consequently, he should be immediately released from jail.[7]

By the time the court came to its decision, the clamor over the Jewish boy's abduction had largely died down. For the liberals and the opponents of the Pope's temporal rule who had taken up the cause, events were moving too quickly, headed toward the unification of Italy, of which they had long dreamed. They had little time to waste worrying about Edgardo and the Inquisitor's fate. Also militating against any protest was the fact that the deci-sion had been reached by a court of the new regime. Indeed, it was one of the very first court verdicts made in the former Legations, now under King Victor Emmanuel's control.

There were other reasons why the freeing of Father Feletti was greeted with little protest in Italy. Just a week earlier, following the crushing of a revolt in Sicily by the armed forces of the kingdom of the Two Sicilies, Garibaldi announced that he would bow to the Sicilian revolutionaries' pleas and organize an expedition of volunteers to come to their aid. This alarmed Victor Emmanuel and Cavour, whose carefully crafted diplomatic arrangements were put in jeopardy and who, most of all, worried that the unification movement would escape from their hands and degenerate into a social revolution. They did everything they could to prevent Garibaldi from sailing off while, at the same time, they tried to solidify their own support, both within their newly expanded kingdom and in the courts of Europe. A head-on assault on the Church was not what they needed, and although the Pope's opposition to their annexation of his northern lands could not have been any clearer, both the King and his prime minister sought to portray themselves as good Catholics, eager to live in harmony with the Church.

For the Jews, it was a different story. The Inquisitor's arrest had been a triumphant vindication, and sweet revenge. The major Italian Jewish newspaper, *L'Educatore israelitico*, describing the verdict, aptly called the proceedings "the trial of the present against the past." Higher political aims were at stake, as the paper recognized. "And so," the Jewish paper observed, "almost suddenly and unexpectedly, a trial concludes that was, perhaps, begun unwisely, because they never foresaw a successful conclusion or, indeed, they wanted, prudently, to avoid it."[8] And the editor of *Archives Israélites*, who had led the French campaign for Edgardo's liberation, took a similarly philosophical view. "At least," he wrote, "this sentence demonstrates the court's impartiality. . . . As for the rest," he concluded, his sights set on higher targets than the Bologna monk, "what good does it do to strike at the arm when it is the head that in this case conceived, carried out, and sanctioned the attack?"[9]

When Father Feletti, praying in his prison cell, received word of the court's decision, he thanked God for being merciful to him, and made his way back to San Domenico. The Archbishop, who was seriously ill, was also thankful that the monk had been released, but he found himself no less embattled than before. He had just been informed that, to celebrate the annexation of Romagna, King Victor Emmanuel himself was planning a triumphal visit to Bologna in two weeks' time, a visit made more propitious for the King, no doubt, by not having to be feted in the shade of a tower holding an imprisoned monk. The authorities were planning gala celebrations to mark the monarch's first visit to his new lands and would, as usual, require the services of local priests to lend the proper religious flavor to the occasion.

On April 26, Cardinal Viale-Prelà sent a letter to the King's aide-de-camp with the bad news: no priest under his authority would take part in the festivities. It was his sacred duty, he wrote, to do everything in his power "to maintain the integrity of the pontifical territory, especially that of Emilia." He could not obey the government's order to illuminate all of the churches on the night of the King's visit: "I would betray my conscience and trample shamelessly on my solemn oaths, I would renounce every principle of honor . . . and I would be dishonored for the rest of my life." He explained: "This illumination is ordered to celebrate the sovereign authority of His Majesty in these lands. Were I to illuminate the churches, I would thereby be recognizing the King's authority." The Cardinal added the hope that the King would see to it that he was not insulted and attacked as he had been the previous summer, when he came to a similar decision regarding Massimo d'Azeglio's triumphal march into Bologna. He could not believe, he wrote, "that His Majesty would tolerate that, under his very eyes, a Bishop, a Cardinal, be insulted because of what his sacred duty forbade him to do." It would take, he added, but one word from the King to prevent such outrages from those people who "sought nothing but scandals and disorder."[10] The same day that he sent the letter, the Archbishop, gravely ill, left the city for the healthier air of the Apennines nearby. He was not in Bologna when, on May 1, Victor Emmanuel rode into town.

Such was the nature of the battleground in the war between Church and state that the point of honor on which the new rulers insisted, and the Church officials resisted, was the ringing of the city's church bells. How, after all, could the sovereign march into town with the bells silent? The day after the Archbishop took to the hills, Bologna's mayor sent a letter to every parish priest in the city, ordering that "on the entrance of His Majesty Victor Emmanuel II in Bologna, they ring the bells of their church to celebrate just as all the other cities have done." But, following their archbishop's instructions, the Bologna parish priests refused.[11]

Through the city's portal and down the flag-draped city streets the King marched, beneath tapestries—hung from windows—painted the colors of the more than two hundred cities and provinces of his newly enlarged realm. People waved flags from windows and balconies and sent a blizzard of flowers down onto the royal carriage. Everywhere the coats of arms of the King and the city were displayed together, alongside the tricolor. The King made his way to the central piazza, newly renamed Piazza Vittorio Emanuele, filled not only by celebrating citizens but by color guards, military battalions, and even firemen. Amidst the cheers, the bands, and the artillery salutes, the King may not have noticed how few church bells rang.

The next day, the local paper excitedly recounted the splendiferous day, but hastened to add a rejoinder to the clerical critics of the celebration: "We note that, contrary to the confusion of our malicious enemies, who wanted to see a disastrous welcome and heavenly disapproval" for the event, "not even a sprinkle of water came to dampen the public joy, even though it rained continuously all morning, and then rained again right after."[12]

What most enraged the Church leaders that day was the ceremony held in the King's honor in San Petronio. On May 2, the Archbishop's second-in-command, Monsignor Ratta, in place of the ailing Cardinal, sent a report of the latest outrages to the Secretary of State, Cardinal Antonelli, in Rome. "What most saddened me," he wrote, "is what happened in San Petronio when the King had barely reached the entrance of the church. There was a horrendous uproar, with people shouting 'Long live the King!' and it lasted through much of the mass and until the King left the church. And so Jesus Christ was insulted in his own home, and the sanctuary devoted to prayer and the holding of sacred services were profaned. . . . Most Eminent Reverence," the Monsignor concluded, "I thought of the scourges sent by Jesus Christ against those who profaned the Temple, and what came to my mind was the words *zelus domus tuae comedit me* [the zeal of your home consumed me]."[13]

The Monsignor would soon have unexpected time on his hands to ponder the new government's sacrileges. Just three days after Monsignor Ratta sent his letter to Cardinal Antonelli, the parliament in Turin decided that May 13 should be celebrated in communities throughout the realm as a festival honoring the Piedmontese constitution, recently extended to the annexed territories. The Archbishop, by now mortally ill, gave his second-in-command instructions to continue the hard line, forbidding any Church action that could be interpreted as legitimating the new government.

When the government ordered Bologna's parish priests to celebrate a special Te Deum on May 13, the clergy received instructions from the archdiocese to refuse. This was the last straw for government officials, who wanted to arrest the recently returned Cardinal Viale-Prelà. Apprised of the Archbishop's failing health, they ordered the arrest, instead, of his pro-vicar, Monsignor Ratta, charged with promoting disobedience of the laws of the land.

Ironically, on the very Sunday of the patriotic festival for the constitution, as the new regime was showing its vigor, Cardinal Viale-Prelà's condition took a turn for the worse, and Monsignor Ratta was urgently called to administer the last rites. As the Monsignor left his lodgings to rush to the Archbishop's side, he was intercepted by police and arrested, an arrest approved by Count Cavour himself. The police escorted him to the Torrone prison, locking him in the cell that Father Feletti had vacated less than a month before. Later that morning, the Te Deum was sung in churches throughout the diocese, led, for the most part, by military chaplains. Bologna's parish priests had heeded their archbishop's last wish.

That night Michele Viale-Prelà, aged 61, died. The man who had been the toast of all Europe—or at least all Catholic Europe—five years earlier when he concluded the new concordat as papal nuncio to the Austrian Empire, the friend of Metternich, the man who might have replaced Cardinal Antonelli as secretary of state, died in the most humiliating of circumstances. In the less-than-two years since the seizure of Edgardo Mortara, the Archbishop had been reduced in standing from the most prominent and influential man in Bologna, the city second only to Rome in the Papal States, to an embattled enemy of the government, openly reviled, unable to prevent his own assistant's being jailed simply for following his orders.

Just how swiftly the tide had turned, and how unscrupulous Bologna's elite were in embracing their new rulers, can be seen in the diary kept by Francesco Nascentori, the same Bolognese chronicler who—then a fearless champion of papal rule—had approvingly quoted from *Civiltà Cattolica* in describing the Mortara case only a year and a half earlier. His obituary notice for the Cardinal showed that Nascentori had been transformed, overnight, from a defender of Church power to a red-white-and-green patriot:

> At 2 a.m. on Tuesday, May 15, the physical sufferings and moral apprehensions of Cardinal Archbishop Viale-Prelà came to an end. We are all glad about this, knowing that he had no homeland here, nor consolations, and aspired continuously to heaven, inasmuch as he found it upsetting and tiresome to feel any human sentiments or charity for this people. We thank God for him while, for ourselves, let us hope that Bologna's next Archbishop is Italian and Catholic, human and pious, like the one we had the other time [that is, Cardinal Oppizzoni], a respected and beloved pastor who, when separated by eternal decree from his flock, merited the mourning of the entire citizenry and not just the usual hypocrites and stupid servants of Austria and the despots of the Roman Curia.[14]

On July 4, Monsignor Ratta was found guilty, sentenced to three years in prison, and assessed an enormous fine. After a Church delegation went to Turin to plead with Count Cavour for leniency, the King pardoned him. Like Father Feletti, he had spent about a hundred days in jail.[15]

As for Father Feletti, Church authorities judged it prudent for him to leave Bologna and move to Rome, which remained under Church control. His principled stance on behalf of the Church, his refusal both to recognize the right of the usurper state to try him and to reveal any of the secrets of the Holy Office, his testimony to the grace that God visited on little Edgardo, all these endeared him not only to his Dominican superiors but to the Pope himself. He was appointed prior of a Dominican convent in the Holy City, where he remained until his death, in 1881, at age 84.

A few years before Father Feletti died, he wrote to the elderly Pius IX, reminding the Pope who he was ("the religious events of 1860, well known to your Holiness, having necessitated that I withdraw from Bologna"), and asked for authorization to be buried at a Dominican convent in Lombardy, in northern Italy. When he did die, he was eulogized—in Latin—by the head of the Dominican order in Lombardy, who recalled the Mortara case in these terms: "With the sadness of all good people, he was made to stand trial, and in this critical situation he behaved so courageously as to provoke the admiration of all those who take religion to heart and, in particular, his ecclesiastical superiors, especially Pius IX."[16]

Both Cardinal Viale-Prelà's and Father Feletti's successors in Bologna faced disastrous situations. With the chaos in which the Church found itself in the former Papal States, it took three years for a new archbishop to be appointed. The Pope's choice for the position reveals a great deal about his attitude toward the Mortara affair. Rejecting any attempt to accommodate himself to the loss of papal power in Bologna, and choosing to ignore the sensibilities of those who had protested the Mortara abduction, he named a Dominican monk, Filippo Guidi, to the post. Indeed, not only was Guidi a Dominican, but he had lived for the previous three years in Vienna, thus combining—from many a patriotic Bolognese's viewpoint—memories of their former inquisitor with their worst memories of their recent archbishop.

The Pope had finally been forced to fill the vacancy because Monsignor Antonio Canzi, bishop of the small northern diocese of Crema, who was serving as acting archbishop of Bologna, had himself been jailed. The Monsignor was but one in what was becoming a long line of high ecclesiastical victims in the ritual struggle between Church and state in Bologna. In January of 1862 he had advised a parish priest not to officiate at the funeral of a prominent judge, because the man was a well-known supporter of the new regime. The jurist's family initiated court proceedings against both the parish priest and the bishop. On April 5 of that year, Bologna police invaded all of Bologna's churches, searching the vestries for a circular that Monsignor Canzi had just sent out. The circular, in line with the policy enunciated by the Holy See itself, called on the parish priests to refuse communion to those who took part in the new government. Monsignor Canzi was arrested for having sent out the offending circular without first getting government authorization. In early August, the Bishop was found guilty and began serving a three-year prison sentence.

When the Monsignor finally got out of jail, in June 1865, there still was no archbishop in Bologna to succeed the now long-dead Corsican cardinal. The government had refused to permit the Dominican to take office, and it was only in 1871 that Guidi finally renounced his appointment, never in those years having set foot in his archdiocese. As a result, upon his release after three years in jail, Monsignor Canzi served six more years as acting archbishop of Bologna.[17]

As for the Dominicans whom Father Feletti left behind, they too suffered. As the government of the new state gave up on its attempts to make peace with the ever-hostile Church, it resorted to tactics that Napoleon had employed at the turn of the century. In July 1866, Parliament passed a law suppressing religious orders and ordering the confiscation of their property. In December of that year, the remaining monks were forced to abandon San Domenico, leaving the bones of their founder behind. The entire convent was turned into a military barracks, while just three Dominicans were allowed to remain to oversee the church itself.

The following year, adding insult to injury, the city council changed the name of Piazza San Domenico to Piazza Galileo Galilei, honoring the Inquisition's most eminent victim. In January 1868, a city councilor, decrying the presence in the square of the statue of Saint Dominic, which had looked down on the picturesque piazza since 1627, proposed replacing it with a monument to those men of Bologna who had died in the struggle to defeat papal power. That, as it turned out, proved a bit much for the members of the city council, and, by a vote of 31 to 7, Saint Dominic's likeness was allowed to stand.[18]

CHAPTER 23

New Hopes for
Freeing Edgardo

T HE MORTARAS HAD put little hope in the Feletti trial. Neither Momolo nor Marianna had had a direct hand in bringing about the Inquisitor's arrest, and even Momolo's father's plea to Farini, which had led to the monk's jailing, had been aimed not at bringing Father Feletti to trial but at getting Edgardo back.

For the first several months after his son was taken, Momolo remained convinced that the Pope could be persuaded to return him. By the time he finally realized that Pius IX would never willingly give Edgardo up, the clouds of unification were already on the horizon. It was the beginning of the end of the Papal States. When papal forces and their Austrian protectors retreated from Bologna and Romagna in June 1859 and the new king and his prime minister, Count Cavour, prepared to send their troops southward into the Marches and Umbria, the status of the Papal States and the future of the Pope's temporal power moved to center stage in European diplomacy. The Pope no longer enjoyed the position he had occupied but a few months before, when, ruling a sizable territory and backed by foreign armies, he could do as he pleased. Now, thought Momolo, whether Pius IX liked it or not, he would have to listen to the foreign powers whose deliberations would determine whether the Pope continued to have any land to rule at all.

In the fall of 1859, in the wake of the revolts in Romagna, Parma, Modena, and Tuscany, plans began to be made for a conference of European powers, to be held in Paris, to discuss the fate of Italy and the Papal States. France and Great Britain would be the two most influential participants.

All of Momolo's efforts to follow the quiet diplomacy urged on him by Scazzocchio and other officers of Rome's Jewish community had failed. Now living in Turin, he was increasingly influenced by the perspective of the Jews of Piedmont, whose public criticism of the Vatican contrasted with the role of humble supplicant assumed by Rome's Jewish leaders. Papal rule, in the Piedmontese view, was an anachronism that the governments of the civilized world could no longer tolerate.

Momolo thus came to see the upcoming conference as his best hope for getting Edgardo back. In its November 28 issue, the Bologna newspaper *Gazzetta del popolo* reported hopefully: "The members of the Congress will probably be fathers of families themselves, and even those who aren't will not remained unmoved by the pleas of a father who asks to be given back a son who was violently stolen from him by a government that the oppressed and outraged peoples have repeatedly expelled every time that it has been left unprotected by a foreign army."[1]

In December 1859, Momolo was in Paris, frantically trying to drum up support for his cause. But the issue that had been so much on the mind of the French ambassador to the Holy See the previous year, and that had irritated the Emperor himself, no longer drew much attention. The French already had more than enough to attend to in Italy, with the defeat of the Austrians in Lombardy, the demise of the Italian duchies, the fall of the old regimes in Romagna and Tuscany, and the uncertain future of the tottering kingdom of the Two Sicilies, not to mention the ticklish question of what to do about what remained of the Papal States.

Isidore Cahen, the *Archives Israélites* editor who had long championed the Mortara case, could see this even if Momolo could not. In January 1860, he described his recent meeting with Momolo, a man who seemed obsessed with the effort to get his son back: "We in Paris saw a father who was desolate," wrote Cahen. "We listened to him, we saw the tears in his eyes, this husband whose wife is still sick from the blow that struck her. We felt that the scar was still open, and we didn't have the courage to tell him how unlikely [diplomatic] intervention seemed to us."[2]

From Paris, Momolo went on to London, where he received the news that Father Feletti had been arrested. He met with Sir Moses Montefiore for the first time and addressed the Board of Deputies of British Jews, pleading with them to get the British government to bring the question of Edgardo's plight before the upcoming congress. Momolo also met with Sir Culling Eardley, head of the Protestant Evangelical Alliance in Britain, who had campaigned so vigorously for Edgardo's release. He met with members of the Rothschild family, who had not only been providing him with financial support but who, he hoped, could use their influence to help his cause at the congress. Yet, after

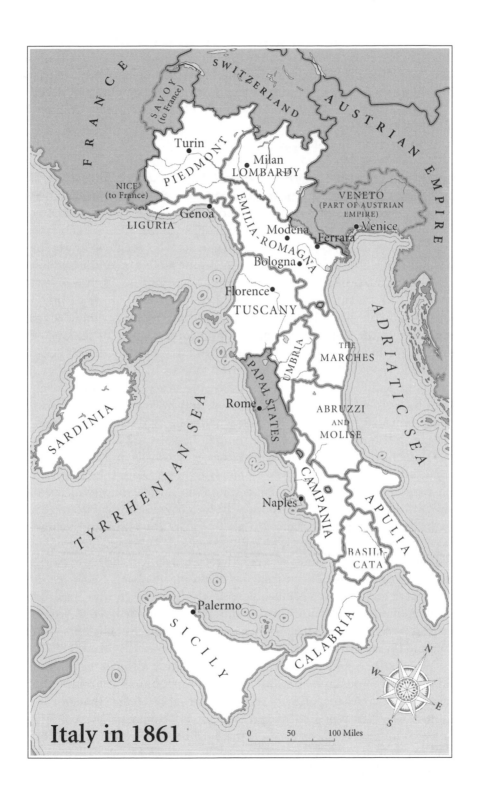

Italy in 1861

FRANCE

SWITZERLAND

AUSTRIAN EMPIRE

SAVOY
(to France)

Turin

PIEDMONT

Milan
LOMBARDY

NICE
(to France)

VENETO
(PART OF AUSTRIAN
EMPIRE)

LIGURIA

Genoa

EMILIA-ROMAGNA

Modena

Ferrara

Venice

Bologna

Florence

TUSCANY

UMBRIA

THE
MARCHES

ADRIATIC SEA

PAPAL STATES

Rome

ABRUZZI
AND
MOLISE

SARDINIA

TYRRHENIAN SEA

CAMPANIA

Naples

APULIA

BASILI-
CATA

Palermo

SICILY

CALABRIA

0   50   100 Miles

N
W   E
S

all this campaigning, Momolo was disappointed. Because of the kaleidoscopic course of political events, the congress was called off, and his dreams of seeing the leading diplomats of Europe discuss his son's kidnapping and devise a plan for the boy's release came to nothing.[3] He returned, dejected and ill-humored, to Turin.

Although the Mortara case was no longer high on the European diplomatic agenda, it remained powerfully resonant among the Jews of Italy, Britain, and especially France. No journalist had crusaded for the Mortara cause more ceaselessly than Isidore Cahen in Paris. For the Jews to find themselves in the same conditions as in the Middle Ages, wrote Cahen, was intolerable. In much of the world, Jews remained subject to the whims of anti-Jewish government officials and exposed to demagogues who delighted in whipping the local rabble into anti-Semitic frenzies. In the wake of the Mortara affair, and with Momolo's visit to Paris still fresh in their minds, a group of Jewish men met in Paris in May 1860, convinced of the need to create an international organization in defense of Jewish civil rights. There they founded what soon became the most important European organization of its kind, the Alliance Israélite Universelle, which still today has its headquarters in Paris.[4]

Those who saw Momolo in this period found a man transformed by the horrors he had lived through over the past two years, a man aged, weighed down by worries. His business was ruined, and he lived on Jewish charity, money provided not only by the Rothschilds but by donations collected at synagogues throughout Europe. Returning to Italy, he testified before Magistrate Carboni, where he let some of his bitterness show, denouncing the former inquisitor's claim about his son's happiness in being taken from his parents, and about the Pope's solicitude. But despite all this, while others had given up hope, Momolo still believed that one day he would be able to get Edgardo back.

In May, Giuseppe Garibaldi led his legendary thousand-man volunteer army by boat to Sicily, where he established rule over the island in the name—although against the wishes—of King Victor Emmanuel. The enlarged Garibaldian army began its march up the peninsula in August, and by early September had conquered Naples, center of the Bourbon court that ruled the kingdom of the Two Sicilies. The remaining Papal States fell to the Piedmontese forces shortly thereafter, leaving only the region around Rome to the Pope and his secretary of state.

With Victor Emmanuel's forces moving so swiftly through the peninsula, and the Papal States crumbling, Momolo had new grounds for optimism. In August 1860, in a letter of thanks to the chief rabbi of the Alsatian city of Colmar, who had sent him the proceeds of his congregation's collection, Momolo wrote: "The happy events that are taking place in Italy give me hope that the day is not far off when justice will be done and I will have my poor, dear little son back again."[5]

Rome's fall now seemed imminent. And if Rome fell, what was to prevent the Mortaras from taking their child back? Officers of the newly formed Alliance Israélite Universelle kept a close watch on the development. On September 17, with Piedmontese troops beginning their march down from Romagna into the Marches and Umbria, they wrote to Count Cavour.

"Like all friends of progress and freedom," wrote the organization's president, Alliance members had been pleased to hear the reports that the French troops would soon be leaving Rome and that the Pope would no doubt flee as well. Yet they were concerned that the Pope, "moved by an exaggerated religious sentiment," might try to take little Edgardo Mortara with him. The Alliance Israélite Universelle, he informed the Prime Minister, was "taking measures to protect this young child, who is today a Sardinian subject, now detained contrary to the eternal laws of nature and of God!" The Alliance "dares to hope," the letter continued, "that with your refined spirit and your noble heart you will not forget the innocent victim of the cruelest persecution, despite the many important questions that will no doubt arise when the kingdom of Italy takes possession of the capital."

Two weeks later, Cavour responded, assuring the Jewish organization that his government would do everything possible to see that the Mortara boy was returned to his family.[6] His letter was properly diplomatic, but he did not really think it likely that the Pope would be dislodged from Rome any time soon. The Prime Minister was, however, genuinely concerned for Edgardo's fate. The following spring, when he had much else on his mind, and when the Mortara case no longer promised any diplomatic advantage, he sent a letter to Count Giulio Gropello, the Sardinian representative to the kingdom of Naples, reminding him of the boy's abduction and the Pope's refusal to budge. Cavour told the Count that he had recently received new pleas from the boy's father, and expressed his enthusiastic support for Momolo's request that his son be returned, reiterating his belief that the boy's abduction was an offense against natural law. He noted, regretfully, that there was little he could do, for his government had no diplomatic relations with the Holy See. Cavour suggested that the French, on whose troops the Pope depended, might be able to act more successfully.[7]

Just five weeks later, at the height of his fame and in the midst of his labors to build the new Italian nation, Cavour was suddenly struck ill and died. He was fifty years old.

Following his letter to Cavour in mid-September 1860, the president of the Alliance Israélite Universelle wrote to Momolo Mortara in Turin with the thrilling—if enigmatic—news that the Alliance had a plan of action in place for liberating his son: "This is what you have to do to find your son and get him back again. You must keep closely posted on events and get the best-informed people in Turin to let you know the time when the Pope is likely to fall. Then you will leave for Rome, and there you will speak to the friend whose name we give you below. He is one of our coreligionists, and you will find that he will give you the most efficient support in Rome." Just who this secret Jewish agent was in Rome, we do not know. The copy of the letter that remains in the Paris archives lacks it, and the original, which Momolo received, is long gone.

The letter went on to offer Momolo reimbursement for what it would cost him to leave his business and go to Rome, for "getting your child back is the cause of all Israel. . . . It goes without saying," the Alliance president added, "that you must employ the greatest prudence in this delicate matter, the most absolute secrecy. Success depends on it."[8]

There seemed to be no lack of conspiratorial plans for seizing Edgardo from the grip of the reeling papal forces. Even Garibaldi apparently got into the act, albeit fleetingly. In his force of volunteers—men willing to risk their lives for the ideal of a united Italy—were, curiously, many foreigners. One of these, an English Jew named Carl Blumenthal, angered by the failure of diplomatic efforts to win Edgardo's release, came up with his own plan for rekidnapping the boy. He and three friends would dress up as monks, win admittance into the Rome convent where Edgardo was being held, and make off with him. Blumenthal asked for Garibaldi's approval of the plan in 1860, and Garibaldi—who would later work the Mortara case into a novel of his own—gave his blessing. But the attempt never took place, aborted, it was said, by the unexpected death of one of the conspirators.[9]

Garibaldi was not the only one to see fictional potential in the Mortara drama. A spate of plays were written and produced in the immediate aftermath of Edgardo's abduction. Most significant was *La Tireuse de cartes* (The Fortune-Teller), whose opening in Paris on December 22, 1859, was attended by the Emperor and Empress themselves. Inspired by the Mortara case, the story was altered to appeal to a broad audience and set in seventeenth-century France. Its dramatic details were reported in the *Monitore di Bologna*, which praised the play for "re-evoking and supporting a cause that moved the whole world."[10] It was quickly translated into Italian and put on in Bologna the same month that Father Feletti was freed from prison.[11]

Given the times, it is no surprise that in Italy dramatization of the Mortara case took the form of an encomium to national unification and vilification of papal rule. But to serve this purpose, a more satisfactory ending was required. *La famiglia ebrea* (The Jewish Family), the best known of these plays, written by Riccardo Castelvecchio in Milan in 1861, was set in Bologna in 1859 but had the kidnapping of the protagonist—a Jewish boy secretly baptized by the family servant—take place twenty-nine years earlier. Although he was raised by the Jesuits, the boy nourished a smoldering hatred for those who had deprived him of his parents, and he became the secret leader of Bologna's unification forces.

In the play's last scene, amidst the uprising of patriotic forces in Bologna, he is at last reunited with his father, who is a rabbi. The Cardinal Legate is arrested, but before he is led off, he sneers at the Rabbi: "But you won't get to enjoy the fruit of your triumph. I leave your family in discord: the father a Jew, his son a Christian!"

"You forget," the Rabbi replies. "The star of freedom has arisen; the fogs of prejudice and ignorance disappear before its light. Christians and Jews, Protestants and Catholics, will form one family alone. They will shake hands on the altar of the nation and will have but a single name: Italians!"[12]

Curiously, both the Italian and the American play based on the Mortara story, written at the same time, renamed Edgardo with the more Jewish-sounding name of Benjamin. Without the patriotic romance that so permeates the Italian play, the American drama became simply an extension of the anti-Catholic polemics that the Mortara case had tapped into in the United States. Leaving no room for missing the point, it was titled *Mortara—or The Pope and His Inquisitors*, and the play's characters included Mortara, his son Benjamin, Pope Pius, a cardinal, monks and inquisitors, and even an English rabbi named Montefiore.

The play could scarcely have been more melodramatic, more violent, or more anti-Catholic. The mad pope screams for the inquisitors to "imprison every Jew." Mortara is cruelly tortured by the Cardinal, who seeks information on the Jew's nephew, a refugee from papal justice. The Inquisitor, while gleefully dislocating Mortara's fingers and pouring hot oil on his arms, threatens to torture his son as well: "to rack thy son and burn his eyeballs out, to flay his feet and make him walk on sand, to roast his flesh and lay him on crushed glass," and on and on.[13]

What both these plays make clear is the fine line that little Edgardo was walking between hero and villain. In the Italian dramatization, the boy's father would kill him if he found that he had become a "Jesuit," although, in keeping with the secularization of the story, the murderous sentiment is justified on patriotic rather than religious grounds. And Edgardo/Benjamin himself sees through the fact that, in educating him, the priests were simply trying to turn him, too, into "an instrument of oppression." There again the reference is ambiguous, the oppression universalized. But for Jews in the audience, the reference was clear enough. Having endured centuries of forced sermons by converts, and having been brought up on cautionary tales of fanatic converts torching Talmuds and baptizing hapless Jewish children, they knew just what kind of devil Edgardo/Benjamin could turn into.

Fear that Edgardo himself might become the enemy of his people was voiced directly in the antipapal literature when Edgardo had barely reached his ninth birthday. A French pamphlet captured these sentiments, writing in 1860 of the fate in store for little Edgardo: "The child will become not a

Christian according to the Gospel but—the pen balks at writing it—he will be a Jesuit! . . . this order whose principles are in opposition to the legitimate, true Christianity. And now what will become of this innocent child, if he does not become the instrument of this order, one of its missionaries, a persecutor of the Jews, a persecutor of his own father." And the author concludes, writing in France before the Castelvecchio play was written: "At that moment, perhaps, will we hear his parents cry, their hearts broken, 'Would to God he were never born!' "[14]

A story appeared in the newspaper *L'opinione nazionale* in the fall of 1860. The paper had gruesome news to report about Edgardo. It seems that Church authorities, having discovered to their delight that Edgardo had a talent for singing, had had him castrated so that he could fill a recent vacancy in the Sistine Chapel choir. The French head of papal military forces in Rome, General Lamoricière, was said to have energetically opposed the operation. The story—if not the operation—hit a nerve. Reports of such operations had long circulated. Alexandre Dumas, for one, had reported that in a trip to Rome not many years earlier, he saw a sign in a barbershop window: "Boys castrated here." In the 1860s, the Spanish traveler to the Vatican Emilio Castelar reported hearing that the soprano ranks of the Vatican choirs were suffering "because they can't find families who are so heartless as to be willing, for the love of gold, to sacrifice their own little sons." For the Holy See, by contrast, the newspaper report only reconfirmed their view that the fuss over Edgardo was simply a scurrilous attack mounted by the Church's enemies. On October 13, in the *Giornale di Roma*, the castration report was firmly denied.[15]

The Pope had good grounds for feeling besieged. Not only had he lost Bologna and Romagna the previous year, but much of what had then remained of the pontifical state—the lands of the Marches and Umbria—had now been conquered as well. On November 4, 1860, a plebiscite in those two regions repeated the ritual enacted the previous year in Romagna, and of 232,685 of his former subjects voting, 230,805 voted for annexation to the kingdom of Sardinia. All that prevented the same military that had marched into these regions from continuing their march to Rome was the French troops, yet it had been the French who had unleashed the disaster in the first place, plotting with Cavour and King Victor Emmanuel. For the Pope, the presence of the French soldiers seemed scant guarantee against the invasion of the godless hordes.

Odo Russell, the British attaché in Rome who had been so helpful to Moses Montefiore the previous year, reported in early December that the Pope was in a foul temper, "although at intervals he is as cheerful and as benevolent as ever." The bitterness with which the Pope berated foreigners for the conduct of their governments, wrote Russell, "has more than once placed the Cardinal Secretary of State in a very awkward position towards the representatives of the Catholic powers." And Pius IX's feelings of persecution were now combined with the certainty that his own life was in danger. This time, he vowed, there would be no repeat of his undignified flight to Gaeta twelve years before. "His Holiness believes," reported Russell, "that the enemies of the Church will lay violent hands on his person and that his end is nigh. He covets the palm of martyrdom which has been borne by so many of his early predecessors. He has abandoned his former plan of withdrawing to the catacombs in the hour of danger and now wishes to fall in his pontifical robes, a victim of his persecutors, on the altar of St Peter."[16]

When, the following month, the delegation of Jews from Rome's Università Israelitica came to the Vatican for their annual meeting with the Pope, they found the pontiff in a very different position from that of their stormy meeting of two years before. But Rome was still under papal control, and the Jews showed their customary deference, although they must have been wondering whether this might be the last of their annual visits. On entering Pius IX's quarters, however, they were surprised to discover at his side a 9-year-old boy in a seminarian's robe whose shoulder the Pope was gently caressing. Of the Jews present, only Scazzocchio had ever seen him before. It was Edgardo Mortara.[17]

By the time the Roman Jewish delegation got their fleeting glimpse of him, Edgardo had been in the Holy City for two and a half years and had not seen either of his parents for more than two years. He was, however, constantly in touch with the man he described as his other father, Pope Pius IX. Just what his fellow junior seminarians at San Pietro in Vincoli thought of this boy whose father was the Pope can only be imagined. Each month a Vatican messenger arrived at the convent bearing the sum of thirty scudi, sent by the Pope for Edgardo's expenses. At Christmastime each year, Edgardo was called to the Vatican for a visit with the Pope. On these occasions, as Edgardo himself later fondly recalled them, Pius IX "always lavished the most paternal demonstrations of affection on me, gave me wise and useful training and, tenderly blessing me, often repeated that I had cost him much pain and many tears." When he was still little, he recalled, the Pontiff, "like a good father, had fun with me, hiding me under his grand red cloak, asking, jokingly, 'Where's the boy?' and then, opening the cloak, showing me to the onlookers." The Pope took special pride in the strides Edgardo was making in his studies, and liked to impress his guests with the boy's religious learning. The Pope beamed with pride as, at his prompting, the little convert translated Latin passages for him, to the delight of his visitors.[18]

CHAPTER 24

Edgardo's Escape

B Y THE TIME the Pope, with Edgardo at his side, met with the delegates of Rome's Jewish community in early 1861, most of Italy had been united under the Savoyard king's rule. Only the Veneto region, in the northeast, remained under Austrian control, while the region around Rome was all that remained of the pontifical state. At the end of January 1861, the first election of an Italian parliament was held, with the Church urging all good Catholics to boycott it. The following month the new parliament, meeting in Turin, proclaimed the formation of the kingdom of Italy, with Victor Emmanuel II as its king. In March, Count Cavour, the prime minister, declared that only by liberating Rome would the new nation be whole; national pride demanded that the Eternal City become its capital. He hastened to warn, however, against any precipitate military action. Rome's annexation should come only after agreements were reached with France, whose soldiers still guarded the papal domain.

France, which had played such a major role in triggering and protecting the Italian unification movement in 1859, remained at center stage in the emotionally fraught battle over Rome's fate. Even though Cavour tried to reassure Catholics by offering safeguards for the Pope's role as the spiritual leader of Catholicism worldwide, opinion in France was mightily swayed by the cries of alarm emanating from the Vatican and taken up by the ultramontane forces. With French public opinion opposed to recognizing the legitimacy of the new Italian state, and the French parliament itself showing unaccustomed independence from the Emperor in denouncing Italian designs on the papal territories, Napoleon III decided to wait until Parliament had recessed before officially recognizing the kingdom of Italy. In May, representatives from Spain and Austria met with Napoleon and urged formation of a common Catholic front to defend the Pope's temporal power and his continued control of Rome.[1] Whatever his personal preferences, Napoleon felt he had no choice but to keep his troops in the Holy City.

In Rome, a siege mentality prevailed. The panic felt at the time of Sir Moses Montefiore's hasty departure in 1859—when news of victorious Italian armies on the march had sent so many in Rome's foreign community packing—subsided somewhat, but the threat of invasion remained. Although cooler heads realized that the Italian troops were unlikely to attack, for they would have had to fight the French, the Vatican had other armed patriots to worry about as well—most notably Giuseppe Garibaldi and his followers, men inspired by dreams of a united Italian nation, with Rome its capital.

The gates of the city were barricaded. After 9 p.m. no one could enter or leave. On every street corner, it seemed, stood two armed guards, checking the papers of passersby. Many of the guards were members of the Vatican's own defense force, volunteers and mercenaries from various European nations. Most spoke no Italian, and although French had become the lingua franca of the protectors of the Holy See, most spoke no French either. For the Romans, tension became a way of life. Year followed year, and Pope Pius IX, with the assistance of his Secretary of State, Cardinal Antonelli, held on, an ecclesiastical island in an Italian sea. Pilgrims continued to make their way to Rome; the cardinals could still be seen, resplendent in their purple robes; bishops clutched their ornate miters; and the Swiss guards, with their broad-striped tunics, lent a carnivalesque air to the area around the Vatican, set in colorful contrast with the guard of noblemen clad in their black velvet cloaks.[2]

The military defeats suffered by Pius IX, far from leading him to make peace with the new regime, prompted him to go newly on the attack. In 1862, his allocution, *Maxima quidem laetitia,* reaffirmed that the Pope could not be free to do his spiritual duty without temporal power, and on December 8, 1864, he issued one of the most famous—and controversial—encyclicals of modern times, *Quanta cura,* with its accompanying Syllabus of Errors.[3]

The idea of preparing an inventory of the errors of modern times had long been championed by the Jesuits of *Civiltà Cattolica.* A team of Vatican experts drew up the list, and the Pope's encyclical and the Syllabus were sent out together to all bishops with a cover letter sent from Cardinal Antonelli. The Cardinal explained: "The Pope has already in Encyclicals and Allocutions condemned the principal errors of this most unhappy age. . . . Therefore the Pope wished a Syllabus of these Errors to be drawn up for the use of all the Catholic bishops that they may have before their eyes the pernicious doctrines that he has proscribed."[4]

For the Pope's enemies, the Syllabus simply confirmed their belief that the pontifical state—if not the papacy itself—was a glaring anachronism in the nineteenth century. Among the pernicious doctrines the Pope condemned were that people should be free to profess whatever religion they thought best; that even those not in the Catholic Church could aspire to eternal salvation; that Catholics could disagree with the need for the Pope to have temporal power; that there should be a separation of Church and state; and "that the Pope could and should reconcile himself to and agree with progress, liberalism, and modern civilization."[5]

Even many loyal Catholics—perhaps most—were shocked by the Syllabus, in which the Pope seemed to condemn progress and modern civilization. For the anticlerical forces, the Syllabus was "manna from heaven," in the words of Roger Aubert, Pius IX's biographer. One Piedmontese newspaper, noting that the Pope had condemned modern science, delightfully (if maliciously) asked whether he now planned to ban trains, telegraph, steam engines, and gaslights from his—albeit recently reduced—lands.[6]

In 1864, another episode involving a Jewish boy demonstrated anew the Vatican's intention to hold out against the forces of secularization. The case involved 9-year-old Giuseppe Coen, who lived in Rome's ghetto. One day Giuseppe failed to return home from his job at a nearby cobbler's shop. His parents soon discovered that he had been taken to the House of the Catechumens, forced there, they said, by the Catholic cobbler. For the Jews and the enemies of Church temporal power, this had all the makings of Mortara redux.[7]

At the beginning of August, when protests about the new case began to appear in the liberal press, the church-allied *Giornale di Roma* painted its own picture of what had happened. Giuseppe Coen, a Jewish boy of the Rome ghetto, had long nourished the wish to become Christian, along with the fear that he would be severely punished if his parents heard of it. "For fifteen days he begged his employer to take him to the House of the Catechumens." Finally, on July 25, taking advantage of the visit by a relative of the cobbler who happened to have a priest with him, Giuseppe's pleas were answered. They took him to the Catechumens, where the boy convinced the Rector of his fervent desire to become a Christian.

The Coens had wasted no time in seeking French aid, for in the wake of the Mortara case they had no illusions of getting their son released simply by petitioning the Church. Three days after the child's disappearance, the French ambassador went to see Cardinal Antonelli on their behalf, and he returned to the Vatican the following morning to renew his angry protests.

The French liberal press quickly took the case up, demanding to know why French soldiers were standing by while Jewish children were being stolen from their parents. On August 13, the papal nuncio in Paris wrote to Cardinal Antonelli to report on his recent unpleasant meeting with the French minister of foreign affairs, Drouyn de Lhuys. The Minister railed against the holding of the boy, calling it an action contrary to the laws of nature, "carried out and sanctioned by the Holy See under the eyes of the French troops." The nuncio reported, "I responded that France's protection of the pope's temporal power did not give it the right to involve itself in measures and actions that regarded the Pontiff's spiritual jurisdiction."[8]

At the same time the Secretary of State was receiving this report from Paris, he was also given a long letter that the delegates of Rome's Università Israelitica had written to the Pope, pleading for the Coen boy's return. The delegates wrote that they had evidence enabling them to "exclude entirely" the notion that Giuseppe had acted on his own.

Giuseppe's mother was, meanwhile, arrested outside the House of the Catechumens as she tried to get a glimpse of her son, or so at least the papers of Italy reported.[9] The Rector's request to the Secretary of State to do something about the noisome woman produced some help, in the form of police patrols, but Giuseppe's mother was not easily discouraged.

Finally, on October 1, a Bologna paper reported the departure of what remained of the Coen family for Livorno, in Tuscany. They had to leave, the paper claimed, "to remove the boy's mother from the violent pain that afflicts her every day as she wanders around outside the House of the Catechumens, where her son is kept, and from which she is often brutally chased away by the police." In a story later taken up by the liberal press throughout Europe, it was reported that "the wretched woman is seriously threatened with dementia."[10]

If revulsion at the Pope's refusal to release Edgardo Mortara had contributed to Napoleon's decision to back the plan to take the Legations from the Pontiff, his anger over the Coen case, according to some observers, contributed to his next step: pulling French troops out of Rome. According to *La nation*, when the French ambassador had spoken to Cardinal Antonelli about the Coen boy, he had warned him that "if the pontifical court persists on a path that so conflicted with the general direction of modern ideas, and particularly of French ideas, the Emperor's government, despite its great sympathy for the pontifical court . . . would be constrained to abandon the Pope to his own forces."[11] And, indeed, just a few weeks after the ambassador's request for Giuseppe's restitution was denied, the French signed an agreement with the Italian government to begin removing all French troops from Rome. Although the agreement bound the Italians not to attack Rome, the Pope had little confidence that the promise would be kept once the French left. A few years later, when the paltry papal guard was finally overrun by Italian troops, the Austrian ambassador in Rome, referring to Giuseppe Coen, told his sovereign, Franz Josef: "Italy should be erecting arches of triumph in honor of this little Jew."[12]

With the phased French withdrawal from Rome under way, the city's status once more became the question of the day. Some conservatives favored a compromise by which Rome would become part of Italy, but with the Pope enjoying special powers over the city. But even then, several years after Edgardo was taken, the Mortara case continued to cast its shadow. In July 1865, when Marco Minghetti, until recently Italian prime minister, explained his opposition to this proposal, he said that Italian soldiers could not replace the French in protecting papal rule in Rome, for "we cannot go to guard the Mortara boy for the Pope."[13]

By this time, Edgardo had already spent half of his life in the Church. Memories of his parents were getting hazy, for he had not seen or heard from them since their last visit to the Catechumens in 1858.

By the time he was thirteen, Edgardo had decided to devote his life to the Church, and he became a novice in the order of the Canons Regular of the Lateran, on his way to becoming a monk himself. He took the name of Pio, honoring his new father and protector, Pius IX. At the initiation ceremony, Father Strozzi, General of the Order, preached on Isaiah 65:1: "I was ready to be sought by those who did not ask for me." The Old Testament passage had itself been quoted by Paul in Romans 10:20, in which Paul expresses his heartfelt wish that all the Jews be saved by embracing Jesus.[14]

On April 12 of the following year, 1866, when the Pope made his annual visit outside the city walls to the church of Sant'Agnese, 14-year-old Edgardo was given a special honor. Stepping out from a group of young seminarians, he recited by heart an original poem of fulsome praise to the Pope. Each of the eighteen flowery verses had eight lines.[15]

Shortly thereafter, in 1867, the Pontiff sent the boy a message that shows, almost a decade after Pius IX's first defense of the decision to hold on to Edgardo, the Pope's unchanged view that he had done God's will, and that for doing so he had suffered grievously. He wrote:

> You are very dear to me, my little son, for I acquired you for Jesus Christ at a high price. So it is. I paid dearly for your ransom. Your case set off a worldwide storm against me and the apostolic See. Governments and peoples, the rulers of the world as well as the journalists—who are the truly powerful people of our times—declared war on me. Monarchs themselves entered the battle against me, and with their ambassadors they flooded me with diplomatic notes, and all this because of you. . . . People lamented the harm done to your parents because you were regenerated by the grace of holy baptism and brought up according to God's wishes. And in the meantime no one showed any concern for me, father of all the faithful.[16]

Later that year, in the wake of Garibaldi's unsuccessful attempt to con-
quer Rome, French troops flooded back into the Holy City. For Edgardo, now
a novitiate of the Canons Regular, the year was memorable for a more personal reason as well. He had finally heard from his parents. "I wrote letters to
my parents many times," he later recounted, "dealing with religion and doing
what I could to convince them of the truth of the Catholic faith." Unfortunately, he added, "they could see that these letters, however much they were
the expression of my own strong personal conviction, could not have been
exclusively my own work, and so they did not respond." It was only in May of
1867 that they did reply, perhaps in the hope that Rome was about to be freed
from papal rule and that they would soon be reunited with him. As Edgardo
later described the letter: "After they assured me of their unshakable affection,
they noted that if they hadn't yet responded to my letters, it was because they
had nothing of me in them outside of my name and signature, but that they
now hoped that I would be able to correspond with them without any surveillance." Momolo and Marianna still clung to the hope that their son, deep
down, had remained faithful to his family and, what came to the same thing
for them, to his religion.[17]

The Mortaras' prayers that the Pope's rule in Rome would fall before the
advancing armies of Italian unification were, at long last, answered in 1870,
eleven years after the demise of the pontifical state in Bologna. For the past
decade they had been following political events closely, praying for the day
when Edgardo would be free to return home. He was 6 when the papal police
came to take him from their Bologna home. He was now 18.

In July 1870, France made the mistake of declaring war on Prussia, and in
a matter of weeks the French army was crushed by Prussian troops. The
remaining French soldiers in Rome were withdrawn, Napoleon himself was
deposed, and a new French republic was proclaimed. With the French troops
gone and France itself no longer a threat, the Italian parliament authorized
that military action be taken, if necessary, to establish Rome as the nation's
capital. In a last-minute effort to avoid bloodshed, King Victor Emmanuel
sent a letter to the Pope, asking him to accede to the Italian army's march into
Rome and guaranteeing the Pope full spiritual independence for the Holy See.
Pius IX, however, would have no part of such a devil's pact, and stood his
ground.

General Raffaele Cadorna subsequently led the Italian army into the
region of Lazio, moving to the outskirts of Rome without encountering resistance. On September 20, 1870, the troops opened a breach in the city walls at
Porta Pia. Following a brief battle with the hopelessly outmanned pontifical
forces, they brought papal rule of Rome to an end. The Pope took refuge in
the Vatican, whose buildings and grounds had been left alone. Six weeks later,

portraying himself as a captive in the Vatican, Pius IX issued an encyclical branding the Italian occupation of the territories of the Holy See "unjust, violent, null, and invalid" and excommunicated the King of Italy and all those who were involved in the usurpation of the Papal States.[18]

General Cadorna, in his memoirs, recalled the giddy early days of Italian occupation of Rome as a time when old wrongs could be put right. Of all these wrongs, the one he singled out for special attention was the taking and holding of Giuseppe Coen, "a fact," he wrote, "that six years earlier had upset the entire civilized world."

The General reported what happened when, within two weeks of the battle of Porta Pia, Giuseppe's parents returned to the city and headed for the Church institute for orphans where their son had been living for the past six years. On knocking on the door, he wrote, the Coens were "brusquely turned away by the director." With an ever-growing crowd of Jews milling angrily in the streets, Rome's police chief himself decided to take the matter in hand. He went to the orphanage but was told that the boy was no longer there; he had fled. "However," wrote the General, "he had in fact been spirited away, and we found where he was being hidden." One of the priests who worked at the orphanage had taken Giuseppe, both man and boy in civilian disguise, to the home of a lay employee of the orphanage. There the police tracked them down and handed the boy over to his parents.

In General Cadorna's report to his superiors on the conquest of Rome, he described all this and discussed the ticklish question of what action to take against those who had kept the boy from his parents. "Although the pontifical laws left me in doubt about the possibility of applying a penalty against those who originally took Coen, I believed it right to order, on my own responsibility, the arrest of the Rector of the Institute of the Orphans and the person who was involved in hiding the boy, in order to satisfy the public conscience. Thus the judicial authorities are proceeding with the case."[19] Both the Rector and the employee who had hidden the boy were thrown in jail.

From the perspective of Rome's Jews, as well as for Italy's liberals, what might have been a triumphal ending to a sad story became, instead, something quite different. When Giuseppe's mother, who had not spoken with her son since he went off to work at the cobbler's shop half a dozen years earlier, finally got to see him again, she threw her arms around the now 16-year-old boy and covered him with kisses. Yet, wrote Cadorna, it was "all in vain. The voice of blood had been snuffed out, he didn't give a rap for his mother, and the cynical rector of the institute said, 'He should be considered to be no longer part of his family.' " Nonetheless, the Rector could not prevent the Coens from taking their son back with them, and on October 9 Giuseppe was consigned to his mother. But, as a local liberal correspondent described the scene, "for his desperate, weeping mother he had only words of disdain and rage, saying he no longer had anything in common with her."[20]

Despite the boy's opposition, a court had ordered his return to his parents, on the ground that his father enjoyed legal rights over him. Hoping that, by removing their son from Rome, his old loyalties would reemerge, the Coens took him to Livorno.[21] Yet Giuseppe never did change his mind, and as soon as he could, he returned to Rome and became a priest.

The Mortara family was also living in Tuscany, having moved from Turin to Florence in 1865, the year in which Italy's capital made the same move. Like Michele and Fortunata Coen, Momolo Mortara trailed the Italian army into Rome hoping to reclaim his son. He may not, however, have been the first in his family to reach Rome, for, according to some accounts, his son Riccardo preceded him. It was the same Riccardo who, twelve years earlier, on that traumatic night in June, had run through the streets of Bologna searching for his uncles, tearfully telling them the news of the police who had appeared in his home in search of his younger brother. Perhaps as a result of that experience, Riccardo had chosen to join the Italian army and, at the time of the battle of Porta Pia, was a young infantry officer.

Although militarily the battle was a travesty of mismatched forces, patriots did what they could to puff it up. As the Italian troops poured through the gate, Riccardo, fighting behind General Cadorna, raced to San Pietro in Vincoli, where he knew that his brother was being held. When, however, Riccardo appeared in the doorway of Edgardo's convent room, wearing the uniform of the Italian light infantry, he was in for a rude welcome. His 19-year-old brother, dressed in an initiate's robes, placed one hand over his eyes to shield them from the sacrilegious sight and raised the other in front of him, signaling Riccardo to stop where he was. "Get back, Satan!" Edgardo shouted. But, the crestfallen Riccardo replied, "I am your brother." To this Edgardo responded, "Before you get any closer to me, take off that assassin's uniform."[22]

The only first-person account we have of Momolo's search for his son in the wake of the fall of Rome is from Edgardo himself. The boy—now a young man—viewed events with mounting panic as he saw a vise closing in on him: "After the Piedmontese troops entered Rome, in those days of anarchy that preceded the formation of the new government, the police were unable to rein in the rabble-rousers. After they used their force to seize the neophyte Coen from the Collegio degli Scolopi, they turned toward San Pietro in Vincoli to try to kidnap me as well."

Pius IX, Edgardo recalled, had many times, in those tumultuous days, sent word to Edgardo's superiors to ask whether he had been taken away from Rome to safety. And it was the fatherly Pope, Edgardo said, who gave him "the strength and the courage not to give in to the pleas and the threats of the liberal authorities who wanted to make me, in violation of my religious vows, return to my family and expose myself not only to the danger of breaking my oaths but, indeed, of becoming an apostate."

The Rome police prefect himself appeared at the convent, "urging and pleading with me to return to my family, in order to satisfy public opinion." Meanwhile, Edgardo learned that his father had arrived in Rome and was waiting for him. Police stood guard outside the convent to ensure that the monks did not try to sneak Edgardo out of Rome. Loath to see his father, and afraid that, like Giuseppe Coen, he would soon be seized by the police and handed over to his parents, Edgardo, no doubt with the help of higher ecclesiastical authorities, arranged to meet with General La Marmora, the King's representative in Rome. In Edgardo's recollection, after he had explained the situation to the General, he was asked what he wanted.

"The police want to make me return to my family."

"But how old are you?" asked the General.

"Nineteen, Excellency."

"Well, then, you are free. Do what you want."

"But, Excellency, I am being threatened with reprisals."

"In that case," replied the General, "come to see me, and I will protect you."

Despite these assurances, if assurances they were, Edgardo's superiors feared that he would be taken. Outrages against the Church were being committed every day, and Edgardo was a symbol of the Pope's temporal power, whose downfall the rowdy masses were joyfully celebrating. Although Cardinal Antonelli had said that he did not think it necessary, a plan was made to send Edgardo abroad. In Edgardo's words:

> On October 22, 1870, at ten at night, accompanied by one of the monks, both of us dressed in street clothes, we made our way through the convent garden in order to elude the surveillance of the guards who were stationed there. We went to the central train station, where, my mentor told me, he spotted my father. Deeply frightened, I begged in my heart that I be spared the encounter, and in fact my prayer was answered and, without any incident, I got on the train for Bologna.

Edgardo and the monk got off the train briefly in Foligno, a small city in Umbria, to get something to eat at a restaurant.

> In front of us sat several young men who, from the red sash they wore, seemed to me to be Garibaldini. They were talking about the recent escape of the young Mortara, attributing it, as usual, to the Jesuits. To tell

the truth, I was shaking like a leaf, but my companion, without losing his composure, began to talk to them and, being clever, was able to change the subject of their conversation, so that they forgot about the fugitive.

Edgardo and his guide then reboarded the train. They reached the Austrian border without mishap and found refuge in a convent on the other side.

Back in Rome, Edgardo's father was despondent. For twelve years, Momolo and Marianna had been waiting for this moment, had been consoling themselves with the thought that the days of papal power in Rome were numbered, that the gloom that had clung to their home all these years would finally be lifted. All his hopes, his appeals for help to everyone who would listen, seemed to have been in vain. And he also felt he had failed his own people, the Jews. For years they had been praying for his son's return to his family and his religion, yet all the while they had harbored the fear that the boy would be won over by his captors and join the long line of former Jews who devoted their lives to denigrating the religion of their ancestors. Momolo returned to his family in Florence a beaten man.

CHAPTER 25

A Death in Florence

W HEN MOMOLO RETURNED from Rome, he was 55 years old, and Marianna 52. Of their nine children, seven still lived with them. Other than Edgardo, only their eldest son, Riccardo, aged 27, lived elsewhere. A second lieutenant in the Italian army, he was based at the Advanced War Academy in Turin. The twin girls, Ernesta and Erminia, 24, helped their mother at home. Augusto, 23, had recently received his law degree and worked for the Ministry of Finance. Arnoldo, 21, had a good job working for a company that provided foodstuffs to the army. Ercole, at 18 just a year younger than Edgardo, had gone to high school and recently taken an exam to get into pharmacy school. The two youngest children, Imelda, 13, and Aristide, 11, born after Edgardo's departure from home and given the same name as the child who had died in 1857, were both students.[1]

In addition to the nine members of the Mortara family in their fourth-floor apartment in via Pinti, they had, as always, a servant. When they had lived in Bologna, the same servant typically remained with them a number of years, Anna Morisi serving the longest, but by the time they moved to Florence they were finding it difficult to keep one for more than a few weeks. One after another quit. Shortly after Momolo returned from his fruitless trip to Rome, yet another of their servants left, and a 22-year-old replacement, Antonietta Vestri, was found. She left after four weeks.

After Antonietta, the Mortaras hired Rosa Tognazzi, a large, lively, redheaded young woman of 23. Rosa was one of seven sisters from a share-cropping family in the Chianti hills of Tuscany. She had moved to Florence a year before, following the example of her older sisters, who had already taken jobs in the city as servants. Since her arrival, Rosa had worked for a succession of families, moving in with the Mortaras in late February. She may have been put in touch with them by her sister Giuseppa, who lived with a Jewish family herself.

At 5 p.m. on April 3, five weeks after Rosa Tognazzi moved in, a servant in the apartment below thought she heard someone running in the Mortaras' apartment. Her ceiling shook, and then, all of a sudden, she heard the sound of window shutters flung open, followed by two awful thuds from the tiny courtyard. She ran to the window and saw Rosa lying on her side on the pavement. Glancing up, she noticed that the Mortaras' window was open. Looking down again, she could see that Rosa's skirts were lifted up over her face, showing her private parts. The screams of the woman who lived on the ground floor fueled her terror. After looking up again and seeing no one at the Mortaras' windows, she wondered if she should go down to help. She decided against it. "I didn't have the courage," she said.

Rosa was still alive and partially conscious as she lay in the courtyard, although she had a broken neck, a broken foot, broken legs, a broken hip, and many other injuries. She even murmured a few words to the neighbors who rushed to her aid. It took an hour and a half to get Rosa to the hospital, where, at 7:15 p.m., she died.

Police soon swarmed over the scene, ministering to the injured woman and talking to witnesses. The initial police report, prepared that evening, concluded that Rosa had killed herself. The policemen had already reconstructed the events that had led to her fateful fall. Around 3 p.m., she had gone, as she did every day, to meet Imelda as she got out of school. While she was walking the girl home, Rosa happened to run into her former employer, Luigi Bartolozzi, who was walking with another man. Bartolozzi accosted Rosa, accusing her of having stolen ten lire, as well as some of his wife's clothes. He warned her that if she didn't return it all immediately, he would report her to the police. With a frightened Imelda looking on, Rosa denied the accusations and hustled the girl away. The men followed the two down the street until they reached the building of the Mortaras' friends the Bolaffis, where Rosa was supposed to deliver a message. The men entered the building after them but soon left. Signor Bolaffi then offered to escort the shaken Rosa and Imelda back to the Mortaras' home, which he did. A few minutes after Rosa's entry into the apartment, the police report concluded, "she threw herself, unobserved, out the window."

The initial police report notwithstanding, within minutes of Rosa's fall, neighbors began to spread the rumor that this was no suicide. The man of the household, a loud and violent type, they said, a Jew, had pushed Rosa to her death.

The morning after Rosa's death, a 36-year-old hatmaker named Luigi

Pierleoni, who had been one of the first on the scene, was called in to police headquarters to testify. He recalled that he had been walking down via Pinti when an old woman came out of a building yelling for help. She rushed him through a door and into a small internal courtyard, where he saw a woman lying on her left side, moaning. Her skirt and petticoats were raised up over her chin, so that he could see her thighs. Her left hand was curled back around her head. Around her forehead a blood-soaked white kerchief was tied, knotted in back. The old woman told him that she had already pulled the woman's skirts down a bit, because she had found her in a shameful state, with "nature" showing.

Attracted by the growing crowd outside the building, another neighbor, Andrea Casalegno, entered the courtyard as well. He told police that "everyone who was there was saying that they had thrown her out of the window of the top floor." He had lifted Rosa's head off the pavement and asked her if she had fallen, or if she had been thrown out of the window, or if she had tumbled down the stairs. She responded to this last question only, whispering "down the stairs," although there were no stairs near where she lay.

Casalegno then lifted the bloody kerchief from her forehead and discovered that it had concealed a nasty wound over her left eyebrow, a wound so deep that her mangled bone stuck out. A civilian employee of the carabinieri, Casalegno prided himself on his powers of detection. "That wound could not have been made by falling on the pavement, because there were no stones or anything else there that could have produced it," he explained. On questioning, both Pierleoni and Casalegno recalled that it was the old woman who had first told them that Rosa had been thrown out of the window of the top-floor flat, the apartment, she had informed them, where the Jews lived.

The old woman was Anna Ragazzini, a 67-year-old widow who lived in her ground-floor apartment with her 18-year-old servant, Teresa Gonnelli. Teresa recalled hearing a big crash, as if someone had slammed a window shut, and right afterward, a big thud in the courtyard. The dog immediately began to howl, and the two women ran to see what had happened. There lay Rosa, her skirts up over her head. "Ragazzini pulled her clothes down to cover her shame," Teresa remembered, "and we could then see that her head was bound with a white kerchief tied by two knots in back." Rosa murmured, " 'Help me, I feel like I'm dying,' and then Ragazzini went to the door to get help. I stayed there, alone, and said to her: 'Poor girl, what happened? Did they throw you down?' and twice she answered, 'Yes.' "

Signora Ragazzini's young servant went on to testify that in the two weeks that she had been living there, "day and night, I always heard loud noises, arguments, and quarreling in the Jew's house."

The Mortara Apartment in Via Pinti, Florence
April 1871

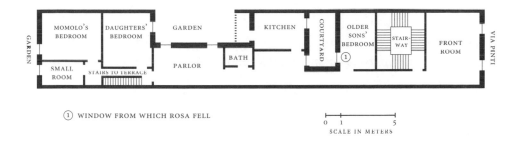

① WINDOW FROM WHICH ROSA FELL

0   1   5
SCALE IN METERS

"I know the Jew Momolo Mortara by sight," Signora Ragazzini testified that same day. Although the Mortaras had lived in the building for two and a half years, she had never spoken to them, nor, for that matter, had she ever met their new servant. The widow had, however, seen Rosa return to the building the previous afternoon with the Mortaras' little girl. Within fifteen minutes of their return, she heard the alarming sounds from the courtyard.

When Rosa, lying bleeding on the pavement, appealed to Signora Ragazzini for help, the woman had frantically raced to the street to find someone. Once outside the building, she looked up at the Mortaras' apartment: "I saw two people—I couldn't make out whether men or women—and I said, 'Come down! Can't you see that it's your servant!' but no one came."

Actually, someone did come, although it was not one of the Mortaras but Signor Bolaffi, the family friend who had accompanied Rosa and Imelda home. He came down with a boy, reported Signora Ragazzini, "and asked what had happened. I told him, 'You know better than I do, because the servant is from up there.' He replied that he was going to the police station. That surprised me," said the suspicious widow, "because it seemed to me that he should have shown more interest in the situation."

Signora Ragazzini did not hesitate to tell the police just what she thought. "There's a constant uproar in the Mortara home, and arguing and swearing day and night. I believe," she told the inspector, "that the servant was wounded on the head before she fell into the courtyard, because she certainly didn't put that kerchief on down there, and she didn't do it on her way down either!"

Finally, the inspector called in Flaminio Bolaffi. Rosa had been dead less than a day. Bolaffi, a Jewish friend of the Mortaras, was also a businessman, at 53 about the same age as Momolo.[2] He testified that when he had returned home the previous day, a little after 4 p.m., he had found Rosa and a very frightened Imelda there. His wife told him Rosa's story of her encounter with her former employer and the man's attempts to follow her into the house. Indeed, Bolaffi's wife had herself spoken to the men when they came to the door. Imelda did not want to return home with Rosa alone, because she was frightened of the two men, nor did Rosa want to go either. "However," Bolaffi recalled, "I persuaded her and accompanied both of them back to the Mortara house."

When they arrived, Bolaffi found Momolo in bed. He had been bedridden for some time because of a painful tumor on his knee. In his large bedroom, his wife and two older daughters also sat, sewing. None of the other children was at home. Bolaffi explained why he had accompanied Rosa and Imelda home, and Momolo asked his wife to go fetch Rosa so they could hear what had happened directly from her. Marianna found Rosa, crying, upstairs on the terrace and told her to come down, saying, according to Bolaffi, "that if she was innocent, she had nothing to fear." But Marianna returned to the bedroom alone.

A few moments later, Bolaffi reported, they heard a loud noise, and the Mortaras' dog started barking. He thought the noise must have been made by Rosa, slamming the front door on her way out, but when he went to the stairs to look, no one was there. He noticed, however, that the window of the room that the older boys slept in, which looked out over the courtyard, was open, and, peering out, he saw Rosa lying below. "I immediately ran down the stairs to notify the police, and once I got downstairs, I saw two women at Rosa's side. I urged them to assist her while I went for the police. And I can assure you," he added, "that no argument occurred between Rosa and any member of the Mortara family while I was there."

It was now time for the investigating magistrate, Clodoveo Marabotti, to go to the morgue to hear directly from the two surgeons responsible for examining Rosa's wounds. It was a gruesome scene; Rosa's body lay atop a marble slab, her long reddish hair spread out around her bloodstained head. A tall and robust woman, she was dressed in the clothes in which she had fallen: a slip, two petticoats, and a gray-and-white plaid dress. The examiners had removed the bloody white kerchief from her forehead. When they inspected her dress, they made a puzzling discovery: in a pocket, they found a razor, stained with blood.

Marabotti was especially interested in what the doctors could tell him about the wound to Rosa's forehead. It was an irregular, rough, serpentine gash, they reported, five centimeters long, with contusions around the edges, so deep that the frontal bone beneath showed through.

Having done all they could with the body in the state in which they had found it, the doctors began the autopsy. They first opened up Rosa's head and discovered that whatever had caused the gash over her eyebrow had also produced an extensive fracturing of the skull beneath. Her brain cavity was filled with blood. As for the cause of death, the doctors concluded that she could have been killed by the traumas caused by a fall from high up, but, they added, the wound to her forehead might have been lethal by itself.

The Magistrate then told the medical examiners of the testimony he had received about the violent behavior of Rosa's employer, and asked them if they could say anything about what kind of implement might have caused the head wound, whether the gash was caused by the fall, or whether it predated the fall. Marabotti particularly urged them to consider the fact that, despite the vicious nature of the wound, the kerchief that covered it, though bloody, was itself not torn in any way.

The doctors hedged a bit, but clearly they saw Marabotti's point. The wound to her forehead "could have been produced by the fall," the doctors reported. Yet, "given that the woman, just before her fall, had folded a kerchief and tied it around her frontal region, in the manner found on the one that has been submitted to us, stained by blood . . . it is more believable and more consonant with the laws of mechanics that the wound . . . came before the fall and was produced a short time before the other injuries, by a lacerating and blunt implement."

When the investigating magistrate returned to his office, he received a report from his assistant, who had reconstructed the events, based on the testimony he had gathered. The assistant's report told of Rosa's unpleasant encounter with her former employer and the man's warning about reporting her to the police. When Rosa returned to the Mortaras, she seemed very upset, "and being near a bedroom window, she must have thrown herself into the courtyard below." The inspector had learned from Imelda that, just before Rosa's death, the girl had seen her with a kerchief in hand, which she had folded lengthwise. When Rosa saw that Imelda was watching, she pretended, the girl said, to blow her nose. The inspector did not think much of the neighbors' wild accusations. It was a simple case of suicide.

Unfortunately for Momolo, Marabotti reached a different conclusion. Something was suspicious. Why would a healthy young woman toss herself out the window because she was accused of stealing a few lire and some scraps of used clothes? If every servant accused of such behavior were to toss herself from a window, Florence would be littered with their bodies. And what about the suspicious gash and bandage on Rosa's forehead? How could that be explained except by an earlier skull-cracking, and probably lethal, blow, followed by a panicked attempt to stanch the bleeding with a kerchief? And then there were all the neighbors' reports about the nonstop quarreling and bellowing that emanated from the Mortara apartment. When put together with reports that one servant after another had quit, a clear pattern was emerging: Momolo was a violent type, and his family's servants bore the brunt of his ire.

Wasting no time, the Magistrate signed arrest warrants for both Momolo Mortara and Flaminio Bolaffi. Citing the testimony of the widow Ragazzini and her servant, Teresa Gonnelli, and the evidence of the gash on Rosa's forehead, the warrant charged that, "far from voluntarily throwing herself out the window . . . Rosa Tognazzi was thrown out by others." It concluded that there was "serious evidence pointing to Momolo Mortara and Flaminio Bolaffi as the authors of the homicide."

The next day, April 6, three days after Rosa's death, the Magistrate arranged for a doctor to examine Momolo at his home to determine whether he was well enough to be taken directly to prison. The physician found Momolo still in bed and concluded that he was, in fact, incapacitated by his ailing knee. Both Momolo and his friend Flaminio were arrested the following day. Momolo was taken not to the hospital, as the doctor had recommended, but to the prison infirmary. Flaminio went directly to a jail cell.

The Magistrate, meanwhile, continued his interviews with the residents of the Mortaras' building. Violante Bellucci, a single, 51-year-old man who rented rooms just below the front of the Mortara apartment, confirmed the other neighbors' reports. "There isn't any peace there day or night. You hear noises, quarreling, and swearing all the time, and they seem to live like animals." Late on the afternoon of April 3, Bellucci testified, he had been looking out his window onto via Pinti and saw Rosa returning home with the Mortara girl, who was carrying a school bag, along with one of the Mortaras' sons. About a quarter hour later, still in his front room, he heard a woman from the ground floor calling for help, shouting that someone had fallen from the fourth floor. When he heard this, he rushed to a window that looked onto the courtyard, leaned out, and spotted Rosa lying below. Before going down to see what he could do, he had looked up at the Mortaras' window. There, he testified, at first he saw the Mortara schoolgirl looking out, and then "I saw a man who was not Mortara but seemed to me to be a Jew, with an olive complexion, a small man . . . and I noted that he was shaking his head while I was looking at him."

There was one thing about the case that bothered the Magistrate: If Momolo was as infirm as he was made out to be, just how had he killed the woman and then lifted the bulky servant out the window? "He always walked with a limp," said Bellucci, "but I can say with certainty that on that same day, April 3, around 9 p.m., I heard him on the stairs, and then I saw him leaving the house with his little son. He had a walking stick."

The other neighbor interviewed that day was 52-year-old Luigi Balocchi, who lived in the building with his wife, children, and servant. "I know the Jew Momolo Mortara," he said, "purely by sight." Like his neighbors, he often heard loud quarrels and swearing coming from their apartment and concluded that Momolo "was a violent and quick-tempered character. It seems," he added, "that harmony did not reign between husband and wife."

Balocchi recalled that he and his family had been at the table eating at 5 p.m. on April 3 when they heard a fearful crash from the courtyard. "I told my children and my wife not to move, imagining that something bad had happened." Hearing cries from below, he peeked cautiously out the window into the courtyard and saw a woman covered with blood. "I immediately closed the window and returned to the room where my family sat, frightened, and neither I nor any of them got up until all the noise had stopped." He told the Magistrate that, "since the matter didn't concern me, and since my wife had begun to sob uncontrollably," he had paid no more attention to the injured woman. But that evening, when he went to pick something up at a nearby store, he found many of his neighbors gathered there, chatting about the woman's death. They claimed that Rosa "was thrown from the window." Ever cautious, he added, "but whether what they said is true, I cannot say."

The only friendly witness interviewed that day was a 49-year-old widow, Adele Berselli, a friend of the Mortaras' since they had moved to Florence. True, she admitted, Momolo "is an irritable man and shouts loudly, but," she quickly added, "he is a good man." Hers was a lonely voice.

At 2 p.m., shortly after his arrival at the Murate prison, Momolo Mortara was visited by the Magistrate in his infirmary bed. In response to Marabotti's questioning, Momolo gave his version of what had happened on the day that Rosa died. Around 4:30 that afternoon, as he was lying in bed, he had heard Rosa come in with Imelda, along with Flaminio Bolaffi and Bolaffi's son, Emilio. Bolaffi told Momolo, Marianna, and their daughters what had happened. Just then, seeing Rosa pass by the room, they called for her to come in but got no response, so his wife went out to get her. Marianna "found that [Rosa] had gone out on the terrace, and she told her to go into the kitchen to make some broth. They went back into the kitchen together, and my wife tried to cheer her up by saying that if she was innocent, she shouldn't even think about it."

Marianna then returned to the bedroom. A few minutes later, they heard a big noise, like a door slamming. Rosa didn't answer their calls, and, being all too familiar with his servants' habit of walking out on him, Momolo told his daughter Ernesta to go to Rosa's room to see if she had taken her clothes with her, a sure sign that she would not be back. Meanwhile, his wife went to look for Rosa down the stairway. As Marianna was returning through the corridor, she heard shouts coming from the courtyard and went to look out the boys' bedroom window. She saw Rosa lying in the courtyard below. "She returned to my bedroom all upset and said that Rosa had thrown herself out the window." Bolaffi, hearing this, ran to see for himself. Returning to Momolo's room, Bolaffi "said he would go to the police station and try to help Rosa. I tried two times, amidst all the confusion, to get out of bed, but I just couldn't." Momolo then sent his son Aristide to run down and try to find out what had happened.

At the time all this occurred, Momolo reported, the only people in his house were Bolaffi, Bolaffi's little boy, Rosa, his own youngest son, Aristide, his wife, and his three daughters. His older sons were all out. His bedroom was far from the room from which Rosa fell, he said, and for the previous two weeks he had never gotten out of bed except to go to the lavatory.

Having completed his interrogation of Momolo, the Magistrate went into the main part of the Murate prison to interview Flaminio Bolaffi. Bolaffi said that he had forgotten to mention to the police that when he had accompanied Rosa and Imelda to the Mortaras' home, he had taken along his 12-year-old son, Emilio. Asked whether Rosa had been wearing the white kerchief on her head when she had come to his house, Bolaffi responded no, she hadn't.

"You should know," said the Magistrate, "that on the basis of our investigations so far, we must conclude that Rosa Tognazzi was wounded on her head inside the Mortaras' house before she fell from the window. Therefore, we believe that the wound was caused either by Mortara or by you and that, following this grave wound, she was thrown from the window."

"That can't be," Bolaffi replied, "unless she injured herself. Mortara was in his room in bed, and I had no reason to lay a hand on the servant."

The following day, the Magistrate, as required by law, prepared a request to the court for permission to hold the men in jail. The immediate reaction to the incident, that it was a case of suicide, he wrote, had been proven wrong by the wound they had found on the victim's forehead and the kerchief that had been tied around it. Rosa had returned home that afternoon, according to witnesses, healthy and calm. The women in the ground-floor apartment had heard angry noises coming from the Mortara apartment, followed immediately by Rosa's plunge. Asked, as she lay moaning on the pavement, whether she had been thrown out the window, she had responded yes.

All the evidence, the Magistrate wrote, led to the strong suspicion that Rosa had been gravely injured inside the Mortara apartment and, half alive and half dead, had been thrown from the window to give the appearance of suicide. Although careful examination of the apartment the following day had revealed no sign of any blood or murder weapon, this was not surprising given the delay.

The accumulated evidence, wrote the Magistrate, "dictated the arrest of

Mortara and the other Jew, Flaminio Bolaffi, the one who had been in the Mortara home when the event occurred." What was the case against Bolaffi? He was the one, wrote the Magistrate, who brought word of what had happened to the police station without first doing anything to minister to the injured woman. He, too, had been trying to get everyone to believe that Rosa's encounter with her former employer had led her to kill herself. And if Rosa had been so gruesomely attacked in the apartment and then thrown from the window, as the evidence indicated, Bolaffi must have known about it.

As for Momolo, he claimed that he was unable to get out of bed, but a neighbor had seen him go out that evening with his youngest son, walking without difficulty. And all the evidence suggested that Momolo was a man of poor character: the household was constantly filled with screaming and profanity, and no servant could stand it for long.

The judge found the Magistrate's case convincing and ordered the two men to remain in jail.

In the aftermath of Momolo's arrest, his family sent a telegram to Riccardo in Turin, telling him to return home immediately because of "a family emergency." Meanwhile, Augusto, who had just finished law school, took on his father's defense.

Marabotti called in twenty witnesses to testify over the next two weeks as the investigation gathered momentum, bringing more disturbing facts to light. But the first few witnesses did nothing to help the prosecution's case. Giovanni Balduzzi, the young carabiniere officer who was the first policeman called to the scene, flagged down by a neighbor, told how, after seeing Rosa lying in the courtyard minutes after her fall, he had rushed up to the Mortaras' apartment. Quickly moving through the rooms, he found that only one of the windows that looked out on the courtyard was open, in a room with two beds. Although he looked quickly for signs of blood or other such evidence around the window, he found none. "I then went," he testified, "into the room where the whole family of the Jew Mortara was gathered, and where Mortara himself lay in bed."

At the request of Augusto Mortara, in his capacity as his father's lawyer, the Magistrate interviewed a number of character witnesses for Momolo. The Mortaras' 26-year-old seamstress reported that she had, for many months, come regularly to the Mortara home to do sewing for them. Although she had heard Momolo raise his voice at times, she said, "I can't say anything bad about the Mortaras." And, she concluded, "I don't think he is capable of having thrown the woman out the window." Momolo's barber was called in, and he testified that in recent weeks he had had to come to the Mortara home to shave Momolo, who was too incapacitated to get out of bed.

But Momolo's neighbors, eyewitnesses to the tragedy, continued to doubt his innocence. Among the most hostile was Enrichetta Mattei, a 38-year-old woman who lived on the third floor of Momolo's building. "I knew the Jew Mortara," she said, "only to say hello to." And though she had been out of the building on the afternoon of the third, something had happened on the previous day, she told the Magistrate, that he should know about.

It was a Sunday, she recalled, and she had overheard Momolo "cursing the servant Rosa, who had just returned from mass, saying: 'This mass takes you an awfully long time, oh, damn you and your mass!' and other words in the same angry tone, so I went to the window and said, 'Damn you and your Rabbi!' And then he closed his window himself, and I could hear that he was in the kitchen and not in bed. After I said those words to the Jew," she added, "Rosa came to the window, shook her head unhappily, and I saw that she was crying."

She concluded her testimony by telling the Magistrate: "People in the neighborhood all say that Rosa was thrown from the window, and I believe it." But, she observed, "Mortara could not have done it alone, because she was a heavy woman." Enrichetta, illiterate, signed the transcript of her testimony with a cross.

Interspersed with the neighbors, other witnesses were called in an attempt to shed more light on the victim herself. Had she ever reported any fears about Mortara to anyone? Was there, on the other hand, any evidence to suggest that she was suicidal? What kind of a person was she?

Angiolo Farzini, in whose home Rosa had lived as a servant for three or four months before she went to work for Luigi Bartolozzi, testified that Rosa had been an excellent employee. "She was always cheerful," he recalled, "and never showed any ideas of wanting to throw herself out a window." There had, though, once been a problem: "She had a sister sick in the hospital, and she often took her things, with our approval. One time, though, my wife surprised her while she was taking a bit of oil and vinegar in a little bottle, and she reprimanded her. Rosa took it badly and left our house without ever returning, even though it was only a matter of a few pennies. For the rest," he concluded, "I always found her to be a good woman, and if she hadn't left, I would have been happy to keep her."

Rosa's sister Maria testified that she had last seen Rosa three weeks before her death. Rosa told Maria that she was happy in the Mortaras' house. "She never in her life seemed gloomy, nor ever had any reason to be." When she first heard of Rosa's death, Maria had assumed that it was the result of natural causes, but then she heard rumors that Rosa "had been thrown out of a window for having burned her employers' lunch." That story was, in fact, gaining wide currency. Police were already trying to locate two women in the neighborhood who, the day after the murder, had informed a third that Rosa had been murdered because she had burned the Mortaras' soup.

The police tracked down the two servants employed by the Mortaras before Rosa. Erminia Poggi, an 18-year-old woman, had gone to work for them three months earlier, just after Momolo had returned empty-handed, and empty-hearted, from Rome. She left after a month, she recalled, "because there were too many people in the house, and the employer was a furious man, as were his children." Momolo Mortara "continuously mistreated me and did nothing but complain all day long."

The Magistrate asked the young woman if Momolo had ever threatened her. "He never threatened to hit me, though a number of times he swore he would throw things in my face. He was violent with his children as well and, out of anger, would throw plates or other things at them." Nor was his wife spared his wrath: "One time, when his wife broke a lampshade, he went into a fury; he took her by the neck, saying he wanted to kill her. He brought her like this into the bedroom." What happened there she didn't know, she said, but afterward, she saw the signora in a faint on the bed, being attended to by her daughters, who were giving her smelling salts. Nor, completing Erminia's unflattering portrait, was the signora herself much better; she was always in a bad mood.

If Erminia had lasted for thirty-three days, her successor, 22-year-old Antonietta Vestri, lasted only twenty-seven. She, too, described the household as plagued by constant quarreling. Her boss was "of furious character, even shouting at his children." And Marianna "was never satisfied with my service."

More direct testimony on how Rosa was faring at the Mortaras came from her friend Augusta Carnicelli, a 19-year-old servant. Augusta had spoken to Rosa when, she recalled, Rosa "had already been working for the Jew Mortara for over a month. . . . In talking to me about her employers, she told me she couldn't stand it anymore, because they were never satisfied with her. They made her take stuff back to the market, and even though she obeyed, when the shopkeepers refused to take it back, they beat her with fists and slaps and were always insulting her." Augusta told Rosa she should quit, but Rosa did not want to leave before she found another job, afraid that "she would find herself in the middle of the street." Just five days before Rosa's death, Augusta had run into her again. The young woman who had always been so cheerful was in tears, Augusta claimed, bemoaning her life at the Mortara home.

The Magistrate heard testimony of another kind from the policeman who had been on duty when Flaminio Bolaffi rushed in with the news of Rosa's fall. Officer Pilade Masini painted a suspicious picture of Bolaffi. Asked to tell what had happened, Bolaffi had said he didn't know anything, and then, when the policeman asked him to accompany him back to the scene, he didn't want to come. When Masini arrived at the courtyard and examined the moribund woman, he was struck by the terrible wound on her forehead and noted the bloody kerchief and the fact that there was so little blood beneath her head. "Right then I got suspicious that she had been thrown out."

Learning that Rosa lived on the top floor, the officer rushed up the stairs and knocked repeatedly on the door, as loudly as he could, but got no response. He went back down, thinking that no one was home, but quickly ran up again when the neighbors told him there were people up there. This time he kicked at the Mortaras' door until finally it was opened by a 12-year-old boy who, Masini said, seemed confused. The officer brought the youngster downstairs with him, but since the boy seemed to know nothing, Masini took him back upstairs. The boy did not knock on the door but whistled, and a girl came to open it. Masini went in and found Momolo in bed. The invalid, reported the policeman, said that he didn't know what had happened. Masini went to investigate the windows that looked onto the courtyard but found them all closed. "I looked on the ground briefly but didn't find any traces of blood."

The matter of blood was on the Magistrate's mind that day as he asked the two medical examiners to do more detailed studies of the forensic evidence, focusing, in particular, on the wound to Rosa's forehead. Could it have been made by the blade that was found in her pocket? And could they shed any more light on whether the wound came as a result of the fall or had been inflicted first? On April 19, they submitted their report.

On the razor the doctors had no doubt: "Such a wound could not have been made by the blade of the razor found in Tognazzi's pocket." The gash was not caused by anything as sharp or as light as a blade. The mysterious razor seemed to have nothing to do with the young woman's death.

The doctors were also able to reconstruct the position in which Rosa had landed. Given the nature of the fractures to her right foot and leg, as well as to her hip, they were confident that, "if not in a perfectly upright position, she was in a vertical position not far from fully upright" when she hit the ground, right foot first.

As for the kerchief, if the wound that it covered had been produced by the fall, "it would have had to be lacerated." It was not.

The Magistrate had also asked whether the limited amount of blood on the kerchief and the lack of much blood below Rosa's head on the courtyard didn't show that the wound must have been inflicted elsewhere. In this, the doctors had to disappoint him. The amount of blood in the handkerchief, they reported, was consistent with the nature of the wound.

In response to the Magistrate's final question, the medical examiners reported that, had the head wound been caused before the fall, Rosa might well have lacked the strength to resist being hoisted out of the window.

For the Magistrate, the pieces of the puzzle were falling into place. On

April 20, he wrote up his preliminary findings, in which, in addition to emphasizing all the evidence about the wound, the kerchief, and Momolo Mortara's violent temper, he gave great weight to Officer Masini's testimony. Why had the Mortaras not answered the door when the policeman first knocked? Why, later, had Aristide come out, closing the door behind him, taking the officer downstairs? And why were none of the family members able to give the officer useful information? The family's behavior could only be explained, he wrote, by their frantic effort "to gather up all the bloodstains, which were consequently not found anywhere in the apartment by later inspections."

Bolaffi's behavior, according to the Magistrate, was suspicious as well. Although he testified that he had already looked out the window and seen Rosa below, when he got downstairs, he had asked Signora Ragazzini what had happened, pretending that he didn't already know. And then, when the widow replied that he should know better than she, he said nothing but simply went off.

Given all this evidence, Marabotti concluded, "the unshakable conviction arises that this is a case of homicide, that this could only have occurred inside the Mortara home, where, it seems from other evidence, Mortara's 20-year-old [sic] son, Ercole, a pharmacy student, was to be found." This new wrinkle to the case had arisen from further testimony from neighbor Andrea Casalegno, who claimed to have seen Ercole at the front window of the Mortara apartment immediately after Rosa fell, and shortly thereafter running out the front door without stopping to talk to anyone. Why would everyone in the household be trying to cover up the fact that Ercole had, in fact, been home when Rosa went out the window?

That afternoon, the judge signed his third arrest warrant in the case, citing Ercole.

CHAPTER 26

Momolo's Trial

T HE MAGISTRATE DECIDED not to execute Ercole's arrest warrant immediately but instead had police deliver a summons for him to appear to face charges on April 23. But as soon as Ercole received the order, he went directly to see the Prosecutor to try to clear himself.

When Rosa fell from the window of his older brothers' bedroom, Ercole recounted, he was out. "I returned home after five o'clock; it was about 5:20. My friend Vittorio Boas, who's a student at the Technical Institute, can tell you. I know that I returned exactly at 5:20 because the church bell in our neighborhood rings at that hour, and because I noted the time on the clock at the pharmacist's in via Alfani."

The Magistrate walked Ercole into a nearby room for a lineup. Andrea Casalegno was brought into an adjoining room, from which he could view three men standing against a wall. He pointed to the man on the left. That was the one, he said, that he had seen at the window of the top-floor apartment of via Pinti when he first got to the scene of Rosa's fall. The young man to whom he pointed, with a dark, patchy mustache and long curly hair, was Ercole Mortara.

The following day, April 22, Vittorio Boas, 17 years old, Jewish, and Turin-born, was called in to be questioned. Ercole Mortara, he said, was his friend. Vittorio recalled that he had gone to get Ercole at the Mortara home, near his own, around noon on the day in question. "We stayed together until he walked me home," he recollected. "When Mortara left me, it was about 4:30 or 5. But I know that the five-o'clock bell hadn't yet sounded."

Marabotti and his team of investigators had by this time, less than three weeks after Rosa's death, gathered a mountain of evidence. He was convinced that she had been murdered. It was time to draw up the formal charges, but first he wanted to have one more talk with Bolaffi. The family would be hard to crack, but maybe he could get the family friend—after two weeks in jail—to confess what he knew.

Bolaffi was not in a particularly cooperative mood. "I've already told you the whole truth," he complained to the Magistrate, "so there's nothing more to say." Responding to the Magistrate's question about Ercole, Bolaffi stuck to his story: the boy had not been home when Rosa went out the window. Marabotti thought the time had come to apply more pressure:

> I warn you to tell the truth, because from our investigations it emerges that Rosa Tognazzi suffered a serious wound to her head before falling from the window . . . so that the injury occurred inside the home. There is reason to believe that someone in the Mortara family did it, and in particular Momolo, who has an erratic and violent character. So you must have witnessed what happened: with Mortara's responsibility for the girl's injury being so clear, the decision was made to throw Tognazzi from the window. . . . Your silence in this regard [warned the Magistrate] leads to the supposition that you, too, took part in throwing the woman down into the courtyard.

"We were all in the bedroom when the woman fell from the window," Bolaffi insisted, "and we're all innocent."

On April 24, unmoved by these protestations of innocence, Marabotti sent the formal charges to the Civil and Criminal Court of Florence. Momolo Mortara was charged with having, "on April 3, 1871, between 4:30 and 5 in the afternoon, mortally wounded his domestic servant Rosa Tognazzi by a blow to the head made by a heavy, lacerating object, and then . . . in order to conceal his crime, threw her from the window with the aid and direct cooperation of Flaminio Bolaffi and Ercole Mortara, his son."

In support of this accusation, the Magistrate offered an array of evidence. The medical inspectors "admitted that the wound to the left parietal ridge was made before the fall." The evidence pointed to Momolo as the one who had struck the blow. He was irritable and bad-tempered and often driven by his foul disposition "to violent acts."

Momolo's entire defense, the Magistrate argued, was based on the claim that he had never gotten out of bed that day, due to the tumor on his knee. But this fact was disproved by the neighbors who had seen that he was up, especially Violante Bellucci, who, the very evening after the death, had seen him leave the building with his little son. And further incriminating Momolo was the delay in opening the door of the apartment to the police officer, "because in those precise moments, it was necessary to get rid of the traces of blood and prepare some kind of alibi."

However, reasoned the Magistrate, once Momolo had mortally wounded Rosa and come up with the idea of throwing her out the window, "it was impossible for him to do it alone. Others needed to help, and these were Flaminio Bolaffi and Ercole Mortara, his son." The evidence showed that Bolaffi had been lying. Here again the Magistrate cited the ingenuousness of Bolaffi's question at the courtyard of "What happened?" and his claims of ignorance about the circumstances of Rosa's fall when reporting the matter to the police.

The evidence pointed to Ercole Mortara as another of the conspirators, claimed Marabotti, for he too had lied about being there at the time of the incident, and why else would he lie but to conceal his guilt?

This was murder, not suicide, the Magistrate insisted. Rosa was a cheerful soul, not engaged in any amorous relationship that could have gone bad, in perfect health, with sufficient means of support. "She would never have been able to conceive, much less execute, such an act, on a moment's notice and without giving any sign." As for the claim that she would have killed herself over the dispute with her former employer, "The accusation of theft that was leveled at her is a ludicrous basis for trying to explain such a disproportionate effect."

The following day, the three-member judicial council of the Civil and Criminal Court, which was responsible for the preliminary phase of murder trials, issued its judgment. The investigating magistrate, Clodoveo Marabotti, was himself one of the three judges. In a decision that largely reiterated Marabotti's charge, the court ruled that there were strong grounds for believing that Momolo Mortara was guilty of voluntary, unpremeditated homicide and that both Flaminio Bolaffi and Ercole Mortara were guilty of being accessories to the murder. The three men were ordered bound over to the next higher court, the Court of Cassation. Responsibility for the next phase of the investigation was placed in the hands of the prosecutor attached to the court.

A few days later, the *procuratore generale* wrote up his preliminary reactions to the mass of documents that had been forwarded to him. The basic question was "determining if this was a case of suicide or, rather, of homicide." The Prosecutor was not entirely happy with the work done by the investigators so far. In particular, evidence for the crucial question of whether the injury to Rosa's forehead had preceded her fall appeared to him to be less clear than it had been to the investigating magistrate. He wanted the medical examiners to reconsider, as well, the issue of whether Rosa might not have landed headfirst, and not feetfirst, thus explaining her cracked skull. And then there was the crucial issue of the kerchief. The Magistrate had reported that it belonged not to the victim but to the Mortaras. How did the defendant claim it had ended up around his servant's head? And what of Momolo's claim that he was too infirm to get out of bed, much less assault anyone? A medical examination of his condition must be ordered. Finally, there was the perplexing question of the bloodstained razor in Rosa's pocket. Whose was it, and was the blood fresh?

While both Momolo and Bolaffi were kept in jail, Ercole was allowed to remain free for the time being.

In response to a request from Bolaffi's lawyer, who sought to show that Rosa was, indeed, in a suicidal mood that afternoon, the investigators interviewed the Bolaffis' 22-year-old servant, Adele Reali. She told how, at about 4 p.m. on April 3, Imelda arrived at their apartment "all frightened, and recounted that two men were downstairs with her servant and they were talking angrily, and that they had followed the servant for a long way along the street. She then said that she did not want to return home with her. A little later," Adele continued, "the servant came in with their little dog, and I saw that her face was red and she was crying, and she told me not to open the door to the two men who were coming up the stairs. Then, a little later, the doorbell sounded. I went to open it, and there were two men there who I didn't know." The men were finally persuaded to leave.

Adele then went to the kitchen, where she found Rosa standing by a window to their courtyard, looking out and crying. "I asked her what happened, and she told me that these men had said that she owed them ten lire, but it wasn't true. She remained in the house until near five o'clock, when my employer Bolaffi returned home." When Rosa left with Imelda and Bolaffi, "her face was red and she was crying, and it seemed she was very upset." She wore no white kerchief.

The investigators succeeded in tracking down Rosa's sister Giuseppa, the one whom she had taken food to in the hospital. I turned out that Giuseppa had last seen Rosa, though only briefly, the day before she died, having come by the Mortara home to say hello. How did she seem? She seemed fine, said Giuseppa. "She told me that she was doing well and was happy. I asked her if her employers were good people or if they mistreated her, and she answered that she was happy."

Had Rosa ever mentioned killing herself? asked the investigator. "My sister never showed the least idea of doing harm to herself or committing suicide. It's unthinkable."

On May 16, the investigating magistrate returned to the infirmary of the Murate prison to interview Momolo Mortara. He had been there now for almost six weeks. The interview was brief. The Magistrate had only a few questions.

Asked about the white kerchief, Momolo reported having heard his daughter Ernesta say that the kerchief was hers, and that she had given it to Rosa on the morning of her death, but he had never seen her wearing it.

The following day, Momolo's physician, Dr. Gonnetti, came to testify. He had been called to the Mortara home on March 22 and found Momolo in pain, with a badly swollen right knee. He diagnosed a tumor and prescribed bed rest and some medication. The next day he had been called back by one of Momolo's sons because the pain had gotten worse. The last time he had seen his patient was the day before Rosa's death. "He was still in bed," the doctor reported, "but he said he was feeling better and that he was getting up to go to the lavatory."

Asked if, in his professional opinion, Momolo could have gotten out of bed on April 3, the doctor responded yes, he could, unless he had gotten worse since the previous day's visit.

Would Momolo have had enough strength on April 3, the Magistrate asked, to administer a blow capable of producing the head wound described in Rosa Tognazzi's autopsy report? He showed the report to the doctor. And could Momolo, in a moment of fury, have had the strength to throw the woman out the window, given that she was only semiconscious?

Dr. Gonnetti, a cautious man, responded: "I lack the information I would need to answer these questions. Having seen Mortara only three times, I cannot say how much strength he might have had on April 3. I would have to know the size of the stick with which the blow was struck. . . . I believe, though, that Mortara was able to administer such a blow with a stick . . . but I do not think it equally reasonable to believe that Mortara, especially given the state of his knee, could have had the strength and leverage to throw an unconscious Tognazzi out the window."

That same morning, May 19, the final witness was called, Marianna Mortara. During the weeks that Momolo had been in jail, the family had moved out of its apartment on via Pinti, but whether they were forced out by their landlord or could not stand the hostile glances and overheard comments of their neighbors, we do not know.

Rosa, Marianna recalled, had begun working for them on February 28. They were so pleased with her that they had given her a salary of twelve lire per month rather than the customary ten.

Marianna then recounted the events of April 3: Bolaffi's unexpected return with Imelda and Rosa, his appearance at the bedroom where she sat with her bedridden husband, and the story that Bolaffi told of Rosa's stormy encounter with her former employer. But in the details that followed, there were some elements that were new to the Magistrate.

While we were talking, Rosa had gone up to her room. Meanwhile, Bolaffi was saying that we should give some careful thought to the matter, and he advised us to fire the servant and report her to the police. Since he was talking so loudly, I asked him to speak more softly so that Rosa wouldn't overhear him. I then called Rosa from my husband's bedroom, and since she didn't answer or come down, I got up to go look for her. Going upstairs, I found that she'd locked herself in on the terrace with the key that is always left in the lock. Her face was all red, and it seemed to me that she'd been crying. I asked her to come down and prepare dinner, but she didn't say anything. She walked ahead of me down the stairs, and I accompanied her to the kitchen, where I told her that she shouldn't get all upset, and that if she was innocent, she had nothing to fear.

Marianna then returned to the bedroom. About five minutes later, she heard a big, sudden noise. Their dog started barking. Momolo thought that Rosa must have slammed the door and left, and Aristide ran to call after her down the stairway.

Bolaffi and I went to the front window to see if she was leaving the building, but since we didn't see her, we started to go back. As we passed the room with the two beds, where the dog kept barking, I saw that the window was open. I approached it with Bolaffi and saw Rosa lying in the courtyard, groaning. Desperate, I went back to the bedroom, no, first I threw myself in Bolaffi's arms. Since none of my older sons were home, I told him that he would have to do what had to be done. He said that he would go down to help Rosa and to report it to the police, and without even going back to my husband's bedroom, he left. . . .

Then I went back to the bedroom and fainted. When, after some time, Bolaffi still hadn't come back, my husband wanted to try to get out of bed, and he fell down. My son Aristide began to shout for help from the window on via Pinti, and after that some carabinieri came, then other police. Let me repeat, none of my older sons were there, and no one was in the kitchen or the room with the two beds, because everybody was in my husband's bedroom.

The Magistrate asked Marianna if Rosa had been wearing a kerchief when she had last seen her. No, Marianna responded, but she did recall something about a kerchief: "On Saturday, April 1," she said, "Tognazzi asked one of my daughters for a handkerchief to blow her nose." The Magistrate showed her the kerchief that had been covering Rosa's wound when she was found in the courtyard. "Yes, that's it," said Marianna.

The case was about to take on a new wrinkle, for the Magistrate was sure that Marianna was not only guilty of perjury, trying to protect her guilty husband, but of something more. We have reason to believe, he told her, that Rosa Tognazzi was mortally wounded on the head in your home. "In order to make it look like suicide, she was thrown out the window into the courtyard with your own help."

"I tell you as a woman of honor," Marianna responded, "that no one in my house ever molested or mistreated Rosa. On the contrary, we were happy with her, and in the thirty-three days she was with us, we never even had occasion to shout at her."

Her sons had told her that the Magistrate was asking about an old razor, and Marianna volunteered that she knew something that might be relevant. "One evening, Rosa said she couldn't walk because of her corns. I told her to put her feet in hot water, and she did. Then she asked for a razor, and she was given one of my daughters', a razor that has written on the outside the word 'special.' When we were recently packing up to move," said Marianna, "we couldn't find the razor anymore."

Before dismissing her, the Magistrate showed her the razor found with Rosa's body. She recognized it as the one that was missing from their home. When asked how long it had been stained with blood, she said she didn't know.

In Marianna's testimony there was one small detail that the Magistrate thought might solve one of the remaining mysteries in the case. The murder weapon had never been found. How was the mortal blow struck? What was that blunt but cutting implement that had smashed Rosa's forehead?

Marabotti asked the two medical examiners who had done the autopsy to come with him to via Pinti. He led them up to the apartment in which the Mortaras had lived. After explaining his mission to the new tenants, the Magistrate and his medical colleagues made their way to the two narrow sets of stairs that led to the terrace and the servant's quarters. He turned to the two doctors and asked: If Rosa had been pushed down the stairway, might she have sustained the injury which they had noted on her left frontal ridge? After careful examination of the steep pitch of the stairs and the old, jagged edges, they replied: "If Tognazzi was violently pushed in such a way as to go headfirst down either the first or, especially, the second staircase, she might well have sustained the wound on her forehead, along with a number of her other injuries."

The Magistrate's evident pleasure at this feat of scientific detective work soon began to fade, however, as he discussed the final preparations for trial with the Prosecutor. The stairs theory created more problems than it solved. What scenario were they to present to the judges? That the Mortaras, enraged at hearing from Bolaffi the news that Rosa was a thief, shouted angrily—as was their habit—up the stairs to the terrace to which Rosa had retreated? That, further enraged by the young woman's refusal to respond, Momolo, cane in hand, made his way up the stairs? That, beside himself with fury, he struck or pushed the woman so that she went tumbling down the stairs? That, as Marianna, Bolaffi, and the others ran to see what had happened, they saw the woman lying at the bottom of the stairs, blood flowing from a horrifying gash in her head? That, after first trying to aid her, taking one of their hand-kerchiefs and, folding it lengthwise, tying it around the wound, it became all too clear that Rosa was mortally wounded? That the prospect of having police once again in their home, and their fear of what people would think of a sus-picious death of a Catholic servant there, led them to panic? That, remem-bering Rosa's unpleasant encounter earlier with her former employer, and her tearful state on returning home, someone had the idea of trying to make the death look like suicide? That, because Momolo could not lift the bulky, semi-conscious woman, his friend Bolaffi helped Marianna and their just returned son Ercole drag Rosa to the courtyard window and hoist her up and out?

Although the prosecutor agreed with the gist of this scenario, he was afraid that tying the prosecution to the tumble down the stairs would leave too large an opening for the defense. First of all, even if Momolo were not nearly as incapacitated as he pretended to be, the idea of his jumping from his bed and rushing up the steep stairway seemed shaky. And, just how would he then have been in a position to push her headfirst down the stairs? The Prose-cutor thought it best not to rely too heavily on the stair theory. And so, although the prosecution's charge to the court on June 7 mentioned the possi-bility that Rosa might have been pushed down the stairs, it also advanced the alternative that the enraged Momolo had struck her with a heavy stick, per-haps the handle of one of his walking sticks.

It was mid-June, and the case was ready to go to Florence's Royal Court of Appeal. Both Momolo Mortara and Flaminio Bolaffi had been in jail for two and a half months. There were now four defendants, for both Ercole and his mother, Marianna, were charged, along with Bolaffi, as accessories to murder, accused of having helped Momolo throw Rosa from the window. Momolo was charged with unpremeditated murder. There were two defense lawyers, and each submitted a lengthy brief to the court, one for Bolaffi, the other for the Mortaras.

Just before the final defense arguments were to be made, the District Attorney, reviewing the prosecution's case, requested that the court drop the charges against Bolaffi, Marianna, and Ercole for lack of evidence. The court, however, was not bound by this recommendation.

It was outrageous, began Bolaffi's lawyer, that a perfectly peaceful, decent family man could be thrown in jail and left there for months without any evi-dence against him. All Bolaffi had ever done was show kindness to the Mor-taras' servant, escorting her back home on that fateful day. Why would such a man "become, all of a sudden, so perverse as to assist in a crime of such incredible atrocity?" What motives could he possibly have had to lead him to help throw the still-breathing Tognazzi out the window? And, assuming someone did help Momolo throw her out, what evidence was there to think that it was Bolaffi? There were several other members of the Mortara family present, including Momolo's wife and, perhaps, his son, Ercole, all of whom, as family members, would have had a much stronger motive for such a cover-up.

And what about the various witnesses whose testimony was being used against Bolaffi? Why did the prosecution regard Bolaffi's question to the old woman on reaching the ground floor as so suspicious? If he had asked her what had happened, it was not to feign ignorance of the fact that the injured woman was the Mortaras' servant or that she had just plummeted four stories into the courtyard. He asked because he wanted to know if she were still alive.

And if Bolaffi, in reporting the fall at the police station, said that he didn't know what happened, there was no cover-up here. He simply meant that he had not been in the room from which Rosa fell and so could not tell the police how it happened. "As for his refusal to return to the Mortara house," argued the lawyer, "it can be explained by his natural desire to return home." Bolaffi had already done his duty by rushing to the police to report the matter. "The spectacle that the Inspector invited him to see was not pleasant, and anyone would have wanted to flee from it."

In short, the lawyer concluded, there was no evidence of Bolaffi's guilt, just a sinew of speculation. "We are confident that you will absolve Signor Flaminio Bolaffi of this accusation and free him from prison." With this, Bolaffi's defense rested.

Bolaffi's attorney had good reason to think that his client's ordeal was nearing its end, since the District Attorney himself had recommended against prosecution. Momolo's lawyer had no such confidence. Momolo's defender, whose eloquent closing argument preceded the judges' verdict, was not his 23-year-old son Augusto, but a more experienced lawyer named Mancini who had come to the family's aid.

For the defense, a clear thread tied the police persecution of the ailing Momolo to another police operation that had, nineteen years earlier, in Bologna, deprived his family of one of its members. Momolo was a Jew, viewed by many of his Catholic neighbors with ill-disguised hostility.

"If there was ever a trial which brings to mind the sad examples of ill-fated legal proceedings, it is this one," Mancini began. You start with some ill-conceived assumptions, add a hearty dose of religious fanaticism, and this is what you get. "What stands out to the eyes of the dispassionate observer," he said, "is the veil of prejudice under which, in this proceeding, they began to suspect that a crime had been committed by the *Jew* Mortara. It's remark-able," the lawyer exclaimed, "that the witnesses do not simply refer to him by his name. Indeed, the prosecutor's office itself does not call him, in the normal manner, the *defendant* Mortara. He is, for everyone, simply *Mortara the Jew!*"

As a result of this attitude, Mancini argued, instead of first asking whether any crime had been committed, "they assumed that it was a crime, prompted by the twisted suspicions of an old bigot and by the [Catholic] paper *Armonia*, to the detriment of *Mortara the Jew*, and both logic and common sense were bent in search of proof."

Immediately after Rosa's fall, the lawyer recalled, the first police report had attributed her death to suicide. The first doctor on the scene had said that the head wound could very well have been caused by Rosa's fall, and what they knew of her upsetting encounter immediately beforehand with her former employer showed that she had been in an agitated state of mind.

But then the servant from the ground floor, Teresa Gonnelli, "who knew that Tognazzi worked for 'the Jew,' hearing the poor woman's moans, says she asked her the following question: 'Oh! What happened, poor girl? Did they throw you down?' and claimed that twice she responded 'yes.' And then Anna Ragazzini," the lawyer continued, "who knew the '*Jew*' and knew that the dying woman was the servant of the *Jew*, says that Gonnelli, trembling with fright, repeated that terrible response to her." Out of this hysteria came the idea that a crime had been committed, and amidst a welter of conflicting ideas, of medical reports and then requests for reconsideration of the medical evidence, came "this monstrous trial."

"Momolo Mortara," the lawyer told the judges, "is the most loving, yet most unhappy, father of the boy Edgardo, abducted from his family as a result of religious intolerance, a fact that produced such a scandal not only in all of Italy but in the entire civilized world. And this intolerance, unfortunately, appears again in the souls of these bigots and fanatics." Having thus set the stage, the attorney began his review of the testimony, and as he did he offered a dramatically new view of what had happened on that April afternoon.

It is curious, said Mancini, that when, right after Gonnelli asked the gravely injured Rosa if she had been thrown out the window, witness Andrea Casalegno asked her "if she had fallen, or if they had thrown her from the window, or if she had fallen down the stairs," Rosa had only reacted to the last of these questions, murmuring, "Yes, down the stairs." Yet the police had only paid attention to what the "two bigoted women" had said, and ignored this. The fact is, the lawyer told the court, Rosa was in no position to respond lucidly to anyone. She had just fallen down four stories, her head was smashed in, her brain cavity filled with blood, and her neck broken. To base Momolo's arrest on the murmured responses to the leading questions of a bigot, under such circumstances, was disgraceful.

First, look at Rosa's state of mind that afternoon. She had run into the employer from whom she had stolen, a man she hoped never to see again. In a public street and in front of her employer's child, he had accused her of being a thief and a liar and had threatened to denounce her to the police. She was humiliated and fearful not only of the police but of being summarily fired when the Mortaras found out what had happened. What would she do? She had nowhere to go if she were fired but into the street. When, crying and upset, she returned to the Mortara home, she saw Bolaffi go in to talk with the Mortaras. Indeed, she may even have overheard Bolaffi advise them to throw her out and report her to the police.

"To say that she had never before shown suicidal tendencies," said the lawyer, "as if to say that she did not have sufficient reason for such a desperate decision, is meaningless. . . . These are ideas that are spoken of when they will not be acted on, and are most likely to be carried out when they are least discussed."

Yet, admittedly, it wasn't easy for Rosa to put her sudden suicidal resolve into practice. Looking four stories down into the tiny courtyard robbed her of her courage, so she got the fateful idea: she would cover her eyes so that she would not have to see the vertiginous sight. She even had something in her pocket that she could use, the handkerchief that the Mortaras had recently given her. But when she began to fold it in order to make the blindfold, Imelda happened by and, embarrassed and afraid that the girl might guess its purpose, the nervous Rosa tried to conceal what she was doing.

Then, said the lawyer, there is the issue that the prosecutors have made so much of: the evidence that Rosa's lethal head injury could not have occurred on the courtyard pavement, that it had to have been inflicted before she hit the ground. I fully admit that in this the scientific evidence is clear. Yet, he asked, must this be taken to mean that the wound had been inflicted in the Mortaras' apartment, as the prosecution, moved by its preconceptions, so stubbornly contends? The answer is no.

The courtyard itself measures just three meters by two meters. In fact, from the window from which Rosa fell to the opposite wall measures exactly 2.09 meters, barely more than six feet. And on each floor down, the wall juts out around the base of the windows. Yet with all the investigations undertaken by the single-minded investigators, did any of them take the trouble to examine these protuberances? Unfortunately, Mancini said, they did not.

And then there is another bit of evidence ignored by the prosecution: the account of the servant Margherita Rosati, who was sitting in the second-floor apartment near the courtyard window. She reported hearing two big thuds, one after the other. Why two?

The explanation is simple, and the investigators would have come to it quickly if not for their assumption that Rosa must have been killed in the

Mortaras' apartment. In jumping, blindfolded, from the fourth-floor window, Rosa had inevitably gone forward as she plunged, and her body smashed off one of the ledges on the opposite wall as she picked up speed.

A whole set of her injuries made sense when understood in this way. Most important, it explained the deep, irregular gash on her forehead, caused by something blunt, and crushing the bone beneath, but also the other injuries on her left side: her smashed left knee and hand, and the peculiarities of her snapped lower cervical vertebra, produced when her head bounced back from the terrible impact of the blow to her forehead as she hurtled downward.

And then there is the final mystery. How was it that Rosa, on being discovered on the courtyard floor, had a white kerchief covering her wounded forehead? The prosecution theory, argued Momolo's lawyer, was absurd. They would have it that in the less than fifteen minutes between Rosa's arrival home and her fall, the bedridden Momolo was first told the whole story of Rosa's encounter with her former employer, then he either called her in or went to find her, then inflicted the lethal wound, then someone found a handkerchief and prepared a bandage, and tied it around her forehead with a double knot, then Momolo came up with the idea that it would be better to throw her out the window, then he convinced everyone else to go along, then they dragged the heavy, semiconscious woman to the boys' bedroom, and finally they hoisted her up and out.

There is something more, though, said Mancini. The prosecution is missing another important implication of the physical evidence they have presented. The medical examiners had concluded, based on her injuries, that Rosa must have hit the ground in a largely upright posture, feet first. Indeed, although the prosecution had not mentioned it, the fact that Rosa's skirt and petticoats had been up to her face when she landed could be explained in no other way.

Now let us return, said the lawyer, to the prosecution's scenario. As the frantic Momolo and his confederates were desperately hoisting the weighty servant up to the windowsill, were they lifting her feetfirst or by her trunk? The answer is clear. They would have done what was natural and hoisted her up by her trunk, followed by her legs. She would have plunged headfirst into the courtyard.

Rosa's bare private parts, when the two women first found her, helped to explain the mystery of the kerchief-covered wound. The force of the air had put upward pressure on her kerchief, just as it had on her skirt. When Rosa's head snapped back from the blow to her forehead as she fell, the position of her head allowed a burst of air to get under her hastily prepared blindfold, lifting the front of it up a few inches. By the time she landed, it had reached her forehead, the knot still firmly in place at the base of her skull.

What of all the evidence that Momolo was lying about his incapacity, or that the Mortaras were trying to cover something up? asked Mancini. Perhaps Momolo was seen in the kitchen. He said himself he got up to go to the lavatory, and so passed right next to the kitchen. The one witness to claim that Momolo was really ambulatory was the neighbor who swore that he saw him spryly leave the building that evening with his son. But he was looking out his third-floor window on a night in which there was no moonlight and only the dimmest of gaslight. What he saw was a product of his fantasy. The man he really saw leave that evening, after hearing the footsteps coming down from the fourth floor, was Flaminio Bolaffi, and the boy he heard and saw was not Aristide Mortara but Bolaffi's son, Emilio. In fact, Bolaffi testified that he had returned to the Mortara home earlier that evening with his son to find out what had gone on in the hours since his visit to the police station. Apparently, to the neighbor, one Jew looked much like another.

And what of that damning bit of evidence, that no one would open the door to the police officer summoned by Bolaffi after Rosa's fall? The prosecution charges that this shows that the family was busy cleaning up blood and concocting an alibi. But, in fact, even before that officer came, the first policeman on the scene, called from the street by a neighbor, had arrived. He had already gone up to the Mortara apartment and been admitted right away. He had gone to the window from which Rosa fell, and found nothing. If the Mortaras were trying to cover something up, why admit the first policeman and not the second? The reason there was initially no response to the second policeman, the lawyer argued, was because of the sad state in which those in the apartment found themselves. Both mother and daughters had practically fainted away, Momolo himself had fallen and was being helped back into bed, and the room in which they were all to be found was itself far from the front door.

As for any material proof that, even were a murder committed—and there was no murder—it was Momolo who committed it, all we have is imagination. "It is worth considering the kind of arguments that were judged sufficient to yank a citizen from his bed while he was afflicted with a painful illness and take him to jail and keep him there for several months," said Momolo's lawyer. "Indeed, we believe that because we are dealing with the *Jew Mortara*, it is all the more important that we employ some common sense."

Even the briefest consideration revealed that Momolo would have had no motive for murdering Rosa. "The interest that an employer might have in discovering that his servant had stolen in a previous job is that of firing her, not killing her. . . . You would have to be dealing with a maniac, and if this is what you thought, the police should have taken him to Bonifazio [insane asylum], not to Murate [prison]."

This gets to the second point, the claim that Momolo Mortara is a violent, hot-tempered person. "Those of us who have the honor of knowing the Mortaras are well able to testify that what hurts Momolo and his family even more than his being in jail and more than suffering this trial is to see him accused of having little love for his family, for he is a man who shows the greatest tenderness toward his wife and children."

The lawyer then returned to the reason for Momolo's renown, as well as for his misery.

> From the time that the papal guards took Edgardo, his favorite child, from him, he was beset by a tremendous anguish! Everyone knows about this scandalous case, and all can imagine how it might change someone's character to see his treasured son torn from his breast and his religion, without warning, in the thick of the night, without pity, amidst the boy's, the mother's, and his brothers' and sisters' screams. From the moment of that agonizing scene . . . he became, it's true, a bit brooding and apt to grumble. But his nature was so gentle and good that, deep down, he has always stayed the same. For him, the old saying is apt: "The dog that barks doesn't bite."

The defense lawyer concluded with an appeal to the judges to rise above the popular prejudices against the Jews, and above the hatred aimed at Momolo in particular, a man viewed by many as having caused the Church much misery. The long-suffering father should be allowed to return to his family, a family that had already suffered enough. With this, the defense rested.

On June 30, 1871, having examined all the testimony, the medical evidence, and the briefs and arguments of the Prosecutor and the two defense lawyers, the three judges of Florence's Royal Court of Appeal issued their decision. They rejected Mancini's arguments and found "that the wound on Tognazzi's head was inflicted by Momolo Mortara in his apartment, as a result of a sudden rage, and that Tognazzi was then thrown from the window to make it look like suicide." The judges noted the medical evidence that Momolo could not have thrown her out of the window without help and concluded that "others must have assisted him in this barbarous deed." At home at the time that the crime was committed, the judges found, were Momolo, his wife, his twin daughters, his son Ercole, his friend Flaminio Bolaffi, and three small children.

Here, however, the judges found themselves in a quandary: "Although there is no doubt that some of the above-listed individuals helped Momolo Mortara throw the unfortunate Tognazzi from the window . . . we have no special reason to conclude that any one rather than any other lent a hand to the wicked deed. We must, then, apply the rule that suggests that it is better to abandon the accusation rather than have it weigh on both the innocent and the guilty together." Clearly, the judges concluded, all of them were lying, trying to protect a husband, wife, parent, child, or friend. But the determination that they were lying did not justify finding them guilty of pushing Rosa from the window.

As a result, the judges decided "not to proceed, due to a lack of evidence, against Flaminio Bolaffi, Ercole Mortara, and Marianna Padovani Mortara." They bound Momolo over to Tuscany's highest court, the Court of Assizes, which was responsible for making the final ruling on all murder cases. Flaminio Bolaffi was released from jail, after spending almost three months locked up.

Momolo, in worsening health, remained in jail for another three and a half months while he awaited his fate, his condition steadily deteriorating. Finally, on Wednesday, October 18, Augusto Groppi, president of the Court of Assizes, called the final trial to order. A stricken Momolo sat in a special chair that had been prepared for him, next to his lawyer. After hearing opening arguments, the three-judge panel, on October 21, heard from the two medical examiners. The newspapers, reporting the trial, focused on their testimony that the mortal wound to Rosa Tognazzi's forehead had not been caused by the knife found in her pocket. Rather, they testified, it had been caused either by a blunt instrument or by the fall.[1]

On Friday, October 27, following the closing arguments, the judges reached their verdict. Momolo Mortara was found not guilty. They ordered him released from the jail in which he had lived for almost seven months. A month later, he died.

EPILOGUE

WIILE HIS FATHER was in jail, accused of murder, and his mother was facing charges of sending a bleeding 23-year-old woman hurtling four stories to her death, Edgardo was living happily under an assumed name in a convent of the Canons Regular in Austria. The following year, he moved to a monastery in Poitiers, France, where he continued his theological studies. Pius IX, now an old man, had not forgotten his son. The Pope wrote regularly to the Bishop of Poitiers, asking how Edgardo was doing and expressing the hope that he would soon be ordained a priest. In 1873, having received a special dispensation—at 21, he was still shy of the minimum age for priesthood—Pio Edgardo Mortara was ordained. The Pope sent Edgardo a personal letter on this occasion, expressing his immense satisfaction and asking the young man to pray for him. According to Edgardo, the Pope also established a lifetime trust fund of seven thousand lire to ensure his support.[1]

Known as a scholarly man—reputed to preach in six languages, including the notoriously difficult language of the Basques, and to read three others, Hebrew among them—Father Mortara dedicated his life to spreading the faith, singing the praises of the Lord Jesus Christ, and traveling throughout Europe, going where he was most needed. As a preacher he was in great demand, not least because of the inspirational way he was able to weave the remarkable story of his own childhood into his sermons. As he recounted it, his saga was the stuff of faith and hope: a story of how God chose a simple, illiterate servant girl to invest a small child with the miraculous powers of divine grace, and in so doing rescued him from his Jewish family—good people but, as Jews, on a God-forsaken path. He might still have been lost, had it not been for the courageous actions of a saintly pope, who braved cruel threats from the ungodly and allowed Edgardo to devote his life to spreading the word of Christ's saving power.

In 1878, Marianna Mortara, now widowed and with all of her nine children grown, heard that Edgardo was preaching in Perpignan, in southwestern France. Accompanied by a family friend, she went to see him. It had been twenty years since she had last laid eyes on her son. It was a poignant reunion, for Edgardo felt great affection for his mother. But try as he might to turn her onto the path of eternal blessing and happiness, he could not get her to agree to enter the Catechumens and convert.

From that moment, Edgardo remained in touch with his family and, as he aged, sought out family members when he found himself in Italy. But while his mother made peace with him, not all of his siblings were so kindly disposed.

In 1890, when Marianna Mortara died, French newspapers reported the dramatic news of her deathbed conversion by her proselytizing son. It seemed that after all those years of holding out, she had finally succumbed to her son's pleas. But in a letter to the paper *Le Temps*, dated April 18, 1890, Father Pio Edgardo denied the report: "I have always ardently desired that my mother embrace the Catholic faith, and I tried many times to get her to do so. However, that never happened, and although I stood beside her during her last illness, along with my brothers and sisters, she never showed any sign of converting."[2]

The following year, to much public curiosity and, in some quarters, enthusiasm, Father Pio Edgardo visited his mother's natal city, Modena, to preach at the Church of San Carlo. A sympathetic local newspaper offered a description of Edgardo a month short of his fortieth birthday: "Of medium height, he is a man with a most pleasing appearance, with a gentle and courteous manner, and an entirely Christian kindness about him." The correspondent told of shaking the monk's hand just before he got up to preach: "His modesty, his simplicity moved us, knowing that his learning and his fame are known throughout the world."

When Edgardo rose to speak, not only were a sister and a number of his brothers in the pews, but the large audience contained, according to the newspaper's account, "not a few Jews, eager to hear the illustrious speaker." Father Pio Edgardo told of his joy upon first returning to Italy after a twenty-year absence, and of his thanks to God for letting him see his beloved land once again. He then spoke of his emotion in returning to Modena, his mother's homeland, of the way his heartbeat quickened at the thought of her, and of the emotion he felt in seeing his sister and brothers sitting before him.

Edgardo then launched into his sermon, expanding on the theme of what a great and wonderful adventure it was to be a Catholic, because as a Catholic a person possesses the truth. What he most fervently desired, he said, was that others come to understand these truths, that others come to share the happiness he had gained by taking them into his heart.

The journalist described the crowd's delight in hearing the monk's inspiring sermon, concluding: "We were extremely pleased to have heard him. We blessed God, who, in the inscrutable ways of his providence, permitted the acquisition to Catholicism of such a powerful champion of the faith." They had all left the church convinced, the correspondent wrote, "that God would, without doubt, concede him great triumphs and the comfort of seeing others embrace that Holiest Religion, of which Father Mortara is a most learned and convinced apologist."[3]

By this time both Cardinal Antonelli and Pope Pius IX were long gone. The Secretary of State, whose merits were more appreciated by the Church's diplomatic enemies than by its own cardinals, died in 1876. It is said that even Antonelli's longtime protector, the Pope, on first being told of his Secretary of State's death, responded: "Let's not talk about him anymore!"[4]

Two years later, the two principal antagonists in the unification battle, King Victor Emmanuel II and Pope Pius IX, died within a month of each other. Indeed, one of the Pope's final acts was to authorize the giving of the last rites to the monarch whom he had excommunicated. The King's body, visited by fifty thousand mourners a day, lay in state in the Quirinal Palace, which had for three centuries served as the official residence of the popes before being taken over by the royal family in 1870. An imposing funeral followed at the Pantheon, a building dating to Roman times and now merging imperial and Christian functions, the church of the royal family.

When the Pope died, the following month, his body lay for a week in St. Peter's basilica as thousands of mourners came to pay their respects. As part of the ceremonies, his coffin was taken in solemn procession out from the Vatican through the nearby city streets. When the procession of carriages, white-tunicked clergy, purple-robed cardinals, mournful bishops, and papal guards reached the bridge over the Tiber, they were met by an unruly mob of anticlerical protesters, who waved the tricolor, chanted patriotic songs, and shouted antipapal slogans. Just as it looked as though they would succeed in removing the Pope's coffin from its carriage and heaving it into the river, a detachment of police arrived to save the day.[5]

Edgardo lived many more years. By the end of the First World War, he had moved into the abbey of the Canons Regular in Bouhay, Belgium. Although he visited Italy occasionally—including a nostalgic visit to Rome's House of the Catechumens in 1919—he preferred to remain in Bouhay, dedicated to contemplation, study, prayer, and devotion to the Virgin Mary, for whom he had a special fondness.[6] Bouhay was renowned for its sanctuary to the Virgin of Lourdes, second in fame only to that found in the Pyrenean town itself, and Pio Edgardo felt a special, spiritual link to the miracle at Lourdes.[7] The Virgin had chosen to reveal herself to the faithful in 1858, and so two miracles took place in the same year, one in a French town, the other in Italy, when the Virgin appeared to a little boy just plucked from his Jewish home, a boy who, in a few days' time, went from the obscurity of life as the sixth child of a modest merchant's family to the heights of celebrity, his welfare of concern to a pope, a secretary of state, ambassadors, a prime minister, and even, fleetingly, to an emperor.

On March 11, 1940, the 88-year-old monk died at the Belgian abbey in which he had lived for many years. A month later, German soldiers flooded into Belgium, soon to begin rounding up all those tainted with Jewish blood.

AFTERWORD

W H Y   H A S the Mortara case attracted so little attention from historians? It represents one of the significant episodes in the unification of Italy, and yet it has been largely ignored, even though a huge amount of historical work has focused on the Risorgimento.

The case of the Jewish child seized from his family, and of the Pope who braved popular denunciation and fierce diplomatic pressure to hold on to him, has all the elements of melodrama, as was recognized by the several nineteenth-century playwrights who rushed to write plays based on the case. From a historian's perspective, the Mortara case is loaded with ties to epochal developments, providing a window into many of the major forces at work at one of the turning points in Italian history. There could scarcely be a better demonstration of the worldview that lay behind the Holy See's commitment to temporal rule, or of the manner in which it came into conflict with the new liberal, secular ideology that spread throughout Europe in the nineteenth century. Also, the involvement in the Mortara case of many of the principal protagonists of the unification struggle offers a valuable vantage point for understanding the mind-set of such crucial figures as Pope Pius IX, Secretary of State Giacomo Antonelli, Count Camillo Cavour, and the French emperor Napoleon III.

So how can we explain the fact that until now the only book-length scholarly study of the Mortara case was one published in 1957 by an American, Bertram Korn, dedicated entirely to the American reaction to the affair, a book by an author who apparently read neither Italian nor French? It should not be surprising that the account of the actual facts of the case given in the opening chapter of Korn's book—before he turns to his main topic, what happened in the United States—is filled with inaccuracies. Unfortunately, insofar as non-Italian scholars around the world (mainly in Jewish studies) have learned about the case, it is through Korn's flawed and, in any case, limited account.

The major historical work to date on the Mortara case was undertaken by Gemma Volli and published in a series of articles around the hundredth anniversary of the boy's seizure. These made a major contribution to Jewish history but were published in places where few people other than Italian Jewish studies scholars ever saw them. For the rest, the Mortara case is known to historians through passing mention in various works of nineteenth-century Church history: no serious biography of Pius IX or Cardinal Antonelli is complete without a discussion of the case, but in these the focus and perspective are understandably limited.

When I first learned about the story, it struck me as so dramatic and so bound up with the major personages and events of the Risorgimento that I assumed that it must be widely known among educated Italians. I was amazed to discover how mistaken I was. Very few had ever heard of it. Even many modern Italian historians, at least those who were not specialists in the Risorgimento, were unfamiliar with the case. Yet, whenever I spoke with specialists in Jewish studies anywhere in the world, from the United States to Israel, Canada to Britain and France, they invariably knew in detail (albeit not always accurately) the story of the little Jewish boy taken at the Inquisitor's order from his home. People who did not know the difference between Mazzini and Cavour knew all about Edgardo and the illiterate Catholic servant who claimed to have baptized him.

The Mortara story, in short, fell from the mainstream of Italian history into the ghetto of Jewish history. It became something of interest to Jews. If it took on a special importance in this arena, it was because the case was not simply one more illustration of the persecution suffered by the Jewish people at the hands of the Christian Church, but was itself an influential chapter in modern Jewish history. What was striking about the case was not the forced baptism and the taking of the Jewish child from his family, but the fact that, after centuries in which such events happened regularly, the larger world finally took an interest, finally rose in protest. But, most significantly, the Mortara affair marked a turning point in helping to catalyze the creation of national and international Jewish self-defense organizations in both Europe and the United States.

Why have Italian scholars taken so little interest in the case? Here, as a foreigner, an American, I tread on uncomfortable ground, but let me forge ahead, however foolishly. The historiography of the battle between Risorgimento forces and papal power contains two large currents. One consists of the

Risorgimento historians themselves, and the other of historians of the Church. Needless to say, both traditions have made major contributions to Italian history, yet each has its limitations. One of the major ones, from my perspective, is that the history of the Church has been viewed primarily as the domain of scholars closely identified with the Church, who tend to take a rather Church-centered view of Italian history. Let me hasten to add that the problem has its parallel in the history of the Jewish people—in Italy and elsewhere in the world—which has been practiced largely by Jews and which has, as a result, often had a somewhat parochial character. For Church historians, the Mortara case has a certain importance, and scholars such as Giacomo Martina and Roger Aubert have made significant contributions to our knowledge of it, but their concern is primarily with the negative impact that the case had on the Church. By contrast, the Risorgimento historians have, for the most part, simply ignored *il caso Mortara*. Major biographies of Cavour, for example, fail to mention it at all. Is this because the matter is viewed as affecting only Jews, and therefore of no concern to those historians who deal with the major issues of the period? The question cannot easily be answered.

It is also true that in those two communities most closely implicated in the Mortara case, the Italian Church and Italy's Jews, the memory is not only painful—for very different reasons—but also embarrassing. If the case has been kept out of public view, it may be because neither Catholics nor Jews in Italy are eager to publicize it. For Catholics, the case is troubling for a number of reasons. It is based on an article of faith that was absolutely central to the Church until recent times but that today is deemed reprehensible: the tenet that presented the Jews as degraded Christ-killers and that sanctioned the use of physical force to take Jewish children from their parents. Moreover, in highlighting the fact that until recent times the Church rejected the ideal of religious toleration and, indeed, continued to promulgate an Inquisition, the Mortara case draws attention to the fact that the Church's transition from a medieval fundamentalism to modernity took place only in the present century. It is no surprise, in this context, that the most common reaction of people today on first hearing of the Mortara case is: "You mean there was still an Inquisition in 1858? I thought the Inquisition took place hundreds of years ago!"

More generally, the Church's treatment of the Jews has not been a favorite topic of Church historians. It raises too many awkward questions, especially after the Holocaust: Who was it who developed the tradition in Europe of requiring Jews to wear colored badges so that they could be readily identified? Who for centuries taught that any contact between Jews and Christians was polluting to Christians and should be punishable by force? It was far better to see Italy's 1938 racial laws as having nothing to do with the Church, or indeed even with Italy, but as some sort of importation, the fault of foreigners.

For Italy's Jews, it is not the pain of the Mortara memories that has made its discussion uncomfortable, but the embarrassment. The battle between the Jews and the Church was played out in a struggle over a 6-year-old boy. For the Jews, the Church's claim that Edgardo could not remain with his Jewish parents because he had been supernaturally transformed by baptism was doubly insulting. Not only did it demonstrate their vulnerability to the Church's political power, but it also asserted a Catholic claim to possession of the true religion, to a privileged relationship with the Almighty, and to the dismissal of Judaism as error, if not worse. When the Church began to publicize reports that Edgardo was showing signs of his supernatural transformation, the discovery of what, in fact, the little boy actually believed, and whether he truly preferred to stay in the Church rather than to return home to the Judaism of his ancestors, became a kind of public test of the relative merits of the two religions. It was a test the Jews lost.

Of course, Italian Jews were well aware of the psychological pressures exerted on the small boy and had no trouble coming up with a secular explanation of his ultimate decision to abandon his family and Judaism and embrace the Church, but this did not make his transformation any more palatable. That he followed the long—and, for the Jews, vile—tradition of such converts and dedicated himself to trying to convert his own family, and indeed Jews everywhere, meant that Edgardo came to be viewed with horror: he was a changeling. The child who had once been portrayed in the most glowing terms, the object of Jewish compassion, became a man who was disdained, whose character had to be discredited. He could not be happy, he could not even be fully sane, for were he happy and sane, it would reflect poorly on the religion of the Jews. It was best not to talk of him at all.

My own interest in this story derives from a mixture of personal and professional motives. I am not a historian of the Risorgimento, nor a Church historian, nor a student of Jewish history. As a social anthropologist who became interested in historical questions, my work in Italian history up to now has focused on social history, trying to shed light on how the masses of people, mainly illiterate, lived in the past and how their lives were transformed in the nineteenth century. Those whose lives I have examined—sharecroppers and day laborers, unwed mothers and foundlings—were people who had largely escaped the attention of chroniclers of the time as well as of historians today. In short, I had never examined the life of anyone famous, never inquired into affairs of state or diplomacy. My work bore the marks of a movement that was rather critical of all the attention paid by historians in the past to the lives of the elite, to the machinations of political leaders, and to the conduct of wars.

How, then, did I come to write this kind of narrative history, telling a story, one that involves some of Europe's major personages, a war for national unification, and the drama of a pope under siege? The professional part of the answer stems from my admiration for those historians who have been able to blend historiographic and literary skills to bring a particular historical case to life. They have focused on the lives of "regular" people, telling gripping stories that shed new light on life in the past. One of the best examples of this genre is Natalie Davis's *The Return of Martin Guerre*, the story of obscure French peasants of the sixteenth century who, unexpectedly caught up in a dramatic case of spousal imposture, came to the attention of the courts, and whose lives became known to the eager readers of pamphlets that recounted the dramatic tale.

The Mortara case differs in some important ways from the story of Martin Guerre, for it involves important historical figures—from a pope to an emperor—and had an impact on events of much broader significance. But as in the French case, at the heart of the story lies an obscure family caught up in a drama—and later a court case—that offers a glimpse of life among a seg-ment of the population that rarely comes into view in historical work. Indeed, one of the surprises for me in doing the research for this book was how rich a view of people's daily lives we can get through the study of court and notarial records of the type used here. Such insight is simply not obtainable if we limit ourselves to the kinds of sources most closely identified with the new social history: parish censuses, baptismal records, land registers, and the like. I have, for example, spent much time in the past using this more demographic type of records to get a better understanding of the lives of the illiterate young women who worked as domestic servants in Italy, but I was never able to get the kind of insight into the relations between servants and their employers, nor among servants, that I found in the records connected with the Mortara case.

But all this said, an admission is in order. What drew me most to the Mortara case was not professional interest at all but forces rooted deep in my own family background. My fondness for Italy dates back to early in my child-hood, when I heard the stories my father told about his experiences in the war. Chaplain Morris Kertzer landed at Anzio beachhead with the Allied forces early in 1944 as part of the effort to drive out the Nazi occupiers. In April, he conducted a Passover seder at Anzio for the Jewish troops. At the adjacent cemetery, he officiated at more than a hundred funerals of young Jewish sol-diers in a few weeks' time.

On Sunday afternoon, June 4, Kertzer entered Rome as the city was being liberated. On the following Friday evening, June 9, together with Rome's Chief Rabbi, Israel Zolli, he conducted the first Sabbath service to be held in one of liberated Europe's major synagogues. Four thousand people crammed into Rome's central synagogue, overlooking the Tiber. That historic service itself presaged, in a number of ways, my own later fascination with the

Mortara case. As the service was about to begin, an American soldier forced his way through the crowd to the front, where my father stood, and explained that he was himself a Jew from Rome, who had been sent ten years earlier to the United States. He had not seen his parents since then. He did not know whether they had been sent off to the concentration camps or had survived, and he pleaded with the Chaplain to do something to see if they were present amidst the throng. My father asked the soldier to stand at his side as the service began, so that his parents could see him if they were indeed still alive. A woman's cry of joy and recognition pierced the crowd, and she ran up. Mother and son were reunited in front of the Ark of the Torah.

Barely half a year later, while Nazi forces still occupied portions of northern Italy, the elderly Rabbi Zolli—enmeshed in a bitter dispute with the leadership of the Rome synagogue—stunned Jews worldwide by announcing his conversion to Roman Catholicism. The embarrassment of Italy's Jews could scarcely have been greater, and denunciations of his character, his past, and even his sanity thundered from Jewish leaders far and wide. My father, who had visited Rabbi Zolli's apartment and gotten to know him a bit, wrote in his defense.

A half century after my father assisted the Chief Rabbi at that emotional and exhilarating service at Rome's Tempio Israelitico, I sat outside the Chief Rabbi's office there, in the adjacent reading room, poring through the 1858 correspondence between the Secretary of Rome's Jewish community and Momolo Mortara, the desperate father of a boy taken from him and from his religion.

I dedicate this book to the memory of my father, who received word of the death of his own father, David Kertzer, after whom I was named, while he was stationed in Naples before the triumphal march into Rome. I dedicate it as well to his granddaughter, Molly, my daughter, who shares with her father not only a love for Italy but a fascination with *il caso Mortara*. I am only sorry that my father did not live to read his granddaughter's undergraduate thesis, or this book by his son, both of which, in some way, are testaments to his memory.

ACKNOWLEDGMENTS

I t   w a s   Steven Hughes who first drew my attention to the Mortara case several years ago. Since he first told me about the boy who was taken from his Bologna home on orders of the Inquisitor, I found myself drawn in, entranced not only by the personal drama, but by what the story told about the battle between the old order and the new, the dawn of modernity. For a number of years I took advantage of trips to Italy designed for other purposes to collect what I could about the case from archives and libraries. It was only in 1995–96, however, that I was able to devote my attention entirely to the project, thanks to a grant from the National Endowment for the Humanities (long may it live!), with additional support from Brown University and from the Paul Dupee, Jr. University Professorship at Brown. Earlier support had been provided by the William R. Kenan Professorship at Bowdoin College. During my year in Italy, I was hosted by the Fondazione Carlo Cattaneo of Bologna, a wonderful group of scholars and staff, which offered both a stimulating environment and excellent research support. Special thanks go to Robert Cartocci, director of research at Cattaneo, for providing me with such a conducive environment for bringing this project to completion.

Many colleagues in Italy helped steer me through the intricacies of Italian and Church history, as well as through the archives and libraries. In particular, I would like to thank my good friends Mauro Pesce, Pier Cesare Bori, and Arturo Parisi, as well as Margherita Pelaja, Gadi Luzzato Voghera, and Paolo Bernardini. I would also like to thank Nancy Green for her help in Paris.

A number of people assisted me in the research. Adanella Bianchi worked closely with me on the library and archival research for this project in Bologna. I would also like to thank Amitai Touval, Arnaldo Ferroni, Miriam

Bellecca, Jennifer Frey, and Kathy Grimaldi for their help in the United States, and Carolina Cappucci for her help in Modena.

In the early days of this project, Mauro Pesce and I talked of working on a book together, and Mauro subsequently directed two laurea theses on press reaction to the Mortara case, by Floriana Naldi and Grazia Parisi. I would like to thank both Floriana and Grazia for sharing the materials they collected with me, and thank Grazia for her kind help at the state archives in Reggio.

Of the many librarians and archivists who helped me in this research, I would like to thank Otello Sangiorgi and Mirtide Gavelli at the Biblioteca del Museo del Risorgimento di Bologna, Elvira Grantaliano of the Archivio di Stato di Roma, Mario Fanti of the Archivio Arcivescovile di Bologna, Simona Foà of the Archivio Storico della Comunità Israelitica di Roma, Luigi Fiorani of the Biblioteca Apostolica Vaticana, and Domenico Rocciolo of the Archivio del Vicariato di Roma. Thanks also to Don Vittorio Gardini, of Bologna's San Gregorio parish, for his kind help with the parish censuses.

Special thanks go to Luisella Mortara Ottolenghi, director of the Centro di Documentazione Ebraica Contemporanea in Milan, whose deep knowledge of the Mortara case is enriched by a special family connection, her husband being Edgardo Mortara's great-nephew. Thanks also to Franca Romano for all her help.

For their comments on an earlier draft of this book, I would like to thank Bernardo Bernardi, Robert Dana, Pamela Goucher, Steve Hughes, Massimo Marcolin, Luisella Mortara Ottolenghi, Tom Row, Aaron Seidman, Daniel Wathen, and Paolo Zaninoni at Rizzoli, editor of the Italian edition of this book. For his infectious enthusiasm for this project, and for his wonderful work as literary agent, I am grateful to Ted Chichak. Thanks also to Tom Dunne, who helped guide me through the world of commercial publishing, to Carol Brown Janeway, my editor at Knopf, whose sharp eye and keen literary judgment helped shape this book, and to Knopf staff members Stephanie Koven and Melvin Rosenthal for their help.

I dedicate the book in part to my daughter, Molly, who has long shared my passion for the Mortara story. While still in high school she transcribed the several hundred handwritten pages of the Feletti trial transcript, no mean job even for a professional scholar. She beat me to the punch by writing her undergraduate history honors thesis at Brown on the Mortara case. I am very proud of her and of my son, Seth.

NOTES

Throughout this book, unless otherwise noted, all translations from Italian, French, and Latin sources are my own. For more information on archival sources used and abbreviations employed, please refer to "Archival Sources and Abbreviations."

PROLOGUE

1. For population figures on the Jews in the Papal States at midcentury, see Ministero del Commercio e Lavori Pubblici, *Statistica della popolazione dello Stato Pontificio dell'anno 1853* (1857).

CHAPTER 1

1. The primary source used to prepare this account of the events of June 23–24, 1858, are the transcripts of the 1860 trial of Father Feletti for kidnapping, found in ASB–FV. Among the other sources employed is Marshal Lucidi's account, dated August 8, 1858, which somehow made its way into ASCIR.

2. Enrico Bottrigari, *Cronaca di Bologna*, vol. 2 (1960), p. 419.

3. In fact, the two cardinals were traveling together that day, visiting the town of San Giovanni in Persiceto. See Giuseppe Bosi, *Archivio di rimenbranze felsinee*, vol. 3 (1858), p. 309.

CHAPTER 2

1. On *Cum nimis absurdum*, see Luciano Tas, *Storia degli ebrei italiani* (1987), p. 64; and Attilio Milano, *Storia degli ebrei in Italia* (1992), p. 247.

2. The passage from Pius V's papal brief is taken from Lucio Pardo, "Il ghetto e la città," in Sergio Vincenzi, ed., *Il ghetto: Bologna. Storia e rinascita di un luogo* (1993), p. 56.

3. There were five northern legations, ranging, north to south, from Ferrara, Bologna, Ravenna, and Forlì—together constituting the region of Romagna—to the legation of Pesaro and Urbino, part of the Marches.

4. Lazzaro Padoa, *Le comunità ebraiche di Scandiano e di Reggio Emilia* (1986).

5. On the history of the duchy of Modena's legislation regarding Jews in this period, see Guido Fubini, *La condizione giuridica dell'ebraismo italiano* (1974); and Gino Badini, "L'archivio Bassani dell' Università Israelitica," *Ricerche storiche* 27, no. 73 (1993): 27–80. More generally on the history of Jews in the duchy in the eighteenth and nineteenth centuries, see Andrea Balletti, *Gli ebrei e gli Estensi* (1930).

6. See Giacomo Blustein, *Storia degli ebrei in Roma* (1921), p. 215.

7. Mario Caravale and Alberto Caracciolo, eds., *Lo stato pontificio da Martino V a Pio IX* (1978), p. 526.

8. Eremanno Loevinson, "Gli ebrei dello Stato della Chiesa," part 2, *Rassegna mensile di Israel* 9 (1934): 164; Augusto Pierantoni, *I carbonari dello Stato Pontificio*, vol. 2 (1910), pp. 21, 99, 117.

9. Umberto Marcelli, "Le vicende politiche dalla Restaurazione alle annessioni," in Aldo Berselli, ed., *Storia della Emilia Romagna* (1980), p. 72.

10. The Austrians left Bologna again in July of 1831, leading to a period of chaos. They returned in January 1832. For details, see Steven C. Hughes, *Crime, Disorder and the Risorgimento: The Politics of Policing in Bologna* (1994), pp. 114–35.

11. For an excellent discussion of Church theology regarding the Jews, and the changes introduced in the sixteenth century, see Kenneth R. Stow, *Catholic Thought and Papal Jewry Policy, 1555–1593* (1977).

12. The quote is from Giovanni Vicini, *Causa di simultanea successione di cristiani e di ebrei . . .* (1827), p. 154.

13. Vincenzo Berni degli Antonj, *Osservazioni al voto consultivo . . .* (1827), p. 70.

14. In addition to Gioacchino Vicini, *Giovanni Vicini* (1897), see discussion in Gadi Luzzato Voghera, *L'emancipazione degli ebrei in Italia* (1994), pp. 83–85.

15. Bottrigari, *Cronaca*, vol. 2, pp. 36–7.

16. Luigi Carlo Farini, *Lo stato romano dall'anno 1815 all'anno 1850*, vol. 4 (1853), p. 139.

CHAPTER 3

1. Francesco Fantoni, *Della vita del Cardinale Viale Prelà* (1861).

2. Bottrigari, *Cronaca*, vol. 2, p. 362.

3. On Viale-Prelà's family relations, see Paul-Michel Villa, *La maison des Viale* (1985).

4. The struggle between the conservative wing of the Church in Bologna and that more open to reform was influenced by the parallel battle taking place in France at the time. See Aldo Berselli, "Le relazioni fra i cattolici francesi ed i cattolici conservatori bolognesi dal 1858 al 1866," *Rassegna storica del Risorgimento* 41 (1954): 269–81. Also see Rodolfo Fantini, "Sacerdoti bolognesi liberali dal 1848 all'unita' nazionale," *Bollettino del Museo del Risorgimento di Bologna* 5 (1960): 451–84; and Fantini, "Un arcivescovo bolognese nelle ultime vicende dello stato pontificio: il Card. Michele Viale Prelà," *Pio IX* 2 (1973): 210–44.

5. Alfredo Testoni, *Bologna che scompare* (1905), p. 119; Oreste F. Tencajoli, "Cardinali corsi: Michele Viale Prelà," *Corsica antica e moderna* 4–5 (1935): 148.

6. Bottrigari, *Cronaca*, vol. 2, p. 363.

7. The two documents by Viale-Prelà, dated 1858, are "Lettera pastorale al clero e popolo della città e diocesi di Bologna," published by the Tipi Arcivescovili of Bologna, and "Circolare ai RR. Parrochi di Città, e Diocesi. Intorno alla S. Infanzia," both found in AAB–N. There is some irony in the Cardinal's description of the heathen practice of infant abandonment, for the practice was common in Italy as well at the time. See David I. Kertzer, *Sacrificed for Honor* (1993).

8. Fantoni, *Della vita*, p. 125, AAB–AC, b. 151, protocollo n. 231, 1859.

9. "L'ebreo di Bologna," *L'osservatore bolognese*, October 1, 1858, p. 2.

10. Enrico Bottrigari, quoted in Tencajoli, "Cardinali corsi," p. 148.

11. Marcelli, "Le vicende politiche."

12. Clifford Geertz, "Centers, Kings, and Charisma," in J. B. Davis and T. N. Clark, eds., *Culture and Its Creators* (1977), p. 162.

13. *Pio Nono ed i suoi popoli nel 1857* (1860), pp. 430, 440. Another example of this genre of report is provided by *Albo a memoria dell' augusta presenza di Nostro Signore Pio IX in Bologna* (Bologna, 1858).

14. Bottrigari, *Cronaca*, vol. 2, pp. 377–8.

15. Caravale and Caracciolo, *Lo stato pontificio*, p. 700.

16. Giacomo Martina, *Pio IX, 1851–66* (1986), p. 28.

17. Protection of this sacred treasure had not been easy, for a parade of potentates had, over the centuries, sought the divine blessings that the holy relics offered. In the late seventeenth century, the monks had turned down the Grand Duke of Tuscany, Cosimo III de'Medici, when he requested a slice of the sacred skull. Going over their heads to get a piece of Saint Dominic's, the Grand Duke enlisted the aid of his brother, a cardinal, who ultimately persuaded Pope Innocent XII to make the monks give the Grand Duke what he wanted. The result was that, on a January night in 1699, in the presence of a delegation from the Bologna senate, a professor of anatomy and two surgeons opened the holy reliquary in San Domenico. Bending the papal order a bit, they decided not to chip away at the holy skull itself but, to the relief of the Dominican brothers, extracted a back right molar instead. Nor was this the last assault on Saint Dominic's bones. In 1787, despite the anguish and protests of the Domini can brothers, they were forced to cut off a piece of skull for the spiritual benefit of the Duke of Parma. See Alfonso D'Amato, *I domenicani a Bologna*, vol. 2 (1988), pp. 630–5, 798–801, 951–2. On the Pope's visit to San Domenico, see, in addition, Abele Redigonda, "Lo studio domenicano di Bologna," *Sacra dottrina*, 2 (1957): 134–5.

18. Martina, *Pio IX*, pp. 27–8. Pasolini's reference to the troops as German betrayed a common popular perception in Bologna at the time, equating the Austrians with Germans. The matter is even more complicated, because few of the troops were either Austrian or German, in the national or ethnic sense. While the officer corps of the Austrian forces consisted primarily of Austrians, the bulk of the troops came from the various outposts of the Austrian Empire: Croatians, Hungarians, etc.

CHAPTER 4

1. ASCIR, dated 24 giugno 1858.

2. See the entry by Giuseppe Rambaldi et al. on "Battesimo," in the *Enciclopedia Cattolica* (1949), vol. 2, pp. 1003–46. That article also notes that "the children of non-Catholics, if they are in danger of dying . . . before reaching the age of reason, can be baptized licitly, even against the wishes of their parents" (p. 1031).

That the position adopted by Pope Pius IX in the Mortara case was fully in accord with existing Church policy is evident by a glance at the compendium of Church doctrine published fifteen years earlier, in Gaetano Moroni Romano's *Dizionario di erudizione storico-ecclesiastico* (1843). Under the entry "Ebrei," on the Jews, in vol. 21 (p. 21), the section on the baptism of Jewish children lists five basic points:

"1. That without parental consent, the Church was never in the habit of baptizing them.
2. That without such consent, one can make two cases for baptism: when the child's life is in extreme danger, and when children have been abandoned by their parents.
3. That baptism given in situations where it is not licit to give it remains, nonetheless, valid.
4. That in such cases the baptized children should not be returned to their Jewish parents, but raised by Christians in the Catholic faith.
5. That for proof that they were truly baptized, a single witness is enough."

3. A series of handwritten documents on the Pamela Maroni case, including a number of letters from Abram Maroni, are found in ASRE–AN, b. 25.

4. These documents are found in the ASRE–AN, b. 25.

5. ASRE–FB, Cancello II.

6. A handwritten copy of Deputy Bottaro's remarks, reproduced from the *Foglio di Piemonte—Supplemento—Camera de' Deputati* (9 giugno 1858), is found in ASRE–AN, b. 8.

7. Copies of all three letters are found in ASCIR.

8. Carlo Cattaneo, *Ricerche economiche sulle interdizioni imposte dalla legge civile agli Israeliti* (1836), p. 22.

9. Original copies of the "Editto sopra gli Ebrei" from both the Inquisitor and the Archbishop of Bologna are found in the AdAB, miscellanea B, 1894.

10. Franco Della Peruta, "Le 'interdizioni' israelitiche e l'emancipazione degli ebrei nel Risorgimento," *Società e storia* 6 (1983): 78n1.

11. ASG–SA, 1850–60.

12. Cecil Roth, "Forced Baptisms in Italy," *New Jewish Quarterly Review* 27 (1936): 129; Gemma Volli, *Breve storia degli ebrei d'Italia* (1961), pp. 62–3.

CHAPTER 5

1. This point could be made more generally about the Jews of Europe before Jewish emancipation, as discussed by Jacob Katz, *Out of the Ghetto* (1973).

2. On the attitudes of Italian Jews toward their emancipation in the nineteenth century, see the articles by Andrew M. Canepa, "L'atteggiamento degli ebrei italiani devanti alla loro seconda emancipazione: Premesse e analisi, *Rassegna mensile di Israel*

43 (1977): 419–36; and "Emancipation and Jewish Response in Mid-Nineteenth-Century Italy," *European History Quarterly*, no. 16 (1986): 403–39.

3. This and, unless otherwise noted, all letters to and from the Jewish community of Rome cited in this book are found in ASCIR.

4. Cecil Roth, "The Forced Baptisms of 1783 at Rome and the Community of London," *Jewish Quarterly Review* 16 (1925–26): 105–10.

5. Abraham Berliner, *Storia degli ebrei di Roma* (1992; German orig., 1893), p. 302.

6. Emilio Castelar, *Ricordi d'Italia* (1873), p. 96.

7. Andrée Dufaut, *Vie anecdotique de Pie IX* (1869), p. 129.

8. *L'osservatore bolognese,* 29 ottobre 1858, p. 3.

9. "Notizia sulle disposizioni d'animo del fanciullo Mortara nella sera 23 giugno p.°p.° e nei seguenti giorni," ASV–Pio IX.

CHAPTER 6

1. G. Bareille, "Catéchuménat," *Dictionnaire de Théologie Catholique* (1905), 2:2: 1968–70; Milano, *Storia degli ebrei*, p. 590. For Turin, see Luciano Allegra, "L'Ospizio dei catecumeni di Torino," *Bollettino storico-bibliografico subalpino* 88 (1990): 513–73.

2. The history of Jewish baptisms in Rome's Houses of the Catechumens can be found in the three-article series (1986–88) written by Wipertus Rudt de Collenberg in the *Archivium Historiae Pontificiae*. See also C. Ruch, "Baptème des infidèles," *Dictionnaire de Théologie Catholique* 2:2:341–55 (1905).

3. Serena Bellettini, *La comunità ebraica di Modena* (1965–66), pp. 212–27.

4. A good example is provided by Giacomo Forti, "Lettera di un ebreo convertito," *Annali delle scienze religiose* 18, fasc. 53 (1844): 345–54.

5. *Civiltà Cattolica*, ser. 2, vol. 2 (1853), p. 197.

6. Ibid., ser. 3, vol. 3 (1856), p. 691.

7. Ibid., pp. 441–2.

8. This view of Jewish converts to Catholicism is also reflected in the Jewish historiography on the Italian Houses of the Catechumens. Cecil Roth ("Forced Baptisms in Italy," p. 120.) writes of the converts: "a disproportionate number were in fact arrant scoundrels."

9. The 1641 constitution of the Bologna House of the Catechumens, for example, states that the institution "will not receive infidels of any kind before first obtaining sufficient information on their life and behavior, and of the sincerity, seriousness, and true desire to receive the most holy Baptism." AdAB–COL.

10. Roth, "Forced Baptisms in Italy," p. 120.

11. Renata Martano, "La missione inutile: La predicazione obbligatoria agli ebrei di Roma nella seconda metà del Cinquecento " (pp. 93–110), and Fiamma Satta, "Predicatori agli ebrei, catecumeni e neofiti a Roma nella prima metà del Seicento" (pp. 113–27), both in M. Caffiero, A. Foa, and A. Morisi Guerra, eds., *Itinerari Ebraico-Cristiani: Società cultura mito* (1987).

12. The image of the *predica coatta* as a ritual reversal was suggested by Anna Foa, "Il gioco del proselitismo: Politica delle conversioni e controllo della violenza nella

Roma del Cinquecento," in Michele Luzzati, Michele Olivari, and Alessandra Veronese, eds., *Ebrei e Cristiani nell'Italia medievale e moderna* (1988), p. 156. An earlier *predica coatta* for the Jews had been tried out in the thirteenth century. On the early history of this practice, see Milano, *Storia degli ebrei*; Volli, *Breve storia*.

13. Gemma Volli, "Papa Benedetto XIV e gli ebrei," *Rassegna mensile di Israel* 22 (1956):215.

14. Roberto G. Salvadori, *Gli ebrei toscani nell'età della Restaurazione* (1993), pp. 107, 146n29.

15. *Ratto della Signora Anna del Monte trattenuta a' Catecumeni tredici giorni dalli 6 fino alli 19 maggio anno 1749*, edited and with an introduction by Giuseppe Sermoneta (Rome, 1989).

CHAPTER 7

1. Raffaele De Cesare, *Roma e lo stato del papa* (1975; orig., 1906), p. 227.

2. *"Un homme très-honnête, mais pas trop à son aise."* Letter from Joseph Pavia, Bologna, 13 novembre 1859, *Archives Israélites*, décembre 1859, p. 708.

3. On attitudes of Italian Jews toward emancipation, see Andrew M. Canepa, "L'attegiamento degli ebrei italiani davanti alla loro seconda emancipazione," *Rassegna mensile di Israel* 43: 419–36, and Canepa, "Emancipation and Jewish Response in Mid-Nineteenth-Century Italy," *European Historical Quarterly*, n. 16: 403–39.

4. "Edgardo Mortara," *Il Cattolico*, November 8, 1958.

5. Giuseppe Pelczar, *Pio IX e il suo pontificato*, vol. 2 (1910), p. 196.

6. I thank Pier Cesare Bori for pointing out this New Testament parallel.

7. *L'Univers*, 11 novembre 1858, reproduced in l'abbé Delacouture, *Le droit canon et le droit naturel dans l'affaire Mortara* (1858), p. 43.

8. "Edgardo Mortara."

9. "Notizie del giovenetto cristiano Mortara," *L'armonia*, 16 October 1858.

10. Dom Jacobus, *Les vols d'enfants* (1859), pp. 34–36.

11. "Il piccolo neofito, Edgardo Mortara," *Civiltà Cattolica*, ser. 3, vol. 12 (1858), pp. 389–90.

12. "Edgardo Mortara."

13. The unsigned letter from the Università Israelitica di Roma to the Baron de Rothschild in Paris, dated September 8, 1858, is found in ASCIR.

14. Letter addressed via Sig. Jacob Vita Alatri, pel Sr. M. Mortara, Roma, 12. settembre 1858, ASCIR.

CHAPTER 8

1. Roger Aubert, *Il pontificato di Pio IX*, Storia della Chiesa, vol. 22/1 (1990), p. 449.

2. Roth, "Forced Baptisms in Italy," p. 130.

3. The Pope also did away with the Carnival tribute, on which see Berliner, *Storia degli ebrei*, p. 300; on the papal commission, see Bruno Di Porto, "Gli ebrei di Roma dai papi all'Italia," in Elio Toaff et al., eds., *La breccia del ghetto* (1971), pp. 35–6.

4. Aldo Berselli, "Movimenti politici a Bologna dal 1815 al 1859," *Bollettino del Museo del Risorgimento* 5 (1960):225.

5. Giovanni Miccoli, *Fra mito della cristianità e secolarizzazione* (1985), p. 49.

6. P. R. Perez, "Alcune difficoltà emerse nella discussione 'super virtutibus' del servo di Dio Pio Papa IX," in Carlo Snider, ed., *Pio IX nella luce dei processi canonici* (1992), p. 237.

7. Fubini, *La condizione giuridica*, p. 10.

8. Aubert, *Il pontificato*, pp. 70–2.

9. Martina, *Pio IX*, p. 40; Roger Aubert, "Antonelli, Giacomo," *Dizionario biografico degli italiani*, vol. 3 (1961), p. 485. For an English-language biography of Antonelli, see Frank J. Coppa, *Cardinal Giacomo Antonelli and Papal Politics in European Affairs* (1990).

10. Carlo Falconi, *Il cardinale Antonelli* (1983), pp. 302–3.

11. Odo Russell letter to Lord J.R., no. 7, Rome, January 7, 1806. In Noel Blakiston, *The Roman Question* (1962), pp. 79–80.

12. Jan Derek Holmes, *The Triumph of the Holy See* (1978), p. 130.

13. Aubert, *Il pontificato*, p. 143n147. Also see Piero Pirri, "Il card. Antonelli tra il mito e la storia," *Rivista di storia della chiesa italiana* 12 (1958): 81–120.

14. Holmes, *Triumph*, p. 135.

15. Giuseppe Leti, *Roma e lo stato pontificio dal 1849 al 1870* (1911), vol. 1, pp. 11, 16n.

16. Perez, "Alcune difficoltà," p. 34.

17. Aubert, *Il pontificato*, pp. 449–52.

18. August Hasler, *How the Pope Became Infallible* (1993), pp. 105–10. On the Catholic belief in supernatural punishment for earthly sins in the time of Pius IX, see P. G. Camaiani, "Castighi di Dio e trionfo della Chiesa: Mentalità e polemiche dei cattolici temporalisti nell'età di Pio IX," *Rivista storica italiana* 88 (1976): 708–44.

19. Frank J. Coppa, "Cardinal Antonelli, the Papal States, and the Counter-Risorgimento," *Journal of Church and State*, 16 (1974), p. 469.

20. Martina, *Pio IX*, p. vii.

21. De Cesare, *Roma e lo stato del papa*, p. 243.

22. Ibid., p. 67.

CHAPTER 9

1. ASV–Pio IX; found in Sharon Mullen Stahl, *The Mortara Affair, 1858*, doctoral diss., Saint Louis University (1987), p. 34.

2. Unfortunately, the central archives of the Inquisition, at the Vatican, are not generally open to researchers.

3. Camillo Cavour, *Il carteggio Cavour-Nigra dal 1858 al 1861*, vol. 1 (1926), p. 206, letter 143.

4. Giacomo Martina, a Jesuit historian and the foremost contemporary biographer of Pius IX, is of a similar opinion, judging Villamarina's remarks as off the mark. Martina, *Pio IX*, p. 33n50.

5. From the Pio IX archive in ASV, cited by Martina, *Pio X*, p. 33n50.

6. In Italy in the Restoration period, however, there was an important body of non-Jewish opinion expressing concern about the Jews' lack of civil rights. In addition to Cattaneo's *Ricerche economiche*, see Massimo D'Azeglio, *Dell'emancipazione civile degl'Israeliti* (1848).

7. Quoted in Gemma Volli, "Il caso Mortara nell'opinione pubblica e nella politica del tempo," *Bollettino del Museo del Risorgimento* 5 (1960), p. 1090.

8. The text is reproduced in Isidore Cahen, "L'affaire Mortara de Bologne," *Archives Israélites* 19 (October 1858): 555–6.

9. Aubert, *Il pontificato*, pp. 145–6.

10. In France in particular, a great deal of emphasis was placed on the paternal-rights argument. See, for example, Jules Assezat, *Affaire Mortara: Le droit du père* (1858).

11. Draft of letter from Momolo Mortara, addressed to Son Excellence Mons. le Duc de Grammont, Ambassadeur de France près le S. Siège, no date (probably September 8, 1858), ASCIR.

12. Giuseppe Laras, "Ansie e speranze degli ebrei a Roma durante il pontificato di Pio IX," *Rassegna mensile di Israel* 39 (1973): 515–17; Giacomo Martina, *Pio IX e Leopoldo II* (1967), pp. 200–1.

13. Falconi, *Il cardinale Antonelli*, pp. 239–40.

14. ASV–SS, fasc. 3, n. 167.

15. Ibid., n. 171.

16. Ibid., n. 220. Letter from Antonelli to Lionel de Rothschild, London, 13 September 1858. This is a draft of a letter and may not have actually been sent. In the margins a note is added: "Non ebbe corso" (not sent).

CHAPTER 10

1. ASV–Pio IX.

2. Letter from S. Scazzocchio to Don Enrico Sarra, Rome, September 29, 1858, ASCIR.

3. As one report put it, the baptism had been performed secretly "at the instigation of the fanatic Catholic grocer Lepori." Alfredo Comandini, *L'Italia nei cento anni del secolo XIX (1801–1900), 1850–60* (1907–18), p. 823.

4. These details come from ASG–SA.

5. ASV–SS, fasc. 1, Allegato E, Ripertorio Generale n. 5358.

6. ASV–Pio IX.

7. For a fuller history of infant abandonment in nineteenth-century Bologna, see Kertzer, *Sacrificed for Honor*.

8. ASV–Pio IX. Both the cover letter and all the notarized testimony from Bologna discussed below are found here.

9. A biography and an autobiography of Pasquale Saragoni, both in manuscript form, are to be found in AMRB.

CHAPTER 11

1. S. Bloch, "Rapt d'un enfant israélite," *L'univers Israélite* 14 (July 1858):11.

2. Cahan, "L'Affaire Mortara," p. 555.

3. Reprinted as lettera C in *Brevi cenni*, "Supplica diretta dai rabini di Germania a Sua Santità," p. 113, ASV–Pio IX.

4. Letter to Sig. Alessandro Carpi, Bologna, August 25, 1858, ASCIR.

5. "Chronique du mois," *Archives Israélites* 20 (January 1859):46.

6. Ibid., p. 61.

7. Momolo Mortara letter from Bologna addressed via Giacobbe Tagliacozzo, Rome, October 10, 1858, ASCIR.

8. Testimony of Momolo Mortara, February 6, 1860, trial of Father Feletti, Bologna, ASB-FV.

9. Letter from the Bishop of Alatri to Secretary of State Antonelli, October 16, 1858, ASV–SS, fasc. 1, n. 7.

10. Letter from Secretary of State Antonelli to the Bishop of Alatri, October 18, 1858, ASV–SS, fasc. 1, n. 9.

11. Letter from the Bishop of Alatri to Secretary of State Antonelli, October 19, 1858, ASV–SS, fasc. 1. n. 75.

12. Letter from Cardinal Cagiano, Frosinone, to Secretary of State Antonelli, October 18, 1858, ASV–SS. fasc. 1, n. 73.

13. Letter from Secretary of State Antonelli to Cardinal Cagiano, Frosinone, October 21, 1858, ASV–SS, fasc. 1, n. 77.

14. Letter addressed "Alle Università Israelitiche dello Stato," dated Rome, October 20, 1858, ASCIR.

CHAPTER 12

1. *Shema*, the Hebrew word for "hear," is the first word of the most important prayer in Judaism, an expression of God's oneness.

2. "Ratto del fanciullo Mortara," *Il piccolo corriere d'Italia*, November 8, 1858.

3. Transcript of trial of Father Feletti, Bologna, testimony of Marianna Padovani, February 20, 1860, Turin, ASB.

4. "Dans les plus recentes visites, . . ." draft of letter written in mid-November 1858, ASCIR.

5. *L'univers*, November 11, 1858, quoted in Delacouture, *Le droit canon*, p. 43.

6. "Edgardo Mortara," *Il vero amico*, n. 49 (December 5, 1858).

7. "Il piccolo neofito, Edgardo Mortara."

8. Letter from Momolo Mortara to Scazzocchio in Rome, sent from Florence, dated December 2, 1858, ASCIR.

CHAPTER 13

1. Giuseppe Massari, *Diario dalle cento voci*, vol. 1858–60 (1959), p. 97.

2. Letter from Count Minerva, Rome, to Count Cavour, Turin, October 9, 1858. Reprinted in appendix of Gian Ludovico Masetti Zannini, "Nuovi documenti sul caso Mortara," *Rivista storica della chiesa italiana* 13 (1959):271–2.

3. Lettera particolare, Count Minerva, Rome, to Count Cavour, Turin, October 9, 1858. Reprinted in ibid., p. 273.

4. Letters from Count Minerva, Rome, to Count Cavour, Turin, October 25 and November 23, 1858. Reprinted in ibid., pp. 273, 274.

5. Letter from O. Terquem, Paris, December 10, 1858, in *Archives Israélites* 14 (December 10, 1858):233–5.

6. Letter (#143) from the Marquis of Villamarina, Paris, to Count Cavour, Turin, November 21, 1858. In Cavour, *Il carteggio Cavour-Nigra*, vol. 1, pp. 206–7.

7. Letter (#149) from Count Cavour, Turin, to the Marquis of Villamarina, Paris, November 25, 1858. In ibid., pp. 213–14.

8. Carlo Sacconi, apostolic nuncio in France, letter to Cardinal Antonelli (#1171), dated January 7, 1859, Paris. Reprinted in Mariano Gabriele, ed., *Il carteggio Antonelli-Sacconi, (1858-1860)* (1962), vol. 1, p. 12.

9. Letter from the apostolic nuncio to Madrid to Cardinal Antonelli, dated Madrid, December 1, 1858, ASV–SS, fasc. 3.

10. Letter from Conte Du Chastel, Rome, to Cardinal Antonelli, November 8, 1858, ASV–SS, fasc. 2, n. 93.

11. Letter from Cardinal Antonelli to the Ministro Residente di S.M. il re de' Paesi Bassi, November 27, 1858, ASV–SS, fasc. 2, n. 95. For the reaction to the Mortara case in Belgium, see G. Braive, "Un choc psycologique avant la guerre d'Italie: L'affaire Mortara," *Risorgimento* 8 (1965):49–82.

12. Quoted in Bertram W. Korn, *The American Reaction to the Mortara Case* (1957), p. 24.

13. Quoted in ibid., p. 42.

14. Ibid., p. 48.

15. Ibid., p. 70.

16. Ibid., p. 95.

17. Ibid., p. 63.

18. Fair Play, "The Alleged 'Mortara' Kidnapping Case in Bologna, Italy" (1858).

CHAPTER 14

1. Stuart Woolf, *A History of Italy 1700–1860* (1979), p. 235. See this work more generally for its account of the evolution of relations between the Church and the European rulers in the eighteenth and nineteenth centuries.

2. *Journal de Bruxelles*. September 18, 1858. Reprinted in *Archives Israélites* 19 (October 1858):558–9.

3. A brief history of *L'armonia della religione colla civiltà* and an analysis of its

writings on the Mortara case can be found in Floriana Naldi, *Il caso Mortara: Il processo nel 1860 e le reazioni della stampa ecclesiastica ed ebraica*, tesi di laurea, Università de Bologna, 1993, pp. 61–87. For an analysis of the writings of the Italian press, see Grazia Parisi, *Il caso Mortara: Il processo del 1860 e le reazioni della stampa italiana*, tesi di laurea, Università di Bologna, 1993.

4. "Notizie del giovanetto cristiano Mortara," *L'armonia della religione colla civiltà*, October 17, 1858.

5. Momolo Mortara's testimony at the trial of Feletti, Bologna, February 6, 1858.

6. "Il piccolo neofito, Edgardo Mortara," p. 406. For a widely circulated pamphlet, in both French and Italian editions, polemicizing with the *Civiltà Cattolica* article, see *Roma e la opinione pubblica d'Europa nel fatto Mortara* (Turin, 1859).

7. "Il piccolo neofito, Edgardo Mortara," p. 400.

8. Ibid., p. 391. *L'armonia* (October 31, 1858, p. 2) took up this theme, blaming the clamor created by the Mortara case on the fact that "the major part of the influential newspapers are in the hands of the Jews."

9. These letters, on *Civiltà Cattolica* stationery, are found in ASCIR.

10. "Al *Journal des Débats*, Parigi," *L'osservatore bolognese*, 29 October 1858.

11. "Edgardo Mortara," *Il vero amico*, December 5, 1858. For background on this and other of Bologna's newspapers of this period, see Isabella Zanni Rosiello, "Aspetti del giornalismo bolognese," in *Il 1859–60 a Bologna* (1961).

12. "L'unione e il popolo," *Il Cattolico*, December 1, 1858, p. 1.

13. For an examination of a fifteenth-century charge of Jewish ritual murder, see R. Po-Chia Hsia, *Trent 1475: Stories of a Ritual Murder Trial* (1992).

14. "Orrendo assassinio di un fanciullo," *Il Cattolico*, January 26, 1859, front page.

15. S. Cahen, "Chronique du mois," *Archives Israélites*, March 1859, pp. 180–1.

16. Vincenzo Manzini, *L'omicidio rituale e i sacrifici umani, con particolare riguardo alle accuse contro gli ebrei* (1925), pp. 143–5.

17. *Civiltà Cattolica*, ser. 15, vol. 5 (1893), p. 269.

18. Ibid., ser. 13, vol. 2 (1886), p. 437.

19. Ibid., ser. 15, vol. 2 (1892), p. 138.

20. "L'ebreo di Bologna e le bombe di Giuseppe Mazzini," *L'armonia della religione colla civiltà*, August 17, 1858.

21. "I papi, gli ebrei, e i giornali italianissimi nel 1853 e nel 1858," *L'armonia della religione colla civiltà*, October 3, 1858.

22. Antonio Gramsci, *Quaderni del carcere*, vol. 3 (1975), p. 2035.

23. Delacouture, *Le droit canon*, p. 44.

24. Ibid.

25. Letter from Carlo Archbishop Sacconi, nunzio apostolico, Paris, to Cardinal Antonelli, December 19, 1859, ASV–SS, fasc. 3, n. 164.

26. Giovanni Battista Clara, *Memorie per la storia de'nostri tempi*, vol. 1 (1863), pp. 206–14.

27. Letter from Cardinal Antonelli, Rome, to the Monsignor Nunzio Apostolico, Paris, December 30, 1858, ASV–SS, fasc. 3, n. 166.

28. Letter from Carlo Sacconi, Paris, to Cardinal Antonelli, January 17, 1859. In Gabriele, *Il carteggio Antonelli-Sacconi*, letter N. 1179, p. 18.

CHAPTER 15

1. The Pro-memoria and the Syllabus are to be found in ASV–Pio IX. These documents were used as the basis of Sharon Stahl's doctoral dissertation, *The Mortara Affair, 1858* (St. Louis University, 1987), and I make use of her translations from the Latin portions of these texts.

2. "Brevi cenni e riflessioni sul Pro-memoria e sillabo, scritture umiliate alla Santità de Nostro Signore Papa Pio IX relative al battesimo conferito a Bologna al fanciullo Edgardo figlio degli Ebrei Salomone e Marianna Mortara." ASV–SS, fasc. 1, n. 88. Addressed to the nuncios of Vienna, Munich, Portugal, Spain, Brazil, Brussels, Naples, The Hague, and Florence; to the representatives to Lucerne and Turin; and to the apostolic delegates to Panama, Bogotá, and Mexico. The names of the Latin American representatives have all been crossed out in pencil, which may mean that the materials were not, in the end, sent to them.

3. See "Cronaca," *Il Cattolico*, November 4, 1858, p. 1.

4. *Brevi cenni*, p. 8.

5. Ibid.

6. Ibid., p. 18.

7. Ibid., p. 12.

8. Ibid., p. 27.

9. Bajesi remains a mystery figure in the Mortara case. She never came to the attention of the magistrate who later investigated the matter in connection with the kidnapping trial of the Inquisitor. The parish records of San Gregorio reveal that she lived near the Mortaras when they first moved to Bologna but then shortly thereafter left the parish. Of course, it is possible that Bajesi heard of the matter not directly from Regina Bussolari but from a third party who had heard of the baptism from Bussolari.

10. Ibid. The capitalization is in the original.

11. Capitalization in original.

12. Ibid., pp. 30–31.

13. *Dubbi critico-teologici sul battesimo che si pretende conferito in Padova alla Signora Regina Bianchini. . . .* (1786), p. 5. A copy of this document is found in the Archiginnasio di Bologna.

14. My account of the Bianchini case is based on the above-cited source, an anonymous thirty-one-page booklet written by a man who describes himself as a "*privato*," responding to the great public interest in the case.

15. *Brevi cenni*, p. 22.

16. Ibid., pp. 22–3.

17. Commandant Weil, "Un précédent de l'affaire Mortara," *Revue historique* 137. Reprinted as pamphlet (Paris, 1921), p. 3. This quote is from Count de Rayneval's letter of June 26, 1840, to M. Thiers in Paris. Weil reproduces much of the relevant French diplomatic correspondence, and the texts of the correspondence I use here are drawn from this source.

18. Ibid.

19. Ibid., p. 5.

20. Ibid., pp. 7–8.

21. Ibid., p. 15. Letter from Count de Rayneval to Cardinal Lambruschini, July 21, 1840.

22. Ibid., pp. 9–10. Letter from Count de Rayneval to M. Thiers, July 17, 1840.

23. Ibid., p. 12. Letter from Cardinal Lambruschini, Quirinale palace, Rome, July 18, 1840, addressed to Monsieur le chargé d'affaires de S.M. le roi des Français.

24. Ibid., pp. 10–13. Letter from Count Rayneval to M. Thiers, July 27, 1840.

25. Massari, *Diario, vol. 1858–60*, p. 95.

26. Frank Coppa, *Pope Pius IX: Crusader in a Secular Age* (1979), p. 129.

27. Luigi Previti, "La circolare del gran maestro della Massoneria," *Civiltà Cattolica*, scr. 13, vol. 12 (1888):391.

28. Dufault, *Vie anecdotique*, pp. 131–2.

29. Louis Veuillot, *Le parfum de Rome. Oeuvres complètes*, vol. 9 (1926), pp. 448–51.

30. Moroni Romano, "Ebrei," p. 29; Di Porto, "Gli ebrei di Roma," p. 30.

31. The account of this meeting is based primarily on Berliner, *Storia degli ebrei*, pp. 305–7. Also see Di Porto, "Gli ebrei di Roma," p. 59.

32. Quoted in Martina, *Pio IX*, p. 34n53. Martina provides no date for this encounter.

CHAPTER 16

1. Letter from Momolo Mortara to S. Scazzocchio, December 3, 1858, ASCIR.

2. Letter from S. Scazzocchio to Momolo Mortara, December 7, 1858, ASCIR.

3. Israel Davis, "Moses Montefiore," *Jewish Encyclopedia* (1901) vol. 8, pp. 668–70.

4. On the extended Rothschild family, see Egon Caesar Corti, *The Reign of the House of Rothschild*, trans. by Brian and Beatrix Lunn (1928); and Virginia Cowles, *The Rothschilds: A Family of Fortune* (1973).

5. This description of Montefiore's Damascus mission is based principally on the account found in Myrtle Franklin with Michael Bor, *Sir Moses Montefiore, 1784–1885* (1984), pp. 41–57.

6. Letter from Moses Montefiore to the Deputati dell' Università Israelitica di Reggio, January 17, 5001 [year given according to Hebrew calendar], ASRE–AN, b. 28. The other documents sent by Montefiore are also found here.

7. Chaim Bermant, *The Cousinhood: The Anglo–Jewish Gentry* (1971), pp. 104–5.

8. L. Loewe, ed., *Diaries of Sir Moses and Lady Montefiore* (1890), pp. 85–6.

9. The exchange of letters between Montefiore and Eardley was reprinted in *The Jewish Chronicle and Hebrew Observer* (London), December 31, 1858, p. 2.

10. Among those accompanying Montefiore was Gershom Kursheedt, a Jewish businessman from New Orleans who was living in London at the time. As noted by Korn, *American Reaction*, p. 157, Kursheedt went as the "unofficial representative of

American Jewry," and as such his trip constituted the first direct intervention of the American Jewish community on behalf of Jews abroad. This is a rather tenuous claim, however, as just what role he had in Rome is hard to see. Montefiore himself makes virtually no mention of him, and Kursheedt did not attend any of the crucial meetings there with Sir Moses.

11. Loewe, *Diaries of Sir Moses Montefiore*, p. 103.

12. "Return of Sir Moses Montefiore," *The Jewish Chronicle and Hebrew Observer*, May 27, 1859, p. 4.

13. Isidore Cahen, "Chronique du mois," *Archives Israélites*, July 1859, pp. 423–4.

14. Ibid.

15. Volli, "Il caso Mortara nell' opinione pubblica," p. 1117.

16. The handwritten account by Enrico Sarra, Rector of the Catechumens, that includes this information is found in ACC #184, entry n. 317, pp. 95–6.

17. Letter from Scazzocchio to Angelo Padovani, Bologna, February 1, 1859, ASCIR.

18. The source for this account is Edgardo himself, from the autobiographical notes he wrote in 1878, which were republished in the appendix of Masetti Zannini, "Nuovi documenti," pp. 264–5. We have no direct verification from papal records.

19. This is the account given in Moroni Romano, in his entry for "Chiese di Roma—S. Pietro in Vinculis," in his *Dizionario di erudizione storico-ecclesiastico*, vol. 13 (1843), p. 6.

20. This passage of Veuillot is reproduced in Dufault, *Vie anecdotique*, pp. 125–9.

CHAPTER 17

1. Giambattista Casoni, *Cinquant'anni di giornalismo 1846–1900* (1908), vol. 2, p. 21.

2. Cited in "Spoglio dei giornali," *Gazzetta del popolo* (Bologna), January 11, 1860, p. 3.

3. Arturo Carlo Jemolo, *Chiesa e stato in Italia dal Risorgimento ad oggi* (1955), pp. 49–50.

4. Martina, *Pio IX*, p. 34. Recall that according to Pius IX's eminent French biographer Roger Aubert (*Il pontificato*, p. 145), it was the Pope's actions in the Mortara case that led Napoleon III to drop his last hesitations before agreeing to the dismantling of the Pope's earthly empire. Or, in the words of the British historian J. Derek Holmes (in *The Triumph*, p. 126), it was the Mortara case that "once again raised the question of temporal power and ecclesiastical autocracy" and "prepared French opinion for a shift in Napoleon's foreign policy."

5. Bottrigari, *Cronaca*, vol. 2, p. 446.

6. "Cronaca contemporanea—Notificazione dell'Em. Legato di Bologna," *Civiltà Cattolica*, ser. 4, vol. 3, p. 103.

7. My description of the events surrounding the departure of the Austrian troops from Bologna is based primarily on Bottrigari, *Cronaca*, vol. 2, pp. 460–4.

8. Alberto Dallolio, "Bologna nel 1859," in *Bologna nella storia d'Italia* (1933), p. 163.

9. Fantini, "Un arcivescovo bolognese," p. 220; also see Fantini, "Il clero bolognese nella crisi del 1859–60," *Bollettino del Museo del Risorgimento di Bologna* 3(1958):109–61.

10. Letter from Odo Russell to Lord J.R., July 22, 1859, no. 94, in Blakiston, *The Roman Question*, pp. 26–7.

11. This description is based on Bottrigari, *Cronaca*, vol. 2, pp. 479–82, including the story from Bologna's *Monitore*, which he reprints.

12. "Popoli della campagna," *Gazzetta del popolo*, August 17, 1859.

13. The text of Farini's declaration can be found as appendix E in Francesco Jussi, *Studi e ricordi di Foro Criminale per l'avvocato Francesco Jussi* (1884).

14. "Notificazione Ecclesiastica," signed M. Card. Viale-Prelà, Arciv., dated Palazzo Arcivescovile di Bologna, August 29, 1859, AAB–N.

15. "Notificazione Ecclesiastica," signed M. Card. Viale-Prelà, Arciv., dated Palazzo Arcivescovile di Bologna, December 8, 1859, AAB–N.

16. Bottrigari, *Cronaca*, vol. 2, p. 509.

17. On the political uses of ritual, see David I. Kertzer, *Ritual, Politics, and Power* (1988).

18. On the rituals of the French Revolution, see Mona Ozouf, *La fête révolutionnaire* (1976).

19. Dallolio, "Bologna nel 1859," pp. 193–5.

20. Bottrigari, *Cronaca*, vol. 2, pp. 514–15.

21. Fantini, "Un arcivescovo bolognese," p. 226.

22. Dallolio, "Bologna nel 1859," p. 205.

23. Letter from Odo Russell to Lord J.R., December 10, 1859, no. 138, in Blakiston, *The Roman Question*, p. 65.

CHAPTER 18

1. Joseph Pavia, letter from Bologna, November 13, 1859, in *Archives Israélites*, December 1859, pp. 708–10.

2. ASB–FV, p. 4.

3. A year later, Curletti would himself end up in a Turin jail, awaiting trial for murder in a complex tangle involving charges of organizing gangs of thieves and committing political assassinations. In the face of his threats that he would tell all about the secret misdeeds of Farini, Cavour, and other architects of the new state, his wardens allowed him to escape. But in 1861, still bitter about the way he had been treated, he published (with a confederate)—apparently richly compensated by ultramontane Catholic backers—a scandalous exposé of Farini and colleagues that was translated into several European languages. Curletti was forced to flee Europe altogether and died in obscurity in Philadelphia in 1876. Rodolfo Fantini, "Due 'buone lane' nelle vicende del nostro Risorgimento: Griscelli e Curletti," *Strenna storica bolognese* 15 (1965): 99–112; Adriano Colocci, *Griscelli e le sue memorie* (1909). The exposé was published under the pseudonymous initials "J.A.," as *La vérité sur les hommes et les choses du royaume d'Italie. Révélations par J.A., ancien agent secret du compte du Cavour* (1861). For the view taken by the Church of the affair, see the notice in *Civiltà Cattolica*, ser. 4, vol. 12 (1861), pp. 121–3.

4. ASB–FV, pp. 12–14.

5. On the transition of the Bologna police force from the old to the new regime, see Hughes, *Crime, Disorder and the Risorgimento.*

6. ASB–FV, pp. 5–7.

7. The literature on the Inquisition is massive. On the various forms of the modern Inquisition, see Gustav Henningsen and John Tedeschi, eds., *The Inquisition in Early Modern Europe* (1986); Romano Canosa, *Storia dell'Inquisizione in Italia dalla metà del Cinquecento alla fine del Settecento*, 5 vols. (1986–90); Stephen Haliczer, ed., *Inquisition and Society in Early Modern Europe* (1987); John Tedeschi, *The Prosecution of Heresy, Collected Studies on the Inquisition in Early Modern Italy* (1991); Andrea Del Col and Giovanna Paolin, eds., *L'Inquisizione romana in Italia nell'età moderna* (1991), especially Andrea Prosperi, "Per la storia dell'Inquisizione romana," pp. 27–64. On the treatment of Jews by the modern Italian Inquisition, see Michele Luzzati, ed., *L'Inquisizione e gli ebrei in Italia* (1994); Nicolas Davidson, "The Inquisition and the Italian Jews," in Haliczer, *Inquisition and Society*, pp. 19–46; Pier Cesare Ioly Zorattini, *Processi del S. Uffizio di Venezia contro ebrei e giudaizzanti*, 5 vols. (1980); Brian Pullan, *The Jews of Europe and the Inquisition of Venice*, 1550–1670 (1983). For a history of the Inquisition and the Jews of Modena and of the Estensi states, see Albano Biondi, "Inquisizione ed ebrei a Modena nel Seicento," in Euride Fregni and Mauro Perani, eds., *Vita e cultura ebraica nello stato estense* (1993), pp. 259–73; and Biondi, "Gli ebrei e l'Inquisizione negli stati estensi," in Luzzati, *L'Inquisizione*, pp. 265–85.

8. Canosa, *Storia dell'Inquisizione*, vol. 5, p. 216.

9. Antonio Battistella, *Il S. Officio e la riforma religiosa in Bologna* (1905). For the early history of the Inquisition in Bologna, see Massimo Giansante, "L'Inquisizione domenicana a Bologna fra XII e XIV secolo," *Il Carrobbio* 13 (1987): 219–29; and Guido Dall'Olio, "I rapporti tra la Congregazione del Sant'Ufficio e gli inquisitori locali nei carteggi bolognesi (1573–1594)," *Rivista storica italiana* 105 (1993): 246–86.

10. Davidson, "The Inquisition and the Italian Jews," p. 35.

11. Vittore Ravà, *Gli ebrei in Bologna* (1872), pp. 17–19. For a dramatic mid-seventeenth-century case of a Jew imprisoned in the Torrone prison of Bologna and tried by the Inquisitor, see Ermanno Loevinson, "Un marrane du XVII siècle à Bologne, Emmanuel Passarino Léon ou Juda Vega," *Revue des Études juives*, n.s. vol. 3(1938):91–6.

12. On the history of the Inquisition in Bologna in the seventeenth and eighteenth centuries, see Alessandra Fioni, "L'Inquisizione a Bologna. Sortilegi e superstizioni popolari nei secoli XVII–XVIII," *Il Carrobbio* (1992): 141–50.

13. "Editto della Santa Inquisizione contro gl'Israeliti degli Stati Pontifici," in Achille Gennarelli, *Il governo pontificio e lo stato romano, documenti preceduti da una esposizione storica* (1860), part I, pp. 304–5.

14. ASB–FV, p. 23.

15. Ibid., pp. 7–12.

16. From the Italian translation in Volli, "Il caso Mortara nell'opinione pubblica," p. 1121n64. The *Times* story is reproduced as well in Isidore Cahen's entry in "Chronique du mois," *Archives Israélites*, February 1860, p. 91.

17. Bottrigari, *Cronaca*, vol. 3, p. 3.

18. Letter by Leone Ravenna, Ferrara, January 17, 1860, *Archives Israélites*, February 1860, pp. 77–8.

19. Letter by Joseph Pavia, January 15, 1860, *Archives Israélites*, February 1860, pp. 79–80.

CHAPTER 19

1. Carlo Colitta, *Il Palazzo comunale detto d'Accursio* (1980), pp. 48–9, 136–8.

2. ASB–FV, pp. 22–41.

3. Ibid., pp. 46–77.

CHAPTER 20

1. Her birth certificate, provided by her parish priest from San Giovanni in Persiceto, gives Anna Morisi's birthday as November 28, 1833, ASB–FV, p. 202.

2. ASB–FV, pp. 105–22.

3. Ibid., pp. 122–30.

4. Ibid., pp. 143–52.

5. Ibid., p. 192.

6. Ibid., p. 329.

7. Ibid., p. 342.

8. Ibid., pp. 205–11.

9. Ibid., pp. 228–35.

10. Ibid., p. 241.

11. Ibid., pp. 241–9.

12. Ibid., pp. 331–3.

13. Ibid., pp. 343–59.

CHAPTER 21

1. These letters are found in ASV–Pio IX.

2. These letters are found in AAB–AC, b. 152, protocollo n. 42. The underlining is in the originals.

3. ASB–FV, pp. 360–95.

4. Ibid., printed document found following p. 406.

5. Ibid., pp. 395–6.

6. Ibid., pp. 397–8.

7. The handwritten manuscript of the poem, "Motto sopra alcuni uomini politici in un verso endecasillabo," which carries no indication of either author or date, is found in AdAB, B. 3849, mss. n. 11. It was apparently written around 1846.

8. Jussi, *Studi e ricordi*, pp. 117–34.

9. ASB–FV, pp. 404–10.

10. The text of the "Conclusioni fiscali" for the Feletti trial was prepared in

printed form, and can be found in the Biblioteca di Storia Moderna e Contemporanea di Roma, as Misc. Risorg. c. 29. The sentence requested is reconstructed, in addition, from Jussi's later account in his *Studi e ricordi*, p. 219.

11. The parish priest was of course not, in fact, a Jesuit.

12. ASB–CR. Several receipts for purchases from the Leporis' grocery, going back to 1843, are preserved there.

13. Here Jussi was a bit confused. It was not Momolo but Marianna's uncle who accompanied Marianna's brother-in-law that day.

14. Francesco Jussi, *Difesa del Padre Pier Gaetano Feletti* (1860).

CHAPTER 22

1. See Aubert, *Il pontificato*, p. 147.

2. "Circolare dell'intendenza di Bologna alle rappresentanze comunali della provincia, Bologna, 29 dicembre 1859," *Il monitore di Bologna*, January 3, 1860, p. 1.

3. Piero Zama, "I plebisciti," in *Il 1859–60 a Bologna* (1961), pp. 303–13.

4. Marcelli, "Le vicende politiche," p. 114.

5. Bottrigari, *Cronaca*, vol. 3, p. 33.

6. Bolla of March 25, 1860. Text in *Corriere dell'Emilia*, April 11, 1860.

7. ASB–FV, pp. 399–400.

8. *L'educatore israelitico* (April 1860), vol. 8, p. 155.

9. Isidore Cahen, "Chronique du mois," *Archives Israélites* (May 1860), pp. 276–7.

10. Rodolfo Fantini, "Il clero bolognese nel decennio 1859–69," in R. Fantini et al., eds., *Clero e partiti a Bologna dopo l'unità* (Bologna, 1968), p. 23.

11. "Lettera circolare del sindaco di Bologna pel suono delle campane all arrivo di S.M. Vittorio Emanuele II," April 27, 1860. Copy found in AAB–AC, anno 1860, prot. n. 128. The joint response to the mayor from the parish priests is found in that same archival folder.

12. "L'arrivo di S.M. il re," *Il Corriere dell'Emilia*, May 2, 1860.

13. In Fantini, "Un arcivescovo bolognese," p. 239.

14. Quoted in Tencajoli, "Cardinali corsi," p. 154. The original Nascentori manuscript can be found in AdAB. Bottrigari's chronicle contains a similarly bitter portrait of the Archbishop. See Enrico Bottrigari, *Cronaca di Bologna*, vol. 4 (1962), p. 62.

15. Francesco Manzi Nascentori, *Cronaca Bolognese. Con annotazioni sui principali avvenimenti mondiali e sulle più celebrate scoperte del sec. XIX*, anno IV (1858), manoscritto depositato presso la Biblioteca dell'Archiginnasio di Bologna (MSS B. 2218); Fantini, "Un arcivescovo bolognese," pp. 242–4; Mario Fanti, "Una missione del clero bolognese presso Cavour, 1860," *Strenna storica bolognese* 10 (1960):17–40.

16. The three-page Latin eulogy, by Fr. Dominicus Toselli, dated July 9, 1881, is found in ASDB, I.16518, n. 1. Feletti's letter to Pius IX is reproduced in Masetti Zannini, "Nuovi documenti," pp. 278–9.

17. Martina, *Pio IX*, p. 674. Monsignor Canzi's encounters with the Bologna police and courts can be followed in Bottrigari, *Cronaca*, vol. 3, pp. 234 and passim.

18. D'Amato, *I domenicani*, pp. 1003–6.

CHAPTER 23

1. "L'affaire Mortara davanti al congresso," *La gazzetta del popolo,* November 28, 1859.

2. Isidore Cahen, "Chronique du mois," *Archives Israélites,* January 1860, p. 46.

3. Ibid.; and Isidore Cahen, "Chronique du mois," *Archives Israélites,* February 1860, p. 90.

4. The key role of the Mortara case in prompting the founding of the Alliance Israélite Universelle is well established. See, for example, Bernhard Blumenkranz, *Histoire des Juifs en France* (1972), pp. 335–6; and Michael Graetz, *Les Juifs en France au XIXe siècle* (1989), p. 13.

5. Quoted in Volli, "Il caso Mortara nell'opinione pubblica," p. 1136.

6. These letters are excerpted in Gemma Volli, "Alcune conseguenze benefiche dell'affare Mortara," pp. 212–13.

7. Letter from Cavour to Gropello, April 29, 1861 (n. 3405), in Camillo Cavour, *La liberazione del Mezzogiorno e la formazione del regno d'Italia. Carteggi di Camillo Cavour,* vol. 4 (1954), pp. 456–7.

8. Letter dated September 27, 1860, reproduced in Volli, "Alcune conseguenze," pp. 314–15.

9. Volli, "Il caso Mortara nell'opinione pubblica," pp. 1136–7. Garibaldi's novel, *I mille* (1982), deals at length with two converted Jews, and reflects his strident anticlericalism and anti-Catholicism. His reference to the Mortara case comes when he discusses the conversion in a Rome church of his two protagonists: "The devotees of these nauseating ceremonies will have seen a specimen of them in the conversion of the Mortara boy, robbed from his Jewish parents by the priests, so that they could make him a Catholic" (p. 165).

10. *Monitore di Bologna,* supplement to n. 11 (January 15, 1860), pp. 1–2. The opening is also described by Isidore Cahen, "Chronique du mois," *Archives Israélites,* January 1860, pp. 47–8. So as not to offend Catholic religious sensibilities, apparently, the playwright arranged to have the child reunited with his mother without rejecting his new religion.

11. *Corriere dell'Emilia,* April 19, 1860.

12. Riccardo Castelvecchio, *La famiglia ebrea. Dramma in quattro atti ed un prologo* (1861). The continued dramatic potential of the Mortara affair in Italy was more recently on display with the 1983 publication of a novel based on the case. See Pier Domiano Ori and Giovanni Perich, *La Carrozza di San Pietro* (1983).

13. H. M. Moos, *Mortara: or the Pope and His Inquisitors; a Drama* (1860).

14. *Edgar Mortara, dedié aux pères et aux mères de toutes les nations et de toutes les religions* (Paris, 1860), pp. 20–1.

15. Volli, "Il caso Mortara nell'opinione pubblico," p. 1136; Castelar, *Ricordi d'Italia,* p. 7.

16. Letter of Odo Russell to Lord J.R., Rome, December 4, 1860 (n. 183), in Blakiston, *The Roman Question,* p. 142.

17. Di Porto, "Gli ebrei di Roma," p. 59.

18. Edgardo Mortara's autobiographical memoir, written in 1878, is reprinted in the appendix to Masetti Zannini, "Nuovi documenti," p. 265.

CHAPTER 24

1. Renato Mori, *La questione romana, 1861–1865* (1963), pp. xix–xxi.

2. For a vivid description of Rome in this period, see Castelar, *Ricordi d'Italia*, chapter one.

3. Jemolo, *Chiesa e stato*, pp. 49–50.

4. Quoted in John B. Bury, *History of the Papacy in the Nineteenth Century* (1930), pp. 8–9.

5. The (Italian) text of the encyclical and Syllabus that I use here is taken from Eucardio Momigliano and Gabriele M. Casolari, eds., *Tutte le encicliche dei Sommi Pontefici* (1959), pp. 262–80. On the political impact of the Syllabus, see Holmes, *The Triumph*, p. 146. For a detailed analysis of the Pope's role in the development of the Syllabus, see Martina, *Pio IX*, pp. 287–356.

6. Aubert, *Il pontificato*, p. 398.

7. Indeed, the records of the Mortara and Coen cases are contained in the same folder of the Roman synagogue's archives, under "Forced Baptisms," and the two cases are filed together in the Secretary of State's archives at the Vatican as well.

8. Letter from the nunzio apostolico, Paris, to Cardinal Antonelli, August 13, 1864, ASV–SS, fasc. 3, p. 237.

9. *Il monitore di Bologna*, August 13, 1864, cites a report published in *Italie* dated August 9.

10. *Il monitore di Bologna*, October 1, 1864, p. 3.

11. Ibid., September 6, 1864, p. 2.

12. Quoted in Fernando Ceccarelli, "1870—La riconsegna del giovinetto Coen alla famiglia," *L'urbe* 12 (1949):20. Ceccarelli also cites Stefano Jacini's claim that Cardinal Antonelli's refusal to accede to the French ambassador's request to have Giuseppe Coen returned to his parents was the last straw for Napoleon III, making him regret his continued military support for the Pope, and helped lead to the Italian occupation of Rome.

13. Letter from Marco Minghetti in Bologna to Count Giuseppe Pasolini, July 20, 1865, in Guido Pasolini, ed., *Carteggio tra Marco Minghetti e Giuseppe Pasolini*, vol. 4, *1864–1876* (1930), letter n. 745, p. 117.

14. Arthur F. Day, *The Mortara Case* (1929), pp. 502–3. The English translation of the verse from Isaiah is taken from *The Oxford Annotated Bible* (New York, 1962).

15. Edgardo Mortara, "Stanze recitate alla presenza della Santità di Nostro Signore Papa Pio Nono da Edgardo Mortara in S. Agnese fuori le mura il dì 12 Aprile 1866," BAV, 8501, n. 22.

16. Quoted in Pelczar, *Pio IX*, p. 200.

17. From Edgardo Mortara's memoir of 1878, reprinted in Masetti Zannini, "Nuovi documenti," p. 269.

18. *Storia d'Italia, Cronologia 1815–1990* (1991), p. 165.

19. Raffaele Cadorna, *La liberazione di Roma nell'anno 1870 ed il plebiscito* (1889), pp. 247–8, 557.

20. Ugo Pesci, *Gazzetta del popolo*, October 10, 1870, quoted in Ceccarelli, "1870—La riconsegna," p. 17.

21. "Il fanciullo Coen," *L'opinione nazionale* 18 (1870): 332–5.

22. This is the account reported in Gemma Volli's classic study of the Mortara case, *Il caso Mortara nel primo centenario* (1960), p. 36. As a piece of drama, it seems almost too good to be true, and unfortunately, I could find no good evidence to support it, although we do know that Riccardo Mortara had become a career army officer. Edgardo himself makes no mention of it in his 1878 memoirs on the events of 1870, though of course there are reasons he might have chosen not to discuss it.

CHAPTER 25

1. This information, and all other materials used in this and the following chapter, unless otherwise noted, come from the records of the trial of Momolo Mortara et al., found in ASF–MM.

2. He may, indeed, even have been a relative. Momolo's brother Moses had married a Bolaffi, whose mother, to compound the in-marrying complexity of Italy's small Jewish population, was a Padovani. ASRE Stato della popolazione israelitica di Reggio, 1849.

CHAPTER 26

1. The Mortara arrest and trial were covered in a number of Florence's newspapers, especially *La nazione*, but also *Fanfulla*, *Il corriere italiano*, and *Le journal de Florence*.

EPILOGUE

1. Mortara, appendix of Masetti Zannini, "Nuovi documenti," pp. 270–1.

2. Raffaele De Cesare, "Il ratto del fanciullo Mortara a Bologna (1858)," *Gazzetta dell'Emilia*, March 15, 1907.

3 "La conferenza del P. Mortara," July 11, 1891, Biblioteca Estense, Modena.

4. Leti, *Roma e lo Stato Pontificio*, vol. 1, p. 16n.

5. *Fatti (I) della nuova Roma contro la salma di Pio IX*, 1885, Ratisbona. Biblioteca Apostolica Vaticana, R.G. Storia IV 10775.

6. The archives of the Casa dei Catecumeni in Rome contain both a postcard and a loose note written to the Rector by Pio Mortara in 1919, ACC.

7. G.P., "La morte di D. Pio Mortara," *L'osservatore romano*, March 22, 1940, p. 4.

ARCHIVAL SOURCES AND
ABBREVIATIONS

Archivio dell'Archiginnasio di Bologna (**AdAB**).

> Costitutioni, Ordini, et Leggi della Casa dei Catecumeni di
> Bologna, Riformati l'Anno MDXCIII. Bologna, 1641 (**COL**).
> Miscellanea B. 1894. "Editto Sopra gli Ebrei," various versions
> seventeenth and eighteenth centuries.
> Giuseppe Manzi Nasentori. 1858. Cronaca bolognese, anno sesto,
> 1858. handwritten.
> B. 3849. mss. n. 11. satirical poem, handwritten, no author.

Archivio Arcivescovile di Bologna (**AAB**).

> Segreteria Arcivescovile, Atti Comuni, b. 145, 150, 151, 152 (**AC**).
> Miscellanee Vecchie (**MV**).
> Notificazioni, 1858–60 (**N**).

Archivio Cardinale Michele Viale Prelà. Biblioteca del Museo del
Risorgimento di Milano.

Archivio Casa Cat. Catecumini Neofiti. Housed in the Archivio del Vicariato
di Roma (**ACC**).

> #184. Liber III. Baptizatorum Neophytorum. Ven. Domus
> Catechumenorum de Urbe, 1827–1887.
> Various.

Archivio del Museo del Risorgimento di Bologna (**AMRB**).

Archivio della Parrocchia di San Gregorio di Bologna (**ASG**).

> Stato d'anime, 1847–1860 (every year) (**SA**).

Archivio di San Domenico di Bologna (**ASDB**).

Archivio Segreto Vaticano (**ASV**).

> Fondo Pio IX, oggetti vari, n. 1433, "Mortara Edgardo" (**Pio IX**).
> Segretario di Stato, anno 1864, rubrica 66 (Ebrei) (**SS**), fasc. 1, 2, 3.

Archivio di Stato di Bologna (**ASB**).

> Corporazioni religiose soppresse nel periodo postunitario, Misc.
> Serie prima 44,383 (San Domenico) (**CR**).
> Tribunal Civile e Criminale di Prima Istanza in Bologna.
> Causa di separazione violenta del fanciullo Edgardo Mortara . . .
> contro Feletti Frate Pier Gaetano, 1860 (**FV**).

Archivio di Stato di Firenze (**ASF**).

Tribunale Civile e Correzionale di Firenze

> Assise 45, Procedimento penale contro Mortara Momolo, Bolaffi
> Flaminio, Mortara Ercole, Mortara Marianna, imputati di
> omicidio in danno di Tognazzi Rosa . . . il 3 aprile 1871. (MM)

Archivio di Stato di Modena

> Arch. Materie—Ebrei.

Archivio di Stato di Reggio Emilia (**ASRE**).

> Fondo Bassani (**FB**).
> Università Israelitica di Reggio Emilia, Archivio Nuovo (**AN**).

Archivio di Stato di Roma

> Misc. Carte Politiche e Risevate, b. 129.

Archivio Storico della Comunità Israelitica di Roma (**ASCIR**).

> Battesimi forzati, Caso Mortara 1858 (**BF**).

Biblioteca Apostolica Vaticana, biblioteca Vali Ferraioli IV (**BAV**).

Biblioteca Estense (Modena), archivio.

BIBLIOGRAPHY

Albo a memoria dell'augusta presenza di Nostro Signore Pio IX in Bologna l'estate dell'anno 1857. 1858. Bologna: Tip. governativa della Volpe e del Sassi.

Allegra, Luciano. 1990. "L'Ospizio dei catecumeni di Torino." *Bollettino storico-bibliografico subalpino* (Turin) 88:2:513–73.

Anonymous. 1859. *Roma e la opinione pubblica d'Europa nel fatto Mortara.* Turin: Unione Tipografico-Editrice.

Anonymous. 1860. *Edgar Mortara, dedié aux pères et aux mères de toutes les nations et de toutes les religions.* Paris: E. Dentu.

Assezat, Jules. 1858. *Affaire Mortara: Le droit du père.* Paris: E. Dentu.

Aubert, Roger. 1961. "Antonelli, Giacomo." *Dizionario biografico degli italiani* 3:484–93.

———. 1990. *Il Pontificato di Pio IX (1846–1878),* trans. by Giacomo Martina. *Storia della Chiesa,* vols. XX/1 and 2. 4th ed. Turin: San Paolo.

Badini, Gino. 1993. "L'archivio Bassani dell'Università Israelitica." *Ricerche storiche* (Reggio Emilia) 27:73:27–80.

Balletti, Andrea. 1930. *Gli ebrei e gli Estensi.* Reggio Emilia: Anonima Poligrafica Emiliana.

Bareille, G. 1905. "Catécuménat." *Dictionnaire de Théologie Catholique* 2:2:1968–87. Paris: Letouzey et Ané.

Battistella, Antonio. 1905. *Il S. Officio e la riforma religiosa in Bologna.* Bologna: Zanichelli.

Bellettini, Serena. 1966. *La comunità ebraica di Modena nell'età moderna.* Tesi di laurea, 1965–6, Facoltà di Magistero, Università di Bologna. Relatore: Paolo Prodi.

Berliner, Abraham. 1992 (German orig., 1893). *Storia degli ebrei di Roma,* trans. by Aldo Audisio. Milan: Rusconi.

Bermant, Chaim. 1971. *The Cousinhood: The Anglo-Jewish Gentry.* London: Eyre & Spottiswoode.

Berni degli Antonj, Vincenzo, 1827. *Osservazioni al voto consultivo del Signor Avvocato Giovanni Vicini*. Bologna: Nobili.

Berselli, Aldo. 1954. "Le relazioni fra i cattolici francesi ed i cattolici conservatori bolognesi dal 1858 al 1866." *Rassegna storica del Risorgimento* 41:269–81.

———. 1960. "Movimenti politici a Bologna dal 1815 al 1859." *Bollettino del Museo del Risorgimento* 5:201–54.

Biondi, Albano. 1993. "Inquisizione ed ebrei a Modena nel Seicento." In Euride Fregni and Mauro Perani, eds., *Vita e cultura ebraica nello stato estense*. Nonantola: Edizioni Fattoadarte.

———. 1994. "Gli ebrei e l'Inquisizione negli stati estensi." In Michele Luzzati, ed., *L'Inquisizione e gli ebrei in Italia*. Rome: Laterza.

Blakiston, Noel. 1962. *The Roman Question: Extracts from the Despatches of Odo Russell from Rome, 1858–1870*. London: Chapman & Hall.

Blumenkranz, Bernhard. 1972. *Histoire des Juifs en France*. Toulouse: Privat.

Blustein, Giacomo. 1921. *Storia degli ebrei in Roma dal 140 av. Cr. fino ad oggi*. Rome: Casa Libraria Editrice Italiana P. Maglione & C. Strini.

Bosi, Giuseppe. 1858. *Archivio di rimembranze felsinee*, vol. 3. Bologna: Tip. Chierici di S. Domenico.

Bottrigari, Enrico. 1960–2. *Cronaca di Bologna*, 4 vols., ed. by Aldo Berselli. Bologna: Zanichelli.

Braive, G. 1965. "Un choc psycologique avant la guerre d'Italie: L'affaire Mortara. Les répercussions en Belgique (juillet–décembre 1858)." *Risorgimento* 8:49–82.

Bury, John B. 1930. *History of the Papacy in the Nineteenth Century*. London: Macmillan (republ. 1964, New York: Schocken).

Cadorna, Raffaele. 1889. *La liberazione di Roma nell'anno 1870 e il plebiscito*. Turin: L. Roux.

Camaiani, P. G. 1976. "Castighi di Dio e trionfo della Chiesa: Mentalità e polemiche dei cattolici temporalisti nell'età di Pio IX." *Rivista storica Italiana* 88:708–44.

Canepa, Andrew M. 1977. "L'attegiamento degli ebrei italiani davanti alla loro seconda emancipazione: Premesse e analisi." *Rassegna mensile di Israel* 43:419–36.

———. 1986. "Emancipation and Jewish Response in Mid-Nineteenth-Century Italy." *European History Quarterly* n. 16:403–39.

Canosa, Romano. 1986–90. *Storia dell'Inquisizione in Italia dalla metà del Cinquecento alla fine del Settecento*, 5 vols. Rome: Sapere 2000.

Caravale, Mario, and Alberto Caracciolo, eds. 1978. *Lo stato pontificio da Martino V a Pio IX. Storia d'Italia*, vol. XIV. Turin: UTET.

Casoni, Giambattista. 1908. *Cinquant'anni di giornalismo 1846–1900. Ricordi personali*, 2 vols. Bologna: Ed. Matteuzzi.

Castelar, Emilio. 1873. *Ricordi d'Italia*, trans. from Spanish by Pietro Fanfani. Florence: Tip. della *Gazzetta d'Italia*.

Castelvecchio, Riccardo. 1861. *La famiglia ebrea. Dramma in quattro atti ed un prologo*. Milan: Tip di f. Sanvito succ. a Borroni e Scotti.

Cattaneo, Carlo. 1836. *Ricerche economiche sulle interdizioni imposte dalla legge civile agli Israeliti*. Milan: Presso l'Editore.

Cavour, Camillo. 1926. *Il carteggio Cavour-Nigra dal 1858 al 1861*, vol. 1. Bologna: Zanichelli.

———. 1954. *La liberazione del Mezzogiorno e la formazione del regno d'Italia. Carteggi di Camillo Cavour*, vol. 4. Bologna: Zanichelli.

Ceccarelli, Fernando. 1949. "1870—La riconsegna del giovinetto Coen alla famiglia." *L'urbe* 12:5:15–20.

Clara, Giovanni Battista. 1863. *Memorie per la storia de' nostri tempi*, vol. 1. Turin: Unione Tipografico-Editrice.

Colitta, Carlo. 1980. *Il Palazzo comunale detto d'Accursio*. Bologna: Officina Grafica Bolognese.

Colocci, Adriano. 1909. *Griscelli e le sue memorie*. Rome: Loescher.

Comandini, Alfredo. 1907–18 (repr. 1956). *L'Italia nei cento anni del secolo XIX (1801–1900)*, vol. *1850–60*. Milan: Antonio Vallardi.

Coppa, Frank J. 1974. "Cardinal Antonelli, the Papal States, and the Counter-Risorgimento." *A Journal of Church and State* 16:453–71.

———. 1979. *Pope Pius IX: Crusader in a Secular Age*. Boston: Twayne.

———. 1990. *Cardinal Giacomo Antonelli and Papal Politics in European Affairs*. Albany: State University of New York Press.

Corti, Egon Caesar. 1928. *The Reign of the House of Rothschild*, trans. by Brian and Beatrix Lunn. New York: Cosmopolitan.

Cowles, Virginia. 1973. *The Rothschilds: A Family of Fortune*. New York: Knopf.

Dallolio, Alberto. 1933. "Bologna nel 1859." In *Bologna nella storia d'Italia*. Bologna: Zanichelli.

Dall'Olio, Guido. 1993. "I rapporti tra la Congregazione del Sant'Ufficio e gli inquisitori locali nei carteggi bolognesi (1573–1594)." *Rivista storica italiana* 105:1:246–86.

D'Amato, Alfonso (o.p.). 1988. *I domenicani a Bologna*, vol. 2: *1600–1987*. Bologna: Edizioni Studio Domenicano.

Davidson, Nicolas. 1987. "The Inquisition and the Italian Jews." In Stephen Haliczer, ed., *Inquisition and Society in Early Modern Europe*. Totowa, N.J.: Barnes & Noble.

Davis, Israel. 1901. "Moses Montefiore." *Jewish Encyclopedia* 8:668–70. New York: Ktav.

Day, Arthur Francis. 1929. *The Mortara Case*. London: *The Month*.

D'Azeglio, Massimo. 1848. *Dell'emancipazione civile degl'Israeliti*. Florence: Le Monnier.

De Cesare, Raffaele. 1975 (orig., 1906). *Roma e lo stato del papa: Dal ritorno di Pio IX al XX settembre (1850/1870)*. Rome: Newton Compton.

Delacouture, [l'abbé]. 1858. *Le droit canon et le droit naturel dans l'affaire Mortara*. Paris: E. Dentu.

Del Col, Andrea, and Giovanna Paolin, eds. 1991. *L'Inquisizione romana in Italia nell'età moderna*. Rome: Ministero per i beni culturali.

Della Peruta, Franco. 1983. "Le 'interdizioni' israelitiche e l'emancipazione degli ebrei nel Risorgimento." *Società e storia* 6:77–107.

Del Monte, Anna. 1989. *Ratto della Signora Anna del Monte, trattenuta a'Catecumini tredici giorni dalli 6 fino alli 19 maggio anno 1749*, ed. by Giuseppe Sermonetta. Rome: Carucci.

Di Porto, Bruno. 1971. "Gli ebrei di Roma dai papi all'Italia." In Elio Toaff et al., eds., *1870: La breccia del ghetto. Evoluzione degli ebrei di Roma*. Rome: Barulli.

Dubbi critico-teologici sul battesimo che si pretende conferito in Padova alla Signora Regina Bianchini nata Salomoni ebrea nell'età fanciullesca di anni quattro non compiti da un'altra fanciulla di anni sette non compiti. Aggiuntavi sul fine la Decisione della Congregazione del S. Ufizio. 1786. Bologna. No author given.

Dufault, André. 1869. *Vie anecdotique de Pie IX*. Paris: Victor Sarlit.

Fair Play. 1858. "The Alleged 'Mortara' Kidnapping Case in Bologna, Italy." New York (November 29; 8-page pamphlet).

Falconi, Carlo. 1983. *Il cardinale Antonelli*. Milan: Mondadori.

Fanti, Mario. 1960. "Una missione del clero bolognese presso Cavour, 1860." In *Strenna storica bolognese*, n. 10, pp. 17–40. Bologna: Tipografia Vighi e Rizzoli.

Fantini, Rodolfo. 1958. "Il clero bolognese nella crisi del 1859–60." *Bollettino del Museo del Risorgimento di Bologna* 3:109–61.

———. 1960. "Sacerdoti bolognesi liberali dal 1848 all'unità nazionale." *Bollettino del Museo del Risorgimento di Bologna* 5:451–84.

———. 1965. "Due 'buone lane' nelle vicende del nostro Risorgimento: Griscelli e Curletti," *Strenna storica bolognese* 15:99–112.

———. 1968. "Il clero bolognese nel decennio 1859–69." In Rodolfo Fantini et al., eds., *Clero e partiti a Bologna dopo l'unità*. Bologna: Istituto per la Storia del Risorgimento Italiano.

———. 1973. "Un arcivescovo bolognese nelle ultime vicende dello stato pontificio: il Card. Michele Viale Prelà." *Pio IX* 2:210–44.

Fantoni, Francesco. 1861. *Della vita del Cardinale Viale Prelà*. Bologna: Tip. di S. Maria Maggiore.

Farini, Luigi Carlo. 1850–53. *Lo stato romano dall'anno 1815 all'anno 1850*. Turin: Tip. Ferrero e Franco.

Fatti (I) della nuova Roma contro la salma di Pio IX. 1885. Ratisbona. [Biblioteca Apostolica Vaticana, R.G. Storia IV 10775.]

Fioni, Alessandra. 1992. "L'Inquisizione a Bologna. Sortilegi e superstizioni popolari nei secoli XVII–XVIII." *Il Carrobbio* 18: 141–50.

Foa, Anna. 1988. "Il gioco del proselitismo: Politica delle conversioni e controllo della violenza nella Roma del Cinquecento." In Michele Luzzati, Michele Olivari, and Alessandra Veronese, eds., *Ebrei e Cristiani nell'Italia medievale e moderna*. Rome: Carucci.

Forti, Giacomo. 1844. "Lettera di un ebreo convertito." *Annali delle scienze religiose* 18, fasc. 53, pp. 345–54.

Franklin, Myrtle, with Michael Bor. 1984. *Sir Moses Montefiore, 1784–1885*. London: Anthony Blond.

Fubini, Guido. 1974. *La condizione giuridica dell'ebraismo italiano. Dal periodo napoleonico alla repubblica*. Florence: La Nuova Italia.

Gabriele, Mariano, ed. 1962. *Il carteggio Antonelli-Sacconi (1858–1860)*, vol. 1. Rome: Istituto per la Storia del Risorgimento Italiano.

Garibaldi, Giuseppe. 1982. *I mille.* Bologna: Cappelli.

Geertz, Clifford. 1977. "Centers, Kings, and Charisma." In J. B. Davis and T. N. Clark, eds., *Culture and Its Creators.* Chicago: University of Chicago Press.

Gennarelli, Achille. 1860. *Il governo pontificio e lo stato romano, documenti preceduti da una esposizione storica.* Parte I. Prato: Tipografia F. Alberghetti.

Giansante, Massimo. 1987. "L'Inquisizione domenicana a Bologna fra XII e XIV secolo." *Il Carrobbio* 13:219–29.

Graetz, Michael. 1989. *Les Juifs en France au XIXe siècle,* trans. from Hebrew by Salomon Malka. Paris: Seuil.

Gramsci, Antonio. 1975. *Quaderni del carcere,* vol. 3, ed. by Valentino Gerratana. Turin: Einaudi.

Haliczer, Stephen, ed. 1987. *Inquisition and Society in Early Modern Europe.* Totowa, N.J.: Barnes & Noble.

Hasler, August. 1993. *How the Pope Became Infallible,* trans. by Peter Heinegg. Garden City, N.Y.: Doubleday.

Henningsen, Gustav, and John Tedeschi, eds. 1986. *The Inquisition in Early Modern Europe.* DeKalb: Northern Illinois University Press.

Holmes, Jan Derek. 1978. *The Triumph of the Holy See. A Short History of the Papacy in the Nineteenth Century.* London: Burns & Oates.

Hughes, Steven C. 1994. *Crime, Disorder and the Risorgimento: The Politics of Policing in Bologna.* Cambridge: Cambridge University Press.

Ioly Zorattini, Pier Cesare. 1980. *Processi del S. Uffizio di Venezia contro ebrei e giudaizzanti,* 5 vols. Florence: Olschki.

J.A. [Griscelli, Giacomo]. 1861. *La vérité sur les hommes et les choses du royaume d'Italie. Révélations par J.A., ancien agent secret du comte de Cavour.* Brussels: Imprimerie de la *Revue belge et Étrangère.*

Jacobus, Dom. 1859. *Les vols d'enfants: Impuissance morale du catholicisme.* Brussels: Librairie Universelle de J. Rozez.

Jemolo, Arturo Carlo. 1955. *Chiesa e stato in Italia dal Risorgimento ad oggi.* Turin: Einaudi.

Jussi, Francesco. 1860. *Difesa del Padre Pier Gaetano Feletti, imputato come Inquisitore del Santo Uffizio del ratto del fanciullo Edgardo Mortara davanti al Tribunale Civile e Criminale di Prima Istanza in Bologna.* Bologna: Tipografia all'Ancora.

———. 1884. *Studi e ricordi di Foro Criminale per l'avvocato Francesco Iussi.* Bologna: Tipografia di G. Cenerelli.

Katz, Jacob. 1973. *Out of the Ghetto: The Social Background of Jewish Emancipation, 1770–1870.* Cambridge: Harvard University Press.

Kertzer, David I. 1988. *Ritual, Politics, and Power.* New Haven: Yale University Press.

———. 1993. *Sacrificed for Honor.* Boston: Beacon Press.

Korn, Bertram W. 1957. *The American Reaction to the Mortara Case: 1858–1859.* Cincinnati: American Jewish Archives.

Laras, Giuseppe. 1973. "Ansie e speranze degli ebrei a Roma durante il pontificato di Pio IX." *Rassegna mensile di Israel* 39:512–31.

Leti, Giuseppe. 1911. *Roma e lo stato pontificio dal 1849 al 1870. Note di storia politica*, 2 vols. Ascoli Piceno: Giuseppe Cesari.

Loevinson, Eremanno. 1934. "Gli ebrei della Chiesa nel periodo del Risorgimento politico d'Italia," part 2. *Rassegna mensile di Israel* 9:159–74.

———. 1938. "Un marrane du XVII siècle à Bologne. Emmanuel Passarino Léon ou Juda Vega (et ses poursuites par l'Inquisition de Bologne vers 1652 à 1675)." *Revue des Études juives*, n.s. vol. 3:91–6.

Loewe, L., ed. 1890. *Diaries of Sir Moses and Lady Montefiore*, vol. 2. Chicago: Belford-Clarke.

Luzzati, Michele, ed. 1994. *L'Inquisizione e gli ebrei in Italia*. Rome: Laterza.

Luzzato Voghera, Gadi. 1994. *L'emancipazione degli ebrei in Italia (1781–1848)*. Doctoral thesis, University of San Marino.

Manzini, Vincenzo. 1925. *L'omicidio rituale e i sacrifici umani, con particolare riguardo alle accuse contro gli ebrei*. Turin: Fratelli Bocca.

Marcelli, Umberto. 1980. "Le vicende politiche dalla Restaurazione alle annessioni." In Aldo Berselli, ed., *Storia della Emilia Romagna*. Bologna: CLUEB.

Martano, Renata. 1987. "La missione inutile: La predicazione obbligatoria agli ebrei di Roma nella seconda metà del Cinquecento." In M. Caffiero, A. Foa, and A. Morisi Guerra, eds., *Itinerari Ebraico-Cristiani: Società cultura mito*. Fasano: Schena Editore.

Martina, Giacomo. 1967. *Pio IX e Leopoldo II*. Rome: Editrice Pontificia Università Gregoriana.

———. 1986. *Pio IX (1851–1866)*. Miscellanea Historiae Pontificiae 51. Rome: Editrice Pontificia Università Gregoriana.

Masetti Zannini, Gian Ludovico. 1959. "Nuovi documenti sul 'caso Mortara.' " *Rivista storica della chiesa italiana* 13:239–79.

Massari, Giuseppe. 1959. *Diario dalle cento voci*. Bologna: Massari.

Miccoli, Giovanni. 1985. *Fra mito della cristianità e secolarizzazione*. Casale Monferrato: Marietti.

Milano, Attilio. 1992. *Storia degli ebrei in Italia*. Turin: Einaudi.

Ministero del Commercio e Lavori Pubblici. 1857. *Statistica della popolazione dello Stato Pontificio dell'anno 1853*. Rome (repr. 1992, Bologna: Calderini).

Momigliano, Eucardio, and Gabriele M. Casolari, eds. 1959. *Tutte le encicliche dei Sommi Pontefici*, vol. 1, 6th ed. Milan: Dall'Oglio.

Moos, Herman M. 1860. *Mortara: Or, the Pope and His Inquisitors; a Drama, Together with Choice Poems*. Cincinnati: Bloch & Co.

Mori, Renato. 1963. *La questione romana, 1861–1865*. Florence: Le Monnier.

Moroni Romano, Gaetano. 1843. "Chiese di Roma—S. Pietro in Vinculis." *Dizionario di erudizione storico-ecclesiastico*, vol. 13, pp. 5–9. Venice: Tip. Emiliana.

———. 1843. "Ebrei." *Dizionario di erudizione storico-ecclesiastico*, vol. 21, pp. 5–43. Venice: Tip. Emiliana.

Mortara, Pio Edgardo. *Stanze recitate alla presenza della S. di N.S. papa Pio IX da Edgardo Mortara in S. Agnese fuori le Mura il dí 12 aprile 1866.* In Biblioteca Apostolica Vaticana #10544160; Ferraioli IV.8501 int. 22.

Naldi, Floriana. 1993. *Il caso Mortara: Il processo del 1860 e le reazioni della stampa ecclesiastica ed ebraica.* Tesi di laurea, Facoltà di Scienze Politiche, University of Bologna. Relatore: Mauro Pesce.

Nascentori, Francesco Manzi. 1858. *Cronaca Bolognese. Con annotazioni sui principali avvenimenti mondiali e sulle più celebrate scoperte del sec. XIX,* anno IV, manoscritto depositato presso la Biblioteca dell'Archiginnasio di Bologna (MSS B. 2218).

Ori, Pier Domiano, and Giovanni Perich. 1983. *La Carrozza di San Pietro.* Milan: Editoriale Nuova.

Ozouf, Mona. 1976. *La fête révolutionnaire, 1789– 1799.* Paris: Gallimard.

Padoa, Lazzaro. 1986. *Le comunità ebraiche di Scandiano e di Reggio Emilia.* Florence: Giuntina.

Pardo, Lucio. 1993. "Il ghetto e la città." In Sergio Vincenzi, ed., *Il ghetto: Bologna. Storia e rinascita di un luogo.* Bologna: Grafis.

Parisi, Grazia. 1993. *Il caso Mortara: Il processo del 1860 e le reazioni della stampa italiana.* Tesi di laurea, Facoltà di Scienze Politiche, University of Bologna. Relatore: Mauro Pesce.

Pasolini, Guido, ed. 1930. *Carteggio tra Marco Minghetti e Giuseppe Pasolini,* vol. 4, *1864–76.* Turin: Fratelli Bocca Editori.

Pelczar, Giuseppe S. 1910. *Pio IX e il suo pontificato,* vol. 2. Turin: Libreria Berruti.

Perez, P. R. 1992. "Alcune difficoltà emerse nella discussione 'super virtutibus' del servo di Dio Pio Papa IX." In Carlo Snider, ed., *Pio IX nella luce dei processi canonici.* Vatican City: Editrice la Postulazione della Causa di Pio IX.

Pierantoni, Augusto. 1910. *I carbonari dello Stato Pontificio,* vol. 2. Rome: Società editrice Dante Alighieri.

Pio Nono ed i suoi popoli nel 1857. Memorie intorno al viaggio della Santità N.S. Papa Pio IX per l'Italia centrale. 1860. Rome: Tip. Palazzi Apostolici.

Pirri, Piero. 1958. "Il card. Antonelli tra il mito e la storia." *Rivista di storia della Chiesa Italiana* 12.81–120.

Po-Chia Hsia, R. 1992. *Trent 1475: Stories of a Ritual Murder Trial.* New Haven: Yale University Press.

Prosperi, Adriano. 1991. "Per la storia dell'Inquisizione romana." In Del Col and Paolin.

Pullan, Brian S. 1983. *The Jews of Europe and the Inquisition of Venice, 1550–1670.* Oxford: Blackwell.

Ravà, Vittore. 1872. *Gli ebrei in Bologna: Cenni storici.* Vercelli: Tipografia Guglielmoni.

Redigonda, Abele. 1957. "Lo studio domenicano di Bologna dalla soppressione del convento alla confisca dei suoi beni (1798–1866)." *Sacra dottrina* 2:117–46.

Roth, Cecil. 1925–26. "The Forced Baptisms of 1783 at Rome and the Community of London." *Jewish Quarterly Review* 16:105–12.

———— 1936. "Forced Baptisms in Italy." *New Jewish Quarterly Review* 2/.11/–36.

Ruch, C. 1905. "Baptême des infidèles." *Dictionnaire de Théologie Catholique* 2:2:341–55. Paris: Letouzey et Ané.

Rudt de Collenberg, Wipertus. 1986. "Le baptême des juifs à Rome de 1614 à 1798 selon les registres de la 'Casa dei Catecumini.' Première partie 1614–1676." *Archivium Historiae Pontificiae* 24:9–231.

————. 1987. "Le baptême des juifs à Rome de 1614 à 1798 selon les registres de la 'Casa dei Catecumini.' Deuxième partie 1676–1730." *Archivium Historiae Pontificiae* 25:105–262.

————. 1988. "Le baptême des juifs à Rome de 1614 à 1798 selon les registres de la 'Casa dei Catecumini.' Troisième partie 1730–1798." *Archivium Historiae Pontificiae* 26:119–294.

Salvadori, Roberto G. 1993. *Gli ebrei toscani nell'età della Restaurazione (1814–1848).* Florence: Centro Editoriale Toscano.

Satta, Fiamma. 1987. "Predicatori agli ebrei, catecumeni e neofiti a Roma nella prima metà del Seicento." In M. Caffiero, A. Foa, and A. Morisi Guerra, eds., *Itinerari Ebraico-Cristiani: Società cultura mito.* Fasano: Schena Editore.

Stahl, Sharon Mullen. 1987. *The Mortara Affair, 1858: Reflections of the Struggle to Maintain the Temporal Power of the Papacy.* Doctoral dissertation, Saint Louis University. UMI microfilm #8805267.

Storia d'Italia, Cronologia 1815–1990. 1991. Novara: De Agostini.

Stow, Kenneth R. 1977. *Catholic Thought and Papal Jewry Policy, 1555–1593.* New York: Jewish Theological Seminary.

Tas, Luciano. 1987. *Storia degli ebrei italiani.* Rome: Newton Compton.

Tedeschi, John. 1991. *The Prosecution of Heresy. Collected Studies on the Inquisition in Early Modern Italy.* Binghamton, N.Y.: Medieval and Rennaissance Texts.

Tencajoli, Oreste F. 1935. "Cardinali corsi: Michele Viale Prelà (1798–1860)." *Corsica antica e moderna* 4–5 (luglio–sett.):134–58.

Testoni, Alfredo. 1905. *Bologna che scompare.* Bologna: Zanichelli.

Veuillot, Louis. 1862. *Le parfum de Rome,* II. Paris. *Oeuvres complètes,* vol. 9. Paris: P. Lethielleux.

Vicini, Gioacchino. 1897. *Giovanni Vicini,* part 2, 2nd ed. Bologna: Zanichelli.

Vicini, Giovanni. 1827. *Causa di simultanea successione di cristiani e di ebrei.* Bologna.

Villa, Paul-Michel. 1985. *La maison des Viale.* Paris: Presses de la Renaissance.

Volli, Gemma. 1956. "Papa Benedetto XIV e gli ebrei." *Rassegna mensile de Israel* 22:215–26.

————. 1960. *Il caso Mortara nel primo centenario.* Rome: Rassegna Mensile di Israel.

————. 1960. "Il caso Mortara nell'opinione pubblica e nella politica del tempo." *Bollettino del Museo del Risorgimento* 5:1087–1152.

————. 1961. *Breve storia degli ebrei d'Italia.* Milan: Associazione Insegnanti Ebrei d'Italia.

————. 1962. "Alcune conseguenze benefiche dell'affare Mortara." *Rassegna mensile di Israel* 28:309–20.

Weil, Le Commandant. 1921. "Un précédent de l'affaire Mortara." *Revue historique* 137:3–20.

Woolf, Stuart. 1979. *A History of Italy 1700–1860.* London: Methuen.

Zama, Piero. 1961. "I plebisciti." In *Il 1859–60 a Bologna.* Bologna: Calderini.

Zanni Rosiello, Isabella. 1961. "Aspetti del giornalismo bolognese." In *Il 1859–60 a Bologna.* Bologna: Calderini.

INDEX

A NOTE ABOUT THE AUTHOR

David I. Kertzer was born in 1948 in New York City. The recipient of
a Guggenheim Fellowship in 1986, he has twice been awarded, in
1985 and 1990, the Marraro Prize from the Society for Italian
Historical Studies for the best work on Italian history. He is
currently Paul Dupee, Jr. University Professor of Social Science and
professor of anthropology and history at Brown University.
He and his family live in Providence.

A NOTE ON THE TYPE

This book was set in Minion, a typeface produced by the Adobe
Corporation specifically for the Macintosh personal computer,
and released in 1990. Designed by Robert Slimbach, Minion combines
the classic characteristics of old-style faces with the full complement
of weights required for modern typesetting.

Composed by Creative Graphics,
Allentown, Pennsylvania

Printed and bound by Quebecor Printing,
Martinsburg, West Virginia

Designed by Cassandra J. Pappas

28 X 4 DAYS

DATE DUE			
FEB 2 6 1998			
MAR 1 1 1998			
APR 0 4 1998			
APR 2 5 1998			
SEP 3 1998			
DEC 1 2 2002			
		WITHDRAWN	